Jelliffe:
American Psychoanalyst
and Physician

&

His Correspondence
with Sigmund Freud
and C.G. Jung

Jelliffe: American Psychoanalyst and Physician

JOHN C. BURNHAM

His Correspondence with Sigmund Freud and C.G. Jung

Edited by WILLIAM M^CGUIRE

Foreword by Arcangelo R. T. D'Amore

The University of Chicago Press
Chicago & London

JOHN C. BURNHAM is professor of history and lecturer in psychiatry at Ohio State University. His
books include *Psychoanalysis and American Medicine, 1894–1918* and *Science in America*. WILLIAM
MCGUIRE is the executive editor of *The Collected
Works of C. G. Jung* and editor of *The Freud/Jung
Letters*.

The University of Chicago Press, Chicago 60637
The University of Chicago Press, Ltd., London

Library of Congress Cataloging in Publication Data

Burnham, John C. (John Chynoweth), 1929–
　Jelliffe, American psychoanalyst and physician.

　Bibliography: p.
　Includes index.
　1. Jelliffe, Smith Ely, 1866–1945.　2. Psychoanalysts
—United States—Biography.　3. Psychoanalysts—Corre-
spondence.　I. McGuire, William, 1917–　.　II. Freud,
Sigmund, 1856–1939.　III. Jung, C. G. (Carl Gustav),
1875–1961.　IV. Title.
RC339.52.J44B87　1983　　616.89'17'0924 [B]　　83-1076
ISBN 0-226-08114-1

Contents

List of Illustrations

Abbreviations

The following references are cited in abbreviated form:

Coll. Works = *The Collected Works of C. G. Jung.* Edited by Gerhard Adler, Michael Fordham, and Herbert Read. William McGuire, executive editor. Translated by R. F. C. Hull (except for vol. 2, translated by Leopold Stein and Diana Riviere). New York and Princeton (Bollingen Series XX) and London, 1953–1980. 20 vols.

Ellenberger, Henri F. *The Discovery of the Unconscious: The History and Evolution of Dynamic Psychiatry.* New York, 1970.

The Freud/Jung Letters: The Correspondence between Sigmund Freud and C. G. Jung. Edited by William McGuire. Translated by Ralph Manheim and R. F. C. Hull. Princeton (Bollingen Series XCIV) and London, 1974.

JNMD = *Journal of Nervous and Mental Disease.*

Jones = Ernest Jones, *Sigmund Freud: Life and Work.* London and New York, 1953, 1955, 1957. 3 vols. (The editions are differently paginated; therefore double-page references are given, first to the London edition.)

NMDMS = Nervous and Mental Disease Monograph Series.

Psychoanalytic Pioneers. Edited by Franz Alexander, Samuel Eisenstein, and Martin Grotjahn. New York and London, 1966.

Standard Edn. = *The Standard Edition of the Complete Pyschological Works of Sigmund Freud.* Translated under the general editorship of James Strachey, in collaboration with Anna Freud, assisted by Alix Strachey and Alan Tyson. London and New York, 1953–1974. 20 vols.

Foreword

In the late 1950's when John C. Burnham and others contacted the Smith Ely Jelliffe heirs to inquire about his papers, they were told that the papers must have been destroyed in a fire which took place at Jelliffe's home on Lake George, New York, in 1953. Fortunately, that was not what had happened to the Jelliffe papers. I shall describe what did take place.

In 1972 I became involved in researching the papers of William Alanson White, which were being prepared by St. Elizabeths Hospital in Washington, D.C., for transfer to the National Archives. I arranged a symposium on White, held in October 1973, at St. Elizabeths Hospital. White had been superintendent of the hospital from 1903 until his death in 1937. Later, I edited the proceedings for publication.

I learned that Sigmund Freud had written a letter to White in 1914 in which he was critical of White and Jelliffe for having founded the *Psychoanalytic Review*. He refused their invitation to contribute a paper to it. This letter was not to be found in the White correspondence. Among those I asked regarding the possible whereabouts of the letter was Dr. Nolan D. C. Lewis. Dr. Lewis had been on White's staff at St. Elizabeths until he transferred to New York in late 1935. In 1936 he became director of the New York State Psychiatric Institute.

In New York Lewis assisted Jelliffe in editorial work for the *Journal of Nervous and Mental Disease*, and for the *Psychoanalytic Review*, which Jelliffe edited after White's death. From 1942 to 1958 Lewis was the managing editor of both publications. Dr. Lewis stated that he had in his possession the letter from Freud to White. In addition, he stated that he had the "Jelliffe Index." I did not understand what Lewis meant by the Jelliffe Index until he explained that he meant that he had Jelliffe's correspondence.

Dr. Lewis was living in retirement just west of Frederick, Maryland, about fifty miles from Washington. On October 1, 1975, I went to his home by automobile and brought back to my home in Washington the Jelliffe correspondence and the Freud letters to Jelliffe and White. The correspondence was in twenty-five Tengwall loose-leaf notebooks. These were hardbacked and canvas covered with three inches of space for contents. On the spines of the notebooks were letters of the alphabet to indicate alphabetically the names of the correspondents included. There were two additional Tengwall notebooks with "White" on each spine. Dr. Lewis had removed the Freud letters to Jelliffe from the file and put them in a separate folder. However, they had the holes in them to correspond to the rings of the notebooks.

Dr. Lewis stated to me that he had been told by Jelliffe to keep the Jelliffe correspondence file. When the Jelliffe library was being moved from the Jelliffe townhouse at 64 West 56th Street in New York to the Hartford Neuropsychiatric Institute (now known as the Institute of Living) in Hartford, Connecticut, Dr. Lewis intervened and set aside the Jelliffe correspondence for himself. Apparently none of the Jelliffe heirs was aware of this action.

Some of the letters received by Jelliffe have "L & P" written on them near the top of the first page. This was Jelliffe's signal that the letter belonged in his "letters & photographs" collection, as he conceived of his correspondence file. When Jelliffe was at his summer home on Lake George, letters were forwarded to him from New York City by his secretary. He would write the reply to each one in longhand and send it to his secretary who would type the letter. In such cases both the longhand reply and the typewritten reply appear in the file. When a colleague died, the correspondence sometimes ended with a copy of an obituary from a newspaper or journal. Some of the correspondents had provided Jelliffe with photographs of themselves which Jelliffe included in the file for that person. This was more likely to be present in the case of colleagues in Europe. There were some newspaper clippings, most commonly from the *New York Times*, when a book was reviewed or an event took place that merited being kept in the file. This was especially true for the Freud file. Reviews of new books by Freud or events in his life that were in the newspapers were part of the file.

While the Jelliffe correspondence was in my home I removed some of the newspaper clippings, photographs, and letters to use them in the historical exhibit, "Psychoanalysis: The American Experience," which I mounted in the Peabody Library in Baltimore, Maryland. This was for the meeting of the American Psychoanalytic Association held in Baltimore in May 1976, to honor its founding in Baltimore on May 9, 1911. Some of the material was used in a second exhibit with the same title for the Thirty-first International Psycho-Analytical Congress in New York in July 1979. The New-Land Foundation of New York had provided me with a grant for historical work in connection with the exhibit in Baltimore. I used some of this grant to copy some of the nine thousand items in the Jelliffe papers.

Dr. Lewis and I discussed where the Jelliffe papers should go. We decided that the best place was the Manuscript Division of the Library of Congress where the Freud Collection and the papers of several distinguished psychiatrists and psychoanalysts are kept. I got in touch with Dr. Ronald S. Wilkinson, manuscript historian at the Library of Congress, who is responsible for the collections on psychiatry and psychoanalysis. Dr. Wilkinson came to my home on June 30, 1976, to examine the Jelliffe correspondence. He agreed that the Jelliffe papers would be a valuable addition to the collections in the Library of Congress.

The Jelliffe correspondence was transferred to the Library of Congress on August 23, 1976. Dr. Wilkinson reported the acquisition of the Smith Ely Jelliffe papers in the *Quarterly Journal of the Library of Congress* (vol. 34, October 1977, pp. 360–363). Within a few months of their transfer the papers became available for research in the Manuscript Reading Room.

In December 1976 I went to New York City for a meeting of the American Psychoanalytic Association. I telephoned Mrs. Helena Jelliffe Goldschmidt, daughter of Smith Ely Jelliffe, and told her that I wanted to give her a copy of the William A. White book which I had edited. Mrs. Goldschmidt invited me to have dinner with her and her husband, Carel. At this first meeting between us I informed the Goldschmidts that the Jelliffe papers were now at the Library of Congress. However, the Freud letters to Jelliffe and White were still in my possession, as Dr. Lewis felt they were very valuable and was reluctant to give them to the Library of Congress. Mr. Goldschmidt and I decided that I would ask Dr. Lewis how much he wanted to be paid to relinquish his claim to the Freud letters which he had held for over thirty years. These Freud letters were then purchased by Mrs. Goldschmidt, who donated them to the Library of Congress on July 26, 1979.

Dr. Lewis was aware of his declining health as we made these arrangements. He died on December 18, 1979, at ninety years of age. He had donated his own papers to the Library of Congress.

Mrs. Goldschmidt asked about the possibility of having a book written about Jelliffe. I said that I would explore the idea. I thought of John C. Burnham to do a biography since he is a historian of medicine and psychoanalysis, and I knew that he was well-informed about Jelliffe. I thought of William McGuire to edit the letters between Freud and Jung and Jelliffe since he had edited *The Freud/Jung Letters*. I agreed to make the contacts and propose a plan for the book.

At a meeting in my home on February 16, 1978, John Burnham, William McGuire, and I planned the Jelliffe book. The proposal was sent to the Goldschmidts, who approved it, leaving entire freedom to the authors. The Goldschmidts came to Washington on May 24, 1978, bringing with them several bags of additional material on Jelliffe. Several boxes of Jelliffe memorabilia were sent to me later. I set aside one room in my home as an archive for the Jelliffe book project. The Goldschmidt Foundation provided the money to aid the preparation of the book.

It took three years, 1978–1981, for the research, writing, and editing. With John C. Burnham in Columbus, Ohio, William McGuire in Princeton, New Jersey, and me in Washington, D.C., coordinating efforts was very important. Carel and Helena Jelliffe Goldschmidt have been continually helpful. It is indeed a great satisfaction to see this book emerge. It substantiates my confidence in John Burnham and William McGuire as the appropriate persons to do justice to Smith Ely Jelliffe.

Arcangelo R. T. D'Amore, M.D.

August 1981

Preface

Most lives are restricted in focus and reflect relatively narrow aspects of their times. A few lives affect and reflect a broad range of human beings and human events. The subject of this book, Smith Ely Jelliffe, led a life of the latter kind. He involved himself in a wide panorama of activities, allied himself with many scientific and cultural currents, and left his impress on countless lives.

Jelliffe, for half a century a major figure in American medicine, was also one of the first actual practitioners of psychoanalysis. His career provides insights into the history of medical science; of medical practice, institutions, and customs (the folklore, as it were, of the profession); of medical journalism; of the mental and nervous disease specialties broadly and of psychosomatics in particular. He was an exemplar of the manifold ways in which society and medicine interacted.

The work of Jelliffe as a medical editor would in itself justify a biography. Furthermore, as one of the first few dozen psychoanalysts in the world, he not only furthered the reception of Freud's teaching in the United States and elsewhere but was one of the few who maintained a personal and professional link with both Freud and Jung after their break. Having come to psychoanalysis in substantial part through Jung, when Jung was an adherent of Freud, Jelliffe maintained, well into the 1930's, personal warmth for Jung and an intellectual curiosity about Jung's ideas that veered further and further away from what came to be a strictly Freudian approach; but the point was reached where he turned entirely from Jung and cleaved with staunch loyalty to Freud. Moreover, Jelliffe from his clinical experience developed his own scientific ideas, and he was one of the founding fathers of modern psychosomatic medicine.

As a case history illustrating the rise of specialization in American medical practice, Jelliffe's career adds a comparative element to a number of existing biographies of physicians with parallel but not often similar professional development. Two of them who show up as important in the narrative and correspondence that follow have been the subjects of major biographical or autobiographical volumes:

William Alanson White (1870–1937), a psychiatrist and prolific writer who as head of St. Elizabeths Hospital in Washington, D.C., the main U.S. government mental hospital, for over thirty years, was of great importance in shaping the entire psychiatric enterprise in the United States and elsewhere.[1]

Harvey Cushing (1869–1939), a pioneer brain surgeon who was a legend in his own time as operator, scholar, and teacher.[2]

It is worth noting that major books have not—as yet—been published about other important figures whose careers paralleled Jelliffe's or intersected with it:

Pearce Bailey (1865–1922), a leading New York neurologist who made many clinical contributions and whose abilities were so great that he headed the important American neuropsychiatric effort in World War I.

A. A. Brill (1874–1948), the first American psychoanalyst; he long considered himself Freud's official representative in the United States. Brill spoke and wrote tirelessly for psychoanalysis, both in medicine and among intellectuals and artists in New York.

Karl Menninger (1893–), co-founder of the famous Menninger Clinic, a younger dynamic psychiatrist whose prodigious efforts in medicine and in American society did much to establish psychoanalytic ideas and humane attitudes toward the mentally ill, especially during and after World War II.

Adolf Meyer (1866–1950), a Swiss-born psychiatrist whose persistent organizational activities in the United States helped introduce first Kraepelinian diagnostics and thorough record taking and then Freudian and dynamic points of view. In his later years, Meyer saw himself as a competitor with Freud. Meyer commanded much deference as professor of psychiatry at Johns Hopkins.

William G. Spiller (1863–1940), an extremely eminent neuropathologist and clinician of Philadelphia, respected alike for his judgment and for his original contributions to medicine.

One area in which Jelliffe worked—editing—is not generally covered in historical accounts. His work as a journal and series editor, especially as it is revealed in his correspondence, is therefore of notable importance. Not only has little been written about modern medical journalism, but few records

1. Arcangelo R. T. D'Amore, ed., *William Alanson White: The Washington Years, 1903–1937* (Washington, D.C., 1976); William Alanson White, *The Autobiography of a Purpose* (Garden City, N.Y., 1938).

2. John F. Fulton, *Harvey Cushing: A Biography* (Springfield, Ill., 1946); Elizabeth H. Thomson, *Harvey Cushing: Surgeon, Author, Artist* (New York, 1950).

exist. Information about Jelliffe, a major figure over a very long period of time, therefore fills a conspicuous gap in our present knowledge.

The history of psychoanalysis, and especially of psychoanalysis in the United States in the years when Jelliffe was prominent, has been relatively well developed by historians, whose work provides backdrop and context for Jelliffe's endeavors and struggles.[3] There are ample accounts of currents and institutions and even factions within psychoanalysis, and of the cultural impact of Freud's and Jung's ideas.[4] A substantial beginning has also been made in understanding the advent of psychosomatics.[5]

To this body of literature the life of Jelliffe brings yet further dimensions. His conversion to a psychoanalytic viewpoint in 1909–1910 is well known; what the details elucidate are the constituents of the appeal of psychoanalytic thinking to an established practitioner and how he moved from being an eclectic, importantly influenced by Jung, to being largely a Freudian. Between the lines of these personal processes, we may see how intellectual and institutional forces constrained the actors in the drama of the evolution of psychoanalysis. Even more revealing in Jelliffe's life is the way in which his biological and medical training played into the stream of dynamic psychiatry to give birth to psychosomatics. Beyond general trends, institutions, and gossip, the Jelliffe records spell out precisely how many social and intellectual forces moved one man who represented much in his culture.

That man in turn did shape events. Here the record is often less distinct, except for strong contemporary statements that Jelliffe had impact and was impressive as a person. Yet enough evidence is left to show at least some of the effect that he had on his times.

Part of Jelliffe's impact lay in his work as an advocate of a new point of view that was well defined: psychoanalysis. His services in Freud's cause— and sometimes in Jung's—were notable, as will become clear. But Jelliffe's impact beyond that, and his total impact, was largely of a variety that Charles

3. John C. Burnham, *Psychoanalysis and American Medicine, 1894–1918: Medicine, Science, and Culture* (New York, 1967); John C. Burnham, "From Avant-Garde to Specialism: Psychoanalysis in America," *Journal of the History of the Behavioral Sciences*, 15 (1979), 128–134; Nathan G. Hale, Jr., *Freud and the Americans: The Beginnings of Psychoanalysis in the United States, 1876–1917* (New York, 1971); Nathan G. Hale, Jr., "From Berggasse XIX to Central Park West," *Journal of the History of the Behavioral Sciences*, 14 (1978), 299–315; George E. Gifford, Jr., ed., *Psychoanalysis, Psychotherapy, and the New England Medical Scene, 1894–1944* (New York, 1978); Jacques M. Quen and Eric T. Carlson, eds., *American Psychoanalysis: Origins and Development* (New York, 1978).

4. Good examples include Douglas Noble and Donald L. Burnham, *History of the Washington Psychoanalytic Society and the Washington Psychoanalytic Institute* ([Washington, D.C.], 1969); Ives Hendrick, *The Birth of an Institute: Twenty-Fifth Anniversary, the Boston Psychoanalytic Institute, November 30, 1958* (Freeport, Me., 1961); and F. H. Matthews, "The Americanization of Sigmund Freud: Adaptations of Psychoanalysis before 1917," *Journal of American Studies*, 1 (1967), 39–62.

5. See especially Robert Charles Powell, "Healing and Wholeness: Helen Flanders Dunbar (1902–59) and an Extra-Medical Origin of the American Psychosomatic Movement, 1906–1936" (unpublished doctoral dissertation, Duke University, 1974).

David Axelrod has conceptualized recently in terms of the stranger—someone who has a defined relationship to the community but who still sees the world from a set of different perspectives. In the intellectual sphere, Jelliffe was such a metaphorical stranger, someone who moved others to see aspects of the world (and, in this case, often of themselves) in a new light. As Axelrod points out, in the history of ideas such figures who move here and there insisting that people hear the stranger's perspective can have as powerful an impact as an unmistakable revolutionary; Axelrod reminds all arbiters of thought of the momentous nature of multiple contributions that cumulate in their effects. A large part of the following account shows how Jelliffe first developed new outlooks and then came to travel among others as a stranger; and one may, moreover, to some extent spell out the means by which he communicated intellectual breakthroughs, as Axelrod calls them, of varying dimensions.[6]

Jelliffe was, it turns out, entirely human; there were foibles as well as strength, charm, talent, and, above all, vision. He enjoyed life. He changed, naturally, as the years passed—not the least in accumulating wisdom that he tried to pass on to others in his writings, speeches, and correspondence. Because he was active in many different areas, Jelliffe obscured his own life patterns and, ultimately, his importance, the exploration of which thus becomes a special task for his biographer. People who knew him in but one role did not fully connect him with the Jelliffe who played another role—editor, teacher, analyst, medical theorist, intellectual, bon vivant.

After the general account and assessment of Jelliffe's life in Part I of this volume, his special relationship with psychoanalysis is examined in detail in Part II through his correspondence with Freud and Jung. These exchanges evoke as nothing else can the three personalities and the historical currents in which they moved. Although Jelliffe conducted an intensive correspondence (it almost merits the terms "avid" and "compulsive") with many professional colleagues, former patients, artists, actors, printers, etc., in America and abroad, and filed it systematically, only the letters exchanged with Jung and Freud have been singled out for full presentation here, owing to their historical, human, and symbolic interest. They were among papers formerly held by Dr. Nolan D. C. Lewis and donated to the Library of Congress under circumstances described in the Foreword. The correspondence files, along with other papers and memorabilia, have been drawn on to supplement what Jelliffe and others published. Additional archival sources, mostly in New York, Philadelphia, and Washington, have also been utilized to give as complete a picture as possible of Jelliffe's own life and the circumstances in which he and his colleagues functioned.

6. Charles David Axelrod, *Studies in Intellectual Breakthrough—Freud, Simmel, Buber* (Amherst, Mass., 1979).

Where necessary to convey the content and style of his thinking, excerpts are included from the correspondence and also from Jelliffe's published and unpublished works. Jelliffe left many admirers but no school of disciples who could perpetuate his ideas directly and extend the benefits of his insights. This book will therefore serve two ancillary functions: to elucidate the nature of his impact and, in describing ideas that made him influential, help his successors to continue to learn not only from his achievements but also from the conclusions that he drew from his studying and experimenting and from the observations afforded by a very rich medical practice.

Unless otherwise indicated, all letters cited are located in the Smith Ely Jelliffe Papers alphabetical file in the Manuscripts Division of the Library of Congress in Washington, D.C. Some Jelliffe originals are from the Jung Archives through the kindness of Mr. Franz Jung. The Jelliffe family has retained a few items, cited as Family Papers, and the Personal Letter File and the Additional Papers are, at the time of this writing, still in transit to ultimate deposit in the Library of Congress. In quoted material, minor errors, especially in carbon copies, have been corrected throughout for readability, but in large part the original form and punctuation have been retained.

Acknowledgments

Although the title page indicates divided responsibility for sections of this book, the work is nevertheless in many ways a collaboration and joint effort.

Funds for expenses involved in the preparation of this book have been donated by the Goldschmidt Foundation. The Ohio State University has in addition provided some assistance.

We are particularly grateful to the following persons for assistance in research: Professor Robert Buerki; Mr. James Capshew; Mr. J. Stephen Catlett, American Philosophical Society Library; Miss Mabel Cohen, Jelliffe's secretary; K. R. Eissler, M.D.; the late Miss Anna Freud; Mr. and Mrs. Carel Goldschmidt; Mrs. Aniela Jaffé; Mr. Franz Jung; the late Professor Walter Kaufmann; Ms. M. Linda Kircher of the College of Physicians and Surgeons; The Kristine Mann Library and its librarian, Mrs. Doris A. Albrecht; Mrs. Helen R. Lansberg, director of the Medical Library, Institute for Living, Hartford; Mr. Ralph Manheim, beyond his work as translator; Mrs. Salli Morgenstern of the Library of the New York Academy of Medicine; Doris Nagel, M.D.; Sir John Pope-Hennessy; Ms. Ruth M. Reynolds of the Library of the New York Psychoanalytic Society; Professor Emanuel D. Rudolph; Mr. John E. Sauer; Dr. R. S. Wilkinson, Manuscript Division, Library of Congress; and Mr. Richard Wolfe, Francis A. Countway Library, Boston.

We gratefully acknowledge the following permission to reprint from:

Extracts from correspondence between Sigmund Freud and Smith Ely Jelliffe reproduced with permission of Sigmund Freud Copyrights Ltd. The Freud letters, copyright © 1983 by Sigmund Freud Copyrights Ltd. Also to Sigmund Freud Copyrights Ltd. for letters from Anna Freud. Miss Freud also gave her personal permission.

C. G. Jung's letters, copyright © 1983 by Erbengemeinschaft Prof. Dr. C. G. Jung. Also for a letter from Emma Jung.

C. G. Jung, *Letters*, ed. Gerhard Adler and Aniela Jaffé, trans. R. F. C. Hull, Bollingen Series XCV, Vol. I: *1906–1950*. Copyright © 1971, 1973 by Princeton University Press. Excerpts, pp. 28–30 and pp. 210–11, reprinted by permission of Princeton University Press. Routledge & Kegan Paul Ltd. are the publishers of Jung's Letters in the United Kingdom.

The letters from Sigmund Freud reprinted in *Psychoanalytic Pioneers*, ed. F. Alexander et al., copyright © 1966 by Basic Books, Inc. (New York and London).

Jelliffe, "The Editor Himself and His Adopted Child," *Journal of Nervous and Mental Disease*, 89 (1939), 545–589.

Mabel Dodge Luhan, *Movers and Shakers* (New York: Harcourt, Brace, 1936). Reprinted with the permission of Kraus Reprint, A Division of Kraus-Thomson Organization Limited.

Arthur Ramos, "A Bio-Dynamic and Evolutional Orientation of Psychoanalysis, Smith Ely Jelliffe: His Work," *Journal of Nervous and Mental Disease*, 84 (1936), 667–675.

Jelliffe, "The Death Instinct in Somatic and Psychopathology," *Psychoanalytic Review*, 20 (1933), 122–124, Human Sciences Press.

Jelliffe, "Address: Glimpses of a Freudian Odyssey," *Psychoanalytic Quarterly*, 2 (1933), 318–329.

Francis L. Wellman, *The Art of Cross-Examination*, 4th Edn. (Copyright 1923, 1936 by Macmillan Publishing Co., Inc., renewed 1951, 1964 by Ethel Wellman).

Jelliffe, *An Introduction to Pharmacognosy* (Philadelphia: W. B. Saunders Co., 1904).

Photograph of Mary Foote's portrait of Jelliffe, in the Mary Foote Papers, Collection of American Literature, Beinecke Rare Book and Manuscript Library, Yale University.

I

Jelliffe: American Psychoanalyst and Physician

JOHN C. BURNHAM

ONE

The Making of a Physician 1866–1900

A Multifaceted Life

Smith Ely Jelliffe (27 October 1866–25 September 1945) was an American physician who made a particular impact on his civilization as an important medical editor and as a pioneer psychoanalyst. In his capacity as analyst he was also one of the earliest advocates of psychosomatic medicine. In many areas of medicine and of life in general he was a follower, reflective of his times and profession, rather than a leader. Harmony with his social and intellectual environment, however, enhanced his effectiveness on the important occasions when he did lead and inspire.[1]

Jelliffe was a boy at the time after the Civil War when the United States was changing from a rural to an urban civilization. By the 1890's, when he was married and had moved his practice to New York City, he personally had changed many of his attitudes from rural and small town to cosmopolitan. Glimpses of his growing up and becoming a physician emphasize how he adapted to his environment and also how he continually sought some destiny, not only in Victorian respectability but in fame.

The route that he chose to follow was science and medicine. In science he devoted himself to botany, particularly field botany, which just at the end of the nineteenth century tended to be isolated from an exciting new cellular biology. In botany Jelliffe never really escaped the amateur, natural history tradition. In medicine the newer developments in germ theory and physiological chemistry were already underway when Jelliffe was completing his training, and he found himself unable to fulfill his ambitions by making

---

1. Standard accounts, besides directories and obituaries, include *National Cyclopedia of American Biography*, vol. 33, pp. 360–361; Nolan D. C. Lewis, "Smith Ely Jelliffe, 1866–1945, Psychosomatic Medicine in America," in *Psychoanalytic Pioneers*, pp. 224–233; John C. Burnham, "Jelliffe, Smith Ely," *Dictionary of American Biography*, suppl. 3, pp. 384–386; *Semi-Centennial Volume of the American Neurological Association, 1875–1924* (New York, 1924), pp. 191–193.

trailblazing discoveries such as had occurred in European laboratories. But for years he kept looking, aware (not unusual among physicians then) that he had to find a specialty in medicine to rise in the profession. Only tentatively did he move toward neurology and psychiatry where ultimately he could and would become a pioneer. Meantime his restless intellect and his success in writing and editing led him in other directions.

In 1924 Jelliffe wrote informally to a Boston physician and psychotherapist, James S. Van Teslaar, evaluating his own work and sending a list of his publications up until that time.

"I would say that what I am particularly interested in may be summarized somewhat as follows: First the history of psychiatry in the evolution of dynamic principles. Secondly the founding of the *Psychoanalytic Review* with Dr. [William Alanson] White in 1913 and then the writing of *Diseases of the Nervous System* in 1915 with Dr. White which almost for the first time has attempted to carry the conception of the body as a whole as a dynamic concept into a text-book. Thirdly I would call attention to my interest in psychotherapy which might be gathered," Jelliffe continued, from a number of translations he had carried out, especially of the pioneer works on psychotherapy by Dubois and by Déjérine and Gauckler.

"The relation of Psychoanalysis to artistic production you will find in the Bibliography; some of these were collected together in the Monograph on *Psychoanalysis and the Drama*. As a contribution to Technique the articles in the *Psychoanalytic Review* were elementary and were then revised and presented in a more advanced form as a Monograph on *Technique of Psychoanalysis*. Finally I might add that from the beginning, as far back as 1900, I had been of the conviction that any consistent radical philosophy would have to include the psychogenic components of conversion processes which by reason of their intensity and chronicity could produce what was called organic disease. For me the problem of so-called constitution is inadequately comprehended without the participation of the symbolic activities which constitute a special attribute of the delivery system of the human body. Along this line, as appears in my reprint on 'Paleopsychology' and 'Psychopathology and Organic Disease,' both of which I send you, I have taken up skin diseases, particularly psoriasis, alcoholism, dementia praecox, epilepsy, tuberculosis, multiple sclerosis, hyper and hypothyroid states, nephritis and bone disease."[2] This summary will be explored in the narrative of Jelliffe's career and contributions in the pages that now follow.

Ten years later Jelliffe offered a more personal retrospect on his life, writing to an old college classmate whom he had not contacted for many years; this retrospect, too, will be expanded.

2. Smith Ely Jelliffe to James S. Van Teslaar, 6 March 1924. (This letter and all other letters not otherwise identified are in the main alphabetical file of the Smith Ely Jelliffe Papers, Library of Congress, Washington, D.C.)

"Time has gone on and both of us are nearing the patriarch's line. Old Father Time has been fairly good to me. There have been some tough times, especially when I lost my first wife and a son who was studying medicine. We had five kids—2 girls, 2 boys, and a girl in a rapidly arriving row. They all married and all had children—there are nine grandchildren now.

"We worked and played hard. I send you a bibliography and a couple of reprints which will give a glimpse of my mental wanderings.

"And now I am up at my country home on Lake George. I remarried in 1917 but had no children by my second marriage.

"Some of my early chemical enthusiasms are here in my boat house and my botanical collections are here also, with a lot of books and other things. I am growing deaf, have arthritic twinges, a poor pump which breaks down periodically, but we carry on. Naturally gray hair, but I still have my teeth so that I am not as of Shakespeare's 'sans everything.' . . .

"Financially the depreciation in values has reduced me to the necessity of keeping on in my medical work, else I might be free for doing only what I most enjoy, that is, careful undisturbed work in my specialty. But one cannot have everything and I am content although on the down hill side of life with its attendant disturbances and discomforts."[3]

These brief glimpses only begin to suggest the complexity of Jelliffe. He was of course a husband and father, and he did have to provide for himself and his family, even, as he notes, in his old age. But it was the great variety of interests that Jelliffe cultivated in his career that offered the most confusing picture of the man—not only all aspects of medicine and psychology but art, chemistry, drama, and botany. The complexity of his life sometimes bemused Jelliffe himself, particularly when he was young. He did, in fact, take an uncommonly long time to find himself. Interested in many subjects, he tended to develop coherence in his life by working in interdisciplinary areas or simply by doing several things at once. But what in his earlier years appeared as irresolution, and even immaturity and at times unwillingness to make a commitment, later developed into the capacity to keep growing intellectually. From that capacity for growth came most of his distinctive contributions.

Interest in Genealogy

Jelliffe as a young man developed an interest in genealogy that he maintained to the end of his life, when he thought that he might devote two whole chapters of a proposed autobiography to his ancestral backgrounds—one chapter to his European forebears and another to the American colonials (see Appendix 2). He had traced a Joli or Jolif to the Norman invasion of England. ("Perhaps," he quipped, "I owe it to this that I never quite understood English, or even more interestingly the English never quite understood me.")

3. Jelliffe to Barton Cruickshank, 2 July 1934.

Successive generations of teachers, clergymen, and other substantial or professional members of their communities led to the Joelliff who went to Connecticut and finally Jelliffe's grandfather, who was a Danbury hatmaker.[4] Through his mother Jelliffe was descended from a Robert Kitchel who was state legislator and judge in Guilford, New Hampshire, in the 1660's.

Jelliffe's interest in genealogy was not necessarily what it might seem. It may have helped him in confirming his self-image as a professional, for he came of a long line of professionals and community leaders, including a sea captain, William Jelliffe (1772–1814). Unlike many physicians of his day, therefore, Jelliffe was not in a social sense upwardly mobile. Certainly he eventually came to be skeptical of the importance of biological factors in human lives. But he always tended to think in Lamarckian terms about the ways in which individual life history altered heredity. And it is true that this outlook may have contributed to his initial systematic interest in ancestry, an interest that would have been conventional in medicine at the turn of the twentieth century. He did not, however, follow his friend and classmate at Brooklyn Polytechnic, C. B. Davenport, who devoted much of his life to emphasizing the importance of hereditary factors in shaping human character and behavior. Jelliffe in the end became more interested in psychological determinants as such.

What genealogy provided for Jelliffe was not only a way of expressing how important his family was to him but also a sense of continuity. What is striking in his genealogical notebooks and sketches is Jelliffe's sense of place. He was not as interested in *who* as much as in *where*. He photographed sites where his ancestors had dwelt; he traced the holders of property. He took endless photographs of what became his own family holdings.

As a young man, he was acutely conscious of whether or not someone came, as he did, from Brooklyn, and later in life he was a confirmed New Yorker. That was, after all, the city in which he was born. This feeling of local place—which could involve a substantial amount of provinciality—somehow gave Jelliffe the basis for his interest in overseas professional developments, and he was by far the most cosmopolitan of all of the American neurologists and psychiatrists of the early twentieth century.

Jelliffe commented on his own pleasure in genealogy, in a fragment probably dating from the 1930's: "Family Tree-itis is a baffling disease. It runs a chronic course, with acute exacerbations, varying in length and intensity, and its remissions also present unexplained and strange features. . . .

"It is not a rare malady. In only a comparatively few number of instances is it at all devastating, although at times, in its more robust forms, it can withdraw the individual very effectively from the world of real events and

4. Smith Ely Jelliffe, "The Editor Himself and His Adopted Child," *JNMD*, 89 (1939), 545–546.

for a long time plunge the individual thus involved into a fever of isolated activity."[5]

Parents and Family

Jelliffe's immediate forebears, his parents, continued in the tradition of solid citizens. His father, William Munson Jelliffe (born in 1835), was a school teacher in New York and then Brooklyn, where as a principal he was an important influence in education. Perhaps his best known accomplishment was establishing in 1886 the first systematic kindergarten instruction in Brooklyn. He was, moreover, well known locally as an elocutionist whose public reading and speaking talents were in demand.[6] Jelliffe, the son, was also an educator: he taught in medical schools for twenty years, and he, too, was often in demand as a speaker. The father, in turn, after his son's graduation from medical school, took a doctorate in pedagogy at the City University of New York in 1891, acknowledging the help of two neurologists important in his son's life, M. Allen Starr and Ira Van Gieson.

Jelliffe referred to his father in terms of Jelliffe's own "paternal superego," suggesting the powerful influence of William Munson Jelliffe. One family story that Jelliffe recounted suggested the kind of character that was involved.

"My father was studying at the College of the City [of] New York here in New York, as my grandmother was very ambitious for her boys. There was a brother Sam, years younger, who standing too near the railroad train at Darien, Connecticut, where they lived, lost his right arm. My father left college, he was but 19, and told his mother he had a job as a teacher in a public school in New York City. 'Sam would need an education.' That was my father throughout his life. I never knew him unready to help others."[7]

Jelliffe's mother, Susan Emma Kitchell, born in 1836, had been a school teacher in New York when she married William Munson Jelliffe in 1856. She was a vigorous, active woman with a keen sense of humor. At the age of seventy she went to Egypt and climbed the Pyramids and rode a camel. She traveled through the Panama Canal the year it opened. Jelliffe often went to see her at her home in Brooklyn, and after he purchased property on Lake George she spent a part of each summer with him and his family.[8]

5. Copy in Additional Papers.
6. *The Brooklyn Teacher*, February 1898, p. 2. William M. Jelliffe, *Good Selections in Prose and Poetry: For Use in Schools and Academies, Home and Church Sociables, Lyceums and Literary Societies, etc.* (New York, 1871).
7. Jelliffe, "The Editor Himself," p. 546.
8. Information from Mrs. Helena Goldschmidt. Jelliffe himself was remarkably reticent about his mother in both his letters and his autobiographical writings, even in the account of his childhood that is excerpted below.

Jelliffe maintained affectionate feelings for his family and stayed in touch not only with his parents but with his brother and sister. His father died in 1898, his mother in 1921.

Jelliffe arrived in the family in 1866, just after the end of the Civil War. The circumstances he later described himself: "I was born in a brownstone house on West 38th Street, New York City. I must have been very much loved by my parents, as one brother, Samuel, aet. 3, had died of cerebrospinal meningitis just before I was born and another brother William, aet. 8, just after my birth. I was probably saved from being absolutely spoiled by the birth of a brother a year and a half later and thus I became the special ward of a sister nine years older. I am proud to say that my most commendable traits are largely of her patterning."[9]

Childhood: An Unpublished Autobiographical Fragment

Jelliffe's childhood and youth were extremely conventional. Indeed, for many years he seemed naive and at least a bit prissy. At the end of the 1930's he recalled to Ernest Jones that "the pale conservative pall of Brooklyn kept me from any extreme gyrations in my adolescent wobbly years—and then there were my botanical enthusiasms and my fiancée, as I was one of those idealistic youngsters who fell in love at 16 and stuck to the same object for some thirty years or more, so I did not go in for any of the 'movements,' such as are now designated as 'left' and 'right,' etc."[10] This youthful stability contrasts with Jelliffe's "break with orthodoxy," as he viewed it, later in his life.

Virtually all that we know of Jelliffe's childhood is what is contained in his autobiographical sketches. He did finish part of a chapter for a longer autobiography, giving as full an account as he could recall; it was never completed, revised, or published.

"Like most children I recall very little of my earlier years. I was not Eidetic. . . .

"It is a fairly well understood principle of psychology that no early experiences are totally lost and the psychoanalytic technique is one whereby much of this early imagery may be recalled. It is often glimpsed in the dream life, and in many illnesses larger or smaller bits of one's infantile experiences come into mental imagery, usually, however, much distorted by the processes of symbolization which are among the results of the repressing mechanisms."

"As my father had about the time of my birth been advanced to a principalship of a public school in Brooklyn and had not yet settled in his new

9. Jelliffe, "The Editor Himself," pp. 546–547. The birth certificate shows 158 West 37th Street. William Munson Jelliffe and Susan Emma Kitchell had five children, Ann Louise (Lulu) (1857–1947), William (1860–1867), Samuel (1862–1865), Smith Ely (1866–1945), and Alfred (1868–1937).

10. Jelliffe to Ernest Jones, 18 January 1940.

home my mother was with her parents in New York City. I was not born in a log cabin but in a big four-story brownstone house somewhere near the car barns on 38th [*sic*] St. between 5 & 6 avenues. . . .

"My earliest recollections are of our home in Bergen Street, Brooklyn. An earlier home in Raymond St. I have never known of. I only recall the horse car tracks that went by the door and I have had an occasional nightmare of 'horses hoofs and sparks of fire.' My sister has told me I was nearly run over by a fire engine while she was leading me across the street when I was somewhere between 2–4 years of age. This is a clear-cut illustration of an eidetic memory image occurring in a dream. Occasional phantasy images of a wistaria vine and an iron second-story porch are either of the same class or are condensations of a later wistaria vine of the home I lived in from my ninth year on. The porch I have never been able to locate. It is a cover memory of some sort.

"Of my earliest childhood activities there are no recollections. . . .

"A story told by my mother seems to indicate I was a quickly learning child. It seems that at about 4 I was sent to a small kindergarten class, somewhere near on the same street. . . . I had been there but one or two weeks when, as it is reported, the teacher came in tears [saying] that I had done the whole year's work in those few weeks and she did not know what to teach me.

"As I may relate later a slight variant of this experience, it may have been so. I have no recollections of the early school to which I went save a general sense that it was around the corner and a block or so north—Dean Street. I think I was a happy child. I have no recollection of unhappy experiences save one to which reference may be made later.

"As my father, being a teacher, had long summer vacations, my chief tenuous images of these early days were of the country. My mother's brother William had a house in New Jersey. I recall the fruit trees, especially the seckel pears. Also the home of the Elys in Hanover—I recall faintly the fruit trees there, ladders and the two girl distant cousins. I do not recall how, dressed in my best, once at the Elys I found the pig pen and it found me, a sight to behold when my mother rescued me. I recall a great-great grandmother at Hanover Neck, N.J., and the Whippany River. She was a great-great grandmother by marriage only.

"The old house at Darien, my father's father and mother's home, brings back the most distinct images. There was a delightful brook at the foot of the meadow, overhung by wild grapes and a mill pond, but more vividly the factory where an uncle, Fanshaw, used to manufacture French shoe high heels. The movements of mill wheel and of the belts were a constant source of pleasure. It was so cool under this old wheel, but most vividly I can smell the wood and see the piles of sawdust and can hear the turning tools as they cut into the blocks of wood and see the high heels turned. All throughout my life brief spells of craving for a turning lathe have come and gone and what slight facility I had with carpenter's tools derives from the Fanshaw shoe-heel factory.

"A big chestnut tree at the upper end of the pond, a cherry tree by the front door and the quince trees by the old fashioned privy—these are vivid recollections of the house at Darien. The familiar patter of the rain on the shingle roof as I slept just under it in the attic came to me for years as a soothing memory and would put me to sleep. I needed no sheep to count. I could always phantasy the patter of the rain. Occasionally we would catch an eel in the old pond and I learned how to hold him with sand in my hands.

"The tide pools and the salt water marshes on the way to Dibble's and Roton Point are also among these early childhood recollections. In particular were the mud flats wherein my brother and I would sink up to our knees almost in the slimy, salty, oozy greyish mud, as we sought for clams or fiddlers.

"I cannot separate the years of these early memories. They are like other children's years, and I am sure I had more happy summers than most boys.

"I know that I was very agile and fleet of foot and quite handy about the house. I have no recollections of fears or punishments of these early years and used to roam widely in these summer months.

"Although my brother was but a year younger I recall very little of him on these summer vacations. His recollections of Darien are more vivid than mine. Nor are there any early childhood recollections of my sister, nine years older. At the age of 10, when my brother was born, she had much to do with me and my behavior closely following his birth. There are repressions here undoubtedly.

"Particularly pleasant childhood memories were those of a boarding house at Ellenville, N.Y., the Deckers', where we summered for some years. How many I do not now recall. High up on the mountain side overlooking the Walkill Valley I saw my first circular rainbow. I was maybe 6–7–8 years of age. Here my chief recollections were of the big barn, the haying, and especially do I recall one incident where the city boy was challenged to race Robbie Decker across the newly-cut oat field, barefoot.

"I can recall as of yesterday, the grim determination not to mind the sharp straw stubble, and literally closing my senses to the pain, how I raced him across the oat field and beat him. . . .

"I also recall a peculiar excitement when, for the first time, when I was about 7–8, I saw a bull mount a cow. I did not know what it was all about, but something within me must have known. I was, so far as I recall, singularly inattentive to such matters.

"As for sickness I knew little of it. I can recall only earaches. I have a dim recollection of my father puffing pipe smoke into my ears when I was living in the Bergen Street house. This must have been before I was nine, for I was at that age when we moved to Sixth Avenue on the Park Slope. I must have had appendix attacks, for I can recall curling myself up on a sofa in dull misery, refusing to eat or be comforted by anybody for a day or two at times. I was even then a stoic, and ever since it has been a bit of me rarely to complain.

"In fact it might seem that the curtain of my childhood memories came down at about this age, for only after this age do my memories become more numerous and vivid. . . .

"One sad memory of childhood is important, since it carried with it, for years, a mood of sorrow with a specific nuance of suffering. I cannot bring anything but the feeling to memory, but the probable reconstruction is not difficult. Christmas stockings were hung up. I could not have been more than four years of age. On one Christmas mine was empty. A sadness, unaccompanied by anything but a dull heaviness of loneliness, was my response.

"I seem to remember, I have been told, although this may be a phantasy reconstruction, it was because I had hit my little brother on the head with a hammer. On several occasions in my later life when I have done some mean or unworthy action, or have had a severe rebuff, I recall, in particular to come later perhaps, this same mood of deep sadness has come over me, but I have rarely felt it save associated with some wave of self reproach for some antisocial act. At all events I feel it is no rationalization to say that this punishment has served as a censorship throughout my life. If I should discuss in a separate section, diseases, family and personal, I may return to this experience as to possible relationship to some things that came later in my life (deafness, heart).

"In the spring when I was nine years old my father bought a house just completed with two others on the park slope," Jelliffe recalled, near neighbors with gardens and fruit trees.

"I have no [feeling] of sadness when it comes to my recollections of depredations of those cherry trees and the pear trees. Being, as stated, agile and very slight in weight at that time, I was the one who did most of the climbing and apparently was the ringleader in these somewhat precarious if not unlawful undertakings.

"The cherry tree pilferings were specially exciting as the trees were in different yards and one could monkey from one to another as the irate maids threatened dire things. We were never caught.

"Once, in a pear tree, however, the under branch broke and left me suspended, hanging by my hands. Being young and not so strong in the arms as was needed I hung until I was forced to drop some 10–15 feet. I must have been hurt as my companions in disgrace and dismay carried me home and left me to nurse my sore sacroiliac joints. No bones were broken.

"These were banal activities known to most boys, rarely to the actual city dweller, save in vacation times, but we lived in an undeveloped part of the city which more or less rapidly filled up with new houses as the years rolled on.

"Being swift of foot, naturally I must have influenced the gang to running games of all kinds. There were Black Tom and scampers from one side of the street to the other over half a block bounds. There was never any dickering as to who would be 'It' in our group. I voluntarily began almost invariably. I learned early that I could catch any of the other boys but I would be the last to be caught, if caught at all. Nightfall would call us to our homes and studies and I would still be darting back and forth across the street with a dozen or so of my companions in the middle trying to catch me.

"Saturdays or long afternoons it would be Catch One–Catch All, the boundaries several blocks of built, half-built and empty lot blocks. This was, with baseball, my favorite game and sometimes might go on all day. . . .

"My brother was an expert pitcher. I almost always chose first base and was among the better batters and base runners. Being swift I rarely had to slide; for here I was a bit clothes conscious, my brother never. Often I would drop out of a game to get a button sewed on; he never. A pin or a stick would hold him together.

"Saturdays almost invariably saw us either playing Catch One–Catch All or out at Prospect Park watching the grownup teams.

"Later, when I was about 15, some Canadian boys came into the neighborhood and we learned to play cricket. Father often went to the Park and was among those who played croquet. Prospect Park had its much reputed croquet teams. Kites, marbles, tops, one-o-cat and the like were popular in the younger years. As my brother was a dead shot at marbles and tops, I never took much to these games. He soon had all the marbles and could split a top with unerring accuracy. Tops had no virtue in my eyes.

"One idiosyncrasy concerning my lessons may be related. For the most part I preferred to get them all done Friday. This left me all day Saturday and Sunday with no tasks ahead. It was, if I do not mislead myself, a general tendency to get the disagreeable or necessary task out of the way first. This trend has persisted all my life to some degree. I have never paused to analyse it. I do not recall ever being priggish about it. I just did it. This was rarely, however, the case with manual labor. This I always avoided if I could. My arms were never the equals of my legs. This never led me to run away from a fight but I avoided fisticuffs. . . .

"Football was not so popular although we played it. I recall at 13 or thereabouts how astonished and annoyed I was when for the first time I met with the device of interference. In spite of my swiftness it took me some time to learn how to circumvent this device. I can recall to this day my perplexity and annoyance when I could not catch the runner because of this maneuver."[11]

11. Ms. autobiography, Additional Papers. Abridged.

Here Jelliffe's recollections break off. They confirm a happy, active childhood of a quite normal boy, and there is little to be added to them. In later life competitiveness in Jelliffe was heavily masked, but the intelligence that his precociousness signaled and his marvelous memory he always put to good use as an adult. His high school career remains largely unknown, as does his frequenting the natural history museum (letter to Freud, 13 April 1937, Part II).

Education

Jelliffe graduated from the public schools in 1882. He then began the study of civil engineering at Brooklyn Collegiate and Polytechnic Institute, later called just Brooklyn Polytechnic. He followed this course because of the belief of his father "that mathematics was the 'best training for the mind.'" Jelliffe's interests lay rather in botany, but he bowed to his father's decision ("the only criticism I had of my father," he later wrote), and he completed the scientific course at "the Poly" in 1886, taking special pleasure in geology and zoology.[12] Although he was not in the arts course that would have enabled him to receive a B.A., he did take many arts courses and, as he was fond of recalling, he gave the French oration at graduation, and the bewhiskered French professor was pleased with his "Qui est ce guerier devant nous?" as Jelliffe quoted it in a letter many years later.[13]

In spite of his reluctance to discipline his mind with mathematical exercises, Jelliffe had fond memories of his college career. The classes were small, and Jelliffe recalled in 1934, writing to his classmate, Barton Cruickshank: "Only a short time ago I was trying to understand a mathematical concept in a book I was reading and musingly I recalled the days when we sat together at the Poly and compared notes. I was as dumb as an egg on math and you had your troubles with logic and the damned Syllogisms. I cursed Sheldon and got you to help me out with analytical geometry. You came to me anent 'All men are mortal, Socrates was a man—Ergo—' and so it went on. Whether Plymton or old Daddy Cochran harassed you I do not now recall, but those were happy days, especially in the glass enclosed laboratory where we made our first essays into chemical lore." On another occasion he remembered fondly how he and his chums customarily took "noonday milk" in a shop in Clinton Street.[14]

Jelliffe in 1886 also obtained a license to teach in the public common schools of Brooklyn. But instead of teaching he went to medical school. Years later Jelliffe recalled that one fall, when he was about eighteen, after a Dr. Bates had showed him the inner structure of the mosses, he had told his father

12. Jelliffe, "The Editor Himself," pp. 547–548. In his last letter to Freud (Part II, 6 March 1939), Jelliffe recalled again how his early interest in natural history grew into a general viewpoint in his mature years.
13. Jelliffe to C. B. Davenport, 4 January 1937.
14. Jelliffe to Barton Cruickshank, 2 July 1934. Jelliffe to C. B. Davenport, 16 August 1897. Davenport Papers, American Philosophical Society, Philadelphia.

that he wanted to study medicine.[15] From an early time, then, botany and the study of medicine were connected in Jelliffe's mind, and as late as 1937 Jelliffe in writing to Freud recalled specifically studying botany in medical school (see Part II).

Entering medical school was a momentous step in his career, and equally momentous was his choice of medical school, the College of Physicians and Surgeons (P & S), of Columbia University, where he took his M.D. in 1889. He developed associations there that he maintained all of his life, not only with faculty but with classmates, including contemporaries, such as Stewart Paton and J. P. Warbasse, who were important in the fields in which he later specialized. He did well in medical school, to the point of winning a prize for his excellent performance on the examinations. Afterward he continued to feel strong institutional loyalty. And, in fact, in New York City the P & S men tended to stand apart from medical colleagues who had other school connections.[16]

Yet in writing one set of memoirs, in 1939, Jelliffe demurred from recalling his three medical school years in any detail. He did mention his work in neurology with M. Allen Starr, who helped Jelliffe's father and was later an important friend and sponsor, although Starr's three lectures on psychiatry constituted but a "pitiful" course. And he also remarked on "a recurring migraine which regularly overtook me at 11 A.M. when I had to listen to the professor of surgery about 'healthy laudable pus'" during a period when the bacterial theory was establishing itself, and when Jelliffe was already working with T. Mitchell Prudden, "staining streptococcus and staphylococcus and the whole germ brood," as he recalled.[17] Only elsewhere and incidentally did Jelliffe comment on his medical school years or on his internship (1889–1890) at St. Mary's General Hospital in Brooklyn.

On one such occasion, in tracing his interest in psychological medicine, Jelliffe did note one particular benefit that he got from his experience at St. Mary's.

"I then entered St. Mary's Hospital as an interne and it was most useful for me. Although my parents were not church going people, I had gone through a typical adolescent conversion reaction and since 17 had been an active though not very emotionally involved member of the Baptist brand of theology. It had been a fractionated concomitant of my adolescent love object finding. I was now plunged into a definitely Catholic atmosphere. At first a bit bewildering, it ultimately became of signal service in getting a better orientation to emotional values and was distinctly serviceable in wearing down narrow prejudices and scotomata of all kinds.

15. Jelliffe to Louise Jelliffe Long, 5 December 1942, Additional Papers.
16. See Jelliffe to A. Malloch, 15 April 1936.
17. Jelliffe, "The Editor Himself," p. 548.

"As a small boy I can recall I rarely was fond of feuds, or violent parti-sanships. . . . Experience had taught me I could catch anybody and no one could catch me. So was it in the hospital. It made little difference to me, creed, or sect, or color or what not and this was, I soon noted, the influence that religious faith seemed to impart to the sisters who were about on their mission night and day. In those early days I pondered much on the functional values of religious concepts.

"Another striking hospital experience, I also recall in the person of a typical 'mythomaniac' of Dupré's terminology. She was a very attractive 21 year old young woman, who had had no less than 28 different operations on different parts of her body trying to cut out mythical diseases of one kind or another. Needless to say my surgical benevolent skepticism has not abated one bit in the years during which I have observed similar efforts to cut ideas out of the body.

"And now to my early introduction to 'dream' psychology which has kept me amused at myself for many years. There was also in the hospital at the same time as the attractive mythomaniac, another even more charming hys-terical patient, a somnambulist, among other of her vagaries. She was a Spanish type, beautifully classic, vivacious and alluring. I well remember my going to the Mother Superior and virtuously telling of my being visited in my room by this charming creature after midnight. The calm, easy and serious way in which this very superior woman assured me I should not be disturbed again has always made me smile at my early ignorance of the wish fulfilling function of the dream. Needless to say I was 'engaged' at the time and still a virgin, for only of such can one believe in such simple unsophistication, at least in a young physician."[18]

A Year in Europe

In 1890, then, Jelliffe was a young M.D. with a moustache who had just finished his internship at St. Mary's. His passport described him as:

23 years
5'9⅞"
Forehead medium high & wide
Eyes light blue
Nose ordinary
Mouth small, lips arched
Chin square
Hair light brown
Complexion fair, freckled
Face oval, thinnish.[19]

18. Smith Ely Jelliffe, "Glimpses of a Freudian Odyssey," *Psychoanalytic Quarterly*, 2 (1933), 319–320.

19. Passport, Additional Papers.

In later years Jelliffe described himself as "asthenic at 21 and weighed 115 lbs.—Athletic typus at 30 and weighed 125 and," he added at age sixty, "now . . . pyknic and 195."[20] In 1890 he was a thin, active young man.

The passport was for Jelliffe's year in Europe. Like many other late Victorian Americans, Jelliffe determined to spend a year abroad for cultural purposes and, since he was also a physician, to take some postgraduate training in the great medical centers of Europe, particularly Vienna. His trip was financed by a loan from his cousin for whom he had been named, Smith Ely, who had been a reform mayor of New York City. "As I looked at his check for $1,000," recalled Jelliffe, "it seemed like all the money in the world. I squeezed a year's joy and profit out of it."[21] His letters written to his future wife, who stayed in Brooklyn, provide glimpses of his activities, his concerns, and his thoughts during what he called his *Wanderjahr*.

These letters show that Jelliffe was a product of the best type of social uplift environment in both home and community. He knew what he was supposed to appreciate, and he bravely undertook to carry out his role. Already he understood what it meant to have a cultured background. He recalled that in the years of medical school and internship "I was much taken up with my fiancée with a vast variety of general readings. There was Emerson and Thoreau and Burroughs, Spencer and George Henry Lewes, George Eliot. Collecting winter buds and arranging our herbarium sheets. At the hospital I recall reading evenings with my to-be-brother-in-law Aeschylus, Sophocles and Euripides with some Goethe and Schiller and Lessing. All in translations for neither Greek nor German were among the benefits conferred by a college course in engineering."[22]

Jelliffe left New York in October 1890. His first important stop was Vienna, where he continued a valiant struggle with the German language. There he took the usual medical classes and also managed to work in the botany department of the university—with more enthusiasm, he indicated to his fiancée, than he reserved for medical training. But, then, botany was an interest that they shared. "It will look fine," he wrote, "for a doctor's wife to be a scientist also."[23]

In March Jelliffe moved on to Berlin, touring on the way. In Berlin he undertook some short course work in medicine and again worked in botany. As he recalled in a letter to Freud (20 May 1936, Part II), he did not feel welcome in the neurological laboratory. In any event, he directed his efforts

20. Jelliffe to George Draper, 4 January 1926.
21. Jelliffe, "The Editor Himself," p. 548.
22. Ibid., pp. 548–549.
23. Letter page 302, 18 April 1891, Personal Letter File. University records show that Helena Leeming Jelliffe was in fact a special student in botany at Barnard during the 1890's, both before and after her marriage. See William Hamilton Gibson and Helena Leeming Jelliffe, *Our Native Orchids: A Series of Drawings from Nature of All the Species Found in the Northeastern United States* (New York, 1905).

more and more toward general high culture. Koch's laboratory, the importance of which he recognized, received short shrift in the letter in which he mentioned it, compared to the art museum, an opera he saw, and other cultural resources. By late spring and summer as he traveled across the Continent he seldom mentioned any medical matters at all, not even the occasion—which he recalled later—when he heard Charcot himself lecture in Paris. Jelliffe instead was seeing every city with every feature mentioned in the guidebooks and was taking in a large number of operatic, musical, and other theatrical productions. In August his father, who was also in Europe for a few weeks, told him that Smith Ely (his namesake, the former mayor) would advance him more money to stay another year.[24] Jelliffe refused. He sailed for home from Liverpool on 23 October 1891.

In view of the maverick quality of much of Jelliffe's later career, what is most striking in these letters, as he himself later recognized, was, again, how conventional he was. His love for his sweetheart he felt very powerfully, but he was unable to express it with any particular originality. "Is this too sickly sentimental?" he asked shortly after their separation. "Well be it so—but then I am."[25] He sometimes quoted love poetry, such as that of Browning. He prayed and greatly enjoyed hymn sings on board ship and in Vienna. Like so many Americans, he was offended by the openness of prostitution in European cities, and he doubted very much that consorting with ladies of the evening "broadened" one. Even the scanty costumes in the theaters he believed contributed to immorality. He perceived a real difference between his native culture and those of the Europeans. During the first month he was in Vienna, at "one of the shop windows I noticed a crowd of people looking at immoral and sensual books & licentious pictures—all in plain sight and men and women, boys & girls, were enjoying them with broad grins & sundry nudges & pokes. I could see where a part of Vienna gained its impure moral training & again I thanked the Lord that I lived in America—even with its Wanamakers & its Anthony Comstocks—the latter I hope we shall never cease to have: to make such displays of gross impurity impossible."[26]

Jelliffe did recognize the cultural superiority of the centers of Europe, although he was not altogether overwhelmed by the quality of medicine as compared to the best in the United States. What did impress him was the completeness of both the clinical material and museum collections and the range of knowledge available to the student. From the herbariums he also took home ideas for arranging botanical collections in Brooklyn.[27] In view of his later propensity to spend time abroad, it is clear that he managed to

24. Letter page 506, 18 August 1891, Personal Letter File.
25. Letter page 9, 4 November 1890, Personal Letter File.
26. Letter page 139, 20 January 1891; letter page 46, 22 November 1890, Personal Letter File.
27. Letter page 309, 19 April 1891, Personal Letter File.

separate the advantages from the disadvantages of the Continent. In this tactic he was again typical of many Victorian Americans who consciously and enthusiastically valued both high culture and conventional U.S.A. moral standards.

The year abroad did little to help Jelliffe find himself. In Vienna he studied pediatrics, ear diseases, eye diseases, and the use of the ophthalmoscope. He soon transferred from pediatrics to bacteriology to learn basic methods and ideas. Between the microscope and the ophthalmoscope he felt that his eyes were being strained. "The morning went as other mornings do—sticking mirrors into people's throats & trying to see something—thumping & tapping & listening to babies' chests, trying to hear something—looking into & at people's eyes that cannot look into and see yours or only imperfectly—& seeing people's ears & eardrums etc., etc." He was, as he recalled, gaining a great deal of clinical experience in his short stay.

When the ear course ended, he substituted instruction in internal medicine, "which is my especial liking," he noted. "I could spend an hour or so over some patient with a heart-lung-kidney or liver trouble & enjoy it—but 15 minutes work in gynecology is tiresome."[28] Later he clarified his early interests: "I am not making throat & lungs a specialty—but people may think so if they please. Heart & lungs is more to my style. [In] . . . heart diseases . . . I am particularly well acquainted with typical symptoms of a durable nature."[29] He also then substituted dermatology for laryngology, noting that the course cost less, and he also did some pathology. The pathology turned out to be particularly useful when he got home.

In this period Jelliffe showed little interest in either neurology or psychiatry. In February he wrote, "I did a little laboratory work this morning. It was not very satisfactory. It was on the human brain—which histologically as well as physiologically & psychologically, what a lot of ollogies, is a study of a lifetime. But still I want to touch the scientific world in as many points as possible for as one grows older, we become more conservative."[30]

Nor did his Berlin experiences help the young physician answer the pressures to specialize. He clearly was not ready to do so. His work there included dermatology and gynecology, but his enthusiasm continued to be botany, even though, as he noted, he had had no instruction in the subject and knew only the rudiments of anatomical botany.[31] He wrote enthusiastically about his work. Schwendener, in whose laboratory he worked, was at that time, Jelliffe noted, "the leading plant anatomist of the world."[32]

In looking back on his *Wanderjahr*, Jelliffe many years later noted his amazing energy in taking in so much culture and also some of the oppor-

28. Letter page 114, 7 January 1891, Personal Letter File.
29. Letter page 118, 11 January 1891, Personal Letter File.
30. Letter page 199, 25 February 1891, Personal Letter File.
31. Letter page 263, 22 March 1891; letter page 279, 1 April 1891, Personal Letter File.
32. Jelliffe, "The Editor Himself," p. 552.

tunities he lost to work in the field of nervous and mental disease—in which, at the time, of course, he had no special interest at all. He particularly remembered his difficulties with the German language. In Vienna, he re- called, "I was working hard at my German, refusing to take English courses and so filled in courses with Fuchs on the eye, worked over Pollitzer's little sketches of the ear drum which he pinned on the shoulders of the polyclinic patients, picked safety pins out of the larynx of a trained patient in the course on laryngology and so on with practical courses on internal medicine by Lorenze, on pathology by Paltauf, etc.

"I had found an excellent zimmer on the Landesgerichtsstrasse and had a very happy and profitable winter at the Allgemeine Krankenhaus making good my clinical deficiencies and also did a little work in singing with the wife of a great tenor I had heard in Wagnerian roles in New York the winter previously.

"I can recall the rebuff I received from the diener in Meynert's laboratory. My German was not good enough. I agreed with him. I recall some spirited lectures of Krafft-Ebing and the round tower, the Narren Turm, of the mental Hospital, but my best comfort I found in the botanical museum where I was received with great courtesy and met Dr. Zahlbrückner, who became the world's authority on the lichens and whose friendship I kept up for thirty years. My herbarium is rich in specimens determined and presented to me by him. . . .

"I did get . . . a working knowledge of German, much clinical experience, but above all a model of how to work independently. There was some splendid skating on the Danube and hockey. Sands, the son of Professor Sands at the P. & S., was there, also W. K. Draper, a son of New York's most respected W. H. Draper and half-brother of our present-day George Draper and a group of other English and American students. Of psychiatry and neurology there was nothing.

"Then when late spring came off, I went on a walking trip from the falls of the Rhine at Schaffhausen to Milan, falling in with one or another fellow traveller. A midnight walk down the Valley of the Ticino in full moonlight still remains in my memory with a vivid thrill of joy. The Certosa at Pavia, the Giotto frescoes at Padua, the Milan Cathedral, Venice, Rome, Naples and a gradual infiltration of Italian. Vesuvius in eruption after an exhausting walk from Pompeii to its summit from 5 A.M. to 1 P.M. made me acquainted with the first major fatigue of my young frame. I was but 115 pounds, as agile as a goat, but seven hours over loose lava almost had me down. . . . Back to Vienna and my belongings after a six weeks' holiday and then on to Paris. As I look over my daily budget to my fiancée I am appalled at what I took in of the cities visited, particularly the art galleries.

"In Paris my father and mother and the step-daughter of my sister joined up with me and medicine fell into the background. Cathedrals, art galleries and scenery with much rapid sketching were in the foreground. I did hear

Charcot give two lectures and visited St. Anne and met Magnan but it is all a haze even though my French was good enough for me to give the French oration at my college graduation.

"London and more art and tourist visiting with much family sightseeing, Kew Gardens, Windsor, Warwick and Stratford and a visit to Coventry, the home of the Jelliffs and precious little medicine. There was Mott at Claybury I recall, and old Bedlam, and Queens Square but I have no recollection of celebrities save Horsley at the operating table and the sprightly clinical talks by that West Indian compatriot of Dumas, Risien Russell.

"I might have seen more in the psychiatric field since my only acquaintance was a young psychiatrist, Eric France, then engaged to Clouston's daughter, he told me, but who later came a cropper on some research work in tuberculosis in the mental hospitals and went out to South Africa for a time. But I can say that apart from this contact there was no predilection for neuropsychiatry, save perhaps a very definite interest in the nervous system which had first come from the Spencer, Darwin, and G. H. Lewes works my fiancée and I had read together."[33]

By the end of the trip, Jelliffe had gained clinical experience and a great deal of "culture." He had also grown in independence, even to the point of being able to criticize his parents to his fiancée. He noted particularly how he resembled his mother in her ability to chatter on and on wittily and pleasantly.[34] But what direction he was to go remained unclear. Nor was his future assured, as is attested by the delay in his marriage and his vivid memories of his early struggles to gain a living from medicine.

Starting the Practice of Medicine

The profession of medicine in the United States was crowded in the 1890's. People holding degrees from diploma mills practiced, equally licensed, alongside practitioners even better qualified than Jelliffe. Every student who graduated M.D. meant more profits for the medical schools, which flourished in the last years before the reform symbolized by the famous Flexner Report of 1910. What happened, therefore, was that when, at the very end of 1891, Jelliffe hung out his sign on his parents' house in Brooklyn and entered practice, even though the sign, as he wrote to one correspondent, "caused the luminiferous ether to vibrate," yet no patients, to speak of, came.[35]

Jelliffe later often referred to those difficult beginning days when, as he whimsically put it, he undertook to "carve my way to fame and fortune,

33. Ibid., pp. 549–551. Jelliffe's overseas experiences are interesting in that they were so typical of those of the many other American physicians who studied abroad at the end of the nineteenth century—except that Jelliffe made a more successful attempt than most to master German; see Thomas N. Bonner, *American Doctors and German Universities: A Chapter in International Intellectual Relations, 1870–1914* (Lincoln, Nebr., 1963).

34. Letter page 507, 26 August 1891, Personal Letter File.

35. May to Jelliffe, [1 January 1892], Personal Letter File.

starting in my parents' home where I had lived since I was nine years of age. A little bit of luck, and a cholera scare and a small pox epidemic and the Health Commissioner, an old school principal friend of my father, Dr. Griffen, insinuated me into the Board of Health as a sanitary inspector and this with a slowly developing practice, night school teaching, pathological and clinical work at the Methodist Episcopal Hospital and other miscellaneous jobs netted me in three years the princely sum of $6,000. As I budgeted it, $2,000 to pay my debts, $2,000 to pay my way at home and $2,000 as capital to get married on."[36]

At first the competition was even greater than Jelliffe suggested in these reminiscences. His application for a civil service appointment was turned down in April 1892. Jelliffe was well qualified and his scholarship ranked high, but he was not as experienced as another physician who got the position.[37] Only later did he get the appointment that, as he mentioned, helped him out. And even when he had patients they, of course, did not always pay. Already by October he was referring one uncollected fee of $45 to a collection agency.[38] He tried to earn money however he could. By 1893 he had become a medical examiner for the United States Life Insurance Company. Altogether, as he recounts, those were frustrating years. He was not making much of a go of medicine, much less any specialty.

Botanical Activity

With his overabundance of leisure time, Jelliffe threw himself into botany. He worked mostly on cryptogamic plants, although occasionally he dealt with higher plants. He was an avid collector even as a medical student, and by the time of his internship was corresponding and exchanging with many other collectors (of lichens and mosses especially) and asking authorities to identify specimens that he had gathered and was classifying as botanical curator of the Brooklyn Institute of Arts and Sciences. His first publication, which he continued to include at the head of his bibliography all of his life, was a list of plants found in Prospect Park in Brooklyn, near his home, and published in the *Brooklyn Daily Eagle Almanac* after he had sailed for Europe in 1890.

Jelliffe continued this botanical activity after he returned. He again did curatorial work for the Brooklyn Institute and associated himself with other amateurs through the institute, the New York Microscopical Society, in which members mounted displays for the edification of other members, and the Torrey Botanical Club. The training in both botany and microscopy that he received in Europe he thus put to use in the setting of local amateur societies, such as were common and typical at the end of the nineteenth century in the United States. In that day the amateur had a high standing

36. Jelliffe, "The Editor Himself," p. 551.
37. Robert L. Dickinson to Jelliffe, 8 April 1892.
38. The Physicians Financial Association to Jelliffe, 27 October 1892.

in science. In 1893 Jelliffe listed himself as "Member of Cryptogamic Committee of Torrey Botanical Club; Curator of Herbarium of Brooklyn Institute of Arts and Sciences." But within a few years increasing professionalization of science tended to diminish the importance of the amateur in both education and discovery. Jelliffe himself managed a transition parallel with his times, although his amateur's interest and delight in botany never ceased.[39]

He exploited his interest in microscopy as well as in the lower orders of plants by publishing accounts of organisms in water supplies. Already in these early papers, extensive bibliographies and historical introductions demonstrated the mastery of the literature that was to mark all of his medical publications. From the beginning of this work Jelliffe showed that he was completely at home with recent developments in the germ theory of disease, which was only just then becoming fully accepted in medicine. He concluded his first water supply report with a discussion of public health considerations:

"Of what sanitary importance is the knowledge acquired?

"Since the advent of the bacteria all other kinds of creatures living or dead have retired into the background as having nothing to do with the production of disease or even of discomfort; but that certain facts have come to light regarding the higher forms in relation to the well-being of a community is a position that within the past few years has been most abundantly proven by a number of observers. A perfectly pure water is free from all organisms, but given a number of organized vegetable and animal forms which may break down by mechanical or other means, there is provided immediately a more or less rich albuminous pabulum which will assist in the growth of both pathogenic and non-pathogenic organisms; in addition to this evident position many of the organisms observed give a more or less definite idea from whence a water supply is drawn; if the 'blue green' algae, Oscillaria, Clathrocystis, Palmella are found, it is an evidence that the water supply is being drawn from some shallow or stagnant pool, and it is a matter of sanitary importance to know that fact: the results thus far in the case of Brooklyn's water supply shows little or no such evidences of this particular kind of contamination.

"Again, there are a number of microscopical organisms which of *themselves* though not pathogenic are distinctly obnoxious as inhabitants of a drinking water on account of their taste and odor, when found in large quantities. This subject of the relation of taste and odor to certain Algae and Infusoria has received more or less attention from biologists both in this country and abroad, and it is definitely ascertained that certain species, apart from de-

39. Charles William Heywood, "Scientists and Society in the United States, 1900–1940: Changing Concepts of Social Responsibility" (unpublished doctoral dissertation, University of Pennsylvania, 1954).

composition, impart distinct tastes and odors to the water in which they are found. . . ."[40]

Teacher of Pharmacognosy

Botany overlapped with medicine in one important area besides bacteriology: in pharmacognosy, in which study in the late nineteenth century the use of botanical preparations continued to be of importance despite the attitude of therapeutic nihilism that predominated in the best medical practices. Jelliffe was able to combine his interests in botany and medicine by working in this area, and as early as the beginning of 1892 he was discussing an appointment to work with a botanical friend, H. H. Rusby, in teaching courses in pharmacognosy.[41] Rusby (1855–1940) was a New York physician and botanist who since 1888 held the professorship of botany, physiology, and materia medica at the New York College of Pharmacy, which later was absorbed into Columbia University.[42] Rusby, like Jelliffe, was very active in the Torrey Botanical Club. Nothing came of their discussion until 1894, when Jelliffe did indeed join Rusby as instructor in the college. Meanwhile, in 1893, Jelliffe became an instructor in materia medica and botany in the Brooklyn College of Pharmacy— evidently what he later described as night school teaching in this period.

One by-product of his association with Rusby was a textbook in vegetable pharmacognosy, in which Rusby wrote the section on "the gross structure of plants" and Jelliffe that on "the minute structure of plants." This division of work reflected accurately the way in which the two men divided the teaching, in which Jelliffe was in charge of microscopic work.[43] In August 1899, the editors of the *Druggists Circular and Chemical Gazette* were kind enough to announce that "Profs. H. H. Rusby and Smith Ely Jelliffe are taking advantage of their vacations to revise their Essentials of Vegetable Pharmacognosy prior to the issuing of a new edition.

"The first edition appeared in 1895. As the authors were limited as to space they had to compress a very big subject into a comparatively small book. This they did with great success, but, nevertheless, it will be a relief to them to be allowed to keep pace with current events and 'expand' a little in the forthcoming revision.

"Some errors which crept into the text of the first edition will be eliminated, and the letterpress and illustrations will be made more in accordance with a book of this class."[44]

40. Smith Ely Jelliffe, "A Preliminary Report Upon the Microscopical Organisms Found in the Brooklyn Water Supply," *Brooklyn Medical Journal*, 7 (1893), 599–601.

41. H. H. Rusby to Jelliffe, 24 January 1892, Personal Letter File.

42. *New York Times*, 19 November 1940.

43. Henry H. Rusby, *The College of Pharmacy of the City of New York* (New York, [1895]), pp. 20, 35.

44. "Profs. Rusby and Jelliffe at Work on their 'Pharmacognosy,'" *Druggists Circular and Chemical Gazette*, 43 (1899), cxv.

Rusby and Jelliffe explained in the preface to their retitled second edition that it was "a matter of great gratification to the authors that the large edition of their Essentials of Pharmacognosy, which the present work is replacing, should have been so soon exhausted, in view of its peculiarly restricted scope and mode of treatment. . . . that work has met with a flattering reception."[45] Since the book went well, within the specialized market Jelliffe experienced success as a textbook writer—an experience he was to repeat many times.

Beginning in Medical Journalism

Jelliffe characterized his activities of the mid-1890's not so much as intellectual activities as attempts to capitalize on his abilities and to make money so that he could marry and support a family. But the record suggests that he was also trying to keep up all of his interests, perhaps attempting to find that one path through which he could find the role in which he would flourish. He had even, as has been noted, taken on the post of assistant pathologist at the Methodist Episcopal Hospital of Brooklyn, where he made friends who later helped push him in the direction of psychiatry and neurology.[46]

Jelliffe often associated his income frustrations with his wanting to get married and was still making the association in 1939 when he wrote:

"Already at the age of sixteen I had found my first object choice. It was an enduring one and a long gruelling time of conquering the anxiety of tension followed. Twelve years we waited and worked together. She wrote that French oration, for I was helpless, and without her definite literary gifts this particular anniversary [of an editorship] would never have occurred. The salary as instructor was low and I soon learned that certain medical journals paid for editorials and book reviews. So first I brought my ideas, put into better phrases by my wife, to Dr. George Shrady of the *Medical Record* and with Dr. Bainbridge as main whip we started a Quiz. $600 was added to the salary for the coming daughter. There was a meagre $75 from the practice of medicine."[47]

It was, then, in that period that Jelliffe started using his pen frequently to supplement the income from his practice. In 1894 the editor of the *Annals of Surgery* paid him two dollars for abstracts printed in the June number and invited him to submit more material. Jelliffe also ventured into the field of popularization. Some flavor of how Jelliffe functioned as a practitioner as well as writer can be gleaned from his article in *Babyhood*, "Some Dangers Resulting from the Use of Cows' Milk:"

45. Henry H. Rusby and Smith Ely Jelliffe, *Morphology and Histology of Plants, Designed Especially as a Guide to Plant-Analysis and Classification, and as an Introduction to Pharmacognosy and Vegetable Physiology* (New York, 1899), p. 111.
46. Jelliffe, "The Editor Himself," p. 552.
47. Ibid., p. 553.

"Although cows' milk, on account of its resemblence to mothers' milk, is considered the ideal food for children who are deprived wholly, or in part, of the mother's milk, yet recent information upon the subject of germs and germ diseases shows that many dangers are to be encountered in the use of unmodified cows' milk.

"It is a fact that nearly 40 per cent. of all children die before they are five years of age, and that of this 40 per cent. nearly three-fourths die of troubles that are directly or indirectly traced to disturbances in the nutrition of the child; it therefore becomes a matter of grave importance to inquire into the causes of disease which can be traced to the universal food, milk, with a view to their prevention if possible.

"The reading public is apt to treat the subject of germ diseases either with flippancy or with an exaggerated dread. To some, the words germ, bacteria, microbe are the toys of scientists, who make infinite evil out of infinitesimal matter, and who have created by this means a number of vague but unpleasant diseases, which the world was quite free from fifty years ago. To others, the germ is an invisible and deadly foe lurking in [every] pool of water, in the air of night, and in all food.

"The truth is that the so-called germs are very minute plants which can grow and multiply if they find a suitable resting place, just as surely as a handful of oats will grow and multiply in a plowed field; but there are means of rendering these germs as incapable of growth as oats would be after being made into oatmeal porridge. Germ diseases have always existed, but it is only recently that scientists have discovered their cause. In many such diseases this discovery is as far as science goes, the remedy has not been discovered; thus *prevention* is so strongly urged, for prevention is their *cure.*"

Jelliffe then went on to describe how milk could spread tuberculosis, diphtheria, and typhoid, although, he noted, many children had natural immunities. Breast feeding is preferable to cows' milk, he said, but even with cows' milk hygienic measures were effective (this was just when pure milk, rather than pasteurized milk, provided protection for consumers). Then he concluded:

"Lest the dread of possible evil in spite of care oppress mothers who are feeding their children upon cows' milk, it may be well to state in conclusion that regular hours of feeding, regular hours of sleep, and plenty of fresh air, do much to keep a child in good general health; so that it can resist possible attacks of illness. It may, moreover, be some comfort, for those prone to dwell on possible dangers, to reflect that the three-fifths of the human race that did not die in infancy have at one time or another eaten some or all of the bacteria that have been mentioned as occurring in milk, and have survived."[48]

48. Smith Ely Jelliffe, "Some Dangers Resulting from the Use of Cows' Milk," *Babyhood*, 10 (1894), 293–297. For background, see Manfred J. Waserman, "Henry L. Coit and the

Becoming Established

The year 1894 was decisive for Jelliffe. To begin with, he had finally become instructor of materia medica, botany, and pharmacognosy in the New York College of Pharmacy, or, as his notice of appointment phrased it, in "Dr. Rusby's department."[49] And he and Helena Dewey Leeming were married, on 20 December, in the Sixth Avenue Baptist Church in Brooklyn.

Helena Dewey Leeming came of a substantial family. Like Jelliffe, she could trace among her ancestors a seventeenth-century legislator, in her case Thomas Ford of Connecticut. Evidence of the importance of her personality and talents appears throughout accounts of Jelliffe's activities, in which, with his encouragement, she participated far more actively than most women of her time would have.

After briefly maintaining an office at 105 West 77th Street in New York City, Jelliffe and his wife bought a house at 231 West 71st Street with, as Jelliffe put it, "the aid of a considerate father-in-law." There Jelliffe lived and practiced, ending what he designated his "Brooklyn period."[50] And with his marriage, incidentally but not coincidentally, the headaches with which he had been bothered his whole life ceased.[51] (Not long after he got rid of the headaches, at about age thirty, Jelliffe had his appendix removed, again ridding himself of an ailment that had been with him occasionally from childhood.)[52]

In the years that followed, Jelliffe's personal life, too, became more comfortable and settled. Scraps of records show that in the late years of the decade he joined the Century Cycle Club (bicycling was one of the fads of the nineties) and the West Side Tennis Club, and he and his wife joined the Barnard Club. Moreover, the children started to come along, all born in the West 71st Street house. Sylvia Canfield (later Mrs. Gregory Stragnell) was born on 2 November 1895. Winifred (later Mrs. Alfred Emerson) came along on 25 March 1897. Smith Ely, Jr., was born on 1 March 1899, and William Leeming on 6 December 1900. Helena Woodruff (later Mrs. Carel Goldschmidt) was the last child, born on 15 January 1903. All of these signs reflected the fact that Jelliffe was becoming an increasingly successful physician.

Moreover, he seemed set to establish himself in the field of pharmacognosy and materia medica. As noted above, while he was waiting for patients

Certified Milk Movement in the Development of Modern Pediatrics," *Bulletin of the History of Medicine*, 44 (1972), 359–390.

49. In Additional Papers.

50. Jelliffe to C. B. Davenport, 10 June 1895, Davenport Papers. Jelliffe, "The Editor Himself," pp. 551–552.

51. Jelliffe to Dorrell G. Dickerson, 6 May 1932. The headaches did come back from time to time; in 1909 he was so disabled that at one time he could not even read proof; Jelliffe to William Alanson White, 29 January 1909, White Papers, Box 4, St. Elizabeths Hospital Papers, National Archives, Washington, D.C.

52. Jelliffe to John Rickman, 5 October 1932.

during the 1890's, he was busy in a variety of botanical activities, some for money, some not. In 1895 he gave public lectures in a botanical series sponsored by the Torrey Botanical Club and the College of Pharmacy of the City of New York. He gave a similar series in 1896 sponsored by the Brooklyn Institute of Arts and Sciences. In 1898 he was in charge of the summer courses there as well as lecturer. He continued to publish on botanical subjects for some time after his doctoral dissertation on the plants of Long Island appeared in 1899. His articles on pharmacognosy continued for another five years after that, until they were completely superseded by his neurological and psychiatric publications. They may also have been written largely for the fees, although the sum could not have been very great; his article on podophyllum in the *Druggists Circular* of 1899 brought a check for only twelve dollars.[53] From 1897 to 1899 he was editor of the *Journal of Pharmacology*, the College of Pharmacy house organ, or, more precisely, alumni journal, which also carried scientific articles. (Jelliffe listed his years of editorship as 1897–1901, but beginning with April-May 1899 he appeared on the masthead as merely a collaborator, and his name dropped off even that list the next year.)

Medical Journalism Continued and Expanded

It is not clear to what extent Jelliffe pursued medical journalism to make money and to what extent he was drawn to editing for its own sake. He seemed to take to the work naturally. His first association with the magazine to which his fate was ultimately tied, the *Journal of Nervous and Mental Disease*, consisted of a book review that he wrote which was published in 1896.[54] Soon Jelliffe contributed an index to the journal and increasingly became involved in helping the editor, Charles H. Brown, under circumstances that Jelliffe later recalled:

"I would that I had the time to describe the unique methods by which Dr. Brown managed to finally produce his monthly chore. For the ten days of the end of every month his house in West 45th Street was in a pandemonium, a going here and there, hunting for this or that proof, this or that ad, this or that bit to fill the magazine. A man of many admirable qualities, he was as capricious as the April weather and system knew him not. I was a godsend, since if I had any one quality it was that of order and system, family, genera and species trained by my botanical allegiance and thus I slipped into the harness almost without knowing it."[55]

53. The scraps of evidence for the foregoing are in the Additional Papers.
54. Smith Ely Jelliffe, review of Frankl-Hochwart, *Der meniere'sche Symptomencomplex*, in *JNMD* 23 (1896), 153–154.
55. Jelliffe, "The Editor Himself," pp. 570–571.

Jelliffe also furnished a brief memoir of his next major editorial venture, this time with an important general medical journal, as he attempted to establish himself economically.

"The small remittances from editorial and review writing finally culminated in the extra job as Editor of the *Medical News* then one of the oldest medical weeklies which I must confess came not as a reward of literary merit but chiefly by reason of that inherent aptness for orderly despatch but even more the capacity to read impossible handwriting and to know names and how to spell and initial them.

"When I came as an assistant copy and proof reader to the *Medical News* about 1900 I found much the same confusion in preparation and lack of method I had met with when first in contact with the affairs of *The Journal of Nervous and Mental Disease*. They pasted their copy instead of measuring it and posting it on a preparation pad. I recall one occasion early in my work there where Dr. Riddle Goffe, the editor, and Dr. Taylor, the office manager of Lea & Febiger, and Miss Nevins, the wiry, thin, underfed cigarette fiend and general copy and proof reader, were getting out a special number of the *Medical News* containing the report of the Congress of American Physicians. Buttressed by dictionaries and directories, they took certain batches of proof and laboriously checked all the spelling and names of the contributors. Dr. J. J. Walsh, as I recall was their chief reporter and his handwriting in spite of years of practice was still an enigma to the office. I sailed through another batch and they in semi-wonder and indignation doubted my ability to read 3 to 5 galleys to their united confusions on one. Here again as I have already noted, handwriting was no trouble for me, even Charles Dana's or Ramsay Hunt's or Abraham Jacobi's had no terrors for me. I knew how to spell, knew the names and the initials and home towns of all of the contributors by heart and it was with a slight trace of irony that I watched the pulling out of the dictionaries and the directories and their confused bemusings. The end result was that in about six months I was made editor and had the *News* running in an orderly fashion and on time, which almost saved my salary on corrections and overtime charges which previously had been a definite budgetary item in this venture.

"Teaching at the College, secretary and treasurer of a successful Quiz, editing the *Medical News* and other enterprises with a growing practice now led to greater economic ease for the growing family and it was but a short step to *The Journal of Nervous and Mental Disease,* another side line in the beginning. . . ."[56]

56. Ibid., pp. 555–556.

For the time being, however, the *Medical News,* as a general medical journal, represented Jelliffe's interests and activities better than did the *Journal of Nervous and Mental Disease.* And to general medicine he of course added botany.

Irresolution

Jelliffe's bibliography reveals the extent to which he pursued his career combining medicine and botany in the closing years of the nineteenth century. In addition, he not only was adding degrees to his name (the doctorate in botany), but by 1898 he was already professor of pharmacognosy and then director of the Microscopic and Bacteriological Laboratories of the College of Pharmacy. With his ties to Columbia, Jelliffe played an important part in the process by which the College of Pharmacy finally in 1904 became affiliated with the academically extremely prestigious Columbia University.[57] Finally, he continued writing—and rewriting—textbook material in the field. Of course he was writing in other fields of medicine as well, but all of them, including neurology and psychiatry, could have remained sidelines to his medico-botanical pursuits.

Among Jelliffe's published contributions of the late nineties were a number of reports on the pharmacognosy of various substances, such as rhubarb, senna, cascara, cinnamon, and ergot. These were straightforward accounts, with microscopical and laboratory research often reported. Prudden, a sponsor and friend even before Jelliffe moved to New York, let him work in the laboratory at P & S. Prudden, recalled Jelliffe, "was a botanist himself in his earlier days and my pathological assistantship with Dr. Belcher at the Methodist Episcopal Hospital in Brooklyn made another tie of common interest. I was made welcome in the new laboratory and library where Dr. E. C. Seguin's books had found a home."[58]

The extensive bibliographies that made Jelliffe's pharmacognostical papers stand out reflected prodigious coverage of the literature, including French and German sources. The introduction to his paper on ergot (which probably was a classroom lecture reduced to print) gives the flavor of his work.

"Much has been written about ergot, and yet it is safe to assume that much of its pharmacognosy is still little understood, and as for its pharmaco-dynamics, we are still in the dark. That this should be so is not surprising when one recalls what the drug is, and bears in mind the complex problems of plant chemistry in a group of plants which have a very simple morphology

---

57. Curt P. Wimmer, *The College of Pharmacy of the City of New York* (New York, 1929), p. 87.
58. Jelliffe, "The Editor Himself," p. 552.

and yet are the exponents of a very subtle series of chemical interchanges. Representing as it does one of the few really potent drugs of the lower plants, its study has always been alluring as well as suggestive.

"The following sketch aims to give a resumé of what is known of the pharmacognosy of this drug, including the deductions of the more recent studies." Jelliffe went on to talk about the growth of the fungus, methods of collection, anatomy and histology, concluding with a long section on its chemistry.[59]

Early Interest in Nervous and Mental Diseases

Meantime Jelliffe's work in pathology was laying the groundwork for his as-yet-unanticipated interest in neurology. The evidence shows up in another paper—again from the year 1894—that took him explicitly from pathology into neurology. This was his "A Report of Two Cases of Perforating Ulcer of the Foot." Jelliffe described two cases of this rare malady and was able to do a microscopic examination of the tissues in one case and confirm the involvement of the nerves. After a full review of the literature and his own evidence, Jelliffe concluded that in degenerative cases the cause is a "nervous lesion." Yet he warned of the "protean aspects" of the affection and the need for further investigation of the actual mechanisms involved. Although Jelliffe was essentially confirming an opinion of previous investigators—mostly French—still he had with this original clinical contribution entered into the realm of an important specialty group, the neurologists.[60]

Years later, as he looked back, Jelliffe could see many incidents in his life that, although not obvious to him at the time, helped turn him toward becoming a nervous and mental disease specialist, just as some of his experiences at St. Mary's Hospital had. Before beginning there, he recalled, "I took a two weeks' vacation at my favorite place of recreation on Lake George in the Adirondacks. A classmate of the Physicians and Surgeons was there courting my father's brother's daughter. A friend of his was also in the offing. With this friend I daily walked to the post office and back, a mile or more, and among other things he told me how happy he had been for the past three weeks or so, especially as he had always had to spend the time about July for a month or two at Bethlehem, N.H., because it had been the only place he had found in which he was free from 'hay fever.'

"This had been a sore infliction now for ten years or more since he was about the age of 12. He was sick and tired of this New Hampshire resort to which other similarly afflicted pilgrims were wont to gather. Curious then, as now, I inquired as to the reasons, the meanwhile congratulating him upon

59. Smith Ely Jelliffe, "Some Notes on the Pharmacognosy of Ergot," *Merck's Report*, 7 (1898), 163.

60. Smith Ely Jelliffe, "A Report of Two Cases of Perforating Ulcer of the Foot, with Notes and Bibliography," *New York Medical Journal*, 60 (1894), 458–461.

the extension of his topographical possibilities and also noting that what was Bethlehem's loss might be our gain. He told me, innocent as we both then were of the appalling allergic possibilities which have since come like a cloud of locusts upon us, that it was due to the fact there was no ragweed here. . . . Virtuous and virginal as I was to psychotherapy, botanically I was an old master and informed him then and there that our mountainlake fastness boasted in abundant and rich growths of at least two *Ambrosiae* (ragweeds) and possibly a third, to say nothing of at least 20–30 of its sisters and its cousins and its aunts, which had bloomed, were blooming or about to bloom, as well as offering a rich summary of other polleniferous possibilities which I offered to catch for him on glycerinated slides and show him under the simple microscope I then owned. In 15 minutes he had an attack of hay fever and fled before I had an opportunity to learn more of his heredity, constitution or physical characteristics, had I then known of such subtleties.

"I have never forgotten the prompt 'allergic' reaction brought on by the massive overwhelming of repressions by the sadistic exhibitionism of my botanical knowledge and always have been ashamed of not having known enough to have tried out graded doses of additions to his ego. Naturally I have had since a benevolent skepticism regarding the 'prickly irritating' processes on pollen grains which formerly were so widely illustrated in the medical literature and even later of the chemical allergic theories now so regnant. My later experiences have tended to confirm rather than to destroy this benevolent skepticism, although the allergic phenomena remain objects of the keenest curiosity."[61]

Looking back in 1930, Jelliffe remembered that he became interested in psychological medicine only some time after he had started practice, and he tended to associate his new insights with his move to New York City.

"Three years later," he wrote, "I severed myself from my Brooklyn mother. I was enabled to part from those influences which pleasing, agreeable and fruitful though they were in many ways, nevertheless I felt were too circumscribing. So I went across the river where the struggle was much more vital, much more imminent, and much more dangerous. Then for the first time I became aware of the fact that something was happening within me, and I said to myself, 'I do not know enough about what is happening in the mental spheres.' At the Methodist Episcopal Hospital I had been working in the pathological laboratory. In St. Mary's in 1889 I had brought Koch's new tubercle bacillus stain into action and was working, not with immersion lenses, but with an ordinary one-fifth dry lens, trying to find the tubercle bacillus in the sputum and I succeeded and was immensely interested. Later I became interested in the study of the human being . . . , but I felt I wanted to know a little more about brain than blood; more about the things of the

61. Jelliffe, "Glimpses of a Freudian Odyssey," pp. 318–319.

spirit as I had been too long immersed in the things of the body. Even at that time I was firmly convinced they were the same. There was no antithesis of body and mind. They were one and inseparable but, above all, function determined structure and then structure directed function."[62]

Psychiatric Summers

By Jelliffe's own account, his interest in nervous and mental diseases was greatly accelerated by his summer spent earning extra income as a physician at Binghamton State Hospital in 1896.[63] Not the least of the results of his tenure was his becoming acquainted with William Alanson White (1870–1937). White, too, remembered the event as momentous in his life when Jelliffe, "an impecunious young practitioner with a growing family managed to get his vacation by spending the summer weeks at Binghamton, where I was stationed. He gave a certain amount of service to the hospital in return for this privilege and, incidentally, acquired at firsthand contact with the patients, which is of such inestimable importance," White noted, "for anyone who is going to deal with problems of psychiatry in his practice." Each of the men influenced the other in many ways, and while each remained very independent, yet their personal friendship led to a most fruitful collaboration. Jelliffe once remarked, "White and I have written and published so many things together that I am not at all certain when I quote from one of them whether to say 'White and Jelliffe,' or 'Jelliffe and White.'"[64]

Beyond this momentous meeting, the summer greatly broadened Jelliffe's experience, as he recounted in several places. "Winters," he explained, "were very busy at the College, the Vanderbilt Clinic, the Quiz and a host of smaller activities but the summers were hot and dry and unproductive and so thinking to take my young family to the country I wrote to the State Commissioner asking for a job in a State Hospital. Here I was again most fortunate. Binghamton was open, Dr. Wagner was receptive and thus I entered psychiatry. This was the summer of 1896 and I was in my thirtieth year." Elsewhere, he admitted that he did not remember "just what led me to Binghamton . . . , but it had something to do with my contacts with Van Gieson and more particularly with an effort to get a Ph.D. degree."[65] (Ira Van Gieson was director of the New York state hospitals Pathological Institute.)

62. Smith Ely Jelliffe, "Psychotherapy in Modern Medicine," *Long Island Medical Journal*, 24 (1930), 153.

63. As is clear from a document cited below and other evidence, Jelliffe confused some of his experiences during the summers of 1896–1899. A search so far has failed to turn up any clarifying official records, and so to avoid further confusion Jelliffe's retrospective account is followed, with the caveat that any date may be off one year.

64. William Alanson White, *The Autobiography of a Purpose* (Garden City, N.Y., 1938), p. 175; Lewis, "Smith Ely Jelliffe," p. 225.

65. Jelliffe, "The Editor Himself," p. 554.

Jelliffe was hardly prepared for his experience at Binghamton, as he observed with some irony, recalling again that "Dr. Starr thought that all that was necessary to be known about psychiatry could be taught in three lectures and although I had listened to Krafft-Ebing for a time in Vienna, my German was almost nil, and thus I came to Binghamton fully equipped in the sciences of the mind. Had I the time or you the patience I would sketch the bewildered state I lived in for some six or more weeks at Binghamton."

"It was," Jelliffe recorded on another occasion, "a perplexing first month with a host of prejudices regarding the 'insane' to be unlearned before a reorientation took place. Dr. Wm. A. White was my guide. I in turn had the tennis court fixed up and there with Drs. White, Cecil McCoy, Gillespie and Menas Gregory did a little to modify the afternoon nap of the hospital interne routine. It was a happy meeting. I continued dragging in botanical and geological specimens, tried to understand the standard nosology of acute manias, secondary dementias and paretics, for only of such were the diagnoses recorded."

He continued his narrative: "One of the things I learned, however, may be worth passing on. . . . One day, being down in Binghamton, which is a very busy little city, I noted the keenness and the cleverness with which the policemen managed the traffic and when I returned to the hospital that evening, my pockets full of geological and botanical specimens, rocks, plants and so on, I spilled them out on the table to the disgust of the internes, and I said, 'This is a great town; I never saw such policemen in my life. How do you account for it?' In response they laughed and Dr. White said, 'Don't you know they have all been attendants up here in the asylum?' Then I learned for the first time, interestingly enough, or at least it commenced to ferment in my [mind] that, after all, what we call 'normal people' may be sicker in some sense of the word than those people in the asylum, only they don't know it, and that the insight that was gained by the policemen when up in the asylum taught them how to manage so-called 'normal' people."[66]

At Binghamton Jelliffe set out initially "to enlighten the world about the stigmata of degeneration," as was appropriate for what he correctly labeled "the Lombroso era." "Instead of Nôtre Dame dragon heads," he continued, "I sketched ears and ears, and then some more ears . . . hunting for definite criteria of bodily anomalies in the mentally disordered."[67] The amusing sequel to this work he revealed in a letter to a friend some years later.

"Away back in 1896 I had an anthropological fever—it was of the Lombrosian bacillus type. I journeyed up to Binghamton with callipers and all

66. Ibid.; Jelliffe, "Glimpses of a Freudian Odyssey," pp. 321–322.
67. Ibid., p. 322.

that and there still hang around my house bunches of cards of measurements and sketches of the then 2400 patients at the State Hospital.

"Osborn had given me a lead on Cercopithecus and Macacus ears, etc., and I had all of the primates in photos and sketches and it was great fun along with my botanical and geological gathering up of brush and shale. When I arrived in New York I rode up on the 9th Ave. Elevated—I was keen as a motion picture lens on ears, and there by Heck were more anomalies than I had collected in the 2400 patients. This sobered me immensely. I never published a word of reams of stuff I had in preparation. It was all fiction—not the kind that was truer than reality—but 'bunk.'"[68]

The next summer, in the midst of another very significant year, Jelliffe, as he put it, "repeated the formula," but on this occasion he ended up at Bloomingdale "with Dr. Lyons," then the superintendent. There the results were somewhat different, as Jelliffe recalled.

"At Bloomingdale I had dived into the records with my tempermental vigor and prepared a full digest of all of the paretics that had accumulated for nearly eighty or more years. Full of enthusiasm I brought the outline of my study to Dr. Lyons, to be met by the conservative rebuff that it was 'not good policy to reveal the secrets of many of New York's most outstanding families.' These records I later turned over to Dr. Raynor when he became Superintendent."[69] Nevertheless, that summer, too, provided valuable experience.

By 1897, then, Jelliffe had made significant efforts in the field of neurology, but he still was mainly located elsewhere by virtue of his teaching and his publications. Indeed, that was the time that he became editor of the *Journal of Pharmacology*. But he did publish that year his report of part of his summer's labors at Binghamton State Hospital, and he also published a technical descriptive paper in neuroanatomy (under circumstances described below). Moreover, he became an assistant in neurology (Starr's department) in the Vanderbilt Clinic, Columbia University, and the outpatient department of the Presbyterian Hospital. Finally, in December, Starr asked Jelliffe to take charge of abstracts for the *Journal of Nervous and Mental Disease*.[70] The next year Jelliffe's title was clinical assistant in the clinic, and he agreed to become associate editor of the *Journal of Nervous and Mental Disease*. By 1899 he also had become visiting neurologist at the City Hospital on Blackwell's Island, and it was that summer that he spent three months at the Craig Colony for epileptics.

68. Jelliffe to George Draper, 4 January 1926.
69. Jelliffe, "The Editor Himself," pp. 554–555.
70. M. Allen Starr to Jelliffe, 20 December 1897.

Craig Colony provided another happy interlude for Jelliffe, as he testified in his memoirs:

"And the summer . . . found me with my family in a nearby farm house at Craig Colony where I had the happy fortune of meeting Drs. Spratling and L. P. Clark and E. Sharp. Here again a reorientation took place, for I was there nearly three weeks, with a population of 800 or more and did not see a single 'fit.' I had not grasped the significance of the numerous 'petit mal' attacks or many other equivalents. The rest of the time brought plenty of 'fits' and other useful bits of observation, some of which Dr. Sharp and I worked up for Dr. Clark for some papers which he published. . . . A year or so later some of my notes on this visit were put in print."[71]

Finally, Starr tried as early as the spring of 1898 to get Jelliffe into the American Neurological Association. That year sixteen candidates were nominated for membership, including Jelliffe, whose sponsors were Starr and the distinguished New Yorker, Christian Herter. It was just at that point that the neurologists decided to limit membership in the Association so as to make it a group of fully dedicated specialists who had substantial qualifications in the field. Therefore only six of the nominees reached membership in 1899, not including Jelliffe, but he was passed over only in favor of extremely well-qualified persons such as Adolf Meyer, Hoch, and Fraenkel. In 1900 when there were more vacancies, the ANA Council sent Jelliffe's name in at the head of the list of nominees—a tribute to Starr's sponsorship—and in the confirming election that year Jelliffe was indeed elected, although his name was placed second, after that of his friend, the distinguished Pearce Bailey. Other outstanding members of Jelliffe's group included J. W. Courtney, L. F. Barker, and D. J. McCarthy.[72]

Teaching and Publication

For most people such a record would have been sufficient to show that a career as specialist was well under way. Jelliffe was no ordinary person, however. He nourished the neurological specialty only as he was playing other roles. Thus 1897 could have been decisive for him, except that he did not give up any other activities. It was after that when he achieved his professorship in the College of Pharmacy. Moreover, and still another par-

71. Jelliffe, "The Editor Himself," p. 555. Smith Ely Jelliffe, "Some Observations, General and Technical, Made at the Craig Colony," *Medical News*, 79 (1901), 846–848, demonstrated that Jelliffe harbored strong humanitarian and reformist tendencies as shown in his nonobjective discussion of victims of epilepsy.

72. Typescript of minutes of the American Neurological Association Council and Executive Sessions, 26 May 1898, p. 44; 23 May 1899, pp. 47–48; 24 May 1900, p. 1; 1 June 1900, p. 54, American Neurological Association Papers, New York Academy of Medicine, New York City.

adox, his most important teaching role in the late 1890's was the "quiz" (mentioned above) that he ran for P & S students.[73]

It was customary in that day for medical students to take private instruction in order to master the courses on which they had heard lectures or in which they had done laboratory work. The quiz masters, each of whom worked with only a few students, held no official posts but instead organized the group and solicited students on their own. A good quiz would produce high examination marks—a system not unlike that followed at English universities in the late nineteenth century. Jelliffe was obviously very happy and successful in this work until, in the next decade, he no longer needed the money. He was an enthusiastic teacher. When his old college chum, the distinguished zoologist, C. B. Davenport, took a position at the Cold Spring Harbor biological station in 1898, Jelliffe promised to send him as many medical students as he could. "I have one. . . . I would like to work out the hypophysis from a comparative standpoint, especially in its relations to the pre oral intestinal canal or whatever it is, and thus to its relations to disordered metabolism. In a peculiar condition, Akromegaly, this body is often affected. Why? Some work has been done but there is room for more."[74]

Jelliffe's publications after 1897 continued to show his activity in the field of pharmacognosy and also in the practice of general medicine. In 1904 he published his last botanical work, "Additions to 'The Flora of Long Island'" (last except for an article on his mushroom hobby, in 1937),[75] and in 1905 and 1907 his last general works not specifically in the mental and nervous disease area, a collaboration on *The Urine and Feces in Diagnosis* and a revision of the *Standard Family Physician*. And then, in 1901, he added a major activity when, as noted above, he became editor of *Medical News*, for which he was already, since November 1899, doing manuscript editing and reading galley proof for $100 a month.[76]

All of this time Jelliffe was finishing up his course work for his formal B.A. at Brooklyn Polytechnic and his Ph.D., which he took in the Faculty of Pure Science at Columbia (a purely formal M.A. was awarded later). In his own account of how he came to add these degrees to his name, Jelliffe pointed up the amusing aspects of his efforts.

"As already related I graduated from the Polytechnic Institute, but as an engineer, and with no special baccalaureate degree. I had no alphabetical appendages other than M.D. and when meeting with Nicholas Miraculous

---

73. Just when the quiz became Jelliffe's exclusively is unknown. The groups were meeting in his home by at least 1902–1903, perhaps from the beginning.

74. Jelliffe to C. B. Davenport, 21 February 1898, Davenport Papers. Jelliffe was flattered to be asked by Davenport to give two lectures at Cold Spring Harbor.

75. See Bibliography.

76. Agreement in Additional Papers.

Butler [Nicholas Murray Butler, President of Columbia University], for so was our designation of him at the time, it soon became evident he had a liking for these appendages in his pedagogic family. But how was it to be done? So over to the prexy at Poly Prep and I was permitted to re-enter on the liberal program and by examinations in thirteen subjects, with a twice-a-week attendance on his Moral Philosophy course I might get an A.B. So here I was, ten to twelve years older than my fellow students, having to learn by rote about the good, the true and the beautiful in the old theological formulae of Prexy at the Poly. It was a true experiment in remembering 'nonsense syllables,' but I made it, including a stiff rubbing by Professor Kellogg in Old English. Three theses, one major and two minors, were demanded for the Ph.D. One I had already up my sleeve for for years I had collected the Plants of Long Island and Dr. Britton's indulgent eye let it pass for my major. Professor Osborne was content with an examination for one of the minors and fortunately for my other minor I chose Dr. Oliver S. Strong and did some hard plugging on the comparative anatomy of the nervous system with a small squeak on the Cytology of the Brains of some Amphibia and some translations and bibliographical gathering for Van Gieson's new Archives, all of which were later put in print"[77] [see Bibliography].

Conclusion

At that point Jelliffe hungered for academic advancement. But altogether the direction that his career was to take was not clear. The only consistent developments were those pushing him into medical journalism.

A summary of Jelliffe's career at the turn of the century is provided by a unique letter that has survived from the summer of 1897. Jelliffe wrote to his old college classmate, Charles B. Davenport, and, scribbling rapidly, described what he had been doing, the divisions of his life, and the tension he felt in his split existence.

"After I left the Poly—86—I went to Columbia, graduated at the P&S: 1889: a young and enthusiastic *med.* with a strong botanical bias: You may perhaps remember our meeting at the Brooklyn Library when you were immersed in Sachs; I confess to a strong liking for the gentleman myself.

"After graduation, I was in a hospital for a year and a half and then went to '*Eurup*' with accent on the last syllable: I had such a fine time: Holland, Vienna, Prague, Dresden; a walking trip through a portion of Thuringia— Through Switzerland, afoot, from Schaffhausen to Bellanzona, in Italy; through Italy by various stages as far south as Naples: Up into France & England &

---

77. Jelliffe, "The Editor Himself," pp. 553–554. See Bibliography. Butler in fact became acting president of Columbia in 1902. Before that he was dean of the Faculty of Philosophy— but known as a vigorous proponent of upgrading.

home: 8 months I studied or tried to: the rest of the time enjoyed myself: It took me 8 months however to learn to drink beer: such was the highly moral effect of my Poly training: At Munich I fell and gloried in my fall; and have been trying to get over my youthful puritanical asceticism ever since: but I do not enjoy the weed.

"When I came home, this was in 1891, I hustled, worked up a practice, obtained a position on the Brooklyn Board of Health and grunted for the dust: I had to work off a lot of dead horse. It took me three years to square myself with the world: then I married a Brooklyn girl and we came to New York to start anew: I left a comfortable practice behind me, but there was nothing but mental stagnation to look forward to, hence the move: I have two girls, 2 yrs & 4 mos. respectively, a comfortable home & here we are: My botanical bias procured me a chair in the N.Y. College of Pharmacy where I enjoy the rights & privileges as a professor of Pharmacognosy: confess you do not know what that is: incidentally also a salary is attached: This takes about 1/2 my time for 7 months of the year: the rest is devoted to my regular work: this as you can see was the plank that enabled me to cross the Rubicon. At present I feel sometimes as though I were between the devil and the deep sea: My particular leaning is towards neurology & Psychiatry: the major portion of my living comes from the microscopy of drugs and I complacently straddle, hoping that no serious divergence will rend me in twain:

"This summer I am spending my vacation at an Asuylam [sic], more euphoniously termed a 'State Hospital,' with 1300 patients of all conceivable types. I am thoroughly enjoying it, going on as a member of the staff, temporarily, and getting what I can out of it: I have sketched and described some 6–700 ears: trying to get at 'stigmata' of which we hear so much nowadays: some couple of score of melancholics have been frightened into several kinds of fits by my getting some of their blood for examination: General paresis blood is also on the go; A couple of brains; and so I am busy with more material to work up than I could finish in a year: and to think of going back to teach 2–300 youths the differences between stone cells & bast fibres: How to tell true from false Cascara; How to stain for tuberculosis? Yet such is life: This letter is running away with me, & if I do not cease soon—you will certainly deem me a patient with uncontrollable graphomania. . . ."[78]

78. Jelliffe to C. B. Davenport, 16 August 1897, Davenport Papers.

TWO

Life's Work
1900–World War I

Introduction

At the turn of the century, Jelliffe was a man of his times. As reflected in his botany, he was a positivist, convinced that describing and classifying would eventually bring all knowledge within the grasp of humanity. So he, too, added to the medical literature, if not new facts and descriptions, then new juxtapositions. In his 1897 paper on some Binghamton State Hospital patients, "Contribution to the Study of the Blood in General Paresis," he tried to correlate the results of studies of patients' blood cells with a particular symptom complex. Similarly, in 1902 he linked "Influenza and the Nervous System"—unwittingly also anticipating his pioneer role in psychosomatic medicine. He was a collector and to some extent an experimenter, maintaining a laboratory in his home and office on West 71st Street and later on West 56th Street. All of this showed up quintessentially in his desire to know the whole literature and indeed the whole history of any subject to which he turned his attention.

Jelliffe was also an optimist who believed that knowledge produced power. His interest in the germ theory of disease and his work in popularizing it best showed this side of an already complex intellect. Soon he would extend his quest to help human beings control their own fates as his view of nature expanded to include different ways of conceptualizing the human organism and its strivings, insights that grew particularly, at first, out of the psychotherapy movement.

In the new century that began after 1900, Jelliffe adapted to fresh intellectual currents without giving up many of his basic life patterns. However reluctantly, he finally did move into his ultimate field of medical specialization, the realm of nervous and mental diseases (neurology and psychiatry, as will be remarked again below, were at that time usually conceptualized as a unit). He published extensively on the history of his specialty, and with the aid of his unusually retentive memory he extended to an astonishing degree his command of the special literature. He was still able to bring his training in materia medica and internal medicine to bear on nervous and mental disease problems, but his focus became increasingly concentrated on neurology and psychiatry.

Jelliffe became an innovator. He early apprehended first the importance of psychotherapy, as it came into medicine at the turn of the century, and then psychoanalysis, and he struggled to expand the impact of these new forces within the medical world. But he also sensed trends beyond the formal teachings of the psychotherapists and psychoanalysts. With his particular background he was able to point out new directions in which medicine might go—particularly toward what, later, others designated psychosomatics.

As a pioneer, Jelliffe had influence and importance because of his relationship to institutions, particularly medical publications. Sometimes institutions resisted his attempts to shape them, and it was thinkers other than he who tended to have an impact. Often, in fact, he was not inclined to try to grasp institutional power. But in the closing decades of his life he became something of an institution himself.

It is worthwhile to inquire why Jelliffe gained great renown but did not realize the full potential of either his position or his innovations, and in the following pages some exploration of this problem is ventured. At this point, however, it is appropriate to note that not only did institutional bases— particularly medical schools—elude him but his intellectual style was only approximately that of the new age in science and medicine. He sensed the trends and the approaches that superseded positivism, but he lacked the singlemindedness and precision of thinking that might have carried him further in some areas. A certain grandeur of vision, with which in fact he inspired many others to rise above themselves, often kept his own attention from the hard and persistent pursuit of the new ideas. E. E. Southard of Boston, a contemporary and one of the most brilliant medical intellectuals of his day, recognized this characteristic of Jelliffe in a defensive reply to a letter from him:

"As for the purity of your language," Southard wrote, "that was not the issue with me so much as the logical categories in question. . . . Briefly put, I do not believe that your paper on 'Symbol as an Energy Container' will really persuade medical men or even be read intelligently by the majority of *Archives* readers. Nor do I mean that the majority of these readers could not understand the paper. I mean merely that they would not read it. You say that you thought the new magazine was to be progressive, but what you are requiring it to be is philosophical."[1] Clearly Southard and many other ex-

1. E. E. Southard to Jelliffe, 24 September 1919.

cellent figures in medicine were unwilling or unable to follow Jelliffe when he could specify his vision only in terms that were essentially general ("philosophical" was Southard's word), and Jelliffe in fact often complained of being misunderstood even as correspondents described him as inspiring.

In practical terms, twentieth-century Jelliffe has to be viewed in four different major roles: neurologist and psychiatrist, pioneer psychoanalyst, a founder of psychosomatic medicine, and editor. During his years of growth he also continued his role as classroom teacher, but this role withered away in the years just before the 1920's, leaving only his writing, editing, and public speaking to communicate his ideas (see Appendix 1).

The Decision to Specialize

By an accident, teaching appointments crystallized his decision to become wholly a nervous and mental disease specialist. At the turn of the century teaching had provided an important part of Jelliffe's income. The quiz continued, meeting in the hallway of the West 71st Street house, which was crowded with children as well as books. Then after 1904 there were more comfortable quarters in the new West 56th Street house. Exactly when Jelliffe relinquished the quiz is not recorded, but probably he never resumed it after his long absences overseas in 1906–1908 and his sudden reorientation. Louis Casamajor, whose first-hand description of the quiz students is quoted in Chapter 4, took his M.D. in 1907.

The appointment critical to the direction of Jelliffe's career was an instructorship in materia medica and therapeutics at P & S, in the medical school proper (as opposed to the College of Pharmacy). This appointment had begun in 1903 and brought Jelliffe as much as $1500 a year as well as prestige.[2] But in the summer of 1907 the following exchange of letters occurred, in part while Jelliffe was overseas attending his first world congress of nervous and mental disease specialists. The exchange is reported in a letter from the dean of the medical school to the president of Columbia University.

October 4, 1907.

Nicholas Murray Butler, LL.D.,
President, Columbia University.

My dear President Butler:

As I informed you verbally the other day, Dr. Smith Ely Jelliffe has resigned from his position as Instructor in Materia Medica. This is more or less the result of the correspondence which has passed between us as follows:

2. Appointment notices in Additional Papers.

130 East 35th Street,
New York, July 31, 1907.

Dr. Smith Ely Jelliffe,
64 West 56th Street, City

My dear Doctor:

I see by the catalogue of the Fordham Medical College that you have accepted the position as Instructor in that Institution. I am informed by the President of the University that this is equivalent to a resignation from the College of Physicians and Surgeons. That it is not customary for members of the staff of instructors of Columbia to attach themselves to the teaching staff of other, and possibly rival, institutions. I have, therefore, instructed the Treasurer's office to hold up your salary check for the month of July. This matter has only just come to my notice or I should have written to you before. Of course it is possible that your resignation has already been sent to the President's office, but he being away it has not come to my attention if this has been done.

Very sincerely yours,
[signed] *S. W. Lambert.*

Hotel Des Pays-Bas,
Amsterdam, Sept. 2, 1907.

Dr. Samuel Lambert,
New York City.

My dear Dr. Lambert:

I received your letter just before leaving the city and have deferred answering it until such time that I was at comparative leisure.

If it is the rule at Columbia that no officer can have any connection with any other institution then I must regretfully tender my resignation, as Instructor of Materia Medica. I have not received my appointment at Fordham, beyond a mere verbal agreement with Dr. Walsh that I would be pleased to give some clinics in psychiatry if there were no objections on the part of Columbia. I made several attempts to see Dr. Butler, Dr. Herter, and yourself, but as vacations had just begun I was unsuccessful. Dr. Butler left for Europe the very day I called at the University.

Nevertheless—it is perhaps better for me to sever my Columbia connection, much as I regret to do so.

I am thankful for the kindly interest taken in my work and for the encouragement given. The work has helped me considerably but it seems best to me that I finally narrow down to the main interests of my work in nervous and mental diseases.

Very cordially yours,
[signed] *Smith Ely Jelliffe.*

COPY OF LETTER TO DR. JELLIFFE

October 4th, 1907.

Dr. Smith Ely Jelliffe
64 West 56th Street,
New York City.

My dear Dr. Jelliffe:
Your letter of September 2nd, from Amsterdam, reached me after a little delay owing to the wrong address, and I have delayed answering it until you returned to the City.

I acceded to your resignation as Instructor in Materia Medica as outlined in your letter and I have notified President Butler of the fact. I think it would be wise if you would send to him a formal letter of resignation for presentation to the Trustees, preferably before their meeting on Monday next.

I wish you every success in your special work in nervous and mental diseases, and remain,

Faithfully yours,
[signed] *Samuel W. Lambert*,
Dean.

If you have not already received a formal resignation from Dr. Jelliffe you should do so before the meeting of the Trustees on Monday. I enclose the checks representing Dr. Jelliffe's salary since July 1st which were in the hands of the Assistant Bursar.[3]

Thus Jelliffe used this occasion not only to cut himself off from P & S but from any appointments that distracted him from a full commitment to his new specialty, and both he and Dean Lambert recognized the nature of the decision to—as Jelliffe put it—"finally narrow down."

Institutional Affiliations

The biggest change in Jelliffe's teaching came in the displacing of his professorship in the New York College of Pharmacy, an appointment that also ended in 1907. (Columbia, as noted in Chapter 1, had absorbed that college formally in 1904.) Resignation from the College of Pharmacy had been foreshadowed by the decline of Jelliffe's publications in the medical botanical field, which effectively came to an end with his 1903 and 1904 textbooks in pharmacognosy (see Bibliography).

Jelliffe's appointment as professor in the medical school of Fordham University, in the Bronx, New York City, constituted his chief teaching post for

3. Samuel W. Lambert to Nicholas Murray Butler, 4 October 1907. This letter and the original correspondence are preserved in the office of the dean of the Faculty of Medicine, College of Physicians & Surgeons of Columbia University, New York City. Copies were most generously supplied through the courtesy of M. Linda Kircher, coordinator, Medical School Administration.

many years. He was, however, only clinical professor, and he left the position after 1913. (No records of that professorship have survived, and he continued to list it in publications as late as 1915. The medical school itself did not survive past 1921.) The appointment did enable Jelliffe to invite Jung to speak there, thus providing Jung with a forum for his first important statement about his deviation from Freud (see Part II).

There also may have been some teaching connected with Jelliffe's clinical appointments in these years. Beginning in 1899, as noted above, he served as visiting neurologist at the City Hospital on Blackwells Island and concurrently, at first, as "Instructor of Therapeutics"—but the teaching appointment apparently soon lapsed while his neurological practice there continued for almost a decade. The other clinical appointment was as clinical assistant in neurology in the Vanderbilt Clinic of Columbia University. To what extent this was a teaching appointment is unclear, but it began in 1898 and was most important in establishing Jelliffe in his new specialty. He was one of twelve assistants and saw patients in the clinic three afternoons a week from two until four. While he was working there he published reports of the kinds of patients seen, as a contribution to epidemiology: They were about one-tenth mental patients of various kinds and the rest diagnosed as suffering from nervous disease, about half organic and about half functional.[4] This appointment of course ended along with his other Columbia appointments in 1907.

Starting in 1911, Jelliffe put much energy into his position as adjunct professor of diseases of the nervous system in the Post-Graduate Medical School in New York, where he served until 1917 and delivered more lectures than any other lecturer in his department. For 1914 his schedule included thirty-seven lectures (an average of almost one a week except during August and the Christmas season). What is most remarkable about Jelliffe's lectures was the fact that he covered an extremely wide variety of topics, from the most strictly organic tumors of the nervous system to explicitly "psychogenic" conditions—anything, virtually, in either neurology or psychiatry. On 16 May, for example, he covered "Anxiety Neurosis, Hemiplegia with Thalamus, Sensory Changes." At other times he might combine "Dementia Praecox, Thalamic Syndrome" (26 January) or "Cerebrospinal Syphilis, Hysterical Aphonia" (18 September). Sometimes a juxtaposition involved differential diagnosis ("General Paresis, Tabes vs. alcoholic Neuritis, Brain Tumor," 8 June); at other times the subjects appeared to be miscellaneous ("Anxiety Neurosis, Cerebrospinal Syphilis," 11 October). Eight of the thirty-seven lectures were explicitly—by name—on Freud's teachings, indicating that by 1914 Jelliffe even in his teaching was playing an important role in spreading psychoanalytic ideas (see below). Nor was he backward about content sen-

4. See especially Smith Ely Jelliffe, "Some Notes on Dispensary Work in Nervous and Mental Disease," *JNMD*, 31 (1904), 311.

sitive even in medicine: on 6 March he took up "Freud's Hypotheses of the rôle of Sexuality in the Psychoneuroses."

How carefully prepared the lectures were is uncertain, but some were formal, for Jelliffe noted at the time that one, "Little Signs of Hemiplegia," 26 February, had been published in the *Post-Graduate*. On other occasions he noted the use of lantern slides, as on 13 June: "70 Slides of Neurological Subjects."[5]

Besides this list of lectures, other materials that might reveal exactly what Jelliffe was teaching and what impact he had are no longer available. The only exception is a number of "clinical lectures" such as those that appeared in the *Post-Graduate* and those published in the series *International Clinics* (see Bibliography). These lectures in print suggest that Jelliffe's presentations were clear and straightforward and that he assumed a certain quota of intelligence and information on the part of his audience and, moreover, that he did not hesitate to introduce qualifications, complications, and contradictory opinions from various authorities. He was also capable of considerable philosophical discussion and even of just plain chattiness. His students from this period knew him affectionately as "Windy Jelliffe."[6]

Jelliffe's hospital posts paralleled his teaching and clinical appointments. His work at the City Hospital continued until 1913 (although again the title was listed in publications appearing as late as 1915). In 1907 he briefly took a position as consulting physician to Manhattan State Hospital and also as senior attending physician at the Home for the Aged and Infirm.

Another brief but important activity was his association with the New York Neurological Institute, which was founded in 1909 as the independent Hospital for Nervous Diseases and much later absorbed into the Presbyterian Hospital. The three founders were neurologists Joseph Collins, Joseph Fraenkel, and Jelliffe's close friend and colleague, Pearce Bailey. The institute served to stimulate and train many New York specialists, and from the beginning Jelliffe served in Bailey's service there as visiting physician. Jelliffe later mentioned this momentous affiliation in describing how he and A. A. Brill walked home from their clinic there across Central Park and how, over a period of time, Brill converted him to psychoanalysis (see below). But the appointment did not last long; by 1911 Jelliffe was no longer associated with the institute. In a letter to Joseph Collins in 1931, Jelliffe alluded to what had happened: ". . . you induced Bailey 'To give me Hell,' as I heard you tell him at the University Club the night I walked home with him and he at that time told me with much tact and kindly feeling that the 'harmony' would be better if I dropped out of the 'Institute.'"[7] The reason that Jelliffe appeared

5. Smith Ely Jelliffe, "Nervous and Mental Disease Dispensary Work, II," *Post-Graduate*, 29 (1914), 578–580.
6. Caro W. Lippman to Jelliffe, 1 December 1936.
7. Jelliffe to Joseph Collins, 18 December 1931.

to be an inharmonious influence is unknown. If anyone was a troublemaker, it was Collins, not Jelliffe. Collins was known as an aggressive "Irishman," and he did indeed insist on administrative unity in the institute to the point that even Fraenkel resigned after only two years. The wording of Jelliffe's letter suggests that Jelliffe was responsible for some of the idiosyncratic proceedings that so distressed Collins when staff physicians acted in the name of the institute.[8] Those actions may of course have involved Jelliffe's new orientation to psychoanalysis, for Collins was also an intemperate opponent of psychoanalysis.

Private Practice

No doubt leaving the institute was painful, but Jelliffe by the 1910's increasingly was giving his time to outpatient practice, and he had no need for extensive hospital affiliations. He was very active in the American Neurological Association, and in 1913–1915 he served as president of the leading local group in the country, the New York Neurological Society.

A growing activity of Jelliffe's, and one that was on occasion very lucrative, was testifying as a psychiatric expert, or "alienist," in court cases. Already in 1907 his friend, White, was anticipating that Jelliffe would do well serving as an expert witness.[9] Within the next few years Jelliffe was, as articles in New York newspapers indicate, involved regularly in various trials, some of which were notorious at the time, and his letters give further evidence of this activity. In May 1911, Jelliffe noted incidentally in a letter to Adolf Meyer that he had just "finished up one medico-legal case this morning. Two more are on the Day Calendar for this week. . . ."[10]

Again Jelliffe's excellent memory served him well on such occasions. In 1914 he wrote to White about one court experience: "I had a very uncomfortable time on the stand, trying to straighten out your very unpragmatic mode of presentation of the whole Idiocy Imbecility problem in your *Outlines*. Permit me to say that I only escaped from saying that it was 'tommyrot,' by telling the prosecuting attorney that it was the second edition he was quoting from and not the fourth, otherwise I might have appeared as having said that you were a fool. It is awful. Look it over. I have not had a chance to look over the fourth edition,—perhaps that is perfect, but the point of view is the thing that needs correction."[11]

8. See especially Charles Albert Elsberg, *The Story of a Hospital: The Neurological Institute of New York, 1909–1938* (New York, 1944), especially pp. 27–28, 32, 162. *Annual Report of the Neurological Institute of New York*, 1910, 1911. From 1930 to 1938 Jelliffe was a member of the courtesy staff.

9. William Alanson White to Jelliffe, 8 February 1907, White Papers, Box 1.

10. Jelliffe to Adolf Meyer, 8 May 1911, Meyer Papers, I-1921-1, Chesney Archives, Johns Hopkins University, Baltimore.

11. Jelliffe to William Alanson White, 22 October 1914.

The most momentous of the trials was a famous one in which Harry K. Thaw was tried for the murder of Stanford White. Jelliffe had been a fellow passenger and socialized with Thaw's brother on a trans-Atlantic crossing earlier. The Thaw family retained Jelliffe as an expert witness, and he continued to be employed on Thaw's case for years afterward. There were two trials, and in the second, in 1908, Thaw was found innocent by reason of insanity. The fee paid Jelliffe in the first trial enabled him to go abroad for extended study in 1906. The case was important also because it put him on good terms with a number of the leading nervous and mental disease specialists who also testified.[12]

European Trips

For many years after that trip to Europe which his testimony financed, Jelliffe traveled abroad for a longer or shorter stay on the average of once every two years or so (except during World War I), a pattern that he tried to maintain.[13] These trips of Jelliffe's were of great importance in shaping not only his career but his function in American medicine.

Jelliffe was a dedicated traveler. Even while feeling impecunious, in 1893, he attended the Chicago World's Fair (see Bibliography), and in August 1896 he attended professional meetings in Montreal where he presented a paper.[14] In 1901 he went to Seattle, again to read a paper. That time he managed a lot of sightseeing on the way, going via the Northern Pacific route and returning by way of Salt Lake City and Denver. In 1905 his duties as one of the leading medical editors of the country took him as far as the American Medical Association meetings in Portland, Oregon, from which he went on to Alaska. Another time he went to Florida.[15]

But it was his few weeks on the Continent in 1902 that set the pattern for his later European trips that began in 1906. He and his wife traveled in first-class luxury. His main task abroad was to produce reports for three medical journals on the second international conference on venereal diseases, a conference that essentially launched the modern social hygiene movement. But Jelliffe also, besides botanizing, visited the mental patient colony at Gheel in Belgium and made a number of calls on eminent figures in the nervous and mental disease specialties, establishing contacts from which he benefited

12. See, for example, Jelliffe to Adolf Meyer, 22 March 1907, Meyer Papers, I-1920-1, addressed familiarly, "My dear Meyer."

13. Jelliffe to Emil Oberholzer, 16 November 1923.

14. Smith E. Jelliffe, "Notes Upon Strophantus Hispidus and Strophantus Kombé," *Proceedings of the American Pharmaceutical Association*, 44 (1896), 226–227. A "Norway trip" noted on a 1900 photo cannot be confirmed.

15. Many details are to be found in the memorabilia books, Additional Papers. Also see Smith Ely Jelliffe, "The Death Instinct in Somatic and Psychopathology," *Psychoanalytic Review*, 20 (1933), 121.

in succeeding years. He later recalled particularly Van Gehuchten at Louvain and Jelgersma (who later went into psychoanalysis) at Leyden.[16]

At the conference Jelliffe showed himself for the first time in what came to be a familiar role: cosmopolitan physician. Already aboard ship he had undertaken to extend his linguistic abilities, and his wife made this note: "Ely has labored with a little Dutch producing a series of swine-like grunts which a Dutchman who is instructing him pronounces very satisfactory." Mrs. Jelliffe reported further in her journal that at the end of the conference when there was a great celebration, "Ely went to the dinner which he found most inspiring. There were ten languages spoken at his table, all of which he insists he understood. There were six kinds of wine. I have always thought that the gift of tongues could be *spirit*ually interpreted."[17]

One important consequence of that trip was that it caused Jelliffe to initiate the translation of Paul Dubois's classic work on psychotherapy.[18] The appearance of that translation, *The Psychic Treatment of Nervous Disorders*, did the most to trigger the psychotherapy movement in American medicine.

Jelliffe as Specialty Student

For some years Jelliffe was not just a medical tourist. In 1906, at the age of forty, he began a series of trips to Europe that were study trips. They served to establish his credentials in the nervous and mental disease specialty, and they also served to make Jelliffe the best acquainted American in the specialty. His own account emphasizes his sense of mastery that was based on his personal acquaintance with the world leaders in the nervous and mental disease areas. Emil Kraepelin, with whom Jelliffe studied twice, in 1906 and 1907, was the most eminent psychiatrist then in practice. Jelliffe afterward felt very cordial toward him and the two of them, it turned out, occasionally botanized together.[19] In 1907 Jelliffe was an official delegate to another international congress, but this time it was on Psychiatry, Neurology, Psychology, and the Nursing of the Insane (Amsterdam, September 1907), not a meeting outside of the specialty but rather one that drew its leaders (as detailed in the opening of Part II). Six months during 1908–1909 Jelliffe spent with the finest neurologists, in Berlin, and then six more months with the neurologists in Paris who had been pioneering psychotherapy for several years. As his account of these events suggests, he not only came in contact with major thinkers but amassed a formidable amount of clinical experience.

"Thanks to a few ducats extracted from the first Thaw trial I was able to go to Kraepelin in the spring of 1906 and spent six months with him with

16. Jelliffe, "Glimpses of a Freudian Odyssey," p. 322. See Part II. HLJ Journal, 1902, Additional Papers, contains many details.

17. Ibid.

18. Jelliffe, "Glimpses of a Freudian Odyssey," p. 323. John C. Burnham, *Psychoanalysis and American Medicine, 1894–1918: Medicine, Science, and Culture* (New York, 1967).

19. Jelliffe to F. I. Wertham, 3 February 1930.

Pearce Bailey, and the next year with Drs. White and Gregory, another semester in Munich. I also met Dubois in person at Berne and became acquainted with real *'filet mignon* with sauce *bernaise.'* . . .

"Dubois was a very clever, keen dialectician. He would talk with his patients and show them how impossible certain things were in view of the natural laws of the world and by very skillful argument, combined with a very acute intellect and an extremely pleasing personality, he did a great work in psychotherapy. He followed the method of intellectual explanation with a sympathetic understanding of what the symptoms might mean to the patient. He tried to help them by various routes so as to get a better intellectual hold of the situation. I tried this method for some time. I led my patients in those days as they attempted to cross a stream of difficult psychical struggles from one stone to another stone and then to another stone and then to another stone until I got them over the stream. But I found that didn't work as well as it should. There was too much intellect and not enough feeling in it. . . .

"This year, 1907, was my first personal contact with psychoanalysis. We met Jung and Maeder and Riklin in Zurich. Drs. White and Gregory and I then traveled to Italy together, visiting Tanzi in Florence, Rossi and Lugaro, Tamburini in Rome, Mingazzini in Naples and a number of others I shall not stop to mention. We also visited Bernheim at Nancy and saw his patients promptly *'dormez'* at command.

"October of the next year, 1908, saw me off with my family of five children to Berlin for six months where I worked with Ziehen and Oppenheim, met Mendel and the Vogts and became acquainted with Karl Abraham. Then there were six months in Paris. Here other types of psychotherapy were being practiced. I followed Déjérine in his wards, became intrigued with his insistence on the emotional factors in medicine; listened to Janet's meticulous case history taking and his brilliant expositions; followed Babinski who was only just beginning his teachings on pithiatism.

"Déjérine was an entirely different type. Dubois was a slight, delicate, ultra-refined, intellectual type. Déjérine was a big, hearty man with a gusto and a laugh and not afraid of a Rabelaisian reference. He was, moreover, a very gifted man with a temperament that had known sorrow and which had given him a great insight into and feeling for mental suffering. He was of the manic depressive constitution.

"He had periods of great brilliancy and enormous capacity for work; then also a few periods when he went into mild depressed phases and could do very little. The appointment of Raymond as [successor] to Charcot possibly precipitated one of these depressions and he went to Dubois for treatment. He developed, however, a psychotherapy of the emotional type. He appealed to the feeling side of the individual. He was a great big, simple-hearted fellow weighing 250 pounds, 6 feet 2 inches in height, with a heart of gold. He would sit on the edge of the bed with the poor little seamstress or the little cellar rat, or somebody else that came into the hospital, and go over their life's history, their family troubles, difficulties in collecting their bills, how the children's teething kept them up all night, and so on and so on. He poured out a sympathetic emotional type of reaction to them. He was the indulgent humorous father, and the hospital the warm embracing mother with its staff of nurses trained by him. And, moreover, he had developed the idea that many cardiopathies, gastropathies, enteropathies, and other internal ills were nearly 80 per cent. of them of emotional origin; and that fully 80 per cent. of the practice of the Parisian profession was concerned with neuroses and they did not know it. The result of this was that they rose up in their might and wanted to smite him. But he was too great to be bothered and eventually became professor of neurology and adorned Charcot's Clinic for many years, giving it a prestige for thorough neurological work which will endure for a long time. I translated his work on *Psychotherapy* and thus marked another milestone on my way.

"I had been with Babinski in his Paris clinic at the Pitié and had heard his formula, namely, that all hysteria (pithiatism) cases were due to suggestion and could be cured by persuasion; a more or less modified form of the Dubois dialect. Babinski would say, 'You see this patient? Whom did he see?' 'Doctor So-and-so?' 'Didn't he push your liver in there, and didn't he say something about your gall-bladder; didn't he say this would happen and the other thing would happen?' And by heck, it happened! This is a caricature of Babinski's idea of suggestion; that is to say, that the doctor handed the patient the disease that the doctor thought the patient ought to have. This did not satisfy me, however, and good neurologist that Babinski was, his formula was too easy. It did not read a bit like the pictures spoken of in the Greek poets."[20]

While Jelliffe's own retrospective account is revealing in and of itself, yet more comment is apt, to give his story full meaning. He talks of experience with three different types of European practitioners: psychotherapists, psychiatrists, and neurologists; clearly his intention was to be broadly trained, not narrowly focused.

It is worth emphasizing, moreover, that Jelliffe worked with figures in nervous and mental disease practice who were absolutely outstanding in the pre–World War I world. By 1909 he had personally seen the very best, and it is against this background that his ultimate conversion to psychoanalysis is so very impressive. Georg Theodor Ziehen and Hermann Oppenheim in Berlin, for example, names that Jelliffe listed so easily, were in their time considered superlative among German-speaking physicians, Oppenheim in neurology and particularly neuropathology, and Ziehen as the chief intellectual competitor of Kraepelin, Jelliffe's other teacher, in the field of psychiatry.

20. Jelliffe, "Glimpses of a Freudian Odyssey," pp. 323–324.

The psychotherapy of Dubois and Déjérine that Jelliffe learned was generally called "persuasion" and later "supportive" psychotherapy. But Jelliffe also learned about "suggestion" from Bernheim—again, the master himself. Déjérine's influence, finally, it should be remarked, was more lasting on Jelliffe than on medicine in general.

One specific document has survived from Jelliffe's middle-period European adventures: an account of his first weeks with Ziehen in Berlin, written to Jelliffe's close friend, Pearce Bailey. This was the last time that Jelliffe took the role of a student. Beyond the personalities that Jelliffe compared, the account is significant in that he states clearly the place of laboratory work, and particularly up-to-date laboratory work, in the best clinical practice at that time. This type of awareness undergirded the image that American neurologists held of what good scientific medicine should be—aspirations that Jelliffe shared and which affected his life profoundly though he was no longer making laboratory contributions. Meantime the account shows how traditional neuroanatomical studies combined with bacteriological and psychological investigations in pacesetting neurology.

"I would that you were beside me now, tied into a clean white pinafore, taking histories in this execrable language and doing ward work with me. I count myself fortunate in that after a week's probation and following the Geheimrath on his daily rounds, he has consented to my trying to serve as a volontär Arzt and put me in G.K.M. II, as it is officially called, in other words: Geisteskrankheiten, Männlichen II. There are about 33 beds in this ward, it being the male receiving ward for the less disturbed patients. I am assisting an assistant and it is a case of the blind keeping the deaf and dumb; he is a youngster with little experience and mine is all shut up by reason of a leitungs-Aphasie, or whatever one wants to call it. I am busy mostly with copying from dictation, with some degree of independence as soon as I feel any assurance beyond asking the patients to stick out their tongues or what not. I go on duty at 8, the chief starts his rounds at 7:30 and gets to our ward about 10—Lecture usually 11–12; then back until 1:30 when I hibernate until 4 & am on duty until 7:30 at night; thus far so tired then I want to crawl into bed.

"I want to give my first impressions but they have already begun to fade. Ziehen is certainly a wonder. He seems au fait with his anatomy, his neurology, psychology, and psychiatry. He is as good a teacher I should say as Kraepelin, but his pitch is just a little lower and more fragmentary. Whether my own increased knowledge makes it appear that he speaks more simply than K. did, I cannot say—perhaps my viewpoint makes it so. His demonstrations are remarkably clear and straightforward.

"He gives a series of psychological lectures that are extremely interesting. In two such he said more than Gaupp did in his whole course, and moreover his psychological laboratory is in beautiful condition. An hour a day I am spending in the anatomical laboratory going over some fibre tracts and I think I shall try to finish my little Epileptic stunt.

"Some excellent work is going ahead in the experimental line on serum reactions; the Wassermann cerebrospinal complement reaction, etc., is very prominent; also syphilitic blood tests. There are a number of men working in the laboratory, but there is no man like Alzheimer about. Köppen his first assistant I have not yet met. My first week was a gorge of lectures and I saw almost everybody in the nervous and mental disease line, but all in all they are second class alongside of Ziehen. Oppenheim I have seen but not yet been around to his Clinic. I shall wait a little for him until I get in better shape to profit more. Thus far the routine work in the wards takes me all day save a couple of hours at midday. My first week's enthusiasm of getting around to 7:30 rounds in the Nervenabtheilung has simmered down to getting around at 8–8:30. The Geheimrath is a wonder for work—but he has to do it rather hastily and somewhat dogmatically. There is much less bedside discussion than at München. There are about 240 beds—60 nerve and 180 mental cases running all the time. The Neurological Poliklinik Service is quite wonderful. 6000 cases a year, with about 12 men working on them daily from 10–1; and they really work and take histories that are worth while. It makes 'Twinkle's' [Starr's] clinic look like 30 cents in the thoroughness of the history taking; and the Geheimrath wants to see every case and verify the diagnosis. He spends about an hour daily with the Poliklinik cases. . . .

"Mrs. Jelliffe and the children with Fraulein are all comfortably settled in Dresden, with a suite of sunny rooms on a park and they are very happy. Skating, the park, and a riding academy are at hand, and three of them started school the first week.

"Ely Jr. [who had had polio] is improving every week. It takes me 2½ hours to run down or for Mrs. Jelliffe to run up [here to Berlin] and it has been a pleasant alternation. . . ."[21]

All of these travels before World War I were significant for a number of reasons. First, and most obviously, Jelliffe became increasingly internationally oriented. Other American physicians, too, had taken specialty training abroad, but hardly any had done so as persistently as had Jelliffe. Moreover, as he himself became better established, he consciously sought out the major writers and practitioners overseas and therefore had a particularly vivid grasp on strong and weak points in neurology and psychiatry throughout the world. He became a major, if not the major, conduit through which European medical innovations in the nervous and mental disease specialties came into the United States, insofar as they came via the printed page.

21. Jelliffe to P. Bailey, 18 November 1908. This experience as student is alluded to again in Chapter 4.

A second significance of Jelliffe's studies in the 1906–1909 period was that, unlike other American practitioners, Jelliffe did not commit himself to either psychiatry or neurology but maintained competence in both areas, in the traditional way. Since the two specialties were tending to differentiate in the early years of the twentieth century, the fact that Jelliffe remained in both left him without all of the professional and elite influence and prestige that a narrower career focus might have provided to him.[22] He himself clearly felt comfortable, however, since he already had a broad base in medicine, and he made breadth his style, along with an overwhelming grasp of the literature of both special areas.

Finally, Jelliffe clearly was prospering. He worked intensely, but he also took extravagant and lengthy vacations. As early as 1903 he not only enjoyed a late summer's holiday at Lake George in the Adirondacks—taken because he was tired from the extra writing that he had been doing that summer— but after Christmas he and Mrs. Jelliffe took a cruise to Bermuda. Despite his continual concern about money, which persisted even after the traumatic struggles of his first hard years, he and his family lived in a very comfortable way, with a summer home on Lake George (purchased 1904) and for the children a German governess (the "Fraulein," mentioned above).[23]

Medical Journalism

As Jelliffe indicated later on, the main bases for his early prosperity lay in his work in medical journalism. Since most of his efforts, particularly the editorials, were unsigned, as was observed earlier no record remains of just how much writing Jelliffe was doing at any particular time nor what the subject of his editorials—or even abstracts and book reviews—might have been. This aspect of Jelliffe's influence in American medicine will never be known fully.[24] Moreover, his wife also contributed editorial matter, especially when he was editor of the *Medical News* (see below). Again, how much Jelliffe may have inspired her work can only be guessed.

His own account (Chapter 1, above) of how he moved into medical journalism, and how much it meant in terms of time and income, is vivid enough. Business records that have survived give further details. The agreement that he signed in 1900 with Lea Brothers, the publishers who owned the *Medical News*, reveals that he was to receive as editor $250 a month, or $3000 a year, which was a very substantial sum for those days, when a laborer with a family could live comfortably for under $1000 a year.[25] Moreover, Lea Brothers

22. Jacques M. Quen, "Asylum Psychiatry, Neurology, Social Work, and Mental Hygiene: An Exploratory Study in Interprofessional History," *Journal of the History of the Behavioral Sciences*, 13 (1977), 3–11.

23. Children's Book, Family Papers.

24. A partial list of abstracts and reviews can be found in Alexander Grinstein, *The Index of Psychoanalytic Writings*, 14 vols. (New York, 1956–1975), vol. 2, pp. 976–990.

25. Copy in Additional Papers.

allowed Jelliffe up to $4000 a year to pay contributors, who included Mrs. Jelliffe and, it would be reasonable to infer, himself. The office of the journal was furnished by the publisher. Payment to authors was clearly optional and negotiable, but the custom at that time, and as long as Jelliffe was editing, was that abstracts and reviews, usually a very substantial part of journals that served to keep members of the profession abreast of new developments, were paid for.

When in 1905 Lea Brothers sold the *Medical News*, Jelliffe published a valedictory trying to explain what his professional goals were in editing a medical journal.

"Five years ago the writer took up the responsibilities and opportunities offered as editor of the *Medical News* with a single ambition clearly defined in his own mind, the determination to do all in his power to further the ideals of medical science in its efforts to conquer disease and to relieve human suffering.

"To this end it has been the desire of the editor of the *Medical News* to place before its readers from week to week the most helpful and progressive work that could be obtained from his fellow practitioners, and from students of the practical problems of medicine throughout the world. . . .

"A medical journal offers special problems not met in many other apparently similar enterprises. Its contributors, as may be readily surmised, are not primarily literary men who are ambitious to achieve distinction and wealth as authors. They are first and foremost workers, investigators, scientists, and their literary work is done under great pressure, and often only at the urgent request of the editor, who feels that he knows the interest that their experience will have for its readers. Therefore every contribution that comes from the office or laboratory or hospital clinic of a busy man is appreciated as a courtesy, and at this time it seems not inappropriate to recognize the personal obligation of the editor to his friends, and to state that any true measure of worth which the *Medical News* may have shown has been possible only through the help of its contributors. That among these may be numbered the foremost men in medicine in this country is a subject for congratulation.

"From this time forward the *Medical News* and its present editor with it enter into new relations. The *Medical News* is to become on the first of January, 1906, an integral part of the *New York and Philadelphia Medical Journal*. . . ."

Jelliffe went on in this farewell to talk about the ideals of the medical profession, quoting Osler to make the point once more that the work consisted of using scientific investigation to relieve human suffering.[26] Again, since the *Medical News* was a venerable and well-established journal, his influence may well have been significant; there is no way to measure it.

26. "The Consolidation of the Medical News and the New York Medical Journal," *Medical News*, 84 (1905), 1273–1274.

Just how much responsibility—and income—Jelliffe had after that, in his new post as associate editor of the *New York Medical Journal*, is not known. His name appeared as coeditor on the title page, but he listed himself merely as associate editor. Since that journal was one of the three or four most influential medical publications in the United States, his duties could have had substantial importance, but no evidence remains. His shift away from an editor's post did coincide with his departure for Europe, just a few months later, and also with the consolidation of his career as a nervous and mental disease specialist. Jelliffe submitted his resignation from the journal on 6 October 1908, and in a month his name was off the masthead. Editor Frank P. Foster understood that in Jelliffe's circumstances he would be glad to get away from editorial responsibilities: "I shall miss your practical wisdom, of which I have had several occasions to avail myself, and shall always remember our association as one of the pleasantest things of my career." Foster went on to note that Jelliffe could still contribute, at five dollars a column for editorials and half that rate for letters.[27]

The *Journal of Nervous and Mental Disease*

Meanwhile Jelliffe's involvement with the *Journal of Nervous and Mental Disease* was increasing. At the instance particularly of members of the American Neurological Association, in 1899 Spiller had been made editor, as Jelliffe years later explained, ". . . attending to the manuscripts and proof reading, and I was Associate as utility man in actually seeing that the *Journal* appeared in time. There were three or four years of this association. In October 1901 Dr. Brown died and I purchased the enterprise with Dr. Hammond's kindly mediation and my mother's small savings and in 1902 began as Managing Editor, with Dr. Spiller as responsible for the editing of the original article material in the *Journal*. I was chore boy for the 'Periscope.'

"Thus we worked in harmony for many years. Dr. Spiller was even more orderly and systematic than I, a much more meticulously accurate proof reader and I do not recall that we ever had any disagreements. His preeminence as an organic neurologist gave well merited prestige to the *Journal* since the major advances in neuropsychiatry were those of neurological accent during these years. . . .

"The *Journal* grew, paid its bills promptly, increased in size and significance so that by 1916, it could publish two volumes a year and had advanced from the $3.00 level of its quarterly existence to $10 a year in price."[28]

It was just at the end of 1901 that Jelliffe purchased the *Journal*. The entire purchase price, $2500, he borrowed from his father-in-law, Thomas Leeming,

27. Frank P. Foster to Jelliffe, 7 October 1908, in memorabilia notebooks, Additional Papers.
28. Jelliffe, "The Editor Himself," pp. 571–572.

with a note that was paid off on 1 April 1904.[29] Whether that payment represented the prosperity of the *Journal* or of Jelliffe's other activities is, again, not clear. He did always, or so he believed, make money on the *Journal;* and other evidences of affluence were his move to a new house (at 64 West 56th Street) in 1903 and, in 1904, his purchase of the property—125 acres of it—at Hulett's Landing. The latter was financed, at least in part, by a small inheritance of Mrs. Jelliffe's.[30] The role of Jelliffe's mother's savings, which he mentioned in his memoirs as capital for the purchase of the *Journal,* is unknown. The formal purchase money was borrowed from Leeming.[31]

While Jelliffe was editing the *Medical News,* then, he had also been working on the *Journal of Nervous and Mental Disease,* with his name on the title page as associate editor beginning in 1899. Spiller was an important mentor. When Jelliffe had first come onto the *Journal,* Spiller had written him a long letter saying, "I am very glad that you are to be associate editor," followed by three pages of instructions and pointing out the necessity for more involvement with specialists in Boston and Baltimore and the low quality of manuscripts that came from most Western contributors.[32]

The standards about which Spiller was concerned were various. On the one hand he urged Jelliffe to be sure that spelling was standardized in the *Journal* ("Dr. Brown and I have been arguing over the spelling of the word 'center'"). On the other hand, Spiller wrote, "In the index of recent literature I think it is desirable to omit the word 'American' and the sentence, 'The editors will be glad to receive any reprints,' etc. This index ought to be very valuable to men who wish the best literature on any subject, and it should not be limited to American writings. The sentence to which I refer indicates that a critical judgment concerning the value of papers is not exercised."[33]

Since Spiller from 1902 to 1918 edited the original contributions, for content Jelliffe had to concern himself only, as he noted, with the reviews and the "Periscope," or abstract section. In addition, of course, he handled the business management itself. Jelliffe's concern with business matters persisted regardless of editorial duties. Many years later he was still writing correspondents to remind them either that there were no subscriptions in their areas or that their proprietary hospitals were not advertising as they should in the pages of the *Journal of Nervous and Mental Disease.*

In 1902 the *Journal* was essentially the only neurological journal in the United States. Since at this time the neurologists were claiming an even larger

29. When the *American Journal of Insanity* was sold to the American Medico-Psychological Association in 1894, the price was $944.50 but did not include the inventory of back issues such as Jelliffe got with the *Journal of Nervous and Mental Disease.* Richard H. Hutchings, "The First Four Editors," *American Journal of Psychiatry,* 100 (1944), 38.
30. See Children's Book, 1903–1904, Family Papers.
31. The note with endorsements is in the Additional Papers.
32. W. G. Spiller to Jelliffe, 30 November 1898.
33. Ibid.

portion of the patients whom they shared to some extent with the psychiatrists, the phrase "nervous and mental disease" tended to reflect not only
the customary combination of "nervous" and "mental" in medical school
teaching but the increasing interest of neurologists per se in mental diseases.
Original papers in neurology did often appear in journals oriented toward
internal medicine, since neurology was still close to that specialty, and Jelliffe
himself published in such journals. But only his *Journal* attempted to give
complete coverage for neurology.

For this reason, Jelliffe's work with the abstracts section was of great
significance. The abstracts were designed, as Spiller had noted, to cover all
of the literature from all over the world that was relevant to practice and
research in the specialty. Since most American physicians, even very good
ones, did not in fact read foreign languages easily, if at all, Jelliffe came to
serve as the agency through which many specialists and other physicians
learned about the existence overseas of both experimental and clinical advances in neurology. It was in this way, along with what he did as translator
and as coeditor of the Nervous and Mental Disease Monographs, that Jelliffe
became in the United States the symbol as well as the effective mediator of
knowledge of foreign medicine.

American neurology, at least before World War I, followed the lead of
Europeans for both innovations and clinical standards, and Jelliffe's work as
facilitator of communication was correspondingly important. Within neurology the abstracts that he published revealed no special bias, and his selection of items to be abstracted was straightforward, usually covering the
contents of standard journals in the field, except insofar as his correspondents—those whom he happened to know both in the United States and in
Europe or elsewhere—sometimes sent reprints or abstracts of their own articles. Jelliffe went to considerable trouble to maintain comprehensive coverage of other journals and to include summaries of papers read at meetings
of the leading specialty groups in the United States, particularly those in
Boston, Philadelphia, Chicago, and New York.

In general the book reviews provided more latitude for Jelliffe as editor,
and the more so when he was himself the author of many of them. Once
again he tried hard to cover all major publications from Europe as well as
the United States. Reviews of neurological works tended to be descriptive,
often with a rather unspecific commendation of the contents. Neither Jelliffe
nor his other reviewers argued fine points of neuropathology in the review
section. Books in the mental disease field were more likely to receive unpre-
dictable and opinionated treatment. Finally, Jelliffe often included a third
type of book, one that would be "broadening" for a member of the profession,
typically a philosophical or biological work or even a novel. He felt that a
nervous and mental disease specialist, or indeed any physician, should be a
cultured person rather than merely a narrow technician.

Sometimes the total mix of the abstract and review sections, the society proceedings, and the original papers appeared miscellaneous in character. The articles were, of course, chosen by Spiller, who had more or less to select from what was submitted to him, and society proceedings represented papers presented at various meetings. Jelliffe had considerable discretion only in the abstracts and reviews, and there he tried to be inclusive. To a large extent, then, the *Journal of Nervous and Mental Disease* reflected the profession at large as well as, or more than, Jelliffe.

When Jelliffe took possession of the *Journal of Nervous and Mental Disease*, the *Journal* had for years suffered an uneven and sometimes stormy relationship with the neurologists of the United States as represented by the American Neurological Association. Several problems were involved. First, the editors did not accept for publication all papers presented at the annual meetings, a fact that distressed the authors. Second, the *Journal* as a profit-making endeavor appeared every quarter or, later, every month regularly, as was necessary in order to meet the needs of the advertisers. The magazine had to appear whether or not quality material was available. (In Europe the editors of the best institute organs just waited until enough satisfactory papers came in to justify an issue.) Moreover, in a monthly or quarterly journal, budgetary necessity fixed the number of pages. Long papers therefore had to be chopped up and continued in pieces from issue to issue. The most prestigious members of the profession found the whole complex of these constraints irritating.[34]

Finally, the *Journal* had for years issued the annual meeting *Proceedings* for the ANA, the publisher agreeing to print the *Proceedings* and give each member a copy. Since much of the material was already set up in type for the *Journal*, the cost was not great. (Jelliffe in 1902, on behalf of the *Journal*, asked for $250 which was the usual sum, plus $5 for proofreading.) The problem was that neither authors who were supposed to send in their papers nor editors ever gave the *Proceedings* high priority, and so the volumes were usually late and many misunderstandings arose. Spiller, trusted by all parties, was editing both *Journal* and *Proceedings* because ANA leaders put pressure on Jelliffe's predecessor, Brown, in an effort to raise standards and reduce other complaints. Further evidence of the influence of the leaders of neurology is revealed in the letter asking Jelliffe to join the editorial group in 1897. The letter came not from Brown but from Starr, who was explicit about the upgrading that was expected in the abstract section. Jelliffe and Spiller therefore must have been gratified when in 1903 Starr successfully moved at the

34. Based on typescript of the minutes of the Council and Executive Sessions of the American Neurological Association, 1892–1902, American Neurological Association Papers. Details are in John C. Burnham, "The Founding of the *Archives of Neurology and Psychiatry*, or, What Was Wrong with the *Journal of Nervous and Mental Disease*?" *Journal of the History of Medicine*, 36 (1981), 310–324.

ANA meetings "a vote of thanks to Dr. Spiller and Dr. Jelliffe for the able manner in which they had conducted the Journal of Nervous and Mental Disease." But the relationship with the ANA still boded ill for Jelliffe.[35]

The position of the *Journal* is more easily appreciated when the competition is considered. Mental hospital physicians—psychiatrists—published the *American Journal of Insanity* (after 1921 known as the *American Journal of Psychiatry*), which, as noted above, was competitive only insofar as the two fields shared patients. The contents were often as miscellaneous as those of the *Journal of Nervous and Mental Disease*, with a heavy emphasis on management and forensics that was absent from Jelliffe's *Journal*, which tended to be strictly scientific, or at least clinical, in orientation. The only other American journal in competition was the *Alienist and Neurologist*, published in a very personal way by C. H. Hughes of St. Louis. It was a journal of low quality and strangely miscellaneous subject matter.

Eventually Hughes decided to retire, and he wrote to Jelliffe in 1916 asking him to take over the *Alienist and Neurologist*. In response to the "very flattering" suggestion, Jelliffe proposed that Hughes set up an endowment. Before negotiations could proceed effectively, Hughes died. The executors of the estate killed off any interest that Jelliffe may have had in acquiring the *Alienist and Neurologist* by asking a ridiculously high price for the journal. "I imagine these people think that they have got a gold mine to sell," Jelliffe wrote to an interested physician, and he joked with White about the asking price.[36]

The *Alienist and Neurologist* finally ceased publication in 1920, which would have left Jelliffe with a more definitive monopoly on specialized neurological publications except for what could go into general medical journals, and only one major psychiatric competitor—but by 1919 new developments affecting the *Journal of Nervous and Mental Disease* had taken place (see below).

The Monograph Series

As noted above, Jelliffe's connection with the *New York Medical Journal* ended when he went abroad in 1908. From then on, until Spiller left the *Journal of Nervous and Mental Disease* (which occurred during another transition period in Jelliffe's life, in the World War I period), Jelliffe's activities in medical journalism were at a low point. The only major activity that was new was, again, within his specialty area—the founding, with William Alanson White, of the Nervous and Mental Disease Monograph Series, in 1907.

35. Ibid. ANA minutes of the Council and Executive Sessions, especially 12 May 1903. M. Allen Starr to Jelliffe, 20 December 1897.

36. These negotiations can be followed in C. H. Hughes to Jelliffe, 24 May 1916; Jelliffe to Hughes, 27 May 1916; Jelliffe to Otho F. Ball, 21 August 1916 and 26 March 1917; and Ball to Jelliffe, 23 February 1917 (Ball was quite mistaken when he believed that Jelliffe could obtain ownership for $200–$500); and in William Alanson White to Jelliffe, 23 March 1917 and 27 March 1917, White Papers, Box 15.

Jelliffe and White apparently got the idea to publish monographs while they were in Europe. White recalled that "when Dr. Jelliffe and I were trying to get publishers in the United States to bring to the American medical profession some of the outstanding products of European thought, we failed completely, but we reached down into our own pockets and started a publishing business."[37] At another time White noted that "in those days the literature of mental disease was exceedingly scanty even in the foreign journals, and the number of books available to us in this country in English was very small."[38] Neurological literature was more abundant but much of it was in need of translation, White commented.

As late as November 1907, White wrote to Jelliffe, "I have not thought of a name for our company yet but I will try to produce some combination within the next day or two."[39] The first of their publications, White's *Outlines of Psychiatry* (1907), was already in manuscript form earlier in the year (the printed preface bears a June date), and they hoped to have it out before they left for Europe again.[40] White's book was a great success and in numerous revised editions kept the monograph series profitable. Many of the other publications were highly technical and, for one reason or another, did not sell well in the limited medical/psychological fields.

Both White and Jelliffe put much effort into the monograph series, and for some time the business tended to be conducted from Jelliffe's New York office. The business gave opportunity for the two friends to have more than a personal and intellectual relationship, and White, especially, over the years took many occasions to lecture his colleague upon attention to business. These exchanges were usually joking and teasing in nature. In 1914 White noted, "One reason business is poor in New York is because you go away for a couple of days with Gregory to play golf." (Gregory presumably was Menas Gregory, distinguished head of the Bellevue Hospital psychopathic department, who had been in Europe with Jelliffe and White and had earlier played tennis with them at Binghamton.)[41]

The fact was that Jelliffe as a publisher was in substantial part playing the role of businessman. In the basement of his home, on steel shelves, he kept the supply of back issues of the *Journal of Nervous and Mental Disease* and of many of the monographs, particularly in the first years of the series. At that time Jelliffe handled most orders and payments for the monographs and sent White checks. After about 1919 the administration of the monographs moved to Washington, where White's secretary, Arnold W. Barbour, handled

37. William Alanson White, *The Autobiography of a Purpose* (Garden City, N.Y., 1938), p. 79.
38. William A. White, *Forty Years of Psychiatry* (New York, 1933), p. 19.
39. William A. White to Jelliffe, 6 November 1907, White Papers, Box 1.
40. William Alanson White to Jelliffe, 18 June 1907, White Papers, Box 1.
41. William Alanson White to Jelliffe, 9 December 1914.

the orders and also took care of the company's journal venture, the *Psychoanalytic Review*. White then distributed any profits.

The *Psychoanalytic Review*

The first issue of the *Psychoanalytic Review* appeared in 1913. Although White as editor was fully responsible for the *Review*, the journal was at the beginning very much a joint venture, and Jelliffe took a strong interest in it and offered the benefit of his previous experience as an editor. Monographs of the series were more often serialized previously in the *Psychoanalytic Review* than in the *Journal of Nervous and Mental Disease*, for White had considerable trouble in filling the pages of the *Review* in the early years. Jelliffe frequently helped out with his own contributions, but not always with the promptness that would have better pleased the meticulous White. In 1917, for example, White wrote teasingly, "Permit me to inform you by way of passing that all the manuscript of the April number of the *Review* has gone to the printer with one exception. Do you think that by any possibility if you made the effort you could guess what that exception was? Of course I don't even imply it in the most indirect way; I would not presume to. However, it would be such a fine thing to be able to get out a number of the *Review* during the month it is supposed to come out, wouldn't it?"[42]

As Jelliffe and White first envisioned it, the *Psychoanalytic Review* was to be psychoanalytic only in a general sense, and they did not mean to exclude any worker on account of viewpoint. In 1912 when they were discussing the new venture, they thought that terms such as "clinical psychology" and "psychopathology" might be appropriate for the journal title or subtitle. When, during their discussions late in 1912, they first approached G. Stanley Hall, the psychologist who was president of Clark University, for advice about starting a journal connected with psychoanalysis, they wrote to him describing this inclusive approach. Hall in response offered White a regular section of the *American Journal of Psychology*, Hall's publication, to edit as he pleased. White and Jelliffe persisted with plans for their own journal but told Hall they would welcome his far-from-orthodox views and his genetic approach.[43]

In fact the *Review* did embody the broad and comparative approach advocated by Jung in the letter (see Part II, below) that opened the first issue. Jung, indeed, had encouraged the founding of the *Review* during discussions when he visited White in 1912.[44] Since this was just at the point of the break between Jung and Freud, the description of the *Review* that Jelliffe offered in 1914 had overtones, whether or not Jelliffe so intended: "The only journal

---

42. William Alanson White to Jelliffe, 5 February 1917, White Papers, Box 15.
43. William Alanson White to Jelliffe, 9 December 1912, White Papers, Box 7. Dorothy Ross, *G. Stanley Hall: The Psychologist as Prophet* (Chicago, 1972), p. 401.
44. William Alanson White to Jelliffe, 26 October 1912.

in English," wrote Jelliffe, the *Review* "aims to be catholic in its tendencies, a faithful mirror of the psychoanalytic movement, and to represent no schisms or schools but a free forum for all."[45] Under the circumstances, Freud, who had after all founded psychoanalysis, could hardly have been expected to feel very cordial. When, in September 1913, White wrote to him to ask for a contribution, Freud's reply was scarcely as gracious or tactful as might have been expected in treating with the publishers of an organ named the *Psychoanalytic Review*.[46] (Details and letters appear in Part II.) Later, Freud and Jelliffe reviewed the incident (again in Part II), but meantime a number of years passed before Jelliffe came into Freud's good graces.

After the *Review* was launched, Jelliffe wrote ebulliently to C. B. Davenport and reported on the *Review*, incidentally asking for contributions (a remarkable demonstration both of the loose way in which Jelliffe interpreted "psychoanalytic" as well as the fact that he was already thinking in terms of inherited archaic mental structures): "The *Review* is going grandly and must have some of the heredity things [such as Davenport could offer] in it. Heredity is accumulated experience, laid down in growth, structure, instinct, unconscious—or what not & hence may explain—must explain—some phases of the workings of conduct. The *Review* is an assured success thus far: We close our books next week on the 1st year with a substantial profit—almost enough to run the review for a second year—'Truth is truth whan it works' says Mr. Dooley."[47] By and large, however, the *Review* was White's, and Jelliffe's responsibilities came to be restricted to soliciting materials and advising on the business procedures.[48]

Such information about the work that Jelliffe did as a medical editor, especially with the *Medical News* and the *Journal of Nervous and Mental Disease*, is of particular significance because little is known about the history of medical journalism in the United States. Sometimes it is a struggle to find out merely who the editors were, as Jelliffe learned when seeking to identify his predecessors at the *Journal of Nervous and Mental Disease*,[49] and equally

45. Smith Ely Jelliffe, "Technique of Psychoanalysis," *Psychoanalytic Review*, 1 (1914), 444.
46. William Alanson White to Jelliffe, 15 September 1913, White Papers, Box 7. Arcangelo R. T. D'Amore, "William Alanson White—Pioneer Psychoanalyst," in Arcangelo R. T. D'Amore, ed., *William Alanson White: The Washington Years, 1903–1937* (Washington, 1976), pp. 82–83, 88–89. Freud did appear as an author in the *Review*, in 1916 when A. A. Brill published there his translation of Sigmund Freud, "The History of the Psychoanalytic Movement," *Psychoanalytic Review*, 3 (1916), 406–454, but that was owing to Brill, not Freud.
47. Smith Ely Jelliffe to C. B. Davenport, 17 November 1914, Davenport Papers, American Philosophical Society, Philadelphia.
48. A. Louise Eckburg, "The Writings of William Alanson White," in D'Amore, *William Alanson White*, pp. 148–149.
49. Smith Ely Jelliffe, "The Editor Himself," pp. 557–572. See additionally Eugene B. Brody, "The Journal of Nervous and Mental Disease: The First 100 Years," *JNMD*, 158 (1974), 6–17; 159 (1974), 1–11; James B. Mackie, "The Journal of Nervous and Mental Disease: The First 100 Years," ibid., pp. 305–318; Nolan D. C. Lewis, "The Journal of Nervous and Mental Disease: The First 100 Years," ibid., pp. 319–324. The extent to which Jelliffe as editor perfectly

to find out how and why editors worked, what the editorial customs were at the time, and under what constraints the staff operated. As noted in the Preface, Jelliffe's experience provides an important example of how a central medical institution functioned in the early twentieth century.

Textbook Writing

Very close to journalism was Jelliffe's popularizing of medicine. Besides occasional articles for popular magazines, Jelliffe undertook another major task in the years before he was fully committed to nervous and mental diseases. In 1903 he signed a contract to serve as editor of the articles on medicine in a new standard reference work, *Encyclopedia Americana*. Several of the major articles were contracted out to various specialists, but Jelliffe was supposed to furnish the rest, at ten dollars per thousand words.[50] He appeared as one of fifteen "Associate and Assistant Editors." The encyclopedia was a success, and his name continued to be listed as a major contributor as late as the 1927 edition. The impact of this work would, once again, be difficult to appraise.

One aspect of Jelliffe's literary work reflected his role as teacher: the writing of textbooks, which already has been referred to. His bibliography shows a large number of such contributions, especially around the turn of the century. While Jelliffe may have been making money by writing textbooks, he also was fulfilling other functions. His presentations were clear and to the point, but, more important, he felt that he was upgrading the contents of learning materials available to American students, particularly by introducing new European research. This general direction of his effort was evident in chapters that he contributed to collective works, in standard texts that he updated and revised, and in his original efforts. His opening words in *An Introduction to Pharmacognosy* (1904) explain the function that he tried to serve:

"The following Introduction has been prepared with the hope that it may meet the needs of students of pharmacognosy in our schools of pharmacy.

"In general scope it follows the well-established lines already laid down by our European confrères, departing in many particulars, however, from most works published heretofore in this country. Thus special emphasis has been laid on the microscopic rather than the macroscopic characters of drugs, although the latter have not been entirely neglected, and considerable attention has been given to the description of drug powders.

"While there have been many manuals in which the student of plant structures could find ample instruction concerning general histological fea-

reflected scientific/professional currents, with less speculative and case history contents and more experimental, appears in Robert W. Lissitz, "A Longitudinal Study of the Research Methodology in the Journal of Nervous and Mental Disease, and the American Journal of Psychiatry," *Journal of the History of the Behavioral Sciences*, 5 (1969), 248–255.

50. R. R. Peale to Jelliffe, 10 February 1903.

tures, no work has been offered in this country which deals with the special individual anatomical characters of different drugs. Such works have been issued in Germany by Moeller, Tschirch, Meyer, Marmé, Flückiger, and others, and the monumental volume of Plancon and Collin, nearly two thousand pages, testifies in a measure to the value set by the French upon such studies. Greenish, of London, in 1903 gave to the English pharmacists a guide similar in general features to the volume here presented.

"The present Introduction has been in preparation for some time, and here appears, not as a stupendous volume such as those of Flückiger or Plancon and Collin, but in a compressed and convenient form. This form, rather than that of an enormous reference book, has been deliberately chosen as complying with what has been considered good pedagogic principles."[51]

No doubt Jelliffe's experience with the quiz as well as in the classroom and clinic helped him see what a good textbook or handbook could accomplish in introducing what he considered to be modern medicine. Thus in revising Butler's *Textbook of Materia Medica* (1906) Jelliffe was able to eliminate many old theories and therapies that had appeared in earlier editions, and in place of obsolete material to describe ideas current in more contemporary medical literature. Likewise in presenting an American version of Reissig's *Standard Family Physician* (1907; originally published in German in 1900), Jelliffe modified a major European work for practical use in the United States (see Bibliography).

The Jelliffe and White Textbook

Jelliffe's career as a textbook writer culminated in the production of a huge volume written jointly with White, *Diseases of the Nervous System: A Text-Book of Neurology and Psychiatry* (Philadelphia, 1915). This was a standard work used in many medical schools, and it went through a number of editions, competing quite satisfactorily with two or three other such works. Jelliffe and White's textbook, however, was not conventional in approach, and Jelliffe, especially, came to see it as representing an important new point of view. Just how much of it represented Jelliffe, who did most of the neurology, and how much represented White, who did most of the psychiatry, would be hard to say. Jelliffe took a strong proprietary interest in the introductions that made the innovative approach increasingly explicit in each succeeding edition.

The original (1915) introduction was bold enough in spelling out the freshness of the viewpoint:

"The diseases of the nervous system are no longer compassed by a description of the gross lesions of the brain, spinal cord, cranial and peripheral nerves. The more limited symptomatology of disorders of these structures,

51. Smith Ely Jelliffe, *An Introduction to Pharmacognosy* (Philadelphia, 1904), pp. 13–14.

which in this work has been called sensori-motor neurology, has been expanded in two directions—in one by the increase in our knowledge of the historically oldest portion of the nervous system, namely, the sympathetic and autonomic (vegetative) nervous system and in the other by the increase in our knowledge of the mechanisms that operate at the psychic or mental levels.

"The vegetative nervous system is in close functional relations with the endocrinous glands, and, although some of the endocrinopathies may ultimately turn out not to be exclusively nervous affections, still these organs of internal secretion are so closely related from all points of view, embryological, anatomical, physiological, pathological, and pharmacodynamic, with the vegetative nervous system that their disordered functions must needs be considered in a work dealing with the diseases of the nervous system. The symptomatology of this region constitutes the borderland of neurology and internal medicine.

"At the highest level stand the mental mechanisms in which action receives a symbolic representation. Here the nervous system is also the medium through which that form of physiological or pathological activity called conduct is brought about. These mechanisms, while operating consciously, largely through the sensori-motor channels of adjustment, are also intimately related to the vegetative levels where through the emotions they act unconsciously.

"The authors have kept in mind the concept of the individual as a biological unit tending by development and conduct toward certain broadly defined goals and have considered the nervous system as only a part of that larger whole. The part, however, partakes of the unity of the whole and, so far as possible, the attempt has been made to arrange the diseases of the nervous system in accord with this evolutionary concept."[52]

In later editions, beginning in 1919, the introduction to the book spelled out at far greater length what Jelliffe, presumably, meant by his profoundly biological point of view. Even if White did modify or contribute to the introduction, Jelliffe worked within the framework of the introduction for the rest of his life. By "biological" Jelliffe meant the idea that life evolved from the simple to the complex, that is, human beings; that in humans is a hierarchy of structures that parallel evolutionary development; and that adaptation explains both function and evolution. Such a point of view was not different from that of Freud (who, like Jelliffe, cited Hughlings Jackson's idea of nervous system hierarchy) and of many other thinkers of the early twentieth century.

Jelliffe's particular viewpoint involved especially three principles. The first was the idea that "the nervous system is the organizer of all experience, phyletic as well as individual, and the coördinator of that experience." Jelliffe

52. Smith Ely Jelliffe and William A. White, *Diseases of the Nervous System: A Text-Book of Neurology and Psychiatry* (Philadelphia, 1915), p. iii.

used Sherrington's conception of the integrative action of the nervous system, but he added a new emphasis on the role of endocrine products. But the centrality of the nervous system, however, he carried further in viewing both life processes and disease. Jelliffe's second principle was that the human being is a transformer of energy, a complex machine, the working units of which can be determined by reductionistic means, analyzing energy transformations. Finally, Jelliffe spoke of the fundamental purpose of the human organism: "the preservation of the individual and the maintenance of the phylum."

The biological purposes of human beings, Jelliffe believed, manifest themselves in the form of instincts, and he gave special emphasis to the reproductive instinct. His view, however, was extremely broad, like the view of Jung elucidated at the Fordham lectures which brought about his final break with Freud. "The biological conception of sex here outlined," wrote Jelliffe (and possibly White), "is the equivalent of Creativeness and it is quite implicitly parallelled by the theologian's God. . . . The formulation in biological terms then states that any deviation of the inner, or instinctive habit, or good, or God-like-sex-pattern—will result in faulty adaptation."

Jelliffe proceeded then to describe the nervous system in terms of three major hierarchical "levels of activity, the vegetative, the sensorimotor and the psychic." What was new about the viewpoint in a textbook was not only the holistic and dynamic approach but the emphasis given the psychological aspects throughout, and the introduction was intended to explain how and why: "It is then toward a more psychological conception that medicine must look if its understanding of dynamic processes is to [be] better founded and the mysteries of health and disease, not alone of the nervous system, but of all the bodily organs, laid bare."

By "psychological" Jelliffe meant particularly the process of symbolization. The idea of tropisms, he remarked, had been discredited, and so the symbol played the part, in the human energy machine, of ultimate energy container (and hence his 1919 paper using that phrase in the title). The symbol had for Jelliffe the advantage that it could be either conscious or unconscious, and he emphasized the exciting new possibilities that opened with the use of the unconscious, sometimes following Freud carefully and sometimes emphasizing a Jungian collective unconscious:

"So long as the unconscious failed to be recognized, just so long was the gap between so-called body and so-called mind too wide to be bridged, and so there arose the two concepts, body and mind, which gave origin to the necessity of defining their relations. Consciousness covered over and obscured the inner organs of the psyche just as the skin hides the inner organs of the body from vision. But just as a knowledge of the body first became possible by the removal of the skin and the revealing of the structures that lay beneath, so a knowledge of the psyche first became possible when the outer covering of consciousness was penetrated and what lay at greater depth was revealed. As soon as this was done, the wonderful history of the psyche began to give up its secrets, and the distinction between body and mind began to dissolve, until now it has come to be considered that the psyche is the end-result in an orderly series of progressions in which the body has used successively more complex tools to deal with the problems of integration and adjustment."[53]

The textbook represented a major effort in the careers of both Jelliffe and White. As early as 1906 they were talking with the publisher, Lea Brothers, about such a text, and in 1907 they signed a contract for the book, with a 1910 date set for delivery of the manuscript. Meantime the two collaborated in editing a huge, two-volume work on the modern treatment of mental diseases, which they completed in 1913. Not until 1915 did they actually get the textbook manuscript off to the publisher, who succeeded in bringing the book out in the same year.[54] Once published, the work, as has been noted, did well by any standard, and Jelliffe enjoyed the comments that he received. They encouraged him to continue in the direction of what he thought was a broadly biological view but what others later named psychosomatic medicine. A particularly gratifying letter came from L. H. Mettler, a distinguished specialist in Chicago.

"I congratulate you upon the work and shall most certainly commend it highly to my classes in the University of Illinois. Indeed, I am considering seriously recommending it as the text-book for senior neurology. I like the broad and up-to-date way in which it is written. Your opening chapters upon the vegetative nervous apparatus are full and scientific and show that you follow biological trends in your neurological thinking, something which is not observable in most of the text-books. Your grouping of the syphilitic and meningitic syndromes in distinctive chapters, instead of having a number of chapters upon all sorts of mere symptomatic groups indicates the same mode of neurological thinking. The recognition of psychiatry, so-called, as really a part of the manifestations of the nervous organ is still further evidence.

"A number of years ago . . . I attempted the same sort of thing, much in the line of the work of Morat, Grasset, Krehl and others. With the newer knowledge you have gone far ahead in this direction and I cannot refrain from expressing my delight to you. However, I do not wish to provoke a chill when I say, that like my own, your book, I fear, will not reach the number of sales that it deserves. The profession is scarcely ready, even yet, to find hysteria placed among the psychoses and general paralysis in the section devoted to organic brain diseases. I am judging from some of the stupid, uninformed, and antiquated reviews (about one quarter of all) that

53. Ibid. (4th ed., Philadelphia, 1923), pp. 17–23.
54. See especially William Alanson White to C. G. Jung, 10 September 1913, White Papers, Box 9; and William Alanson White to Jelliffe, 16 July 1915, White Papers, Box 11.

were given my book when it first appeared. A few will recognize your advanced neurology as they recognized mine. Some of us must be pioneers, however, so I congratulate you upon joining our company.

"I sincerely hope your work may have a wide distribution and go far toward getting the profession out of the habit of thinking along the old, erroneous, cut-and-dried ways of the average text-book."[55]

As their textbook went through many editions, Jelliffe and White attempted, as was customary, to improve it as they could. They saw the book in terms of how different it was from the competition, and yet at the same time they recognized that the publisher and, implicitly, the market, limited what they could do. Thus in 1923 the preeminent neurologist Constantin von Monakow of Zurich wrote to Jelliffe his praise of the book, particularly the "biological point of view" applied to both brain diseases and psychoses. "Of course," von Monakow wrote, "certain chapters . . . are insufficiently handled," especially those concerning brain localization and pathology, including some sections in which von Monakow's views were not fully elucidated. Jelliffe was grateful for the praise from such an eminent figure, and in replying he commented candidly on the constraints within which he worked: "You are quite right in pointing out the lack of description of the brain pathology. . . . with each edition we have been able to bring the book nearer to a practical ideal. If you knew the kinds of text-books our professors still cling to you would be amazed at our bravery in trying to do what we have done. . . ."[56]

Jelliffe as Nervous and Mental Disease Specialist

The textbook did help to establish Jelliffe's place as a senior figure in the nervous and mental disease specialties. His late arrival as a specialist continued to be a disadvantage, but he moved as quickly as he could to change his junior status to senior. It was not until 1907 that, with White's help, he applied to become a member of the American Medico-Psychological (later Psychiatric) Association, and it was 1910 before he became one of the exclusive twenty-five members of the New York Psychiatrical Society (he was president during 1922–1924). Of course he was primarily a neurologist, but as noted above he had to work within both specialties to maintain the kind of "nervous and mental disease" competence that he sought to attain. He had established credentials in neurology much earlier (described above), and he was forty-nine years old in 1914–1915 when he served as president of the New York Neurological Society. Not until 1929–1930, when he was nearing retirement age, did the national membership of neurologists elect him president of the American Neurological Association (see below, and Chapter 3).

55. L. Harrison Mettler to Jelliffe, 13 September 1915. L. Harrison Mettler, *A Treatise on Diseases of the Nervous System* (Chicago, 1905).

56. C. von Monakow to Jelliffe, 30 January 1923 and 7 April 1923; Jelliffe to C. von Monakow, 30 April 1923.

It was in part, of course, his continued attempt to try to combine neurology and psychiatry when the two were drifting apart[57] that prevented his gaining a more distinctive medical identity than as editor of the *Journal of Nervous and Mental Disease*. Furthermore, despite his many trips to national medical meetings, his practice was based in New York City. Only occasional court cases took him away, and his primary referrals of patients were local.

To some extent, of course, Jelliffe did not choose to play the politics of the medical profession, even locally, particularly when he was shedding other kinds of appointments. That he had the potential to gain organizational recognition is evident from his service in 1904–1905 as chairman of a national committee on drug addiction in the Section on Nervous and Mental Diseases of the American Medical Association.[58] But after that Jelliffe restricted himself to membership in a few groups, mostly specialty groups, except sometimes as an invited public speaker at the meetings of various organizations.

One avenue to what later would be called "national visibility" in his profession, above and beyond his editorship, would have been medical school and hospital appointments on the one hand, or on the other hand the publication of original investigations—and, again, the two often went together. Jelliffe chose neither, because he was, in addition to his writing, busy with his practice. What original material he did publish was of a modest kind— usually, after he stopped his laboratory and microscopical work in the 1900's, reporting clinical cases. Since he included in his publications his mastery of bibliography and, increasingly, his knowledge of the history of various syndromes and traditions, his contributions were significant, substantial, and informative. But they did not involve notably new functions, disease pictures, therapies, or anything else that might have compelled immediate or widespread attention to his work from either a national or international audience. He even published—in the *Alienist and Neurologist,* not in his own journal— a long series of translations and abstracts of the great classics of psychiatric history. By the early twentieth century that sort of publication did not pay off in terms of national professional reputation.

Since Jelliffe put so much effort into his practice, it is regrettable that little evidence is left of what he did do in this period, especially during the 1910's. It is clear that increasingly he practiced psychoanalysis, or at least psychotherapy. In 1935 he wrote concerning his registration to prescribe narcotics: "I have done no prescribing of practically any kind in some past 20 years, limiting my practice chiefly to Psychotherapy and to Forensic Medicine. I

57. Jelliffe's own comments on the problem, in V. C. Branham and R. B. McGraw, "Are Neurology and Psychiatry Separate Entities?" *JNMD*, 73 (1931), 157–158, indicated that even at that late date he did not think that it made any difference which specialist was used so long as the physician had a broad approach: "The material should be apportioned on the basis of the individual need and not on the basis of a nosological abstraction."
58. "Drug Addictions. Preliminary Report of the Committee in Section on Nervous and Mental Diseases," *Journal of the American Medical Association,* 46 (1906), 643–644.

have not written a prescription for any of the narcotics on the list for 20 years."[59]

His impression was, then, that his practice changed around 1915, which was shortly after he became involved in psychoanalysis. That commitment to psychoanalysis increasingly affected his entire career, not just his practice.

Jelliffe's Adherence to Psychoanalysis

In Jelliffe's account of his "Freudian Odyssey," he explained how he had met the Zurich group and how Brill argued with him and convinced him of the soundness of Freud's approach while they were walking home through Central Park from the Neurological Institute. "And thus," recalled Jelliffe, "I became a convinced Freudian." "Our walks through the park started something in me of inestimable value," he wrote Brill in 1943. "I had been reading Freud, but you made it vital and real for me."[60]

With his thorough knowledge of the European literature, Jelliffe had of course already long known about psychoanalysis, as he later recalled to Freud (letter of 6 March 1939, Part II). In 1905 he discussed Freud's views in two book reviews in a manner that suggested that everyone ought to have known about Freud's teachings at that time.[61] His presence at the famous 1907 debate over psychoanalysis and his acquaintance with Jung there and subsequently are detailed in Part II.[62] Jelliffe was as yet, however, far from easily convinced that psychoanalysis was of fundamental importance, even though he understood the possibilities of dynamic symbolization. In 1909 he wrote to White from Vienna:

"This whole Freud business is done to death. The lamp posts of Vienna will cast forth sexual rays pretty soon. They keep writing new stuff. The poor unborn children cannot be told fairy tales any more because of their sexual significance. I suspect William Tell's apple must have been a pair of testicles and as for George Washington's cherry tree—well, perhaps you with your refined intuitive perceptions with these matters can illuminate the dark places in my mind."[63]

59. Jelliffe to Narcotic Department, 22 October 1935.
60. Jelliffe, "Glimpses of a Freudian Odyssey," p. 325. Jelliffe to A. A. Brill, 2 April 1943, A. A. Brill Papers, Library of Congress.
61. Review of Emil Raimann, *Die Hysterischen Geistesstörungen*, in *JNMD*, 32 (1905), 479–480; review of Willy Hellpach, *Grundlinien einer Psychologie der Hysterie*, in *JNMD*, 32 (1905), 683.
62. See introduction to correspondence, Part II.
63. Quoted in Nolan D. C. Lewis, "Smith Ely Jelliffe: The Man and Scientist," *JNMD*, 106 (1947), 239. (Jelliffe was always willing to tease White on the subject of sex; in 1910 he wrote: "Let me thank you for your biblical texts, they have been a source of entertainment, and a stimulus to the higher life. At the same time, remember that there are stringent laws concerning the sending of biblical literature through the mails" [Jelliffe to White, 17 March 1910, White Papers, Box 5].)

That same year White and Jelliffe published in their Nervous and Mental Disease Monographs series the first English translation of Freud's work, Brill's rendering of *Selected Papers on Hysteria and Other Psychoneuroses.*[64] By 1911 Jelliffe was routinely pointing out in reviews and abstracts (in which editorial matter was not routine) the contributions of Freud and criticizing authors who failed to mention the psychoanalytic viewpoint.[65] He was even prepared to accept the idea that "the complex" might determine symptoms in dementia praecox, although he did not take the extreme position that the complex could cause the disease—an example of "ultra-Freudian views of which it would appear A. Meyer is an advocate," as Jelliffe put it.[66] Despite his walks across the park with Brill, then, Jelliffe was far from being a sudden convert. In 1910, for example, he refused to become a founding member of Jones's new organization, the American Psychoanalytic Association (formally founded in 1911), although he did join in 1912. Jelliffe later (writing to Freud, 9 January 1933, Part II) characterized as "largely accidental" his not being a charter member of another group, started at the same time, Brill's New York Psychoanalytic Society, and he did soon join. But as late as 1913, when he and his wife published a translation of Déjérine's large work on psychotherapy, Jelliffe thought that psychoanalysis was appropriate for only a small proportion of the neurotic illnesses and instead recommended Déjérine's method of "persuasion," an approach that had the virtue, according to Jelliffe, of going beyond Dubois's rational psychotherapy by emphasizing "the instinctive, or, more widely speaking, the emotional side of the human machine, in its psychical situations." As was noted above, Déjérine impressed Jelliffe deeply, and his attraction to Déjérine's emphasis on the emotional and instinctive in psychopathology represented a way station in Jelliffe's transit to a psychoanalytic viewpoint; Freud's great contribution was precisely to render affect and drive understandable in a rational psychology.[67]

If Jelliffe still appeared hesitant, nevertheless his practice was changed substantially. In 1910 he spoke of using all kinds of psychotherapy, including

64. Sigmund Freud, *Selected Papers on Hysteria and Other Psychoneuroses*, tr. A. A. Brill, NMDMS No. 4 (New York, 1909).

65. See *JNMD*, 33 (1911), 634; 766–767.

66. Smith Ely Jelliffe, "Predementia Praecox: The Hereditary and Constitutional Features of the Dementia Praecox Make Up," *JNMD*, 38 (1911), 19.

67. Nathan G. Hale, Jr., ed., *James Jackson Putnam and Psychoanalysis: Letters between Putnam and Sigmund Freud, Ernest Jones, William James, Sandor Ferenczi, and Morton Prince, 1877–1917* (Cambridge, Mass., 1971), pp. 247–248; Smith Ely Jelliffe, "Translator's Preface," in J. Déjérine and E. Gauckler, *The Psychoneuroses and Their Treatment by Psychotherapy*, tr. Smith Ely Jelliffe (Philadelphia, 1913), pp. iii–iv. Mrs. Jelliffe's role was acknowledged in the Jelliffe preface but not on the title page. Déjérine's work in neurology also impressed Jelliffe, and he utilized Déjérine's textbook in writing the Jelliffe-White textbook to the point that Spiller commented on it (W. G. Spiller to Jelliffe, 3 October 1915); borrowing is evident only in the number of diagnostic charts acknowledged from Déjérine's work, *Sémiologie des Affections du Systeme Nerveux* (Paris, 1914).

hypnosis, suggestion and reeducation, and psychoanalysis, along with word association and dream analysis.[68] As noted above, his teaching in the Post-Graduate Medical School included many psychoanalytic topics. Finally, as early as 1913, Jelliffe reported on his experience with psychoanalysis in what he characterized as his first psychoanalytic communication. This was a paper later read at the annual meeting of the American Psychopathological Association, an essentially eclectic group of which Jelliffe served as president in 1918.

For the occasion, Jelliffe chose the subject of transference: "The psychoanalytic method fortunately enables one to deal with the subject of transference much more definitely than ever before. It affords positive criteria whereby one is enabled to watch its development, realize its tendencies, guide its direction, and, at times, regain its losses for the sake of the patient. At the same time it provides the most exquisite sensitizer which, rightly used, compels the psychoanaly[st] to search his own complexes and resistances, and forces him to keep clearly the goal in view—*i.e.* the patient's best interests, and not his own gratification or glorification."

Jelliffe characterized the goal of the psychoanalyst as "to bring about an intelligent synthesis of a disturbed personality." Since Americans understood that Freud at this time was emphasizing the therapeutic value of unmasking resistances, Jelliffe's emphasis was in part an anticipation of the new directions in which Freud was trying to steer psychoanalysis. Jelliffe's formulation also, however, harkened back to the idea of reintegrating a split personality, or, more to the point, Jung's stress on individual striving and integrity.

Jelliffe in his presentation underlined the practical results of psychoanalysis and especially of the use of the idea of transference. He cited a passage repeated elsewhere in his writings: "The *bon mot* of that famous pragmatic philosopher, Mr. Dooley, that 'truth is truth when it works,' is as applicable to the psychoanalyst as to the patient, and if the transference is not working, the operator is compelled to examine *himself* to see if *his* own truths are truths and are not self-deceptions."

The paper also suggested that Jelliffe had by this time acquired a substantial amount of psychoanalytic experience:

"I take it to be the experience of many here who have put the psychoanalytic methods to the test of experience that they soon commence to recognize themselves in the patient's dreams. At first the stereotypy struck me—it was only later, that I began to see how various might be the symbolizations which expressed the identification and the transference at the same time.

"For me to be a *policeman*, a *priest*, a *chauffeur*, is quite understandable to those of you who look at me now. As policeman I have 'shielded from harm,' have 'kept away enemies,' have 'arrested impudent intruders,' and 'frightened

68. Reported in *Medical Record*, 78 (1910), 926–930.

away naughty boys'; as priest, confession has been ready and admonition invited, while as a chauffeur or engineer positive transference has permitted dangerous journeys over rough roads and in stormy weather, and even invited to flight and a new life.

"These are all every-day occurrences, I feel, to those of you at all interested in psychoanalysis."

Jelliffe then gave a number of examples of the way in which a particular patient's dreams revealed her attitudes toward him. He concluded:

"This patient has shown the most marked ambivalence in her transferences—at times the rising barriers have threatened to drive her away, but with the subtle barometer of the dream-revealed transference, stormy scenes have been avoided, and the analysis has almost laid bare the entire contents of this Pandora's box.

"This patient has also taught me the value of the keen suggestions in Freud's paper on the '*Dynamik der Uebertragung*' in the *Zentralblatt* of last year, for here the resistances were chiefly due to the infantile regressive factors.

"The battle of intellect and instinct, which is present in these psychoneurotics, is a stirring one, and the physician who would succeed must needs look sharp to the transference."

Finally, Jelliffe added, "I am aware of the somewhat simplistic nature of this my first psychoanalytic communication. I tender it as a slight earnest of my purpose to understand."[69]

Jelliffe was well aware of the fact that speaking out in favor of psychoanalysis could have unpleasant consequences, and so his announcement of a "psychoanalytic communication" was of considerable moment in his career. Not only did many important American colleagues denounce Freud's teachings (or what they imagined to be Freud's teachings), but leading European physicians also launched vicious attacks. W. J. Sweasey Powers, an American taking further training in Germany at Jelliffe's suggestion, wrote a vivid eyewitness account to Jelliffe as early as 1913 spelling out how the leading nervous and mental disease specialists were attempting to discredit psychoanalysis. The occasion was the 1913 congress of German psychiatrists in Breslau. The first event was the address of the most powerful early ally of psychoanalysis, Eugen Bleuler of Zurich. Bleuler, Powers reported, "explained Psychoanalysis, explained he believed in psychoanalysis itself but was not willing to back psychoanalysis based upon the sexual theories of Freud." (This statement of Bleuler's coincided with Jung's backing off from sexual elements in psychoanalysis; Jung of course had begun his psychoanalytic work years before when he was Bleuler's subordinate.) After Bleuler spoke, the leaders of German-language psychiatry took turns denouncing psycho-

69. Smith Ely Jelliffe, "Some Notes on 'Transference,'" *Journal of Abnormal Psychology*, 8 (1913), 302–309.

analysis. Afterwards, back in Munich, Kraepelin, Jelliffe's old teacher, asked Powers what he thought of the congress. "I told him that I was not much impressed by the argument put up against [psychoanalysis]. He asked if I did not realize that all of the members and that is to say all of the prominent psychiatricians in Germany were against it. I replied that I had hoped to hear some scientific facts brought against it. He then said that was not the purpose of bringing up the discussion. The purpose was to give Bleuler the opportunity to publicly back-slide from the Freud-school as his name was considered to have had a great influence in keeping the Freud theories alive. The purpose was also to place the German psychiatricians on record as being against the Freud theories."[70] With such reports from overseas and what Jelliffe knew firsthand both in Europe (as at the 1907 congress) and in the United States, he was cognizant of the significance of the commitment that he was making.

Jelliffe as Analyst

At some point between 1910 and 1913, then, Jelliffe's practice became substantially psychoanalytic.[71] He himself had had no didactic analysis, he later recalled, "but my patients were analyzing me from hour to hour and I had the rare association, especially during the summer months with Dr. White," when he and White professed to analyze each other. (This was before White's marriage in 1918, when for years he usually spent time at Lake George during the summer.) Jelliffe also apparently started an analysis with Federn, the Viennese analyst, who was visiting New York in 1914, but it was cut short by the outbreak of World War I.[72] As late as 1915 (letter of late July, Part II) Jung was underlining to Jelliffe the importance of the analyst's being analyzed.

As Jelliffe was accumulating experience, he presented in the *Psychoanalytic Review* for 1913–1917 a series of articles on "The Technique of Psychoanalysis," afterward gathered into a monograph.[73] Since in the later installments he cited publications from as late as 1915, his articles clearly were in part a running account of the way in which he was learning to view and embrace psychoanalysis. He was going to provide a travel guide in a new country for the novice, he said, and he urged everyone who could to try the new method. "I believe that every sincere practitioner can practise psychoanalysis just as he can practise surgery," wrote Jelliffe. "He may limit himself

70. Burnham, *Psychoanalysis and American Medicine;* W. J. Sweasey Powers to Jelliffe, 25 May 1913.

71. By early 1913 his correspondence to G. Stanley Hall indicated he was practicing psychoanalysis. Ross, *G. Stanley Hall,* p. 398.

72. Jelliffe, "Glimpses of a Freudian Odyssey," pp. 327–328. C. P. Oberndorf, *A History of Psychoanalysis in America* (New York, 1953), pp. 118–119.

73. Smith Ely Jelliffe, *The Technique of Psychoanalysis,* NMDMS No. 26 (New York, 1918).

to minor surgery, or he may attempt more difficult and complicated operations. So with the methods of psychoanalysis, if the practitioner will make an earnest attempt to understand them, he will be enabled to be of enormous service even when only using the simplest fundamentals."[74] Although Jelliffe assumed that the practitioner had had training "in neurology and psychiatry," especially psychiatry, clearly his instructions could be used by any well disposed person such as those he employed in his office (a subject taken up in Chapter 3).[75]

Mostly what Jelliffe wrote in these detailed descriptions of what he understood went on in a psychoanalysis was commonplace for the time except that he tried to incorporate the latest Continental publications. Indeed, he used the occasion to translate or summarize long passages that would not otherwise have been easily accessible in the United States or Britain, especially after World War I started, including Freud's 1915 paper on transference.

But in general Jelliffe's practice conformed to what appeared standard for the day. He observed that in general "patients who really need a psychoanalysis—who are not indulging in a luxury so to speak—need at least two to three months treatment. Most severe hysterias need from five to eight months, and patients with compulsion neuroses usually need more time. One can often aid a compulsion neurosis to such an extent that they are very much relieved after four or five months or even a shorter time, but to cure them takes often a year, or more. Naturally there are some patients who cannot be cured."[76]

Jelliffe apparently was a very active therapist. He noted that early in his practice patient's dreams repeatedly showed that he was moving too fast in his interpretations. And on another occasion, he recalled, "in the early days of my psychoanalytic work, I had announced the Oedipus principle rather crudely" to a patient, with undesirable results. The testimony of former patient Mabel Dodge Luhan (quoted in Chapter 4, below) confirms that Jelliffe talked and interpreted very freely during the analytic hour. It appears that, like Dubois and Déjérine rather than Freud, he even exhorted patients to "stand up to their tasks" and develop backbone.[77]

Jelliffe's active approach to the patient involved trying to get the patient to follow his rapidly moving and often imaginative trains of thought. He saw psychoanalysis as educational, "a form of teaching the patient to grow up." Although he differentiated clearly between the scientific investigation of patients (including those unlikely to benefit from psychoanalysis) and effective

74. Smith Ely Jelliffe, "The Technique of Psychoanalysis," *Psychoanalytic Review*, 1 (1913), 67.
75. Ibid., 1 (1914), 441.
76. "Technique of Psychoanalysis," ibid., 2 (1915), 79.
77. See especially ibid., 3 (1916), 41–42; 2 (1915), 409; 1 (1914), 186.

therapy, Jelliffe was not always clear about precisely who was the object of his concern when he urged that one element or another in the case needed to be understood—understood, that is, by the doctor or by the patient? In either case, Jelliffe required his patients to absorb very large amounts of explanation. By the last installments of the series on technique he was using diagrams to show the patients' levels of development in various areas and types of libido direction (the idea of archaic modes he developed further elsewhere).[78] He alluded to one such stratified case in a letter to Freud (printed in Part II, 19 December 1925).

Unlike most analytic therapists, Jelliffe took substantial interest in the use of psychoanalysis in cases of psychosis. Although his statements were very cautious, and he held out little or no hope that psychoanalysis would benefit the patient, he did believe that psychoanalysis might help the physician to understand the case. Jelliffe evidently came to his conclusions on the basis of personal experience as well as of injunctions in the literature. "I have sat by a mute katatonic for an hour," wrote Jelliffe, "attempting a variety of openings with all the zest which in my younger days had been given to a game of chess."[79]

Altogether Jelliffe's idea of psychoanalysis was not what would later be considered orthodox, even in the 1920's, despite the conformity of his recommendations for technique. Since at least as early as 1913, when Freud refused to contribute to the *Psychoanalytic Review*, as detailed in the correspondence in Part II, Freud had doubts about Jelliffe because of his theoretical stance and free interpretation of what psychoanalysis was. These doubts, as will become evident in the next chapter, were shared by a number of Americans into the 1920's. In part the doubters were misinformed, and Jelliffe certainly thought of himself as a loyal Freudian, but even in the "Technique" papers there were idiosyncrasies that provided a basis for the doubters' thinking.

As Freud felt himself beleaguered by Stekel, Adler, and Jung, the "free forum" of White's and Jelliffe's *Psychoanalytic Review* was not the kind of support for which he was looking. Jelliffe attacked the "stupid critics" of psychoanalysis and spoke of how much he benefited from each rereading of Freud's *Interpretation of Dreams*. But at other times Jelliffe borrowed heavily from Adler and Jung, and he also put psychoanalysis into the context of the ideas of Bergson and even "Pawlow." As the correspondence in Part II below shows, Jelliffe was aware of schisms in psychoanalysis (Jung's letter of 28 November 1912 reported Stekel's departure, for example, a change that seemed to bemuse even Jung himself). Clearly, as Jelliffe later told Freud (17 April 1923), Jelliffe did not take the schisms very seriously in their details.

78. See especially ibid., 4 (1917), 70; 1 (1914), 183; 2 (1915), 194–199, 289–291.
79. See especially ibid., 1 (1914), 306; 2 (1915), 78; 1 (1914), 185.

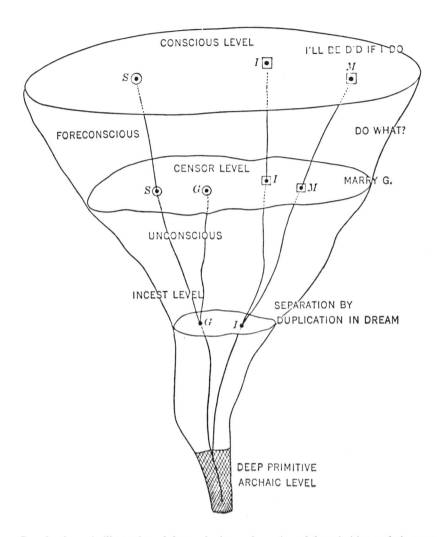

Rough schematic illustration of the gradual transformation of the primitive archaic reproductive instincts wish as it passes to conscious expression in the dream as indicated in text. The chief points illustrated are the distortion by duplication. Dreamer I and M are brothers. G, a sister. S, wife of M, and the marriage wish of the dream. G and I are settled down. M and S come to visit us. Originally published in Psychoanalytic Review, 4 (1917), 188.

Freud and others, of course, did, and even Jung chided Jelliffe for his eclecticism.[80]

Freud, therefore, certainly had sufficient cause after a few years to wonder
about Jelliffe's ultimate loyalties. Not only was Jelliffe obviously on cordial
terms with Jung, but he was involved in translating a major work by Alfred
Adler and another by a Jungian, A. E. Maeder, who spoke openly of representing, as the translation put it, the "Zürich school." Jelliffe, in his own
mind, reconciled these various Freudian and non-Freudian points of view,
and, moreover, he stood up publicly for both Freud and psychoanalysis even
on occasions when he engendered sharp criticism for doing so.[81] He went
over the whole matter in correspondence with Freud in 1926 (27 March, 11
April, Part II).

In practice, too, Jelliffe was not always orthodox. At one point in his
"Technique" series he stated that his patients sat in a chair instead of lying
on a couch. But the most extraordinary of his technical deviations was, as
he revealed in a 1916 "Technique" installment, that he was using assistants—
"the persons assisting me in psychoanalytic work," as he put it. In Jung's
letter of late July 1915 (Part II), Jung advised Jelliffe about the use of assistants on the basis of his own experience. Two of Jelliffe's assistants, Elida
Evans and Louise Brink, are known, and both are discussed in the correspondence with Jung and Freud in Part II, where it becomes evident (4
November 1938) that Brink was "Zenia X" with whom Jelliffe collaborated
in presenting her case history (see Bibliography). As will appear below (Chapter 3), Jelliffe's use of assistants made trouble for him after World War I,
and he renounced the practice.[82]

As late as 1920, when he revised his monograph on psychoanalytic technique, the approach that Jelliffe took to psychoanalysis still had not changed
greatly from that which he had developed in his first years as an analyst.
Except for cosmetic and expository changes such as adding a distinction
between descriptive psychiatry and psychoanalysis and a long translation from
Freud's most recent major work (*Introductory Lectures on Psycho-Analysis*),

80. Ibid., especially 4 (1917), 187–197; 1 (1914), 439–444; 3 (1916), 38; 4 (1917), 80; 2 (1915),
73. Freud's attitude toward American eclectics at this time is explored in John C. Burnham,
"Sigmund Freud and G. Stanley Hall: Exchange of Letters," *Psychoanalytic Quarterly*, 29 (1960),
307–316. Jelliffe cited Hall extensively in his articles, and the two of them for years had
sympathized with each other in their independence from Freud's or any other particular psychoanalytic viewpoint. See Ross, *G. Stanley Hall*, pp. 348, 408.

81. See Bibliography; and A. E. Maeder, *The Dream Problem*, tr. Frank Mead Hallock and
Smith Ely Jelliffe, NMDMS No. 22 (New York, 1916). Examples include Smith Ely Jelliffe,
"A Rejoinder: Maeder's Dream Problem and Its Critic, L. H.," *Journal of Abnormal Psychology*,
11 (1916), 337; Smith Ely Jelliffe, "Address of Retiring President," abstracted in *JNMD*, 42
(1915), 507–511. Among those alienated was Jelliffe's teacher and sponsor, Starr. For details
of what it meant to stand for psychoanalysis in medicine, see Burnham, *Psychoanalysis and
American Medicine*.

82. Jelliffe, "Technique of Psychoanalysis," 3 (1916), 268. Obviously the possibility must be
considered that Jelliffe took from Jung the idea of using assistants.

which was not resolved with the rest of the text, Jelliffe's chief changes involved adding his own schemes and diagrams and emphasizing regression a little more.[83]

While it is clear that in those early years Jelliffe drew in important ways on the inspiration of Jung, it is extremely difficult to show exactly the extent to which Jelliffe was a Jungian, or, indeed, even the particular ways in which he was one. How much, for example, he emphasized the immediate circumstances of the onset of the neurosis—which could have been distinctively Jungian at that time—is not clear, although his tendency to intervene actively might have reflected some such approach. The most important of Jelliffe's Jungianisms was his use of the libido concept, endowing libido with almost anthropomorphic characteristics as it operated in individual patients. This emphasis is hard to document and became largely a matter of style—but it made a substantial difference in both theory and therapy, as will be shown in the case of Mabel Dodge Luhan (Chapter 4).

In fact Jelliffe's style was compatible with much of Jung's. Both moved easily into an extraordinarily wide-ranging interpretation of associations and particularly symbolizations. While it is true that supposed universals, such as found in myth and in elements of what Jung came to call the collective unconscious appeared in the writings of Freud's closest associates, still Jung took such materials and connections far more seriously than the Freudians, and Jelliffe seemed to follow Jung. Texts do not easily demonstrate matters of emphasis and style in which Jelliffe's ideas resembled Jung's, but in the early years of Jelliffe's analytic practice such resemblances were both substantial and consequential. As late as 1921, for example, Brill found himself hard pressed to tell Jelliffe exactly what was wrong with Jelliffe's *Technique of Psychoanalysis.* Brill resorted to saying, "I assume that you realize that your whole mode of approach is more of the Jung Anschauung than Freud's. After all, it matters little," Brill apologized for his lack of specificity, "except that you gave me this feeling and your book certainly speaks the same language."[84] Jelliffe's style, language, and outlook, then, rather than specific ideas, gave him his Jungian aura.

Yet it is possible to make too much of what appear to be similarities between Jelliffe's ideas and those of Jung. Jung recognized, for instance, that Jelliffe's mental archeology with stratification was not wholly like his own (Jung to Jelliffe, 15 July 1920, Part II), thus in a way legitimizing Jelliffe's claim to originality. And, finally, while Jelliffe's leaps of logic and association often continued to unsettle his psychoanalytic colleagues, so that Jelliffe could commiserate with Jung about being called a mystic, still Jelliffe ultimately found Jung's ideas insufficiently empirical (or perhaps he meant insufficiently

83. Smith Ely Jelliffe, *Technique of Psychoanalysis*, NMDMS, No. 4 (2d ed., New York, 1920), especially pp. 31, 40–42, 88–91, 133.
84. A. A. Brill to Jelliffe, 1 May 1921.

reductionistic). As both the next chapter and the correspondence in Part II will show, Jelliffe found eventually, between 1920 and 1930, that he was forced to make a choice between Jung and Freud, and the significant fact is that he chose Freud, even though continuing to follow Jung's later writings.

A Glimpse of Jelliffe's Practice

One document has survived that contains further information on Jelliffe's practice, psychoanalytic and otherwise. In 1916 Jelliffe was called in as a consultant on the case of a psychotic patient who was receiving private treatment at home, and Jelliffe's report is still in existence. "I have come to the general medical conclusion," he wrote, "that the patient is, and has been, involved in that form of mental disease which in current terminology (Bleuler-Kraepelin) is symbolized under the terms, Schizophrenia or Dementia Precox, and manifesting itself chiefly in that variety or trend known as the catatonic form. The patient is seriously and deeply involved in the mental disorder and the prognosis in my opinion is extremely grave."

Yet, Jelliffe went on, the patient had not deteriorated mentally as far as might have been expected, and he was in good physical condition. The management and nursing of the patient had been of high quality, but Jelliffe thought that altered housing arrangements and more planned activities could permit further improvements: "The patient should not be compelled to go into a restraining sheet. By reason of his excessive violence he spends most of his time in a restraining sheet. . . . There may be times when this is absolutely needed but I think they will probably be very few, or at least much fewer, if a better adjustment of his housing and physical environment . . . can be brought about."

Jelliffe was critical of the attending physicians. "I fail to find in the notes of the case . . . any radical departure from the old orthodox list of descriptive phrases. This renders them to me sterile and therapeutically worthless. I find them of value as a detailed list of what is happening and they are useful as affording some insight into the patient's diseased behavior, but to me they are lacking in any real and exhaustive comprehension of the patient's thought-processes. Particularly are they superficial, hackneyed, and unintelligent when viewed from the more modern aspect which views minute study of every symptom, no matter how seemingly trivial, as of great significance.

"The notes at times speak of the patient's utterances, remarks, conversations, etc., without giving the same, as 'meaningless,' or 'trivial,' or 'unintelligible,' or 'unimportant.' . . . The notes are extremely unsatisfactory in this particular, even when judged from the general standpoint of the trends of modern psychiatry, as practised by all, but when viewed from the psychoanalytic standpoint this lack stands out more glaringly. Not only are stenograms missing but there are practically no clues as to following out of the patient's actual conflicts and complexes, and hardly an inkling that this most important aspect of psychiatry is even a problem."

Jelliffe did go on to say that "no claim is here advanced that the psychoanalytic methods are going to cure Dementia Precox patients. . . ." What Jelliffe wanted was as full an understanding of the patient as possible, for "the patient is entitled to results which may possibly accrue from the use of these newer methods. . . ." Jelliffe did admit that the new methods were controversial in their details, but his advocacy of psychoanalytic psychopathology without promise of therapeutic benefit, merely the understanding of the case, was consonant with his published writings.[85]

Jelliffe was, in short, a consistent enthusiast for psychoanalysis in his publications and in his private practice at a time when most specialists had not gone so far in their opinions. Only a small group of Freud's followers had taken so consistent a stance. Clearly Jelliffe was among them. But he also had his own style. In the consultation report just quoted he also urged a more thorough neurological workup, pointing out that certain symptoms suggested the desirability of "a more careful and systematic analysis of the vegetative nervous system including possibly some Abderhalden studies if it is possible."[86]

After his conversion to psychoanalysis, Jelliffe tended always to think in terms of both soma and psyche, although he often wrote in a more conventionally psychoanalytic mode that involved, particularly in the United States, a psychological/environmental stance. As his statement of his viewpoint in general terms in 1917 shows, he also included the social orientation that was typical of American followers of Freud:

"A profounder insight into human character and conduct seeks a new evaluation of determining causes and their manifold elaboration through the intricacies of individual and social life. It serves to clear away the obscurity and confusion which lie about these infantile reactions. It discovers the definite points of fixation and the reason for their attraction for the otherwise outgoing libido, while a consideration of them assists in opening the channels afresh to progress. It reveals in a new way, perhaps, that a sense of priority may have a regressive and therefore unproductive meaning, or it may stand as the servant and very inciter of progress.

"Analyses of human nature, the province and the definite work of psychanalysis, have revealed certain universal modes of obtaining power, of securing or retaining mastery over one's surroundings."[87]

85. This consultation report was most kindly furnished to the writer by Doris Nagel, M.D., out of the William Alanson White Papers.

86. Ibid. For background, see Burnham, *Psychoanalysis and American Medicine*.

87. Smith Ely Jelliffe, "Priority and Progress," *Journal of Philosophy, Psychology and Scientific Methods*, 14 (1917), 895. Or see similarly, Smith Ely Jelliffe, "The Physician and Psychotherapy," *Medical Record*, 90 (1916), 362–363.

Early Psychosomatics

Jelliffe's particular orientation grew out of the circumstances of his life and career. When he became a psychoanalyst, he was a well-established practitioner and editor, already entering middle age. No matter how far he went ultimately in subscribing to and supporting a developing and changing orthodoxy in American psychoanalysis, his orientation and previous experience continued to influence deeply the uses that he made of psychoanalysis. His unique viewpoint in fact reflected his original interest in internal medicine and biology, and his most original and significant publications were those which went beyond psychoanalysis into the area later known as psychosomatic medicine.

Very early Jelliffe began to see the direction in which his work and thinking were taking him, but he expressed the trends of his ideas in such general terms that before 1920—and, indeed, until much later—his readers (or listeners, if he was speaking) were not aware of the unity of his efforts, unless after 1919 they put his work in the context of the *Text-Book* introduction. Thus in 1922, for example, a San Francisco colleague who was pioneering psychoanalysis on the West Coast wrote: "Like your other publications your 'geistreicher' article in the December number of the *Archives of Neurology and Psychiatry* is fascinating and to the point. Perhaps a little trying for the dei minorum gentium, as I noticed from remarks made by some who could not make 'head and tail' of it."[88] By 1920 Jelliffe was able to explain in brief, allusive terms to his longtime colleague, L. Pierce Clark, how his thinking had developed.

"My first paper at Am. Neurological, 1914—'Hypothyroid and Hyperthyroid States and Psychogenic Antecedent Factors'—outlined a general program I have been interested in for some years previous to that. That paper is not finished.

"'Psoriasis as Hysterical Conversion Syndrome' was published by *N.Y. Med. Jl.* December 2, 1916, in furtherance of the program. Which had been fairly well formulated in *Introduction to Diseases of Nervous System*, I Ed. 1915, q.v.

"In order to ultimately push it over I had finished up Déjérine and Gauckler. Had started the 'Technique' articles, did the 'Compulsion Neurosis and Primitive Culture' article, started *Vagotonia* translation and encouraged Kraus to go on with translation of Higier, as I knew the material would be needed.

"The *Text-Book* then came out, 1915. At first I only put the notion in in small doses, here and there. I wanted to see how it would go. The book did go and there was more of it in II edition, big chunks here and there. See Introduction 'Classification' II and III Edition. . . ."

Jelliffe then listed more of his works and continued:

88. C. Renz to Jelliffe, 6 December 1922.

"III Ed. of *Text-Book* pushes the idea still further. 'The Symbol as an Energy Condenser [i.e., Container],' *Jl. of N. & M. Dis.* Dec. 1919 I consider essential.

"All of the time I have been running an organic series, The Thyroids, then Skin Syndromes. I have 3 or 4 papers almost finished on these, but was unable to push to a conclusion until now Cajal's new work on the Vegetative Skin Supply gives me the necessary anatomical details and Tretiakoff's new work on the Substantia Nigra and Bloch's work on the Melanins and the relation to adrenalin has closed up that gap, now I can finish them up not on a basis of a happy speculation but sound foundations.

"'Tuberculosis and Psychotherapy'—*Am. Rev. of Tbc.* Sept. 1919 was the next. I am letting this slumber as it would swamp me with clinical work I don't care to do yet. It is not a good piece of work yet, but it is as far as the profession, as a whole, can stand.

"I have in press, *Am. Jl. Med. Sc.* when? a study on the vascular situation, this one on Multiple Sclerosis, also another on Hypertension, a monograph almost, not finished.

"Two papers, one on Pernicious Anemia, one on Hirschsprung's Disease [dilation of the colon], and Diabetes in one Family and the Psychical Correllates, a fine job, if I can finish it.

"So I might go on, but I spare you any more."[89]

An Important Case and Contribution

Jelliffe's initial chief claim to specific originality, then, lay in his extending the idea of conversion hysteria to a chronic disease, namely, psoriasis. In 1916, he recalled a decade and a half later, "I published the first case of a chronic skin disease as a conversion symptom."[90] The paper was actually coauthored with Elida Evans, one of Jelliffe's students and assistants, to whom he had referred the patient reported on.

In the introduction to the paper Jelliffe spelled out how his concept of pathology had changed radically. "The present paper," he wrote, "will confine itself to a study of some resymbolizations as showing themselves in the skin area. . . ." By conceptualizing all diseases as symbolization processes, Jelliffe expected to show that "dynamic" factors were involved in all pathologies. Moreover, he continued, "in dermatology, as is true for all other disorders of the body, no real dynamic and genetic disease concept is adequate if it neglects the massive truth that the most important and undeniable fact of human existence is man's psychical inheritance. Without a study of man's thought fossils as intimately related to the health of every structure of the human body, no human pathology is complete.

89. Jelliffe to L. Pierce Clark, 22 December 1920. A comparison of projected work with the Bibliography shows that Jelliffe indeed never completed a number of his projects.
90. Jelliffe to P. Bailey, Jr., 24 November 1931.

"What we, as physicians, have been satisfied to call pathology may be and has been practically expedient, but it is far from being a satisfactory pathology. Psychical factors, it is true, have less and less genetic significance as we move from the purely psychogenic disorders, such as hysteria, compulsion neurosis, etc., to such purely physical ills as hemorrhage from a bullet wound, or the burning of the skin by means of a fire, or rhus toxicodendron poisoning, but nevertheless, such psychical factors, if present, should be understood in terms of energy."

While Jelliffe did not wish to assert that the skin disease, psoriasis, is "always an hysterical conversion syndrome," yet he did believe that "this particular psoriatic affection in this patient is chiefly psychogenic in origin." Moreover, Jelliffe was particularly concerned with the therapeutic implications of his findings: "The present case represents an attempt to understand the dynamics of the skin reactions in terms of the hidden psychological factors of the individual life, the patient's thought fossils, to wit, the more primitive and earlier (phylogenetically speaking) ways of accomplishing life's destiny. No amount of working on the outside of this patient's body is likely to change her mode of expression of this life desire. A reconstruction of her attitude toward life and its realities must be gained, or she will bear the marks of her failure to live up to life's opportunities."

The clue to the psychogenic nature of the affliction was that the first complaint was not about the skin but about a pain in the head. Jelliffe concluded that the study of the case revealed that her psoriasis was "a symptom of a hysterical conversion, whereby the patient sought relief and an outlet for the libido with infantile desires."

The case that Jelliffe used as illustration was that of a twenty-six year old woman who was otherwise physically healthy and worked regularly. When he saw her he sized her up as a typical hysterical patient—a fact abundantly confirmed in further clinical study—and he "accordingly advised this patient to consult one of his assistants, as the superficial rapport, easily established, gave unconscious evidence of a new attachment whereby the hysterical symptoms could serve as a direct unconscious sexual gratification in the restricted sense, so that a very strong transference would result in new symptoms of the neurosis. He therefore telephoned to his assistant that he was sending a case of psoriasis for analytic study. . . ."

The treatment proceeded with much dream interpretation and sometimes very strong confrontations, along with frequent shows of resistance by the patient. The patient was using her skin symptoms, especially those in the pubic area, to make symbolic statements to the physicians (male) whom she had been consulting. Under Evans's and Jelliffe's treatment, the symptoms decreased dramatically. The therapists summed up at the end their interpretation of her case:

"We begin to see, here, the regression of the libido from her work and environment, and later the lost libido strives to effect a transference to the young, unmarried brother. He, however, does not prove a sufficient outlet, perhaps from his own efforts to free himself from the family. He loses his health and has a severe illness in a hospital; she has no one to depend upon and reverts to the past, where the father was the ideal, and finally constructs a sexual exhibitionistic substitute—a resymbolization in the form of red spots on the skin—psoriasis."[91]

Jelliffe's ideas continued to develop from this point, and in the realm of ideas the last decades of his life showed, as has been remarked, substantial and important continuity, as will be taken up in the next chapter.[92] It was in other areas of his existence that the pattern of events was very different.

Break and Transition

For several years before the United States entered World War I, Jelliffe, productive in his medical calling, enjoyed his professional life, his social life, and his family life. The children were growing and spent happy summers at Lake George, as Jelliffe's daughter could testify (see Chapter 4, below). Items from fragments of correspondence that have survived show how much Jelliffe relished recreation and travel, some evidence of which was noted above. After war had cut him off from Europe, as noted in the correspondence, he wrote Jung from Arizona, where he was vacationing (see Jung's letter of 2 January 1917, Part II). At home, too, Jelliffe was extremely active in play as well as in his profession, attending the Vanderbilt Cup auto race in 1909, for example. Altogether a picture emerges of a vigorous, spirited person who savored life. He described himself as "large and stout—5['] 10", 200 pounds, clean shaven, with a roundish face."[93]

Then around the time of American involvement in the war, 1917–1918, a number of occurrences signaled substantial changes in Jelliffe's life. Old routines and ties were interrupted, and by the 1920's his professional life was dominated completely by his practice; by the *Journal of Nervous and Mental Disease* and to a much lesser extent the monograph series; by his

91. Smith Ely Jelliffe and Elida Evans, "Psoriasis as an Hysterical Conversion Symbol," *New York Medical Journal*, 104 (1916), 1077–1084. The fact that only one address was listed at the end of the article suggests that Evans was working in Jelliffe's office and that the patient was sent to her there, not elsewhere, but the statement that Evans had to be telephoned argues otherwise. See Chapter 3.

92. Déjérine, who made a powerful impression on Jelliffe, had early come to believe that psychological factors were essentially involved in many organic afflictions, and he may have encouraged Jelliffe in his tendency to think in psychosomatic terms. See Jelliffe, "Glimpses of a Freudian Odyssey," pp. 323–324, quoted above.

93. Jelliffe to C. B. Davenport, 1 November 1909, Davenport Papers. Smith Ely Jelliffe, "Technique of Psychoanalysis," 3 (1916), 162.

championing of psychoanalysis; and by his own particular ideas, which, had Adolf Meyer not preempted the term, might be called psychobiology.[94]

For two years, 1917–1919, Jelliffe was coeditor of the important weekly journal he had left ten years before, the *New York Medical Journal*. In February 1917, the publishers added his name to that of Charles E. de M. Sajous of Philadelphia, who had been sole editor. Both names disappeared from the masthead on 25 January 1919. Jelliffe's accession to the coeditorship occasioned a welcome to a former associate editor and a writeup of who he was and what his qualifications were, emphasizing his general medical orientation. As Jelliffe's life was changing, this statement provided a significant look backward.

"While Doctor Jelliffe has devoted special attention to nervous and mental diseases and has built up a large consultation practice in this line, he has at no time lost touch with the general practice of medicine, and brings to the work which he is undertaking a wide knowledge of medicine and of men, a varied and valuable experience, a sound judgment and lofty ideals, which will make him an important acquisition to the staff."

And after reviewing Jelliffe's editing and writing activities the publisher concluded:

"These literary and journalistic activities have all been carried on subsidiary to Doctor Jelliffe's main work in clinical and hospital practice. For fifteen years after his graduation he devoted every afternoon throughout the week to laboratory, hospital, or clinical work, thus laying a broad foundation of clinical experience, which has been invaluable to him in both his literary and his professional work, and which will add much to his value as a member of the editorial staff of the *New York Medical Journal*."

Finally, the statement included an excerpt from Jelliffe's letter of acceptance, in which he talked about his aspirations and also the conditions under which he accepted the assignment.

"'Notwithstanding the urgent demands of an arduous practice, I have always wished to contribute my bit towards the spreading of that concept in medicine which views the disorders of the human body, not as happenings isolated in this or that organ, but as a failure of the body as a whole successfully to carry on its functions, and in which the particular cell groups, which show the defect, do so for specific reasons. This, I know, is an old Hippocratic ideal, too frequently overlooked in an era of absorbing specialistic investigation. I am in heartiest sympathy with the trend of this mass of analytic research; but what I especially prize is the opportunity to assist in the synthesis of this invaluable material and to make it available for practical purposes.

94. Robert Charles Powell, "Healing and Wholeness: Helen Flanders Dunbar (1902–59) and an Extra-Medical Origin of the American Psychosomatic Movement, 1906–36" (unpublished doctoral dissertation, Duke University, 1974). See below, Chapters 3 and 4.

" 'In trying to present to your readers from week to week the most profitable and productive work which is going on I would seek to avoid a narrow and dogmatic materialism on the one hand and an equally dangerous diffuse and mystic spiritualism on the other. Matter without spirit is dead; spirit without matter means nothing for human beings. A living medicine must consider both.

" 'Your willingness to have me continue my regular practice, and to relieve me of many mechanical details in the editorial office, permits me to accept your generous offer. I wish to remain in the world of action and to be in touch with sick people, for only by so doing can I know at first hand the problems of the profession. . . .' "[95]

Personal Transition

On 3 March 1916, when Jelliffe was forty-nine years old, Helena Leeming Jelliffe died of a brain hemorrhage. She was at home and died shortly after she became ill. Her significance was such that the editor of a strictly medical journal, *Medical Record*, gave a special notice of her passing. "Helena Leeming Jelliffe, the wife of Dr. Smith Ely Jelliffe, who died on Friday of last week of cerebral hemorrhage, was a woman of unusual ability in many lines of human endeavor. Although not a physician herself much of her literary work was in medicine. She was the translator of a number of works in neurology and psychiatry and was also the writer of many editorial contributions appearing in various medical periodicals, especially in the *Medical News* during the years that her husband was editor of that journal."[96]

Her passing was chronologically the first of the major changes in Jelliffe's life. Exactly what this loss meant to Jelliffe he characteristically did not reveal. Only hints remain, such as the dedication that appeared in subsequent editions of the Jelliffe and White textbook:

To
HELENA LEEMING JELLIFFE
whose lofty purpose,
ideal striving, and never-failing coöperation,
have been a constant stimulus to progressive endeavor,
this book is dedicated
as a token of love and esteem.

And Jelliffe did allude to the event in his letter to Freud, 19 December 1925 (Part II).

On 20 December 1917, Jelliffe married Bee Dobson[97] (1892–1979), a nurse. The second Mrs. Jelliffe had literary aspirations (and published an autobio-

---

95. "Dr. Smith Ely Jelliffe," *New York Medical Journal*, 105 (1917), 369–370.
96. *New York Times*, 4 March 1916. *Medical Record*, 89 (1916), 479.
97. Mrs. Jelliffe used the first name "Bee" when she was married. Later she used "Belinda" and wrote under that name.

graphical novel, *For Dear Life*, in 1936). She had little interest in close personal relations with the more dignified and powerful members of the New York medical fraternity and their wives. Theater people, whom Jelliffe also enjoyed, were more to her liking. This was an important but subtle nonintellectual factor in Jelliffe's increasingly independent and, indeed, lonely role in the medical profession in the last decades of his life.

A second change, and one that tended to confirm his inclination to professional isolation, was the termination of the rest of his medical school and hospital affiliations. His appointment at Fordham petered out, and he no longer lectured at the Post-Graduate Medical School after 1917. Even his hospital consultantships ended in 1917. He was left with only private practice and his editing and writing.

Helping to make the break was an interim during World War I when he served the army as contract surgeon examining recruits in Plattsburgh, New York. He wrote to White describing his activity in the summer of 1918: "We have been snowed under with work for the past 10 days—2800 youngsters have arrived for training camp & we have examined them all neurologically in about 6 days. It was some stunt I can assure you and by night, with hot weather we were all in. Timme, Barrett, Hutchings, Payne, Jas. W. Putnam of Buffalo [all eminent specialists] are all here & we took turns working in relays of 3 or 4. We polished 673 off one day & I turned out neurologicals in 1 minute—doing about 100 in 2 hours with hardly a stop—until I had them 'Stand on your head' 'Stick out your knees crossed' Say 'truly—open your mouth' & similar mix ups. The pace was so hot—but it was great fun and we picked out a large & interesting group of endocrinous anomalies."[98]

The *Archives of Neurology and Psychiatry*

Finally, the place of the *Journal of Nervous and Mental Disease* in American medicine changed, as did Jelliffe's relationship to it. Beginning in 1918, when his long-time collaborator, Spiller, withdrew, Jelliffe became responsible editor of all parts of the journal. At almost the same time he became involved in an unpleasant controversy that eventuated in the founding of a first-rate rival journal with the same format as his *Journal*. Spiller later said that the prospective competition between the two journals caused him to retire. The newcomer was sponsored by the American Medical Association and was called *Archives of Neurology and Psychiatry*. The first issue was January 1919.[99] The man who took the initiative to found the *Archives* was Hugh T. Patrick, a nervous and mental disease specialist in Chicago, which was where the AMA operated national headquarters.

98. Jelliffe to William Alanson White, 28 July 1918, White Papers, Box 17.

99. William G. Spiller to Jelliffe, 10 April 1939. Details concerning the events discussed in the following paragraphs are to be found in Burnham, "The Founding of the *Archives*." That account emphasizes the professional aspirations of the neurologists who founded the *Archives*.

Two very different kinds of policies brought Jelliffe into conflict with his colleagues who started the *Archives*. The first was that he followed the custom, well established in the nineteenth century, that a medical journal, and particularly the editor, took no responsibility for the contents of advertising. A group of reformers in the profession, working with the AMA, campaigned against the advertising of proprietary or, in any case, undesirable medical preparations.[100] Since the *Journal of Nervous and Mental Disease* did not reflect the reformers' policies, Jelliffe as publisher came under attack.

The other policy that brought Jelliffe and the *Journal* into disfavor with many of his colleagues was his open advocacy of psychoanalysis. Many leading and powerful members of the profession campaigned actively not only against the movement that Freud started but against the agents of its dissemination. For a few years the *Psychoanalytic Review* funneled off some of the psychoanalytic content of the *Journal*, but by 1916 Freud's work was prominent again, particularly in the abstracts and reviews, to the point that the *Journal* did not represent either the specialty or the profession. American physicians were relatively friendly to, or at least tolerant of, psychoanalysis, but many neurologists felt that Jelliffe did not adequately reflect their concerns with other matters, especially ordinary organic illnesses.[101]

Thus it was that Jelliffe complained to White about how "the Chicago bunch sore on the ad. situation uses the N.Y. bunch sore on the psa. [psychoanalysis] situation and so I get raked fore and aft." Jelliffe was, in fact, having to fight for the *Journal*. He found friends and even subscribers deserting him, and as late as 1920 he noted to White that the *Journal* would only just pay for itself, with perhaps a mere thousand dollars in profit for Jelliffe's labor, because of the attacks of "the Chicago bunch."[102] The most immediate and serious loss, however, was in the authors. The neurosurgeon, Harvey Cushing, for example, no longer contributed to the *Journal*, but he did thereafter place papers in the *Archives*.

Late in life Jelliffe provided his own account of the events surrounding the founding of the *Archives*.

"But all was not well with some of the older organic neurologists, especially as psychiatric material was given more and more notice and more particularly since 1910 psychoanalytic views introduced from time to time began to irk, even to irritate the older solons of neurology and psychiatry.

"Some effort was made to mollify certain of the more outspoken opponents to the Freudian conceptions. Thus I took out most of the psychoanalytic material and in 1913 with Dr. William A. White started our *Psychoanalytic*

100. See, for example, "Special Report of the Council on Pharmacy and Chemistry," *American Medical Association Bulletin*, 10 (1915), 333–338.
    101. See Burnham, *Psychoanalysis and American Medicine*.
    102. Jelliffe to William Alanson White, 1 November 1918, White Papers, Box 17; Jelliffe to William Alanson White, 31 December 1920, White Papers, Box 20.

Review. But apparently this separate and independent venture only added insult to injury and your very patient spokesman was actually threatened by the then reigning patriarchs. 'They would ruin the *Journal*'—'withdraw their approval'—and thus in some sort of subtle Machiavellian spleen was the *Archives of Neurology and Psychiatry* born. Dr. Spiller felt that he could no longer be the editor and since then the entire burden has been on my shoulders.

"There was one stormy scene in the senate chamber of the honorable American Neurological Association and I think I told the gentlemen with more heat than suavity that the American Neurological Association had done very little to support the *Journal,* only a third of its membership had ever subscribed and as far as crippling the *Journal* was concerned I promised that my hostility would be mobilized to greater effort and so it happened. Since then the circulation and advertising has gone up steadily from year to year. But I sincerely welcomed the *Archives* whole heartedly in spite of the initial slippery politics, since there was room for and need for more and better neurology and psychiatry and to which the *Archives* has contributed abundantly. I have always believed that a healthy rivalry was advantageous to the development of science."[103]

There was in fact more competition in the offing than Jelliffe probably knew about. At the beginning of 1916 Jelliffe and Spiller announced that each issue was to be increased from sixty-four to one hundred pages because "neurology has been advancing so rapidly within the past decade that it has become necessary to expand the media of communication between those interested in its progress and its achievements. . . . [With the founding of the *Psychoanalytic Review* for special psychical problems, it was hoped] that there would be enough space to deal with the central field of sensori-motor neurology, which the *Journal* had chiefly represented. This hope has been outgrown and the editors feel that they can best give expression to the growing interest by an increase in the size of the *Journal.*"[104] But the growth of interest not only in neurology but in psychiatry was spawning ambitions of other American specialists who wanted to upgrade the profession in ways that the *Alienist and Neurologist,* for example, had failed to do earlier. Thus the founders of the *Archives* had a hard time themselves in heading off still another journal to be edited by the extremely eminent psychiatrist, August Hoch. Hoch had earlier, in 1915, been in on the maneuvering for the editorship of the as yet unnamed journal of the National Committee for Mental Hygiene, still another potential rival for Jelliffe, although eventually it was not really competitive.[105] Clearly the field of nervous and mental diseases was expanding.

103. Smith Ely Jelliffe, "The Editor Himself," pp. 574–575.
104. *JNMD,* 43 (1916), 104. Although no evidence exists, it is likely that the increase of price for the enlarged journal helped set off the movement to found the *Archives.*
105. See Burnham, "The Founding of the *Archives,*" and A. Hoch to Adolf Meyer, 30 August 1918, Meyer Papers (copy kindly furnished by Doris Nagel, M.D.). Adolf Meyer, "August Hoch, M.D.," *Archives of Neurology and Psychiatry,* 2 (1919), 576.

Nevertheless Jelliffe felt that he was the victim of sometimes unseemly tactics on the part of the *Archives* founders. He was particularly unhappy when one of his collaborators, listed on the front of the *Journal*, E. E. Southard, a Bostonian, was asked to serve on the editorial board of the new publication—but on condition that he take his name off the cover of the *Journal of Nervous and Mental Disease*. Southard's vacillation and finally desertion led Jelliffe to write this letter:

"Many thanks for your courtesy in the matter of your new job. May you prosper in it. I have no particular comments save that if they have chosen you editor they have chosen the very best man in the field.

"I had understood that you were simply one of an editorial board and that Weisenberg [*sic*] was the responsible editor. If on an editorial board alone I think the action of Patrick quite arbitrary and distinctly autocratic. I presume it applies to your connection with the *Journal of Abnormal Psychology* as well and to other connections. Or are you lending yourself to some more of the Chicago politics in the hope of personal aggrandizement? The explanation interests me. That is; the 'democratic' choice. In one of Patrick's letters the choice was expressed for the purpose of 'cornering' the neurological material in your vicinity. Fine democracy? I guess not. At all events God bless you and rest assured that I would rather have your honest frankness than the slippery, slimy Chicago filth. Be careful you do not become a 'plaster saint' like your Chicago friends.

"This is the first time in history when a Bunker Hill man was told what he had to do." Jelliffe then added in handwriting: "There is no ethics. It is politics. They have been trying to destroy the *Jl.* for 15 years because I won't be dictated to in the ad. business. Their hypocrisy is nauseating."[106]

This contentiousness around the *Journal* was distressing to Jelliffe, who did not relish controversy and tended to hide his feelings in professional as well as personal matters. He did prove to be an able competitor, however. He even went to the extreme of obtaining (through persons unknown) "unofficial" reports of society proceedings which had spitefully been taken away from the *Journal of Nervous and Mental Disease*, where they had previously always appeared, and which were supposed to run exclusively in the *Archives*—leading to amusing, and hardly professional, recriminations about leakage within at least one society.[107]

In later years Jelliffe was able to take a detached view of the events, as reflected in his rather mellow reminiscences above. In 1939, anent his memoirs, Jelliffe commented to Spiller:

106. Jelliffe to E. E. Southard, 1 November 1918. Norman Dain, *Clifford W. Beers: Advocate for the Insane* (Pittsburgh, 1980), pp. 181–183.
107. Minutes of the Boston Society of Neurology and Psychiatry, 1919–1920, Countway Library, Boston. In March 1920 the society finally gave up and voted to publish reports of the proceedings in both journals.

"There was so much more that might have been said about the discomforts when some of the New York solons were so angry over my psychoanalytic proclivities and made very definite trouble for the *Journal of Nervous and Mental Disease*. You and Mills, however, both stuck by me and the ground lost was soon made up.

"The *Archives* were needed for the wealth of pathological and neurological work which was rushing forward into the foreground and the early antagonistic efforts of some of the elements there soon fell by the way side and we have been good friends ever since.

"The Book Review columns of the *Archives* have never come near those of the *Journal* and so we go merrily on our way. . . ."[108]

This event represented, as Jelliffe finally saw, not merely "politics"— although they were certainly involved, as an unelevating scramble for the *Archives* editorship showed. The movement to found a new journal represented the distress of many organically oriented specialists, a distress growing out of the coming of psychotherapy, especially psychoanalysis, and the mental hygiene movement which originated its own journal in 1917, *Mental Hygiene*, as it ultimately came to be known. The *Archives* in fact would contain more material than the *Journal* did in the sphere of neurology and neuropathology, not psychiatry, and it certainly would not be a synthesis such as Jelliffe was striving to reach in his own writings. The *Archives*, too, as Jelliffe implied to Spiller, did not achieve the international, cosmopolitan professional orientation that marked Jelliffe's work as editor of the *Journal of Nervous and Mental Disease*. Indeed, Jelliffe had a good laugh when the *Archives* founders offended an eminent English neurologist, F. W. Mott, who was already editing a journal with the same title—*Archives of Neurology and Psychiatry*, published in London by that title beginning in 1909—and the "Chicago bunch" did not seem to know about it! "I note what you say about the Chicago crowd," wrote the indignant Mott to Jelliffe; "I had the same information from Dr. Gordon Wilson."[109]

Jelliffe's position with regard to advertising of course soon became untenable. He was just surprised when he was overtaken by the winds of reform that were bringing to an end a standard—and profitable—practice.[110] But it is possible to detect the pleasure with which he wrote to the editor of the *Archives* in 1935:

"I have been telling Hoffmann Laroche they should not advertise Allonal since it contains pyramidon which brings about a lethal blood disorder. They should change its composition. They say the *Archives* carried their ad which they refuse the *Journal* on this attitude of mine [*sic*].

108. Jelliffe to W. G. Spiller, 11 April 1939.
109. See especially F. W. Mott to Jelliffe, 10 February 1920.
110. This general controversy over advertising flared up again more than fifty years after the *Archives* founding. References are in Burnham, "The Founding of the *Archives*."

"Will you ask the Advertising Manager what their stand has been about advertising an unknown poisonous product?"[111]

The members of the American Neurological Association found that the American Medical Association charged about 10 percent less for the 1918 *Transactions* than the *Journal of Nervous and Mental Disease* had for 1917, but by 1920 AMA officials were saying that members who delayed sending in their papers were going to force a raise in costs. Clearly the old problems had not been solved. Within another year the *Transactions* were causing a large deficit for the neurologists. Events suggested that his colleagues were soon looking on Jelliffe in a much more kindly way. He continued to attend the neurological meetings faithfully and, in 1920, was named chairman of the history committee. In 1928 it was an ANA committee of Jelliffe's old antagonists, Tilney and Weisenburg, along with Hunt, who nominated Jelliffe for the first vice-presidency of the association, and the next year another committee, on which Tilney and Weisenburg continued, that nominated him to succeed to the presidency in 1929.[112]

The founding of the *Archives* was just the most public of the events that by the beginning of the 1920's had substantially altered or redirected much of Jelliffe's life. Thereafter, beyond his functioning as medical editor, Jelliffe's role in medicine crystallized into taking a stand and representing certain positions, positions about which he wrote and spoke and which took him far ahead of his own times. Only in the 1930's did the rest of the profession begin to catch up.

111. Jelliffe to H. Douglas Singer, 25 May 1935. No answer to this letter has been found.
112. American Neurological Association Council and Executive Session minutes, especially 18 June 1919, 1 June 1920, 19 February 1921, and 27 and 28 May 1929.

THREE

The Mature Jelliffe

The Pattern of Jelliffe's Daily Life

Jelliffe lived for a quarter of a century beyond the World War I era in which his life underwent so many changes. During the 1920's he enjoyed success and prosperity, but after 1929 he, like many other Americans, found his life altered by unfavorable economic events. As noted in Chapter 1, he felt that he had to postpone his retirement, and he continued to be active until only shortly before he died, even though his working hard and playing hard finally gave way to the infirmities of old age. Meantime, regardless of external circumstance, he identified ever more closely with psychoanalysis and at the same time developed his own viewpoint.

Jelliffe's letters provide glimpses of the nature and pace of his life as his children grew up and went out on their own. As he told White in 1919, he was working from 8 A.M. to 8 P.M. without lunch, and going to bed exhausted. In 1922 he wrote to Otto Rank that he was busy revising his textbook "so that with a monthly Journal, seeing patients from 9 A.M. to 7 P.M., taking my wife to the theater or seeing friends in the evening, looking after a big house, the affairs of five children—two girls fortunately married—two grand-children, some nieces and nephews, etc., etc., you can imagine my life is fairly busy." To another correspondent about the same time Jelliffe wrote that his activity as editor and publisher was "a 'side issue' from my practice which keeps me busy all day."[1]

Almost a decade later, in 1930, Jelliffe indicated to another correspondent that little had changed in this busy, active pattern of life: ". . . there is so much of interest to be done and what with seeing patients every day from 9 to 6, running a couple of highbrow magazines, nights, holidays and Sundays; plugging away on new stuff, reading, to say nothing of sandwiching in a few

1. Jelliffe to William Alanson White, 27 April and 16 May 1919, White Papers, Box 19. Jelliffe to Otto Rank, 14 February 1922. Jelliffe to Dr. Bratz, 3 April 1923.

hours for a wife—helas, 'tis a dog's life."[2] But by then Jelliffe's children had left; the last one to be married was Helena, in 1925.

Jelliffe was proud of all of his children and then also of his grandchildren, as they came along; the first was Helena Leeming Emerson, born 16 February 1921. "My Holland daughter [Helena] has had a son," he wrote in 1928, "and this completes my quiver biologically. All five have carried on another series of 'spreselings.'"[3] In 1924 Jelliffe did note that his son, Smith Ely, Jr., now twenty-four years old, who had had a severe case of polio when he was eight, "is still a source of much anxiety to me." And then in 1925 his second son, William Leeming, a medical student at Yale and a champion swimmer, died in a gun accident in his room. This was a profound blow to Jelliffe, although as usual he tried to mask and displace his emotions. It is remarkable that in his letter to Freud, 19 December 1925 (Part II), Jelliffe discussed his feelings openly, even more than he did in writing to the warm-hearted Jung (20 February 1925). In 1926, when his friend, the surgeon Harvey Cushing, in turn lost a promising son, Jelliffe was almost unable to work. "To-night I am feeling like hell," he confessed. "I can hardly hold myself together. The tragedy that has come to Cushing is so like what came to me a year ago that life hardly has any value." Jelliffe was, he continued, doing his work and trying "to be valiant and go on with the game."[4]

As the children grew up and departed, Jelliffe made other adjustments. At times guests and roomers helped fill the big house on West 56th Street. He wrote to his young friend and sometime confidant, Karl Menninger, in 1933 that he was welcome to stay "if the roomers are out of the house— Bee's penchant for helping the down and outers. . . ."[5] Increasingly the house on Lake George came to be a haven for Jelliffe, and he spent as much time as he could there each summer, even though he had great difficulty in getting his practice started again when he returned to New York. White came to know Jelliffe's annual reestablishment plight. In 1926 White wrote:

"Let me know as soon as you get back as I have a little envelope to send you by registered mail that will help tide you over the period of readjustment which I have watched over throughout the years following your vacation, during which you are convinced that your business is ruined and that you never will get any patients and when you look forward to the winter expecting that the world will come to an end. I trust this will be a therapeutic effort that will prove successful, although, as usual, your contribution to the success of the business has been very feeble."[6]

2. Jelliffe to K. M. Payne, 7 January 1930.
3. Jelliffe to Ernest Jones, 13 November 1928. Jelliffe to R. Mourgne, 31 December 1923.
4. Jelliffe to T. Weisenburg, 14 June 1926. See also Jelliffe to Jung, 20 February 1925, in Part II.
5. Jelliffe to Karl Menninger, 31 March 1933. From World War I to the early 1920's, Dr. Caroline F. J. Rickards had an office in the front of the building.
6. William Alanson White to Jelliffe, 29 September 1926.

At the lake Jelliffe's family gathered around him, and the grandchildren reenacted the happy times enjoyed by his children a generation earlier. As the physical problems of old age became more prominent in his life, this haven at the lake meant more and more to Jelliffe. Only a tragic speedboat accident in which he was involved in 1934, with a subsequent lawsuit, marred his contentment there.

The place on Lake George was not an estate but consisted rather of a large amount of land (125 acres, as noted above) on the hills facing the lake, with some rough but comfortable dwellings in various buildings. Electricity was installed in 1934. Jelliffe's main domicile was ultimately a converted boat house that had once housed an earlier owner's steam launch. What appealed to Jelliffe about his Lake George existence was the natural beauty and isolation as well as simple life style. In 1926 Jelliffe described his lake routine for Ernest Jones: "The servants have gone home and I am the breakfast chef. I confess to a gourmet's accomplishment in omelets, hashes and morning dishes running quite a gamut. My indulgent B. D. J. stating she thinks I even incorporate oak leaves to advantage. Then follows a long day for we are devotees of a two meals a day regime. I have not eaten lunches for 20 years, so it is quite au fait with me. For two, three or four hours I prepare the abstracts for the *Journal,* write those stodgy book reviews and do some work on miscellaneous papers. Witness the 'Respiratory Encephalitis' monograph in the *Journal*—and then some more. Revising the Jelliffe and White *Textbook:* Osler, Hysteria article and other odds and ends.

"What those odds and ends are—some breaking the 18th Amendment, for my chemical flair has degenerated into a brewer's vat and I make most excellent beer. The motor boat, for the mail, and sundry commissariat purposes—a swim and general review of the farm, building, repairing, tree planting, etc., etc.

"Mrs. Jelliffe prepares the chicken, and a meal de luxe at 5, and now late in September a long evening in which I read all the past season's novels, detective stories, the *International Library of Philosophy;* Koffka, Koehler, Ogden, Rignano, and others, and then settle down to the *International Journal [of Psycho-Analysis].* . . ."[7]

In New York the Jelliffes' social life during the 1920's was extraordinarily stimulating. Glimpses of it appear in his correspondence and other places. In 1928, for instance, Jelliffe invited the famous writer, Max Eastman, to tea in order to meet the even more celebrated actress, Helen Hayes. On another occasion Jelliffe attended a banquet in honor of New York publisher Horace Liveright and there consorted with a group of luminaries any of whose names were well known in literary and social circles.[8] Other examples

7. Jelliffe to Ernest Jones, 30 September 1926.
8. Jelliffe to Max Eastman, 9 February 1928. The second occasion was recorded by Sigmund Freud's nephew, Edward L. Bernays, in *Biography of an Idea: Memoirs of Public Relations Counsel Edward L. Bernays* (New York, 1965), p. 285.

will be noted below. Jelliffe's existence, in short, was lively and full in his senior years and even as old age drew near.

Growing Significance of Jelliffe's Physical Aging

Jelliffe, like so many physicians, was very open about his physical complaints. He did not hesitate to write to medical correspondents about his various ailments, often showing a resigned good humor as well as a detached professional interest. In 1925 he told Walter Timme, also referring repeatedly to the death of his son, Leeming:

"Somewhere around Marseilles or on the steamer a particularly offensive pneumococcus strain attracted by my glancing eyes chose to raise a brood of obnoxious relatives on my conjunctiva. This kept me in a darkened chamber more or less for a couple of weeks and then the damned brood moved on into my naso-pharynx and now for a month all of my resistance has gone to the bow wows. I have managed to crawl around and do enough work to pay the ice man but I would say that life has had little joy save in groaning over one's wretchedness.

"I am coming out of it now—there is some colonic residue but if I can get to bed at 8 and get up at 10 I manage to pull through the day, but Richard is far from being himself I can assure you. There is some subtle psychic background undoubtedly for I have a curious right arm syndrome—a relic of my unassimilated struggle with the wound of last Spring, but this too is passing. On the whole I have to hold on tight to hallucinate that 'silver lining' so easily wished on us by the hurdy gurdies of the market place. Leeming's wife had a son born on September 8th. That also goes in the picture. It should make me very happy, but it is hard to see it when a goal of one's Ego ambitions is pushed ahead another generation."[9]

In 1939, surgery left Jelliffe particularly uncomfortable. He suffered, as he told a European correspondent, "a severe attack of arthritis from the ischaemia of the Trendelenberg position ($1\frac{3}{4}$ hrs.) while the surgeon was doing a transurethral prostatectomy. After six months of pain and disability, I am back to relative comfort." In fact he was not recovering well. "I start things," he wrote to his old friend Casamajor, "and am unable to push them to a conclusion. My feet go to my head, as it were, and I am heavy and only feel adequate for the most routine procedures." But in general Jelliffe's infirmities left him more good natured. "My German," he wrote characteristically in 1936, "is falling out in spots; like my hair it grows thinner."[10]

Jelliffe did not think his fortune or his life was especially notable. In 1932, replying to an inquiry addressed to many prominent persons about cases of courage that they had witnessed, Jelliffe wrote:

9. Jelliffe to Walter Timme, 2 December 1925. Jelliffe mentions the conjunctivitis incident in a letter to Freud, Part II.
10. Jelliffe to Michael Danyl, 19 January 1940. Jelliffe to Louis Casamajor, 10 February 1940. Smith Ely Jelliffe, "My Arthritis and Me," *Medical Record*, 152 (1940), 85–87. Jelliffe to Ives Hendrick, 1 December 1936.

I am unfortunate in that my life has been so humdrum as never to have been a first hand participant in what usually goes by the name of "Courage." By this I refer to the more frequently cited forms dealing with more obvious difficult situations. My own observations only encompass the more subtle denials of narcissism and of events which have little understanding from the dramatic viewpoint.

Regretting my lack of ability to assist,

Believe me,

Very sincerely yours. . . .[11]

Beginning in the 1930's, two of Jelliffe's disabilities particularly distressed him because they got in the way of his earning a living at the very time that he did not feel that he could retire (he turned sixty-five in 1931). The first was his hearing loss, which of course could be very serious for a psychoanalyst. He was finally fitted with a bulky hearing aid, of great help for private conversation and for interviews, but it did not permit him to hear people speaking at a distance, and so he was unable to carry on discussions at meetings or to give seminars. When he refused to become permanent vice president of the American Psychoanalytic Association at Brill's behest, Jelliffe cited his deafness as well as other personal reasons, and he told Freud (28 January 1933, Part II) deafness was the reason he declined office in the New York Psychoanalytic Society.[12]

The second disability that disrupted his pattern of professional activities was an auricular fibrillation from which he suffered particularly on public occasions. In 1936 he told White that he was "feeling well and able to stand the upsets in the ticker which in spite of their fateful periodicity sometimes let up gratuitously." On another occasion he spoke triumphantly of being "free from my tormenter" when he had managed to make a public presentation at medical meetings.[13] Again, he mentioned this now permanent disability casually when writing Freud (4 November 1938, Part II).

The signs of Jelliffe's aging increased at the end of the 1930's. In 1938, for example, he asked G. W. Henry to review Henri Baruk's *Psychiatrie médicale, physiologique, et expérimentale* because after writing "a couple of" drafts himself, he still could not seem to get a satisfactory statement—an experience that he had not theretofore reported. By the early 1940's, too, he no longer maintained his membership in the last professional association in which he had been particularly active, the New York Psychoanalytic Society.[14]

11. Jelliffe to Webb Waldron, 2 February 1932.

12. Jelliffe to Macdonald Critchley, 30 July 1937; Jelliffe to C. C. Burlingame, 14 March 1940; Jelliffe to A. A. Brill, 25 May 1933. The deafness came up in Jelliffe's letters to Freud of 2 August 1934 and 4 November 1936, Part II, and again below, in this chapter.

13. Jelliffe to William Alanson White, 25 November 1936 and 2 January 1934.

14. Jelliffe to G. W. Henry, 21 September 1938. Minutes of the New York Psychoanalytic Society, A. A. Brill Papers, Library of Congress, Washington, D.C.

Amidst his discomforts, Jelliffe was aware of the facts of old age, and he explored ways of reducing his responsibilities and passing them on to younger people. In 1937, after the death of White, he remarked that "I have taken over the *Psychoanalytic Review* and the Monograph Series and if fate does not rip up my arteries or clamp down too hard on my prostate I may survive long enough to get them in reliable hands," and he was making similar statements in his last letters to Freud (Part II). Two years later he was still looking for a successor to carry on the *Journal*, the *Review*, and the monographs: "There may be one," he wrote, "but who and where is he?"[15] Even though he appeared reluctant to give up his editorial work, he was aware of his own mortality. Not only did White die in 1937, but other friends were gone as well, including neurologists with whom he could identify, J. Ramsay Hunt and S. A. K. Wilson—"and so," Jelliffe commented, "the circle narrows." Indeed, White's death Jelliffe took as a reminder to slow down himself.[16]

The failure of Jelliffe's search for a successor was part of the reason that he felt compelled to carry on his work long after retirement age. In 1930 the publishers Williams and Wilkins had offered $30,000 in 7 percent bonds for the *Journal of Nervous and Mental Disease*, but the depression prevented consummation of the arrangement. In 1935 he discussed selling the *Journal* to Karl Menninger for $20,000, but nothing came of that idea, either.[17]

Jelliffe also was conscious of the magnificence of his book collection, and he was concerned for many years about where it might go. At first he thought of leaving it as a memorial to his dead son. After the depression struck, however, and throughout the 1930's he was actively seeking a purchaser, hoping that it would go "somewhere where it can be held together as a unit and be really used and appreciated. It is a burden in a way although I would still go right on adding to it. I am asking a fair price, far more than it would bring at auction and more than dealers would give for it but about half of what it actually cost which has been close to $50,000. The binding alone has cost in the 40 years $15,000. I would be willing to sell it on the so much down and so much a month for ten years plan, the plan to be worked out like $150–$200 monthly." In 1941—four years before his death—title to the collection was transferred to the Hartford Neuro-Psychiatric Institute, now the Institute for Living.[18]

15. Jelliffe to A. A. Roback, 28 June 1937. Jelliffe to Robert S. Carroll, 20 May 1939.

16. Jelliffe to James S. Reeve, 21 August 1937. Jelliffe to A. A. Brill, 7 May 1937. Privately, Jelliffe had some bitter comments on the way in which White had let himself be pushed by others.

17. Jelliffe to William Alanson White, 7 March 1935. Jelliffe was actively looking for a purchaser in 1931; Jelliffe to Gregory Stragnell, 17 November 1931. Jelliffe to Karl Menninger, 17 June 1935. Harry Stack Sullivan twice maneuvered unsuccessfully to acquire the *Psychoanalytic Review* in the 1930's; Helen Swick Perry, *Psychiatrist of America: The Life of Harry Stack Sullivan* (Cambridge, Mass., 1982), pp. 382–383.

18. Jelliffe to Frederick Tilney, 18 March 1926. Jelliffe to Karl Menninger, 27 March 1936. *New York Times*, 3 March 1941.

Changing Financial Status

It was ironic that Jelliffe ended his career concerned again about money as he had been when he began in the 1890's. During the teens and the 1920's, however, Jelliffe was relatively free from financial worries, although he still functioned as a businessman concerned about profits. His prosperity permitted him the luxury of working for what he believed in, in medicine. Writing to Henry Viets of Boston in 1923, Jelliffe noted that only twenty copies of the Jelliffe and White textbook were sold each year at Harvard: "I don't give a D—— myself economically, as the whole year's proceeds of the book in royalties I can equal in one or two days' work in my office, but I am interested in getting the *ideas* across."[19] At about the same time he wrote to a European about the editing he and White were doing: "Our two magazines are practically philanthropies of our individual time and interest."[20]

Jelliffe's losses from the Great Depression were immediate and substantial. "I knew absolutely that the bubble of '29 was going to burst, but I blithely go to Europe and when I return things are so flat one could hardly crawl out from under," he recalled. "Like many another I hesitated and was lost. I actually cabled from Europe to sell out and at the top but used the fool phrase 'use your own discretion however.' I am $15,000 the flatter because they did use their discretion and did not sell. But it is all in a life time and it would happen again." Very soon after the crash hard times affected practice, and Jelliffe was thereafter deeply involved in the general depression. In 1932 when serving as vice president, he was unable to preside over the American Psychoanalytic Association meetings in Brill's stead because he had to be present at a meeting of stockholders of a company in which he was substantially involved.[21]

As early as 1924 Jelliffe was aware of the extent to which his assets were tied up in real estate. "Commerce is commencing to invade the section where I live and practice. . . . Already my property is being sought for commercial purposes. This is gratifying financially but provoking as to making my plans very unsettled. . . . If I sell or lease my house I shall have to move and that will take some time for a house in which one has lived for 25 years, brought up 5 children, accumulated a library of 10,000 volumes and other things of all kinds; it will be a very annoying thing. . . . If not this year it may be another."[22] In the end Jelliffe held on, despite his taxes and the temptation of profit. As late as 1932 he was congratulating himself that he had not lost as much as many people had because his assets were in real estate, but by 1933 he admitted that he was taking a loss on real estate investments.[23]

19. Jelliffe to Henry Viets, 29 January 1923 (italics in original).
20. Jelliffe to H. Silberer, 12 October 1922.
21. Jelliffe to Ernest Jones, 19 May 1933. Jelliffe to A. A. Brill, 31 May 1932.
22. Jelliffe to Emil Oberholzer, 14 January 1924.
23. Jelliffe to Ernest Jones, 2 June 1932; Jelliffe to James J. Walsh, 8 December 1933.

Meantime practice continued to languish. "Here things are beastly quiet," he wrote to White in 1931. "No patients, no money, nothing but a gray pall of waiting." When there were patients, he complained, collections were down, a circumstance common to most physicians in the United States in those years. In 1935 he told Karl Menninger, "Practice is nil—nearly all of us are in the same boat. We have not gotten down to chewing the wax in the comb but there is precious little honey." And as late as 1940 he noted to another colleague, "Practice is very slow. No one has any funds but we labor in the vineyard."[24] In the late 1920's Jelliffe had acted as consultant to at least two New York state hospitals, Kings Park and Manhattan, but by the mid-1930's these appointments were no longer being renewed—whether on his initiative or because of institutional changes is unknown.

Nor did Jelliffe's editorial work provide much cushion. White was very reluctant to declare any dividends from the Nervous and Mental Disease Publishing Company (nothing at all in 1933), and recovery was slow. In 1934 Jelliffe did get $800, and in 1935 $1200, but given the way the partners ran the business, it is not clear whether or not they were making much money. Yet the *Journal of Nervous and Mental Disease* apparently lost few subscribers, and by 1934 Jelliffe could note that "the *Journal* is $500 ahead of last year to date. Expenses up, so net profit is nil, but if total receipts mean anything, something is doing."[25]

That same year Jelliffe wrote at length to a European colleague about his economic position. He was, he said, taking longer vacations as his fibrillation got worse (as he also wrote to Freud), even though the time lost represented great financial sacrifices. "I see no use in leaving money for children to wrangle over. My parents left me no money and I am glad of it. I had to work and it was good for me." (Jelliffe was trying to explain why he and White could not publish an unprofitable monograph, and he may have dramatized matters a little; it seems unlikely that any of his children would have wrangled about money.) He continued, describing how he occasionally took a patient during the summer at "a simple camp in the woods and lakes of the Adirondacks" and so just barely paid his way. He had resigned all hospital affiliations and devoted himself to his own work, he said, "which is quite meagre." And he added what may have been somewhat closer to a strict accounting than he was accustomed to using, "The *Journal* is a philanthropic enterprise and also just self supporting. I work for nothing." And to White he confessed at almost the same time, "In fact the last two years I have really been in the red."[26]

24. Jelliffe to William Alanson White, 25 November 1931. Jelliffe to Ernest Jones, 2 June 1932. Jelliffe to Ives Hendrick, 4 March 1940. See also Jelliffe to Freud, 17 April 1933, Part II.
25. Jelliffe to William Alanson White, 27 May 1932 and 15 October 1934.
26. Jelliffe to Siegfried Cohn, 13 August 1934. Jelliffe to William Alanson White, 15 October 1934.

By 1936 Jelliffe's editorial work appeared more important to him, as he explained to Karl Menninger: "The *Journal* I would want to hold longer as it will be more and more of an asset if my increasing deafness makes practice impossible, especially catching free associations in whispered mumbles. You know you either neglect them or wait for correction on resumé. If I put more time on the *Journal* I can increase its earning power sufficiently to live on it alone, in camp, or in some less expensive castle than 64 [West 56th Street] where the taxes eat me up."[27]

Jelliffe's accounts of his daily life and economic fortunes indicate the general trends in his practice. He carried on psychoanalyses much of the time, but exactly how orthodox his procedures were, or how many patients he treated by other means—presumably psychotherapeutic—is uncertain. Only a small minority of his patients in the 1920's and 1930's used the couch in his office; most sat in a big chair instead, as in the years when Jelliffe first began psychoanalysis. Throughout the interwar years by far the largest fees came from court cases, but they disrupted his office practice when they came up.[28]

Court Cases

Jelliffe savored his experiences with the lawyers. "Barring a few minor accident insurance bullies," he wrote in 1937, "I have been very well treated. I enjoy this type of wit matching. . . . It may be a mistaken impression," he continued, "and one intermingled with wish fulfilling bias, but I have tried never to go on the stand unless I were very sincerely convinced of the reasonable equity or justice of my position. I have then backed it to the limit, maybe a bit beyond, in the fire of combat, but if I do not seriously fool myself I have never been influenced apart from the evidence. My records show I have turned down nearly 75% of the applications made to me for supporting what I could not go to bat on. Hence I have never made any real money in the forensic field."[29]

The occasion of Jelliffe's letter was legal scholar Francis L. Wellman's publication of most of the record of a lawyer's cross-examination of Jelliffe in one of the most celebrated cases in which he gave expert testimony. The cross-examination was so shrewd that Jelliffe's opinion was discredited in a strictly legal way, although not substantially. The case offers an example of Jelliffe's work in forensic psychiatry. It involved the claim of the lawyers of a banker, Joseph W. Harriman, that he was not competent when he carried out certain illegal business transactions, and in 1933 Jelliffe testified to that effect.

27. Jelliffe to Karl Menninger, 27 March 1936.
28. Interview with Marion Cohen, 13 December 1978.
29. Jelliffe to Francis L. Wellman, 11 August 1937.

Jelliffe was a formidible figure on the stand; Wellman observed that "it seemed fairly clear that Dr. Jelliffe would be the defendant's star witness. His international prestige and highly specialized training and experience in nervous and mental diseases were outstanding and unimpeachable."

Jelliffe's testimony showed that he had conducted a very thorough examination of Harriman, using both physical and psychological tools of inquiry. The examination elicited evidence of the defendant's mental impairment, including defective memory, lack of emotional control, the latter manifested in part by his telling in inappropriate circumstances off-color stories that Jelliffe in an amusing way declined to repeat in court.

The vigor of the verbal sparring in this trial appears in excerpts from the cross-examination and Wellman's discussion.

> Q. Doctor, I would like to put it this way: It is clear, then, that he knew that you were talking about the Harriman National Bank?
> A. Yes, he knew that he had been president of the Harriman National Bank, and—
> Q. And he knew that that was what you were talking about?
> A. Yes, he did.
> Q. He knew that you were talking about a securities company account?
> A. He did.
> Q. He knew that you were talking about the accounts of certain depositors?
> A. He did not know whether they—those accounts—that they were accounts; he was not aware of those. That was a function, he said, of his underlings.
> Q. Do you mean to say that he said that he did not know of those accounts, or that he did not know of the transfers to those accounts?
> A. I don't know that he said—I never asked him if he ever heard of those accounts. He didn't know of the transfer of those accounts.

"It was quite clear at this point that Harriman had been fully aware of the charges made against him and that, in his conversation with the doctor, he had simply denied his guilt." (The legal issue in the hearing was chiefly whether or not the defendant understood the charges. Jelliffe therefore was not effective in Harriman's defense, since Jelliffe's concern was with Harriman's mental illness.)

On one occasion the lawyer did best Jelliffe:

"Dr. Jelliffe had testified that he believed Harriman to be incompetent because he was unable to confine himself to a single subject. Throughout the cross-examination of the witness he indicated a similar tendency to stray from the subject of the examination. There was a perceptible ripple of laughter in the courtroom when the witness was asked:

Q. Did you observe any perceptions of repetition of ideas on his part, when you asked him about other matters—if you asked him about one thing he would go off to another subject and stick to the other subject?

A. Yes, he did that quite frequently. . . .

Q. Now, doctor, when I ask you a question, will you please stick to the question I ask you and not go off to something else?

On other occasions Jelliffe more than held his own.

Q. Is the thought of self-destruction necessarily evidence of incompetency?

A. The thought of it? No.

Q. Are efforts in that direction necessarily evidence of incompetence?

A. In general, yes.

Q. Then you think anybody who attempts suicide is mentally incompetent?

A. In general, yes.

Q. You say that unreservedly?

A. Unreservedly, yes. There might be very few exceptions, but I have never met them.

Q. You would say that everybody that you have seen who has attempted suicide was mentally incompetent?

A. Every person that I have ever met that I know of, see, anything at all about, I found them to be incompetent, yes.

Q. By incompetent you mean unable to take care of their own affairs, unable to give any normal judgment on the ordinary processes of life?

A. No, I don't mean that absolutely. I mean that with reference to the act that they performed.

Q. Well, outside of the act they performed?

A. But that is the act.

Q. I know. Having attempted to commit suicide, would you say that such a person is not competent to manage his own affairs—that is, give a business judgment, decide on whether to borrow money or lend money, decide on whether to make a lease or not make a lease, decide on whether to move or not to move?

A. During the time that he is committing that act, no, he is not.

Q. And when it is over with?

A. He might return again to such a condition that you have described, yes, or he might not. It depends on the particular kind of illness that he suffers which brings about the suicide.[30]

30. Francis L. Wellman, *The Art of Cross-Examination* (New York, 1937), pp. 397–412. Jelliffe and Brill discussed the testimony in the case in their letters of August 1933 (in the Jelliffe papers).

Jelliffe was well aware of the cleverness of the lawyer and commented on the cross-examination when writing to Brill at the time. Jelliffe's judgment then was that "altogether this is the damnedest case that I have ever been involved in, and there is no end to it."[31]

Neurology

Jelliffe's legal work was, of course, not necessarily rewarding in all senses. He liked practice. Like most physicians with extensive contacts with people, Jelliffe treasured human relationships that he had with his patients over the years, even though they existed within a professional setting. Jelliffe recalled how he developed ties to the family of a banker who "retired to cultivate a neurosis," for example. "I first, many years ago, saw a young daughter, for years treated as an epileptic, who, as she came into the office immediately showed an evident brain tumor and without so much as another glance [I] packed her off to Cushing. It was an infiltrating glioma and too far gone, but they were struck with my prescience and immediate tender of the only thing available and have remained strong friends now some twenty years or more."[32]

Neurological cases were of course unhappy cases, like the daughter in this family, for until Cushing and other brain surgeons evolved their techniques, all that a physician could do was diagnose the illness and predict a (usually) melancholy outcome. As neurological surgery developed, the surgeons who could manage virtually the only therapy in the field tended to dominate it. By the end of Jelliffe's career, the three major neurological institutes of North America were each headed by a surgeon, although clinical neurology did of course survive.[33]

Jelliffe's forte in neurology was, beyond his clinical abilities, his grasp on the bibliography of the field, and he was, among the relatively small number of specialists, one of the outstanding figures. When his colleagues finally recognized his eminence formally, he wrote to his sister, in October 1929: "They have made me President of the American Neurological Association this last year, having passed me by a bit to punish me for my radicalisms, but finally gave in. It is good fun."[34]

31. Jelliffe to A. A. Brill, 7 August 1933.
32. Jelliffe to Merrill Moore, 5 October 1938. See also Jelliffe to Freud, 16 February 1926, in Part II.
33. Louis Casamajor, "Notes for an Intimate History of Neurology and Psychiatry in America," *JNMD*, 98 (1943), 607; and in general, Henry Alsop Riley, "The Present Status of Neurology in the United States," *JNMD*, 106 (1947), 262–282; and H. Houston Merritt, "The Development of Neurology in the Past Fifty Years," in Derek Denny-Brown, ed., *Centennial Anniversary Volume of the American Neurological Association, 1875–1975* (New York, 1975), pp. 3–10.
34. Jelliffe to Mrs. Theodore Lyman, 18 October 1929, Additional Papers (scrapbook). This honor is discussed in other contexts, above.

A few years later another neurological meeting moved Jelliffe to observe: "Our A.N.A. was as usual—fewer and fewer psychological contributions but more and more tolerance for them. I presume I am the grand old man now— as was Putnam and in another manner was Prince. . . . The youngsters are in the saddle and going strong. The physiological work is excellent. Cushing rides the Pituitary and Crile the Thyroid. It is all vastly interesting. . . . I still am able to say something once in a while and they still seem to like it. . . . Were I a good demagog I should shift my ground and exploit it, but no, I must enter into discussion of details of small generality and of philosophical concepts of greater generality, and the poor dears who have no idea of adventure in their souls pucker up their foreheads and wonder, when they are not moved to jeer."[35]

Jelliffe was well aware of the uncongenial trends in the field of neurology. "Why did Grinker [Roy R. Grinker, Sr.] jump to Michael Reese [Hospital]— was it the neuro-surgery crowd?" he asked Karl Menninger in 1936.[36] And even aside from the surgery, neurological research tended to turn, as Jelliffe suggested, into highly refined microscopical and physiological investigations rather than the clinical studies with which he had grown up. As early as 1925 he noted that he was too old for histology although he was still interested in neurology in general.[37] By the 1930's his total grasp of the field was open to criticism, and Jelliffe felt hurt when an English reviewer suggested that the 1935 edition of the Jelliffe and White textbook did not include adequately "recent developments in neurology."[38]

Psychotherapy and Psychoanalysis

But by that stage in his career, Jelliffe's major writing efforts had long been going into psychoanalysis and its relationship to biology and medicine. So, too, his practice, as noted above, was primarily psychotherapy.

It was within the practice of psychotherapy and psychoanalysis that Jelliffe developed so many of the stimulating social relationships that brightened his last decades. The best known of his patients and friends were theater people, including the set designer, Robert Edmond Jones, the playwright, Eugene O'Neill and his first wife, and the producer, Kenneth Macgowan. Other friends, such as members of the Barrymore family, were probably not patients. At one time the practice included any number of other celebrities such as Betty Compton (Violet Halling Compton), the famous actress who created a neighborhood sensation by coming to her appointments in the car of the mayor of New York (James J. Walker, who later married her).

35. Jelliffe to Ernest Jones, 19 May 1933.
36. Jelliffe to Karl Menninger, 27 March 1936.
37. Jelliffe to P. Bailey, 8 April 1925.
38. Review of Jelliffe and White, *Diseases of the Nervous System*, in *Lancet*, 229 (1935), 1183. Presumably this is the review referred to in Jelliffe to C. M. Smyth, Jr., 20 October 1937.

To outsiders, Jelliffe's practice must have looked impressive, with important patients and flattering descriptions of his reputation. From his own perspective, the operation was somewhat more modest. He wrote all case history material himself, letting his secretary (from 1922 to 1944, Marion Cohen) handle the business of the *Journal of Nervous and Mental Disease*, including all billing and ordering. His fees per hour ranged from a modest ten dollars to twenty-five, and he got one to two hundred dollars a day for a court appearance. Moreover, many of his bills went uncollected, and he very seldom had recourse to law to try to collect. (When he did in one case, that of Thaw, the newspapers gave the story a big play because of the notoriety of the trial. Jelliffe had received nothing since the first trial, and he ultimately had to settle in the late 1930's for $750.)[39]

Grand Old Man of Medical Journalism

Besides his practice and the personal relationships that grew out of it, the other main professional sources of satisfaction in his later years were of course his editing and writing. Not only did Jelliffe maintain the *Journal of Nervous and Mental Disease* against the increasing number of competitors and also the depression, but he actively edited it until 1944. A few years before he gave up the position, he wrote to one colleague: "I am hunting for the name of any freak similar to myself who has owned, run, and managed singlehanded a special journal of medical science for 35 years. I doubt if any such animal is known in American Journalism."[40]

There did continue to be reverberations from the founding of the *Archives of Neurology and Psychiatry*, and partisanship persisted for some time on both sides. As late as 1925 Spiller noted to Jelliffe, "You know there have always been some of the older men who have been hostile to the *Journal*"—to the point, he observed, that they would be unwilling to contribute papers for a festschrift for C. K. Mills if the papers had to appear in the *Journal*.[41] Yet the other side was warm in support of the *Journal*. At the beginning of the 1920's Henry Viets of Boston, who had stood by Jelliffe, felt compelled to comment about the *Journal* in a way that indicated its strengths: "I find it is better than ever before and far excels any journal of its kind in this country. I have been so disgusted, as have others in Boston, with the *Archives* that I refuse to send them anything more. The illustration with Frazier's paper in the last number was the last of a series of blunders such as I have never seen duplicated. Such errors I am sure would never appear in your journal. I personally will make every effort to see that your journal is kept in its right

39. Interview with Marion Cohen, 13 December 1978. For example, the *New York Times*, 12 March 1931; clippings in memorabilia book, Additional Papers.
40. Jelliffe to James T. Pilcher, 23 March 1938.
41. W. G. Spiller to Jelliffe, 16 November 1925.

place at the top of the list of American publications."[42] Jelliffe himself continued to believe that the book reviews were the outstanding asset of the
Journal of Nervous and Mental Disease. (Modern reader surveys of scientific
journals show that book reviews are indeed very heavily used by subscribers,
who typically depend on them to help keep up in a discipline.) Jelliffe wrote
many of the reviews himself, and together with those he did for the *Psychoanalytic Review* they constituted a heavy burden. Throughout the 1920's
and 1930's he complained repeatedly of having over a hundred books waiting
to be reviewed. In 1925 he was "2 years behind in my abstracts . . . and 150
volumes behind on book reviews."[43]

Jelliffe was in fact firmly entrenched as a senior figure among medical
editors, and he functioned easily in that role, particularly in his specialty.
He was of course consulted when Weisenburg of the *Archives* tried to get
uniformity in the terminology used to refer to paresis. (Other editors opted
for "dementia paralytica," but Jelliffe demurred and in the end apparently
won.)[44] But when Jelliffe tried to get the various specialty journals to cooperate
in a journal that would publish abstracts so that the *Archives*, the *American
Journal of Psychiatry*, and the *Journal of Nervous and Mental Disease* would
not duplicate needlessly the same material, the others were not willing to
follow such a rational—and economical—policy.[45] Jelliffe especially attempted to overlook the *Archives* battle in the normal course of business. As
early as 1921 he was corresponding in a friendly way with the chief figure
in the enemy "Chicago crowd," Hugh T. Patrick, who wanted advice on
what to do about Stekel, who was making a bad impression in Chicago (in
this case Patrick's suspicions were better taken than Jelliffe's attempts to be
tolerant), and whether or not Patrick's assistant, Lionel Blitzsten, might see
Freud.[46]

The only obvious major change in policy that Jelliffe made as managing
editor of the *Journal of Nervous and Mental Disease* was (after 1920–1921) to
stop publishing signatures on the book reviews. To one unhappy author he
wrote: "I am still the managing editor of the *Journal of Nervous and Mental
Disease* but I do not write all of the book reviews. Our policy has been to
publish them unsigned. We publish many and when we did sign them there
was such an interminable correspondence that I had no time for making a
living in my regular medical work. Authors—and I am no exception—are
quite narcissistic about their thought children."[47] In fact at all times Jelliffe

42. Henry Viets to Jelliffe, 1 September 1920.
43. For example, Jelliffe to William Alanson White, 11 March 1933. Jelliffe to G. Stanley
Hall, 11 February 1924.
44. T. H. Weisenburg to Jelliffe, 17 October 1929. Jelliffe to T. H. Weisenburg, 27 February
1930.
45. Jelliffe to E. N. Brush, 14 January 1925.
46. Hugh T. Patrick to Jelliffe, 22 September 1921.
47. Jelliffe to Hulsey Cason, 17 March 1936.

tried to find sympathetic reviewers. That was for him an editorial canon, and the surviving correspondence shows that he consistently pursued such a policy.

The *Psychoanalytic Review*

The publications of the Nervous and Mental Disease Publishing Company, including the *Psychoanalytic Review*, provided concerns similar to those of Jelliffe's *Journal*. White continued to be entirely responsible for the contents of the *Psychoanalytic Review*, which often put Jelliffe into a difficult position. White was eclectic, catholic indeed, in his policies, a position of which Jelliffe approved in 1914 (as noted above) but from which he moved away in the 1920's. While still sympathetic toward a tolerant stance, yet Jelliffe was under continuing and increasing pressure from his psychoanalytic colleagues to purify his idea of what constituted high quality psychoanalysis, and over the years he more and more resonated with the more narrowly Freudian. This tension was not resolved until Jelliffe took over the *Review* after White's death. Jelliffe referred repeatedly to this problem in his letter to Freud of 23 September 1929 as well as in his last letters (see Part II).

In the early 1930's the *Review* was threatened in two different ways. To begin with, the depression hit the *Review* far harder than it did the *Journal of Nervous and Mental Disease*. At one point, in 1932, White noted with alarm that they had lost fifty-two more subscriptions.[48] By 1934 the *Review* was barely breaking even, and White was considering using profits from the monograph series to keep it going.

It was just at that juncture that the second threat appeared, a new journal, the *Psychoanalytic Quarterly*, founded by other New York analysts led by Dorian Feigenbaum. Jelliffe had been very friendly to Feigenbaum in the late 1920's, at one point essentially teaching him how to edit and manage a medical journal.[49] Jelliffe, who had been through a similar experience already with the *Journal* and the *Archives*, tended to be philosophical and sanguine.[50] White, however, was quite upset. He added a subtitle to the *Review* to preempt any further competition: *An American Journal of Psychoanalysis*. Then he maliciously had printed on the subscription blank the word "Quarterly."

There was an issue in the establishment of the *Quarterly*, the issue on which Jelliffe found himself with conflicting loyalties. Ives Hendrick, a younger Boston analyst, "came in and had a little talk," Jelliffe wrote White at the beginning of 1934. "The same story of not being in 'line with newer con-

48. William Alanson White to Jelliffe, 23 May 1932.
49. For a full account, see Arcangelo R. T. D'Amore, "Psychoanalysis in America: 1930–1939," *Psychoanalytic Quarterly*, 50 (1981), 570–586.
50. In 1926 L. Pierce Clark, Jelliffe's eccentric friend, started an *Archives of Psychoanalysis* that expired in 1927 after a few issues, a circumstance that led Jelliffe to be glad that he had maintained a consistently generous and supportive attitude toward the enterprise.

ceptions,' not in 'sympathy with the advance guard,' etc. I laid it down pretty strong even though it was all prefaced by the half believed palaver that 'you' were the 'culturally longed for ideal' but trafficked too much with the hoi polloi. This chiefly anent the *Review*. He was not even aware that the July *Quarterly* was still not yet out. They are dickering with W. W. Norton to unload on. This I get sub rosa from 'Norton.' I put a flea in his ear to the tune of if you wish well for the *Review* and wish to see up to date stuff in it, why not send it along."[51]

Jelliffe's point that good papers submitted would of course be published was valid, but he overlooked or ignored the sensitivities of the "purer" analysts who were concerned about appearing in an eclectic context, since dilution and eclecticism represented a threat to the developing new orthodoxy, a term that Jelliffe and some non-Freudians used to describe an emerging set of standards. On many occasions Jelliffe did see the virtues of a narrow and disciplined, even orthodox, approach, and the new journal could, he admitted, serve a very useful purpose.[52] Meantime he passed on to White more gossip about the problems encountered by the *Quarterly*. In 1932 he wrote:

"This leads me to the *Quarterly*. It is very excellent and I hope they can go on with it. I suspect that Lewin and the crowd would get into hot water if someone read his paper and was after pornographic stuff; they could make it very hot. I do not know if I should warn Feigenbaum about it as it might also include others, as you know the R. C. gentry are not asleep.

"The *Quarterly* has no special prospects. They will have to dig into their jeans or find an angel and I suspect they think W. will find one. He is treasurer. We had a dinner last week, Wednesday. It was all very jolly, the board were there and Mayer and Kardiner, Brill and myself and Blaauboer [a printer who also contracted with Jelliffe] was invited and was there. He seemed just a bit preoccupied—but we had a fairly good time. They all talked of their hopes, etc. They have about 300 subscribers and a grand in the treasury. Evidently they had not received the first bill.

"As to the ads, subscriptions, etc., the boys have done some work but not much has come in. They are both first trying to get something to support themselves and I don't see much luck there."[53]

Jelliffe and White were not the only ones to have a little fun at the expense of the *Quarterly* editors' pretensions. The eminent Franz Alexander, who had only recently left Berlin, wrote to Jelliffe that Feigenbaum had already solicited his paper for the *Quarterly*, "but I am not sure whether the editorial board will find my article good enough on account of the very high standards which they are going to establish. As you remember, one of the members of

51. Jelliffe to William Alanson White, 2 January 1934.
52. Jelliffe to Paul Federn, 12 December 1931.
53. Jelliffe to William Alanson White, 27 May 1932.

the editorial board found my article extremely revolutionary and in contradiction to certain 'sentences' in one of Freud's early writings. I am sure you
will be willing to publish my article even as a rejected paper." Jelliffe in
reply laughed at "their 'high standards' or other nonsense."[54]

As the *Quarterly* thrived, the journal most threatened was not the *Psychoanalytic Review* but the superorthodox *International Journal of Psycho-
Analysis* published in England by Ernest Jones. This all came out early, as
revealed in an exchange of letters that began when Jelliffe wrote to White in
1933:

"One matter I am writing about. Wittels and Brill have just gone. We
dined together and Wittels, who has just returned, brought some matters up
for discussion that I am transmitting as I understand them. They concern
the *Psychoanalytic Review*. He has gathered a number of opinions and attitudes from the European men. Among them he talked with Jones.

"The general summary seems to be that Jones would like to effect some
coalition between the *International Journal* and the *Review*. Just what form
is a matter for discussion. The 'International Psychoanalytic Review,' as a
title, is the most concrete way of expressing the wish. The details are for
discussion also.

"What you may have to say I could not answer for, except that I thought
we might make some change in our policy a bit. As a starter, this can be
expressed in the old idea I have spoken of before: i.e. to put an editorial
board on our front cover including such names as Brill, Jones, Wittels,
Oberndorf, etc., etc. Details open for discussion.

"Wittels emphasized our non-orthodoxy and I emphasized our belief that
if more of the Freudian group would send us good material it would perforce
crowd out the less valuable material that they objected to, instead of their
maintaining the attitude of non support of the *Review* because of 'Steckel'
and other similar presentations.

"This might be a good plan since Jones—particularly—feels quite antagonistic to the *Quarterly*. Around this pivotal point there is much to discuss
which I cannot go into now. I repeated some of our attitudes about the 'more
the merrier' but this does not entirely meet the conflicting issues.

"Among other things if no coalition is possible the thought came into the
arena that we might apport on different aspects of the psychoanalytic activities
and thus not have so much repetition in the various vehicles of psychoanalytic
thought. I feel this is a valuable item to consider. Just how such division of
material could be made practical is to be discussed.

"Will you make some notes and bring them along with you when we get
together.

54. Franz Alexander to Jelliffe, 6 May 1932; Jelliffe to Franz Alexander, 18 May 1932.

"Personally as you know I wish the January *Review* could start some such expression along lines here suggested. At least on the title page."[55]

White's reply was much to the point: "I have your letter which I have read with much interest, but let me please call your attention to the fact that all the journals that want to cooperate with us are bankrupt. Furthermore, I am not willing to renounce my independence and take my orders from anybody else—an editorial board, or whatever it may happen to be called. I am not much on orthodoxy. Of course some of the people involved would quietly slit my gullet with one hand and hold out the other for a friendly grasp. I do not want to mix with that group. More anon when I see you. My general reaction is k.m.a., if you get what I mean."[56]

As late as 1937 Jones was still worried, as Jelliffe wrote to Karl Menninger: "Jones is catawauling (?) about the *Psychoanalytic Quarterly* as a competitor and others not mentioned. I am quite of a different mind. There are good ecological adaptive problems for intellectual 'growths' just as there are for grasses, sedges, oaks, swallows, etc. etc. etc., and to make all living growing things or ideas comport to one model—beyond the fundamental ones of free competition for food, light and air, not to mention Eros and Thanatos, is to me irrational, small minded and also 'snobbish.'"[57]

When in 1937, after White died, Jelliffe took over editorial responsibility for the *Psychoanalytic Review*, he did make numerous changes to try to eliminate the miscellaneous character of the *Review* and upgrade the contents. Although he had not approved of all of White's editorial policies, of course up until that time he had not interfered other than gently to offer information and advice, as in the letters quoted above.[58]

Jelliffe and White naturally had many differences of opinion about their other joint publishing ventures, too. The monograph series particularly presented opportunities for divergent judgments. White often reminded Jelliffe that the whole series was kept afloat by the profits from the *Outlines of Psychiatry* by White, and this was close enough to the truth that Jelliffe used it frequently himself in letters of rejection to hopeful authors.[59] Jelliffe was so cowed by White's economic stance that he even went to the extreme of financing the publication of one of his own monographs that he, but not White, felt would sell sufficiently well to pay off.[60]

55. Jelliffe to William Alanson White, 8 November 1933.
56. William Alanson White to Jelliffe, 9 November 1933.
57. Jelliffe to Karl Menninger, 14 July 1937.
58. Evidence of his intentions and actions after 1937 is to be found, for example, in his correspondence with Karl Menninger. Again, his general sentiments appear in the letters to Freud printed in Part II.
59. In addition to the example above see, for example, Jelliffe to L. P. Clark, 3 February 1927.
60. William Alanson White to Jelliffe, 26 January 1927. See also Jelliffe to William Alanson White, 29 January 1917.

But mostly the two friends, who greatly enjoyed each other's company, settled any differences with joking good humor. "I have your demented letter of the 11th instant," White wrote to Jelliffe in 1925 on some business matter. The next day another letter from Jelliffe set White off again in the same vein: "I have your second series of deliria. . . ."[61] Jelliffe of course replied in kind, although he was not usually as biting in his humor as was White. He did tell White in 1929 that "if you drink more of my wine [next time you are in New York] you might become intelligent, in time."[62]

The death of White was the one event that profoundly changed the pattern of Jelliffe's activities before his own retirement and death. Indeed, as early as 1935–1936, before White died, Jelliffe was more and more often reading proof in order to relieve the pressure on his friend.

Jelliffe and the Foreign Relations of Medicine

In his editorial work, Jelliffe continued to act as mediator for European ideas, and he felt that he served the same function in his other major joint venture with White, the textbook. "As for the newer work in Psychiatry," Jelliffe wrote to his collaborator, "I feel that our jumping right into the Freudian Psychiatry put us way ahead from the beginning and that practically little of the older Kraepelinian Psychiatry is of very much value. Still at the same time, I feel sure that a certain amount of linking of French and German ideas with our own may be advisable. They are reaching out for some more dynamic explanation even behind the descriptive mask, and from this point of view I feel sure that some systematic reading of the chief Psychiatrical Journals would give a number of useful correlations [for the textbook revision]."[63]

By the 1920's, as Jelliffe was already recognizing in that letter, the relationship of the United States to Europe was changing. European psychiatry was increasingly discouraging innovation, and the neurosciences suffered great disadvantages there, not least of which was the fact that the wartime destruction and dismantling of the laboratories were only very slowly being repaired (and then often with American money, chiefly from the Rockefeller Foundation). During the 1930's Jelliffe wrote to a correspondent: "As you may not know, Vienna was my 'Wanderjahr' city in 1891 and its people and locale have always appealed to me strongly. It was sad to visit it after the war when compared with previous visits."[64]

After the war Jelliffe had been reluctant to resume the traveling to Europe that he had so often done before. Not the least inhibiting factor was the expense involved.[65] But he soon fell into his old habits.

61. William Alanson White to Jelliffe, 12 and 13 August 1925.
62. Jelliffe to William Alanson White, 2 April 1927.
63. Jelliffe to William Alanson White, 16 December 1921, White Papers, Box 20.
64. Jelliffe to J. J. Michaels, 14 January 1936.
65. Jelliffe to William Alanson White, 16 May 1919, White Papers, Box 19.

In 1921 he was abroad from 21 May to 21 October, visiting France, Switzerland, Austria, Italy, Germany, the Netherlands, and England.[66] It was on
this trip that Freud and Jelliffe met personally, although in a way that left
Jelliffe discomfited (see the correspondence in Part II). In 1924 Jelliffe was
the official American Neurological Association representative to the Congress
of French Alienists and Neurologists in Brussels in August and in September
to the meetings of the German neurologists in Innsbruck. He also was in
England, the Netherlands, and France. In 1925 he was gone from 15 August
to 20 October and attended the International Psychoanalytic Congress at Bad
Homburg and the meetings of the German Society for Psychiatry. In 1927
between 20 August and 11 October he visited Paris, Innsbruck (attending
the International Psychoanalytic Congress), Vienna (more professional congresses), Semmering, Merano, Amsterdam, and London. The records give
indications of the kinds of professional ties he was maintaining. At the psychoanalytic meetings he had luncheon with a group that included important
international figures in the movement such as Eitingon, Alexander, and Kardiner, and in Vienna one of his luncheons included world leaders of general
psychiatry such as the Nobel Prize winner, Wagner-Jauregg. Wagner-Jauregg
in 1926 sponsored Jelliffe's election as corresponding member of the Vienna
Society for Psychiatry and Neurology, one of many honors that came to
Jelliffe in his international role. Part II includes a record of his meeting with
Freud on this trip.

Jelliffe was abroad again in 1928, from 23 June to early August, attending
many professional meetings and including visits to Paris, London, Antwerp,
and Amsterdam. Then in 1929 he made the last of his great pilgrimages (16
July–16 August), this time to the Psychoanalytic Congress at Oxford, with
side trips elsewhere.[67] It was while on that trip, apparently, that he failed to
sell out before the Wall Street Crash. That he did not thereafter continue
his travels is eloquent testimony to the financial as well as physical changes
that he experienced in the 1930's.

The trips—some of which figure in his correspondence with Freud—of
course served merely to facilitate and reinforce Jelliffe's work as American
mediator of European neurology and psychiatry. Obviously, he and White
went systematically through the newest literature looking for items that might
serve well in translation (and much of the monograph series in fact consisted
of such translations). In 1926, for example, Jelliffe wrote to White about the
writings of two senior European analysts:

"I have read Sadger's letter and am in somewhat of a quandry as to know
how to answer it. We have one of Sadger's works in the Series and you know
how well it sells. Sadger is an important person and does good work but is
very obscure in his writing. He probably could be put into good English

66. Smith Ely Jelliffe, "A Neuropsychiatric Pilgrimage," *JNMD*, 56 (1922), 239–248.
67. Scrapbooks in the Additional Papers document these travels.

however and be made available. The special work on the Psychopathia Sexualia [sic] mentioned in the letter never impressed me very much as a work itself. But I do feel that we could advantageously add some material of this kind because it does have an appeal. I will go over it a little more carefully with your inquiry in view.

"This leads me to a further thought that I was turning over the other night when I could not sleep very well—namely the advisability of putting some of Abraham's works in our Series. I feel, as I think you do, that good English translations of psychoanalytic material are very much needed. I know, as I know you do also, that as yet the buying public is hard to reach, and that the really scientific people in the United States are few and far between and that we always have to pitch our note a little lower than we ourselves would like. But with our two magazines we ought to be able to get out some books that would be of benefit to the Series."[68]

Jelliffe, conscious of his role as international broker of ideas, was disgusted with Americans who could not see the value of cultivating a transnational medical-scientific community. In 1936 the American Neurological Association embarrassed him by refusing to follow his recommendation to elect a South American neurologist to honorary membership. Jelliffe concluded unhappily that his U.S. colleagues were narrow-minded snobs who in the bargain could not read Spanish or Portuguese.[69]

Jelliffe was by no means overly impressed by imported ideas or overseas dignitaries. He especially resented the way in which some Europeans, particularly those in the sphere of psychoanalysis (and especially, as Jelliffe saw it, Alfred Adler) tried to exploit Americans. At one point in the 1920's he described to his English friend, S. A. K. Wilson, how in the United States "a surplus of psychoanalysts is among us lusting after the American dollar. How they all hate us because we have it and 'give it to them.' Ferenczi came first, then Rank and now Adler. It is all very amusing."[70] To an American analyst who in 1930 had solicited financial contributions for a psychoanalytic hospital in Germany Jelliffe wrote a polite but firm refusal: ". . . it is largely due to having too many irons in the fire already, and I have some resistances which lie chiefly along old lines of European criticism of our 'bourgeois scholarship' and 'preoccupation with the almighty dollar.' I have noted now for 40 years this depreciation of our culture at the same time that they plead for our money."[71] And in fact Jelliffe had repeatedly to inform Europeans who submitted manuscripts in the hope of making money that "no scientific publication in the U.S.A. pays for contributions."[72]

68. Jelliffe to William Alanson White, 23 March 1926.
69. Jelliffe to H. A. Riley, 3 January 1936.
70. Jelliffe to S. A. K. Wilson, 11 January 1927.
71. Jelliffe to Dorian Feigenbaum, 7 July 1930.
72. For example, Jelliffe to Richard Brachwitz, 21 April 1938.

By the early 1930's Jelliffe's position as agent of international good will led him into another activity: trying to help refugees from Nazi persecution. His correspondence files contain a large number of melancholy letters begging his help for people whose livelihoods had been destroyed and whose lives were soon in grave danger. Many of the writers underlined the desperate nature of their plight by describing the actions of German and American officials or detailing the fates of family members. Traces of this kind of correspondence appear also in Part II. A shadow across Jelliffe's last years, therefore, was his inability really to help many of the Europeans who turned to him. In September 1933, he wrote to the eminent neurologist, Robert Wartenberg, in Freiburg:

"I do remember you very well and I regret most sincerely the difficulties which have arisen not only for you but for so many of your compatriots. You can readily imagine that your plaint has been preceded by many others and now for nearly a year we have been doing what we could for others in similar situations.

"It has not been easy since our own economic situation while incomparably better than in Europe, has nevertheless been much damaged. Credit extension has left us all in a very unenviable position.

"Six months ago . . . I made a personal and letter canvass of all of our institutions, nearly a hundred of them, Hospitals, Clinics, private and University, etc., etc. They were all turning our own men away, reducing their staff, cutting their salaries, and making strenuous efforts to keep in their budget limits.

"Matters seem a little on the mend at the present time although for myself, the private physician, I see another poor winter ahead. So that I would be an 'ignis fatuum' to hold out much hope to you at the present time.

"My view is purely an individual one but it reflects fairly accurately the entire situation. Some of your colleagues began coming to us 3–4 years ago. Many of them have been fortunate in taking some root in the new soil but not all, like Schilder, for instance, have found a safe resting place.

"If anything advantageous should develop I shall certainly remember you."[73]

Wartenberg was both early and lucky, for he ended up at the University of California medical school in San Francisco. Other letters from Europe, particularly those later in the 1930's, had unhappy sequels.

Increasingly therefore Jelliffe felt frustrated by his inability to aid refugees. He wrote many letters—at considerable cost to himself—searching for places that might be available for people who had to have employment before they could enter the United States. In one of these letters, to White, he complained that "you know I have little influence anywhere other than the *Journal*'s backing and I do not know how much that stands for. If you think of anything

73. Jelliffe to Robert Wartenberg, 12 September 1933.

in this connection, let me know."[74] Many professionals who did escape from Nazi persecution were appropriately grateful to Jelliffe for what he did.[75] But others, who were beyond his aid, were very troubling, and for once Jelliffe's independence, a relative lack of institutional and personal ties beyond a certain level of sociability at meetings, constituted a distinct handicap, as he felt it. Of course American colleagues with excellent connections also felt the same frustrations in trying to aid refugees, but they were mostly much less well acquainted overseas than he.

Jelliffe the Analyst

Among the analysts, Jelliffe did become more and more central and acceptable—but that affiliation in turn tended to set him apart from mainstream neurology and psychiatry.

Jelliffe's involvement with psychoanalysis went through a number of stages that reflected changes in psychoanalysis as much as in Jelliffe. During the 1910's, when he first identified himself with Freud's movement, he was, as was noted in Chapter 2, still in part eclectic, but as the years went on his involvement and his conviction grew. He continued freely to make everyday interpretations of himself—and sometimes others—that indicated how habitually he thought in psychoanalytic terms. To one correspondent he wrote, for example, in reductionistic ways characteristic of the time: "Sea stories have always left me a bit cold. Repression of my homo component probably but the salt water on the skin and fingers has always been a bit annoying. Urinary no doubt."[76]

But exactly what psychoanalytic terms Jelliffe used did finally make a substantial difference. His sometimes cavalier embracing of various viewpoints—in the American eclectic tradition—alienated him for some years from Brill, his friend who had converted him initially, and from Brill's increasingly exclusive group, the New York Psychoanalytic Society. In their eyes Jelliffe's enthusiasm was no substitute for correct beliefs about a number of matters, and Jelliffe's relationship to the Society over the years paralleled and reflected his relationship to psychoanalysis in general.

Although Jelliffe was not a founding member of the New York Psychoanalytic Society at its beginning, on 12 February 1911, he joined within the year, on 28 November 1911, and in February 1912 the small group met at his house.[77] In 1913 the society made the *Psychoanalytic Review* its official organ "purely," as the secretary noted, "as a favor to Drs. Jelliffe and White."

74. Jelliffe to William Alanson White, 25 May 1936.
75. There were also, of course, those like Paul Schilder, who had received an extraordinary amount of recognition and also help from Jelliffe, but after settling in the United States hurt Jelliffe's feelings by not citing his work and offended him by referring patients to European émigré analysts only. See Karl Menninger to Jelliffe, 30 June 1938.
76. Jelliffe to Louis J. Bragman, 4 December 1936.
77. This point is covered in Chapter 2, in another context.

That same year Jelliffe was suspended because of a "misunderstanding" (the exact nature of which is not known) and later reinstated. Then at some point (of which there is no record) Jelliffe came to be no longer a member. The society, at about the same time, began to reflect a far more restrictive point of view than was customary then in America (denying membership, for example, to a Jungian analyst, Beatrice Hinkle, as early as 1915). In March 1919, the society resolved to initiate action with the county medical society to prevent four lay analysts in New York from practicing medicine without a license. The effort came to nothing, but it is significant that two of the four, Elida Evans and Thomas Libbin, were associates or former associates of Jelliffe (and also, as noted in letters printed in Part II, of Jung). Yet later that same year, on the initiative of a phone call from Jelliffe to Brill, the society also considered protesting a play that portrayed psychoanalysis unfavorably.[78]

In March 1920 Jelliffe applied for renewed membership in the society. He evidently had reason to think that his application would be accepted. In July he wrote to Ernest Jones: "During the war the Psa Society languished a good deal, now I think we will revive and get down to brass tacks again."[79] But the society refused to recommend his membership. It was at that point, after more than a year, that Brill wrote to Jelliffe, in response to Jelliffe's book on technique, and told him frankly what was wrong with his ideas about psychoanalysis, as Brill saw it. Brill was pleased with Jelliffe's assertion that he was in accord with Freud's generalizations, "but maybe the very few generalizations make the distinction." Brill hoped that a second edition of Jelliffe's book on technique would be more favorable to Freudian views, especially because some beginners, he said, had been misled by Jelliffe's words.[80]

Brill then took Jelliffe to task for supporting lay analysis. "You have, in my opinion, done no good to [psychoanalysis] by harboring and encouraging such persons as Libin [sic]. I have seen some people who went to him just because of his former connections with you. . . . I wish to assure you that despite this one disapproval I have the highest regards for you as a scientist and a man whose motives I do not question."[81] As noted above, and suggested in Jung's late July 1915 letter (Part II), in Jelliffe's case, at least, sympathy with Jung and with lay analysis were associated.

At some point in the early 1920's Jelliffe must have cleansed himself of his Jungian aura, for a year and a half after Brill's letter Oberndorf, one of

---

78. New York Psychoanalytic Society minutes, A. A. Brill Papers, Box 3. The other two lay analysts were Herman DeFren and James Oppenheim.
79. Jelliffe to Ernest Jones, 8 July 1920. Because of the use of the term "society" it is presumed that this was the New York group, not the American Psychoanalytic Association.
80. Ibid. A. A. Brill to Jelliffe, 1 May 1921. See Chapter 2.
81. Ibid. Libbin appears again in Part II. Jelliffe in 1928 forwarded to him in Los Angeles a reprimand for representing himself as certified by the Vienna Institute.

the New York society's most zealous officers, was assuring Jelliffe that his "attitude" concerning lay analysis was the only barrier to his being elected to society membership. By the beginning of 1923 Jelliffe was trying to pressure his way back into the group. He wrote to Oberndorf:

"I still would like to be a member of the New York Psa. Society.

"I also maintain that a society's by-laws are not meant to control members' conduct apart from those which are the chief reasons for the existence of a special society.

"From what Dr. Brill mentioned in our recent talk it would seem that the old problem of independence of action relative to the subscription for the old *Zentralblatt f. Psa.* still rankles. The subsequent fate of this Journal; the internal difficulties in the psa. movement, etc., etc., are all evidences, I believe, that the position maintained by me at the time was sound.

"I never refused, even to demur, as to my personal subscription. My controversy was a personal one, then, with an arbitrary secretary ruling, which interestingly enough was utilized for personal motives, since there were others who were not at all subjected to the same rulings. But this is old stuff and hardly worth recording, save as material bearing on individual motivation."[82]

Later that year the extremes to which pressure was put on Jelliffe appeared in a letter from Oberndorf recounting what happened when Jelliffe was nominated to be secretary of the American Psychoanalytic Association, in which the New York group, represented by Brill, Oberndorf, and Stern, was increasingly influential: "I am very sorry that after you had been kind enough to accept the nomination for secretary of the American Psychoanalytic, when nominations were read, objection was made from the floor and Dr. Stern also nominated. He was subsequently elected. I regret that you and Dr. Clark left so early that there was no adequate explanation of your position in regard to the psychoanalytic movement."[83]

Finally, early in 1924, Brill wrote to Jelliffe: "I am paving the way to have you and some others return to the P.A. society, which I hope will come soon." Jelliffe was, indeed, elected to membership on 24 February 1925. Two months later the group met again at Jelliffe's house, and by January 1926 he was serving as a member of the council of the society.[84]

Clearly these institutional changes reflected intellectual changes also. Throughout this period Jelliffe's appreciation of Freud deepened continually.

82. Jelliffe to C. P. Oberndorf, 6 January 1923. This matter is also taken up in Freud's letter to White; see below.

83. C. P. Oberndorf to Jelliffe, 6 June 1923. Linking Jelliffe to Clark, who was an old friend but eccentric sometimes to the point of dishonesty, was a sly maneuver of Oberndorf's.

84. Minutes of the New York Psychoanalytic Society, Brill Papers. A. A. Brill to Jelliffe, 15 February 1924. See Nathan G. Hale, Jr., "Freud's Reich, the Psychiatric Establishment, and the Founding of the American Psychoanalytic Association," *Journal of the History of the Behavioral Sciences*, 15 (1979), 139.

In 1923 he criticized reservations that he found in J. T. MacCurdy's book
on dynamic psychiatry. "I can readily imagine," he commented to Jones,
"certain limitations [arising] from paucity of psychiatric material in Freud's
statements but every time I reread something of his I see he sees deeper than
I first interpreted it."[85] It was this process of seeing deeper that continued
over the years, as was reflected in Jelliffe's increasingly harsh criticism of
Jung and other non-Freudians (see, for example, Jelliffe's letter to Freud, 8
June 1926, Part II). In 1932, at about the time Jelliffe and Jung ceased
corresponding, Jelliffe commented to the psychologist, Gardner Murphy, as
he had to Jung himself, that Jung's work was too much like Husserl's and
not close enough to the facts for Jelliffe's taste or understanding.[86]

Jelliffe nevertheless often found it difficult to mesh with the European
Freudian community, even though, as noted above, he very early had good
personal relations with Abraham and many others. Jelliffe and White were
unable to publish in the monograph series translations of many major psychoanalytic works because, as Jelliffe explained in 1928, the Internationaler
Psychoanalytischer Verlag, the official publishers of the analytic movement,
"have asked impossible prices for translation rights. . . ." In 1932 Jelliffe
told Alexander that he and White had done the best that they could with the
Review "in the light of practical compromise situations. . . . I think as your
study of American conditions becomes more and more filled out you will see
that we have done a good piece of work with the environmental realities.
. . . We cannot hope to be of . . . service without survival." Alexander, in
reply, stated frankly, "I understand that the policy which you have pursued
with the *Psychoanalytic Review* was the absolutely necessary compromise with
the given situation."[87] Under the circumstances of course it galled Jelliffe
when he found colleagues less understanding than Alexander, especially as
Jelliffe was moving toward a more orthodox position, and at a considerable
cost, as is suggested in his correspondence with Jung (Part II).

For years, however, Jelliffe was very far from orthodox, as has been noted.
It is ironic, therefore, that his initial major publications in psychoanalysis
were in the area of method. In addition to his technique monograph, his
particular interest in transference and countertransference caused him to
publish separately on that subject and refer to it frequently in print.

Jelliffe and His Lay Assistants

His concern with transference coincided with his work with lay assistants—
work, noted in several places above, and in the correspondence published in

85. Jelliffe to Ernest Jones, 6 May 1923.
86. Jelliffe to Gardner Murphy, 16 February 1932. Again Jelliffe spoke very bitterly about
Adler in the same letter.
87. Jelliffe to Mary R. Barkes, 9 April 1928. Jelliffe to Franz Alexander, 18 May 1932. Franz
Alexander to Jelliffe, 21 May 1932. Freud's own works were already committed—or overcom-
mitted—but other writings could have been translated.

Part II, that was so unusual as to be of great historical interest. One aspect of transference that led to his employing an assistant was his experience that transference was difficult to effect with psychotic patients. Comparing three persons in a therapeutic relationship to both a family and the Christian Trinity, Jelliffe suggested that "by utilizing such a deeply psychical principle, a different approach might be made in dementia praecox on an earlier level and a transference accomplished, not toward one person but toward two." The patient addressed the "specially trained nurse or attendant . . . gradually permitting the extroversion of interest at lower intensities, so that the excessive affect has opportunity tentatively and gradually to release itself."[88] For whatever reason, Jelliffe's recommendation here to use lay assistants was endorsed by the distinguished pioneer in the psychoanalysis of psychotic patients, Edward J. Kempf.[89]

The other aspect of transference that impelled Jelliffe to introduce lay assistants was his observation that many patients, male as well as female, did better in analysis with a woman rather than a man, and in fact the assistants of whom any detailed records exist were all women. Sometimes the advantage occurred only at the beginning, where "the woman analyst can thus in some cases take the brunt of the first libido," and the male analyst could then continue the therapy. Other patients, Jelliffe continued, should have all of their analyses with a woman.[90]

Aside from a few allusions in print and the correspondence with Jung and Freud printed in Part II, little evidence remains to indicate the full extent of Jelliffe's involvement with assistants or exactly how he dealt with them. One exchange of letters does provide a glimpse of Jelliffe's activity and attitude just as he was moving toward a more "medical" position. In 1922 Elida Evans, who was treating patients by means of psychoanalysis and who had worked with Jelliffe as a lay analyst and collaborated with him on the psoriasis paper, wrote asking him to refer patients to her. "I presume that you have so much demand for cases," she ventured, "since Dr. Stragnell and Miss Brink, and goodness knows how many others are with you, that there are no left-overs to come here. But, just the same, I shall never forget how extremely kind you were once upon a time."[91] Louise Brink, as noted above, was a long-time collaborator with Jelliffe, and Gregory Stragnell, M.D., was Jelliffe's son-in-law; there is, however, no other evidence that Stragnell ever conducted his practice in close collaboration with Jelliffe. Since there was another office in the house, Jelliffe's use and supervision of collaborators was easy for him, and Mabel Dodge Luhan (quoted below, Chapter

88. Smith Ely Jelliffe, "Contributions to Psychotherapeutic Technique through Psychoanalysis," *Psychoanalytic Review*, 6 (1919), 11–12.

89. Edward J. Kempf, "Psychoanalytic Treatment of Dementia Praecox, Report of a Case," *Psychoanalytic Review*, 6 (1919), 18–19.

90. Jelliffe, "Contributions to Psychotherapeutic Technique," pp. 11–14.

91. Elida Evans to Jelliffe, 29 November 1922.

4), describes one in the house who sounds much like Brink. Years later Jelliffe, in writing to Freud (4 November 1938, Part II) mentioned that he, Jelliffe, had taken only two lay assistants "under my wing," and this figure may be the more accurate one, in contrast to "a number" of assistants he mentioned to Jones in 1927 (see below, this chapter).

In replying to Evans in 1922, Jelliffe did not comment directly on her question but indicated that he did give strong supervision. After discussing certain cases that he had referred to her and she to him, noting that he "had really very few to refer," Jelliffe concluded, "The cases you cite are everywhere. They surround us on all sides. People are only just beginning to realize their importance. In working with them I can only advise one thing, even though it seems unnecessary. Always keep in touch with the medical man that sent the case, and if they come without insist you get a letter from their doctor asking your aid. This you should keep as your guarantee.

"I feel that one has to be extra careful to avoid the *"lay-Freudian"* criticism. No matter how stupid the profession has been in this as well as in many other newer discoveries in medicine, in the end they test out the hypotheses the most stringently, and the steady advance of a solid medicine has always given the calling a preeminence in the collective unconscious which it really deserves."[92]

By the time that Jelliffe was writing to Evans, the pressure of Brill and other Americans (in contrast to Europeans) to keep psychoanalysis within the profession of medicine, as already remarked, was affecting Jelliffe. In 1926, before the New York Psychoanalytic Society, he made an explicit recantation.[93] The next year he wrote an autobiographical letter to Jones explaining how he had come to stand against lay analysis as he did.

"You may know, that of the New York men I have from the beginning espoused the cause of the necessity for a broader utilization of psychoanalytic assistants, medical, lay, or otherwise. This was as early as 1910 on my return to New York, after a broken three year interregnum spent in Europe, as I felt, that unless I cut myself from the slavish neuropsychiatric models that I had been forced into, nothing but a repetition compulsion of older attitudes of mind would be my lot. I made the break and flung myself into the newer movements for better or worse.

"Through many discussions with Brill, I came to a clearer conception of the general psychoanalytic conceptions, towards which both White and myself in our many years of close personal contact, had been veering. Both of us,

92. Jelliffe to Elida Evans, 4 December 1922. Evans's book, *The Problem of the Nervous Child* (New York, 1920), contained an introduction by C. G. Jung; Jelliffe's name did not even appear in the index. Earlier she had worked with Trigant Burrow and others in Baltimore and in New York, and at one point, when she had opened a large house to care for "delicate or nervous children," she gave both Burrow and Jelliffe as references. Elida Evans to Adolf Meyer, 5 February 1915 and 18 November 1920, in Adolf Meyer Papers, I-1088-1.
93. *International Journal of Psycho-Analysis*, 8 (1927), 308.

White and I, were dissatisfied with the Socratic static absolutisms, as were the reigning attitudes, and felt that a dynamic psychology was necessary. This I found in the Freudian conceptions, and the conflicts were resolved in a wholehearted desire to apply the principles and see where they led. Thus for me, the psychoanalytic method of investigation became of primary significance. It satisfied the urgings of research and gave adequate proof of its pragmatic values in therapeutic efforts. . . .

"Believing as I did, and do, that the psyche was as old as the soma (White's favorite phrasing), I arrived at a Neo-Hippocratic attitude and was not afraid to meet the issues.

"You probably know how this, of necessity, precipitated a break, with the reigning attitudes in this, the U.S.A. neurological crystallizations. This is personal history and possibly of secondary importance.

"So when I came to utilize psychoanalytic principles I soon found the necessity for accessory aid. Many problems came to my consultation room and I sought assistance where I could find it—not always wisely as later experience demonstrated. I developed a number of semi-trained and more fully trained assistants. These might be envisaged as 'lay analysts.'

"My activities in this line naturally produced the reactions pro and con which are now under discussion. In actual relations these kept me out of our local psychoanalytic society which were more or less dogmatic contra, on the situation. Some of the members, it is unnecessary to mention their names, considered me anathema because I had lay assistants. And I watched and learned and, in short gradually swung to the opposite pole, and now rest, for the time being, in this attitude.

"This seems to be reinforced from several angles. May I mention some?

"Primarily, I believe that every maladjustment, which in our frame of activity may be called 'disease,' has a psychogenic component. Naturally I am not asinine enough to include therein the realm of pure 'accident.' A dislodged brick on a corner stone that hits a passer by, I do not include as of psychogenic importance. The infectious diseases may also be excluded—although constitutional studies may show some psychogenic capacity for 'dispositional' implication; these apart, psychogenesis cannot be a priorally excluded. Hence my studies in organic disease, coincident with and parallel to Groddeck's similar researches. Thus I handed over patients with epileptic manifestations, tuberculosis, tumor formation, diabetic situations and others to my assistants, as research problems.

"Apart from a detailed recapitulation of these problems I finally arrived at disappointment, and why? These problems which I myself could envisage since I had a biological and medical background, could not be seen by my assistants in the necessary larger frame which would hope for solution.

"So after 15 years of reality testing I have come to believe that only those thoroughly trained in biogenetic lines can adequately envisage the 'proteus' of 'medicine.' . . . that only a student well versed in the *machine*, as well as its *functions*, can really deal with the situation. So long as the machine per se is considered of paramount importance no advance can be made. Here is the dilemma of the structuralist as opposed to the functionalist. . . ."

Jelliffe believed that physicians, however inadequately they dealt with psychological factors, could be sensitized.

"As for the so called 'practical' issues, it is well recognized by those who see the many problems to be met that the 'physician' is illy equipped to meet the situation. The many 'cults' offer evidence of this 'medical' unpreparedness. These never would have come into prominence—Christian Science, Mental Healing, Couéism, and innumerable other aspects of pseudo-medical practices, if the 'doctor' had been *on the job*—i.e., if he had really, sincerely and deeply appreciated the 'human being as a whole' instead of the partitioning of the body into its 'diseases.' "[94]

One of the factors that apparently influenced Jelliffe against lay analysts was the fact that a number of them came from Europe and exploited Americans and often discredited psychoanalysis. Reverberations of Jelliffe's indignation, suggested above, continued in his correspondence for many years, including that with Freud (6 March 1939).[95] In the 1930's, when more really well qualified non-M.D. analysts came to the United States, Jelliffe was sympathetic but explained to them that lay analysis had acquired a bad reputation. Even domestic lay analysts disappointed Jelliffe. "The more I see of lay analysis and those who are in favor of it," he wrote to Jones in 1927, "I feel certain that the economic basis behind it is a very important element."[96]

Jelliffe and Mainstream Psychoanalysis

Jelliffe's heavy commitment to psychoanalytic practice continued in spite of the fact that it was not the most profitable practice. "Psychoanalysis, after all," he wrote to an old friend in 1926, was, because of the time it took, "not a paying business." Moreover, Jelliffe continued to have various kinds of reservations and difficulties with psychoanalysis. In 1933 he wrote to another friend about his "chief difficulty in the psychoanalytic situation, namely, the increasing conviction of the chronicity and malignancy of most of the psychoneuroses; especially the narcissistic ones. They are hell and I get dis-

94. Jelliffe to Ernest Jones, 10 February 1927. One minor correction has been made as Jelliffe requested of Jones (8 April 1927). Excerpts from this letter were published in "Discussion on Lay Analysis," *International Journal of Psycho-Analysis*, 8 (1927), 223–224. The discussion of lay analysis continued to rankle with analysts on both sides of the Atlantic, and Jelliffe and Freud were still corresponding about it in the late 1930's (see Part II).

95. See especially Jelliffe to W. Stekel, 27 March 1926. Jelliffe to Paul Federn, 9 April 1928, was concerned that Ferenczi, who was speaking in New York, would, like Adler, discredit psychoanalysis by associating it with social or political radicalism.

96. Jelliffe to Ernest Jones, 10 March 1927.

couraged not with the inadequacy of the conceptions, but with the pegging of the patients. They slip away so easily."[97] And the next year he noted that "I prefer to call myself a 'physician' rather than anything else. 'Psychoanalyst' is one using a circumscribed method of study and is too limiting a title."[98]

Jelliffe's relationship with psychoanalysis was complicated not only by his persisting medical—"uncircumscribed"—orientation but by a sharp generational conflict among the analysts, a conflict that led to Jelliffe's getting bruised badly on occasion, and one that, as has already been noted, complicated his relationship to the *Psychoanalytic Review*. Younger, "orthodox" analysts tended even before the formal advent of ego psychology to emphasize rigid, rigorous technique and theory and to eschew constructs that were not clearly parsimonious. Jelliffe, by contrast, always remained partially a Jungian. He never surrendered the use of ancestral psychological accretions, recapitulation, and neo-Lamarckianism in general. From his point of view the result was the same, he said, whether one followed Mendel, deVries, or the neo-Lamarckians.[99] Jelliffe even welcomed Freud's idea of a death instinct, a concept the most narrow of the new orthodox analysts pointedly ignored.

Jelliffe's chief effort to contribute to psychoanalytic theory was his "paleopsychology," an idea that he first developed in his pre–World War I Jungian period. Jelliffe paralleled this view of psychical functioning to paleobotany or paleozoology and suggested that the investigator could find evidences of ancestral forms of thought in traces of the unconscious. Jelliffe, as he suggested in the *Text-Book* introduction, believed that energy came from the cosmos not only through ordinary metabolism/catabolism but also through impressions upon sensory organs, which created what Freud conceptualized as psychical energy. Paleopsychology consisted of tracing patterns in the ways that human beings processed energy of all kinds, patterns that in the here and now in part recapitulated earlier stages. Knowing the earlier stages helped explain current thinking and behavior.

It was within this schema, then, that Jelliffe came to speak of "the symbol as energy container," meaning that symbolization represented the patterns through which the energy was processed. He went on to develop graphic representations of what were appropriate and what were inappropriate archaic elements in individual patients' symptoms. The representations also paralleled the levels of functioning taught by Hughlings Jackson and absorbed by Freud in his day and Jelliffe later. Jelliffe expected by this approach to contribute to a holistic view of the patient, in which physical and mental,

97. Jelliffe to Stewart Paton, 25 November 1926. Jelliffe to J. Ramsay Hunt, 14 January 1933. The similarity of some of Jelliffe's disillusionment to that of Freud is striking.
98. Jelliffe to Karl Menninger, 21 May 1934.
99. Smith Ely Jelliffe, "Technique of Psychoanalysis," *Psychoanalytic Review*, 2 (1915), 411. Jelliffe never changed his mind on this point.

constitutional and acquired, could be conceptualized in one single, dynamic pattern.[100]

It was in this sense and in this context that Jelliffe became very much a hereditarian. "In my clinical work," he wrote, "I have seen so many neuroses which were exact replicas to the second, third and fourth generation that I feel assured that we as physicians can not dismiss our problems by invoking Mendel or other authority to solve them."[101]

In his emphasis on energy and on teleology, with his idea that the bodily entity was trying to do something, as in the death instinct, Jelliffe was moving in a direction precisely opposite to that in which psychoanalysis was developing in the closing years of his life. From the 1920's on, he attempted in his correspondence, speaking, and writing to convey his notions, but his colleagues tended to ignore his ideas, ideas that never did find an appropriate ecological niche in the competition in the marketplace of ideas. Jelliffe therefore felt profoundly frustrated in his endeavors.

A good example of the barriers that Jelliffe met was the review that John Rickman, the English psychoanalyst, wrote of Jelliffe's monograph on technique. Since the monograph represented Jelliffe's early work (2d edition, 1920), and the review appeared in 1923, before he was in the good graces of many strictly Freudian analysts, Rickman was very harsh. He praised the long passages translated from Freud and Rank, but he contrasted them with directives out of Jelliffe's own analytic practice. "The advice," Rickman remarked, "obviously does not originate in deep psycho-analytical experience," and in any event the work would not be needed since Freud's papers on technique were now translated. Jelliffe's "philosophy" Rickman characterized as "unique." Like so many others, Rickman found Jelliffe's speculations hard to accept. "His intellectual daring, which sometimes strikes deep, sometimes goes astray. . . ." Rickman continued with a specific and central example. "The author is overwhelmed by the age of the earth and the antiquity of man. . . . This psycho-paleontology, I have no doubt, means a lot to Dr. Jelliffe, but does he not concentrate too much on 'thought fossils' (p. 135) to the neglect of the dynamics of his subject?" Rickman then went on to quote Jelliffe's idea that psychoanalysis consisted of tracing back the life history of the patient to the archaic. "The author's advice on technique finds characteristic expression in the use of libido-charts or 'psychograms,'" which are to be discussed with the patient, and Rickman noted that, while examples of the charts were given, "the patients' comments on them are not." Rickman

100. See Bibliography. Jelliffe's aspirations were parallel to and contemporary with those of the architects of personality theory who achieved intellectual dominance before and after World War II.

101. See especially Smith Ely Jelliffe, "Paleopsychology: A Tentative Sketch of the Origin and Evolution of Symbolic Function," *Psychoanalytic Review*, 10 (1923), 121–139; and Smith Ely Jelliffe, "The Death Instinct in Somatic and Psychopathology," *Psychoanalytic Review*, 20 (1933), 121–132.

concluded by saying explicitly that Jelliffe was not orthodox: "Thus we see that for him analysis is not the overcoming of resistances—a proof that he has not moved with the times."[102] "The overcoming of resistances" was at the time still the brief description Freudians were using to describe their goal.

Jelliffe's Broad Approach to Psychoanalysis

Throughout his career as an analyst Jelliffe persisted in taking a broad and tolerant view of various kinds of psychoanalysts, and for some time in the early years this was the general stance (apart from the lay analysis issue) that estranged him not only from Freud personally but from the New York group. Thus in 1920 he complained that, when Johann Rudolf Katz, a Jungian, had visited New York, he gave what Jelliffe considered a fine presentation, "but the Frink-Oberndorf-Brill contingent almost spoiled the situation" by their hostility to Katz's particular orientation.[103]

In the closing years of his life Jelliffe continued to maintain a broad approach. In writing of the dilution of psychoanalysis as it spread through American psychiatry, Jelliffe observed that "certain superlative natures have been happy to view this enormous extension as an expression of American superficiality." But, he added, "it takes a hot fire to have wide-spread irradiations."[104] Jelliffe just was not overwhelmed by anything or anyone orthodox. In a private letter to a neurotic physician seeking treatment, he commented on Ernest Jones in 1924: "In spite of Jones' 200 hours [of analysis], I am certain that he, Jones, has become so acid—about life in general and his own situations in particular, that he has become incapable of love and hence could not help you in your dilemma."[105]

Yet Jelliffe also, beginning in the late 1920's, as suggested by his relationship to the New York Society, operated within the strictly Freudian psychoanalytic establishment. He even savored in-group gossip—as much as he savored any gossip, which was not much. In 1929 he wrote to a young analyst about a European colleague: "As for 'Seif.' I know of him. If he had cured [Stanley] Cobb of his stuttering I would say fine—but Cobb is afraid to get to the bottom of his trouble and so would go to an Adler disciple who all dodge the real issues."[106]

Or, again, when the New York group was experiencing much personal conflict, he wrote to Karl Menninger: "I also heard from White of the Boston fracas. Behind the scenes there were fierce reprisal suggestions going as far

102. John Rickman, review of Jelliffe, *The Technique of Psychoanalysis*, in *International Journal of Psycho-Analysis*, 4 (1923), 207–208.

103. Jelliffe to William Alanson White, 5 November 1920, White Papers, Box 20.

104. Smith Ely Jelliffe, "Sigmund Freud and Psychiatry: A Partial Appraisal," *American Journal of Sociology*, 45 (1939), 339. See Freud correspondence in Part II.

105. Jelliffe to Charles R. Payne, 27 May 1924.

106. Jelliffe to John Murray, 4 September 1929.

as dropping [Zilboorg] from the Society and other punishments. It struck me as typically paranoid as I have already written you. Z. has already semi-disrupted the New York group. B. had resigned a few months ago and Z. is of the rule or ruin variety. I wish we could get a good film close up on that final cannibalistic oral grin of his when he finishes a sentence. It is highly characteristic. It is malignant O.K., O.K. Don't fool yourself however that Chicago has not some of the same sort."[107]

Although Jelliffe allied himself with Brill, he was, as noted above, unable to serve as permanent vice-president of the American Psychoanalytic Association. In the New York group, however, he did find himself useful, as he explained, again to Karl Menninger:

"As for the V.P. game—It doesn't amount to a pea on a Kansas prairie. I have been getting deaf and I told them I did not want to run and there you are. The amusing part is however, they dared not attack Brill—which I have no doubt Kardiner, Zilboorg, Lewin et al. wanted to do. You know this small coterie has been handing out the analytic applicants to each other for Lehr Analyse and Control Analyse until it assumed a minor graft situation. So they pitched on me—why not? It was useful to get the lines drawn as to factions.

"At all events they only succeeded in being boosted off the Educational Committee and the graft is stopped for a while."[108] Jelliffe was referring to an outstanding service of his, which consisted in heading up the new education committee, the members of which were nontraining analysts who could parcel out trainees (highly desirable, even at cut rates, in the hard depression years) without favoritism or bad feelings.[109]

All of this maneuvering occurred when the subspecialty of psychoanalysis was changing as European-trained analysts, both native and immigrant, undertook to purify American psychoanalysis, especially after about 1930. Jelliffe first suffered personally (to the point of reacting strongly) in 1928 when Ives Hendrick, a young Boston analyst, wrote harshly about Jelliffe's work on encephalitis: "It is chiefly his cosmic outlook, his insatiable urge to synthesize all attitudes toward human life—the most advanced psychoanalytic theories, demonstrable physico-chemical properties and possibilities, neuropathology and metaphysics—that handicaps Jelliffe in demonstrating a few simple and fundamental truths which those not admitted into the Inner Temple of the 'Ultra-Eruditi' can comprehend." Jelliffe wrote at once to Harry Stack Sullivan, White's friend, to ask who Hendrick was. "He spits a tobacco cud on my 'Erudite' pretensions. When they go to Boston they all seem to get that way. I am amused, as well as annoyed—for my cortical

107. Jelliffe to Karl Menninger, 12 June 1933.
108. Jelliffe to Karl Menninger, 24 February 1933.
109. Jelliffe to Ernest Jones, 2 February 1935.

pretensions are thought of as in reverse proportions to my lipoid accumulations! Maybe!"[110]

Subsequently Jelliffe was forgiving as over the years he and Hendrick corresponded in a friendly way about psychoanalysis in America and described for themselves the generational gap. "It certainly is a most extraordinary thing," wrote Hendrick, "that there should be so much cleavage between your generation of analysts, in collaboration if not in actual work, and those of us who have studied in Berlin and Vienna during the past decade." And later Hendrick noted that (as was suggested above) the *Psychoanalytic Quarterly* represented the younger group, the analysts, and the *Psychoanalytic Review*, the older group, those who had merely learned from Freud's work and used psychoanalysis in an eclectic way.[111]

Jelliffe was nevertheless capable of making an excellent case for his own analytic credentials. Not only had Freud himself mentioned Jelliffe's work favorably but Freud apparently in the 1920's had recommended Jelliffe as an analyst. Freud's nephew, New York public relations pioneer Edward L. Bernays, once sent the well-known journalist, Heywood Broun, to Jelliffe on the recommendation of the illustrious uncle.[112] In 1934 Jelliffe modestly but firmly reviewed for Hendrick his own record as a pillar of the analytic movement:

"It may be of secondary interest to you to know that I was the first to send to Alexander analytic applicants from the U.S.A. I was certain there was something of special value for certain personalities in Alexander's work.

"I have advised others to go to others—Helena Deutsch, Edward Glover, Van Ophuijsen, Groddeck, for from my knowledge of these men, their work, their personalities, and other considerations I have believed that there were variables of value not to be overlooked.

"It may be over credulousness but I am certain I am fairly well acquainted with most of the recent European viewpoints. At times, it seems to me much better than many a returned student who has but one viewpoint, that of his teacher. I therefore agree with you that many of such returned students have much to learn and I too have found many of them quite difficult.

"As for the older men I find few of them diligent enough to keep thoroughly abreast of what is going on. They are mostly over burdened with numerous cases of variable nature. I agree with you in part about certain difficulties in certain directions but in a field so new and so difficult to check up on results

110. Ives Hendrick, "Encephalitis Lethargica and the Interpretation of Mental Disease," *American Journal of Psychiatry*, 40 (1928), 990–991. Jelliffe to Harry Stack Sullivan, 28 May 1928. There is a similar review with Jelliffe's reply in *Archives of Neurology and Psychiatry*, 30 (1933), 237–239.
111. Ives Hendrick to Jelliffe, 3 January 1933 and 16 January 1933.
112. Sigmund Freud, "Two Encyclopedia Articles," *Standard Edn.*, vol. 18, p. 250. Bernays, *Biography of an Idea*, pp. 630–631.

of application of theoretical formulations I am inclined to greater charity in criticism.

"Just how the groups will develop I do not know. At present I find myself a bit encumbered with personal somatic hindrances. They make it probable that I shall soon be hardly more than an interested and appreciative spectator of the march of the newer young men now so busy in carrying the banners."[113]

In fact the time-soon came when Jelliffe did feel that he was losing his mastery in psychoanalysis. In 1939 he noted in a memo: "Sprightly evening with Lorand to meet Roheim: Rado, Stern, Zilboorg, Ames, Wittels, & Blumgart. Lively anthropological discussions, first concerning ideas of Lewin & Kardiner, then more general & then stories—at which Zilboorg distinguished himself. Felt out of it a great deal & envious of younger men."[114]

It was ironic that Jelliffe, who had been relatively lately, in the 1920's, accepted into the restricted circles, was within a few years associated with Brill as the object of conspiracy and attack by the young Turks of analytic orthodoxy in the New York group. And it was the more ironic because during the 1920's and 1930's Jelliffe gained a reputation among his colleagues as being an "extreme psychoanalyst."

Psychosomatic Medicine

Jelliffe's extremist reputation grew out of his pioneering work in psychosomatic medicine, which he carried much further and made more explicit after World War I. He was not content to work merely with the psyche of the patient but also wanted to explore somatic modes of adaptation. Likewise he spoke about the psychological aspects of plainly organic illnesses. At one point, in 1930, he even published, in the *Journal of the American Medical Association*, a suggestion that curing organic difficulties could be counterproductive, citing instances, for example, in which the effectiveness of a physician's ministrations precipitated the patient into severe mental illness.[115] Jelliffe's medical colleagues were in general flatly skeptical of his invoking mental factors in somatic illnesses. When Adolf Meyer missed a meeting in 1920, the acerbic C. Macfie Campbell of Boston wrote to him: "You were spared hearing Jelliffe outline the relationship of the sub-conscious to multiple sclerosis."[116]

Jelliffe felt that his work was very close to that of Freud's friend, Georg Groddeck, although independent of it, for both Jelliffe and Groddeck used psychoanalytic insights to open "the way to an attack on organic disease," as Jelliffe put it.[117] Groddeck wrote to him in 1921: "Your recommendation

113. Jelliffe to Ives Hendrick, 23 January 1934.
114. Memorandum in Additional Papers.
115. Smith Ely Jelliffe, "What Price Healing? A Fragmentary Inquiry," *Journal of the American Medical Association*, 94 (1930), 1393–1395.
116. C. Macfie Campbell to Adolf Meyer, 5 January 1922, Meyer Papers, I-595-11.
117. Jelliffe to Karl Menninger, [November] 1922.

of your using [psychoanalysis] in physical disorders was really very interesting for me. I believed me very lonely with the idea of beating physical diseases in that way; now to hear about your studies on the other seaside is a great satisfaction. I take it a [proof] of the reality of experience." And when he was reading the proof of Groddeck's book, of which he was publishing the first English translation, Jelliffe commented to Groddeck: "I am amazed at the wealth of suggestive material, and, feeling its great emotional value, am telling you how much the book means to me, as I now read it again. I read it in 1923 in German but only now really appreciate it. I know that you know that my own thoughts have been paralleling many of yours now for some years and I wish to say how fruitful for me yours have been."[118] But Jelliffe was more than an American version of Groddeck.

Jelliffe's work over many years in trying to introduce what in the 1930's became the psychosomatic medicine movement led to many misunderstandings besides the idea that he was an extremist in psychoanalysis. "Some critics," he complained, "have tried to make me say that the 'encephalitis' is a psychogenic syndrome. This is absurd. I have simply tried to show that the breathing disturbances—eye disturbances—etc., of *certain types* that show symbolic meanings *when studied by the psychoanalytic methodology*, are indicative of cravings and drives that cannot be handled properly because of the loss of dynamic potentials due to the failure of a part of the whole mechanism to function."[119]

On another occasion, in 1920, when he felt misunderstood, he and his audience were involved in different levels of discourse. After one of Jelliffe's papers, Adolf Meyer commented that Jelliffe had not demonstrated, nor tried to demonstrate, the specific connection between multiple sclerosis and psychological trends and types. Meyer was sympathetic to Jelliffe's point of view, Meyer said, but he believed that science compelled investigators to focus on what had actually been demonstrated, and in this case what Jelliffe had demonstrated was strictly physical. In reply Jelliffe said that he was talking diathesis, a classical medical concept involving predisposition, not the disease process itself. Clearly for Meyer and for others in the post–World War I era the connection had to be more substantial.[120]

The fact was that Jelliffe often relegated physical changes to a secondary rather than the usual primary place. In 1922, for example, he wrote that gonadal changes in patients were secondary to and derivative from the patients' libidinal development—even though, he admitted, "I cannot remain totally impervious to the implications of constitutional inferiority factors." And a decade later he declared that "Even the so-called allergic cases are

118. Georg Groddeck to Jelliffe, 20 August 1921; Jelliffe to Georg Groddeck, 14 May 1928.
119. Jelliffe to J. W. G. Ter Braak, 6 February 1933.
120. Adolf Meyer and Smith Ely Jelliffe, reported in *Archives of Neurology and Psychiatry*, 4 (1920), 595.

mostly psychological." On still another occasion he advocated using psychoanalysis in cases of senility, even where there might have been evidence of organic degeneration.[121]

Jelliffe, while viewing himself as a physician rather than an analyst, nevertheless knew that his psychosomatics came from a fundamentally psychoanalytic viewpoint. "I like to think," he wrote Hendrick in 1939, "I have made a contribution to Psychosomatic Medicine in that I have left generalizations to others and have dug into the details with Freudian tools."[122] But he did not enjoy being classified as an extremist in any context. He saw his point of view in entirely different terms, he noted, when he took "exception to one remark of Dr. [William] Healy's in which he classes me among the extreme psychoanalysts. I have no objection to being cast as stressing an extreme psychoanalytic point of view but that does not make me an extreme psychoanalyst, any more than a sharp shooter who wants to make a 100% score necessarily is a 100% shooter."[123]

Perhaps the most amusing instance of Jelliffe's being cast in an extremist's role was when both the lay and the medical press picked up his remarks about the origin of the rhythm of Irving Berlin's "Alexander's Ragtime Band." The story, as recounted in a contemporary medical journal, was attributed to White:

"Dr. White prefaced his story by saying that it seems fairly well established that the sense of time and rhythm are acquired in utero from listening to [the] mother's heartbeats. He then went on to say that Dr. Jelliffe was attending a medical meeting and the question of the remarkable rhythmical sense of a famous composer of jazz music was brought under discussion. Dr. Jelliffe suggested that possibly his mother suffered from cardiac disease. The physician who had attended the composer's mother was present. He said that she had suffered from heart trouble all of her life and had died of it." The moral that was drawn from the story was that "psychoanalysis as a method is to be distinguished from the speculations which psychoanalysts find so fascinating and which they sometimes carry to unbelievable lengths. . . ."[124]

Jelliffe and the Psychobiological Tradition

Jelliffe is best understood as perhaps the chief representative of what Robert C. Powell has called the American psychobiological tradition, which underlay

121. Jelliffe to F. W. Mott, 17 February 1922. Jelliffe to Dorrell G. Dickerson, 6 May 1932. Smith Ely Jelliffe, abstracted in *JNMD*, 61 (1925), 274–278.

122. Jelliffe to Ives Hendrick, 22 May 1939.

123. Jelliffe to E. W. Taylor, 7 February 1928.

124. Frank Whitmore, "Some Psychoanalytical Considerations," *Minnesota Medicine*, 9 (1926), 311. The publicity is described in *New York Herald Tribune*, 26 February 1945. Smith Ely Jelliffe, reported in *JNMD*, 60 (1924), 168–169.

and galvanized the development of psychosomatic medicine.[125] Jelliffe's point of view was holistic, and inclusive—which was what made him function at times as an eclectic (see the exchange of letters with Jung in 1932, Part II). By the 1920's, despite his increasing commitment to orthodoxy in psycho-analysis, Jelliffe was publishing almost exclusively about his own biological/ psychological viewpoint.[126]

One of the most finished expressions of Jelliffe's approach to illness, health, and life was in his 1933 essay on "The Death Instinct in Somatic and Psychopathology":

"It had been a commonplace observation to note a frank psychotic expression of conflict clear up and find as an alternative in the same patient a disturbed renal function, skin disorder, sinus, diabetes, or a hyperthyroid state. In a number of cyclothymic individuals there was observed a regular replacement of the one group of manifestations, by the other. When the neurotic or psychotic phenomena were in the ascendant the anomalous somatic behavior sank beneath the horizon, to emerge into definite form as the more evident 'mental' expressions in their turn faded out of the picture. And thus the replacement cycle went on.

"Finally the generalization became more clear as the conception of the holistic nature of man became more evident and the human being as a whole was seen in a constant state of unstable equilibrium and that further functional variability as evidence of the struggle of energy systems within and without the body was the rule rather than the exception."

Jelliffe went on to note that medical science had provided a precise understanding of both internal metabolic and external inputs, particularly trauma and infection. Freud, Jelliffe believed, had provided a similar understanding of "mental systems," with external social factors on one side and instincts and psychical structures on the other. Then Jelliffe spoke of his own efforts. For years, he said, he attempted to work out the dynamics of a variety of disease processes, "*trying* to separate out the conflict of the Life and Death instinctual processes that finally became encysted or segregated in an organ or organs where the fight was carried out either as a temporary moratorium or in the form of a final adjustment of claims with partial or complete destruction of the organ unconsciously chosen as a site for the conflict. . . .

"Much as I might like to comfort myself that the presentation of these analyses has been incomplete and unsatisfactory because of difficulties surrounding or bound up in all psychoanalytic case histories—some factors of which, medical secret, for instance, are of major significance, I must regret-

125. Robert C. Powell, "Helen Flanders Dunbar (1902–1959) and a Holistic Approach to Psychosomatic Problems. I. The Rise and Fall of a Medical Philosophy," *Psychiatric Quarterly*, 49 (1977), especially 135–136. For a less synthetic evaluation see Harold I. Kaplan and Helen S. Kaplan, "Historical Survey of Psychosomatic Medicine," *JNMD*, 124 (1956), 546–568, especially 554–557.
126. See Bibliography; and Jelliffe to Fritz Wittels, 27 December 1932.

fully acknowledge that the carrying through of the theoretical considerations necessary for real proof has been far from satisfactory especially when I look back upon the work of analysis where I have been late in grasping a truer significance of many situations with that firmness which later experience has permitted. . . . As it takes great patience to persistently dissect the complex and subtle psychical processes, infinitely more compounded than any other in human activities, so it would require volumes of the words and concepts now available to report such micropsychical dissections. It is revealing that Freud in his 'Fragment' of an Analysis of a Case of Hysteria, as he calls it, fills 146 large octavo pages, in English translation, and for myself there is not a useless or redundant phrase in this whole presentation."[127]

The New Emphasis in Jelliffe's Psychosomatics

Jelliffe's friends and critics alike had trouble understanding his psychosomatic approach because in condensing he tended to jump from the very specific to the highly general ("philosophical," as will have become obvious from the foregoing, was the term usually applied). But historical factors also obscured what Jelliffe was doing. His first venture into psychosomatics (Chapter 2) was showing psoriasis as a conversion hysteria, that is, an organ-specific psychosomatic disorder, with relatively specific psychical conflicts expressed somatically, as was typical of the Alexander school of psychosomatics a generation later. Only later did Jelliffe emphasize the whole body functioning as symbolic of general psychobiological adaptation, in what Powell described as the American school of psychosomatic medicine.[128]

Within this context Jelliffe's concern with two of his later works (1930–1931 and after) becomes more understandable. In both the work on oculogyric crises and on Dupuytren's contracture, Jelliffe was dealing with specific cases and specific organs but putting them into the context of the patient's general functioning and adaptation, without dividing body and mind or the various organs of the body. The oculogyric crises were not hysterical forced movements, according to Jelliffe, but represented "essential instinctive processes" that were being filtered through Jacksonian levels of nervous system functioning within which both organic damage and psychological striving and representation were determining factors. Jelliffe was trying to use specific disorders to convey his belief that the complete physician treated the whole person, and he was therefore a precursor of later holistic approaches to medicine. His concern with the details of organic processes as well as psychological dynamics, however, added up to his attempts to grasp more factors than his readers could follow or than could be included in any reasonable printed exposition. He therefore left gaps in his exposition; as, for example, in discussing a case of contracture of the hand, Jelliffe wrote, "Details of

127. Jelliffe, "The Death Instinct," pp. 122–124.
128. Powell, "Healing and Wholeness," especially pp. 55–72.

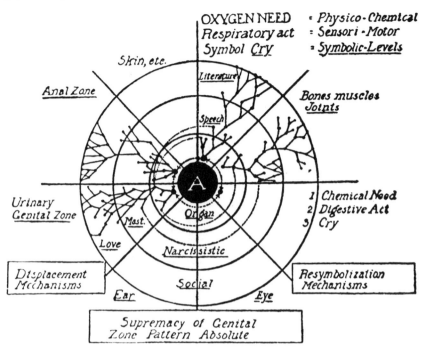

Diagram of Jelliffe's psychosomatic schema as finally developed. From Jelliffe, Sketches in Psychosomatic Medicine, *p. 18 (this figure originally published in 1932).*

this all-powerful grasping tendency, through repressed masturbatory inner urge, cannot be entered into here," for Jelliffe wanted there to describe many other details perhaps not so obvious and also more connected with the patient's general adjustment patterns. Holism, as he found, required consideration of an unmanageable number of complex factors, and most readers and listeners were unable to follow adequately and understand his ability to hold in mind simultaneously an extremely large number of variables and both specific and general levels of discourse.[129] What they often heard instead, then, was unsupported assertion and psychoanalytic extremism.

Despite his passing for "orthodox" in psychoanalysis, Jelliffe continued to be impatient with any particular or dogmatic or narrow viewpoint, and he could not mention one point of view without maintaining the concurrent validity, at some level, of another. In 1929 he wrote analyst Gregory Zilboorg: "The psychodynamics of constitution, as you know, interests me greatly. I am thoroughly sold on the idea that form and structure are strongly under

129. See especially Smith Ely Jelliffe, "Dupuytren's Contracture and the Unconscious: A Preliminary Statement of a Problem," *International Clinics,* 41, series 3 (1931), 184–199. Smith Ely Jelliffe, *Psychopathology of Forced Movements and the Oculogyric Crises of Lethargic Encephalitis,* NMDMS No. 55 (New York, 1932), especially p. 107; and other items in the Bibliography, below.

the influence of early psychological factors. They do not entirely annihilate the hereditary tendencies but they certainly force them or inhibit them. At least I think I have a lot of evidence that tends to put a reverse English on the Adlerian point of view."[130] On another occasion he spoke of the wry neck problem: "There are many wry necks which are not covered adequately by the terms functional or organic. This distinction is I think very old fashioned—every function needs an organ and that's that; so everything organic is functional and everything functional organic."[131]

Karl Menninger recalled that "Jelliffe saw no borderline between medicine, neurology, psychiatry, and psychoanalysis. This seems obvious enough today, but in 1920 this was more than heresy; it was either 'dilettantism' or 'psychosis.' I have heard Jelliffe described by envious and hostile critics as belonging in both categories. Nothing could be more inaccurate. The profundity and orderliness of Jelliffe's investigations were evident in whatever field or aspect he wrote about. He was an exceptionally fine neurologist and an exceptionally fine psychiatrist and an exceptionally fine internist."[132]

Jelliffe found fundamental defects in each of the particular viewpoints that were fashionable in the decades of his maturity. "My only quarrel with the behaviorist," he wrote in a letter, "is that he forgets the inside stimuli and only thinks of the outside ones—both are there. The instincts, which the behaviorist denies, are of these inside stimuli." Or he commented regarding Walter Cannon's work on emotions that Cannon had blind spots, "especially when he tackles symbolic derivations. He has little appreciation of such reconstructions. He is in many respects a naive realist." Or in another moment of candor he noted that George Crile's books "are chiefly ads for his thyroid removing factory in Cleveland." In general, he commented to another correspondent, "Personally I am not a bit impressed by any of the endocrine material, except possibly the parathyroid. . . ." Jelliffe was too much an analyst to ignore the psychological aspects of life, too fundamentally a biologist to forget that humans are animals with cells and organs subject to at least some reductionistic analysis, and too much a physician to believe that laboratory conditions replicate or theories describe individual human experiences. "Redlich believes in a 'disease,'" he exclaimed to one correspondent. "This is nonsense. I have had cases with true 'narcoleptic,' true 'pyknoleptic,' 'hypnoleptic' and 'epileptic' attacks in one and the same person at different ages and under varying circumstances."[133]

Several times, as in his death instinct paper just quoted, Jelliffe tried to express his viewpoint positively, what it was that he favored. He particularly

130. Jelliffe to Gregory Zilboorg, 16 April 1929.
131. Jelliffe to A. C. Matthews, 26 June 1929.
132. Karl Menninger, *A Psychiatrist's World* (New York, 1959), p. 827.
133. Jelliffe to Ethel Dummer, 10 April 1936. Jelliffe to George Draper, 21 December 1935. Jelliffe to Louis J. Bragman, 23 February 1936. Jelliffe to Arthur Birt, 6 June 1932. Jelliffe to A. A. Weech, 4 February 1927.

utilized the introduction to the later editions of the textbook that he and White coauthored as one place where he spelled out what he was trying to do (see above, Chapter 2). In 1939 he noted how up-to-date he felt: "'Psychosomatic' is in the air and emphasizes again the 'Introduction' of Jelliffe & White's 'Diseases of the Nervous System.' It is very simple after all and but restates the old 'Homeric' doctrine that body and mind are but different phrases for the same thing. Everything that an 'organ' does is 'organic' and throughout I have tried to state whether a change in an organ is reversible or irreversible. The evidence [is] becoming more and more pronounced that there are more reversible processes than were thought possible. The 'Metrazol' activities [shock therapy] have made this clearer and clearer."[134]

Elsewhere that same year, in introducing a collection of his papers on psychosomatic medicine, Jelliffe commented again on the new timeliness of his work:

"The general ideas stem from the Socratic principle of the wholeness of the body and as related in Plato's Charmides, 'one looks to the cure of the "soul" in order to cure the body.'

"Freud for the first time rendered the 'soul' accessible to conscious perception and offered a method for gaining insight into dynamic principles of creative and destructive tendencies without which no real psychosomatic unity is understandable.

"Whereas the principles involved are derivations from others, a modest claim for originality in the application of these conceptions to the study of specific medical situations is made. I do not need to accent this further than Freud's own bracketing of these efforts and those of Groddeck as novel and important.

"From an actual historical point of view my earlier papers were written before I knew of Groddeck's work, in which latter the principles here worked out at times in considerable detail are but suggested in Groddeck's intriguing contributions.

"It is furthermore of considerable satisfaction to present this group of studies. When I brought some of these and related papers before my neuropsychiatric confrères, psychoanalytic and otherwise, at the best they were received in conservative silence. Today psychosomatic medicine is almost a byword of progress. Thus I lay my offering before the Temple of Aesculapius with the fond hope it may find favor in the eyes of my colleagues. Should this prove to be so, as these are but a portion of related studies, I may find courage to collect others in the form these have achieved."[135]

134. Jelliffe to Fred B. Western, 13 December 1939.
135. Smith Ely Jelliffe, *Sketches in Psychosomatic Medicine*, NMDMS No. 65 (New York, 1939), p. v. In 1938 Jelliffe signed a letter (to Monroe Meyer, 10 January 1938), "With best wishes from one much frowned down upon in the early days when these relationships were [never] more than speculatively advanced."

But if Jelliffe was so timely, it must still be asked, Why was he not among the leaders of the psychosomatic movement, as a movement, when it came into American medicine? The answer is of course what he himself said: he was ahead of his time, and while his work helped create the atmosphere in which psychosomatics finally crystallized, the leadership of that movement belonged to younger people like Flanders Dunbar and Franz Alexander, who represented respectively the two major varieties of psychosomatics. Dunbar recognized Jelliffe's place in 1936 when she wrote him, "Dr. Wolfe and I would be particularly glad to have your suggestions concerning an assistant for our work in psychosomatic relationships because, as you realize, we are working in the field which you yourself opened up many years ago."[136] Dunbar was of course collaborating with colleagues, in contrast to Jelliffe, who worked alone, not within the institutions and groups that were necessary for the formation of a movement.[137]

Even at the end of his life, then, Jelliffe was being left behind in one area, psychoanalysis, while in another area, psychosomatics, he was either an extremist or a prophet of later developments such as the late twentieth-century holistic medicine movement. Jelliffe had come into psychoanalysis at a time when it was an innovative procedure advocated by a very small group of unconventional practitioners. At that time Jelliffe associated with other social innovators in artistic and intellectual circles, within which he helped popularize Freud's—and Jung's—teachings. Then, as psychoanalysis became more and more a medical subspecialty, Jelliffe provided a model by moving into a strictly medical approach to psychoanalysis.[138]

In the last years of his career, Jelliffe came to serve as a grand old man in neurology and psychoanalysis and even in the new field of psychosomatics. He was still playing a number of roles and refusing as a public figure to be confined to and identified with one line of endeavor. As his public appearances and practice shrank, his editing activities expanded, within which, true to his life pattern, he maintained a variety of interests and enthusiasms. The life of such a person as Jelliffe, who defies simple categorization, is difficult to evaluate. The problem of evaluation is in this case the more intriguing because Jelliffe was nevertheless a significant figure in his culture.

136. H. Flanders Dunbar to Jelliffe, 20 May 1936.
137. It is instructive to note the place of Jelliffe's work in the first general survey of the field: H. Flanders Dunbar, *Emotions and Bodily Changes: A Survey of Literature on Psychosomatic Interrelationships, 1910–1933* (New York, 1935). Jelliffe was mentioned fourteen times, for eighteen different publications. Dunbar cited only ten authors more than Jelliffe: Cannon, Deutsch, Freud, Groddeck, Heyer, Mayer, Pavlov, Schmitz, Schindler, and Wittkower.
138. John C. Burnham, "The Influence of Psychoanalysis Upon American Culture," in Quen and Carlson, eds., *American Psychoanalysis: Origins and Development* (New York, 1978), pp. 52–72.

FOUR

The Complexities of a Man's Influence

Honoring Jelliffe

Smith Ely Jelliffe died on 25 September 1945 of uremia caused by carcinoma of the prostate. The body was interred in the family plot in Dresden, New York. He had been increasingly ill for some time, in and out of hospitals, and at the end he even suffered from occasional confusion, although he had good days when he was much his old self. A trusted younger colleague, Nolan D. C. Lewis, took over Jelliffe's editorial responsibilities, and his son-in-law, Carel Goldschmidt, managed the business side. The transition was completed sometime in early 1945, and so Jelliffe's ventures in medical journalism did not come to an end with his death but instead continued on as social, not personal, institutions.[1] Fortunately, too, he had been honored by his friends when he was still alive and in full possession of his powers, at a symposium and formal dinner, 22 April 1938, attended by a large number of the medical elite of New York and the United States.

On that occasion Jelliffe's colleagues, in paying tribute to him publicly, assessed his impact as physician, editor, and teacher. Such formal statements provide a beginning for a more comprehensive historical evaluation. A few other sources, too, are available to give evidence, beyond the letters and documents so far cited, of the nature of the man and his impact on other people and on his times.

At the celebration, A. A. Brill reviewed Jelliffe's career and many publications and then concluded with this attempt at evaluation:

1. Belinda Jelliffe to Nolan D. C. Lewis, 17 May 1945, Nolan D. C. Lewis Papers, Library of Congress, Washington, D.C. Lewis began acting as managing editor in 1944; Nolan D. C. Lewis, "The Journal of Nervous and Mental Disease: The First 100 Years," *JNMD*, 159 (1974), 319–320. See *Psychoanalysis and the Psychoanalytic Review*, 45 (1958), 2–4.

139

"When I first read Jelliffe's papers on the technique of psychoanalysis, which, as I said, he began in 1913, I was at first more or less irritated by his mode of approach, but my temper changed as I continued reading. I noticed that Jelliffe accepted everything Freud said, but utilized the psychoanalytic concepts in accordance with the expressions of his personality. Jelliffe was really a naturalist to start with; he was a botanist, a chemist, a hygienist, and above all, a deep and daring thinker to whom nothing difficult was an impossible task. . . .

"When one reads his *Ecological Principles in Medicine*, or his *Historical Notes on Constitution and Individuality*, or any of his greater works written during the last few years, one can readily see the value of this *schematization*, as Jelliffe likes to call it. Thus, he compares 'a cross section of the human mind, of which one gets a glimpse in studying the unconscious,' to the Grand Canyon of the Colorado, wherein almost the entire geological history of the North American continent lies revealed to the geologist, but in which some can see only 'a big hole.' To the student of humanity, a cross section of the mind as seen in studying symptoms—thought-fossils, he calls them—represents an infinity of possibilities. . . .

"Jelliffe is fully appreciated even in distant lands, and justly so. In psychiatry, and in the psychoanalytic movement of this country, Jelliffe has done yeoman's work, not only as a prolific contributor of weighty and stimulating literature, but also as a pioneer in the application of psychoanalytic investigation to organic diseases. Professor Freud has always appreciated his work, and has given him due credit for it. I am sure that if the times were different in Vienna, we would be hearing from him this evening. That Jelliffe was appreciated by his colleagues is attested by the fact that they elected him to the highest offices in their professional ranks. I know that his friends love him, his fellow workers admire him, and his opponents fear him."[2]

The next speaker, neurologist Henry Alsop Riley, also reviewed the activities of Jelliffe as writer, editor, educator, and professional figure. But Riley spoke directly of the intangible elements that he was unable to count and evaluate adequately.

"Any individual's contribution to a science is not appraised by his written contributions to the literature of that discipline alone. Many individuals who have never published an article have influenced the development of a Science much more profoundly and purposively than other individuals from whose pens have flowed constant and never ending streams of articles.

"To exert an influence, contact is the one indispensible quality necessary—contact by which thought and deed may be moulded, determined and activated. There has been no one in his generation who has been more prodigal

2. A. A. Brill, "Jelliffe: The Psychiatrist and Psychoanalyst," *JNMD*, 89 (1939), 534–536.

of his contacts, generous with his contributions or unstinted in his response to the demands made upon his great gifts. In every one of his dichotomies, Smith Ely Jelliffe has exhibited the same wealth of expression and fulness of life."[3]

Finally, Louis Casamajor spoke about his personal experience with Jelliffe's influence.

"I am glad to be called upon to talk about Jelliffe—the man—for that is how I have known him over many years. My memory goes back to the far days in Brooklyn, when I was a small boy and he was a very big boy. Later when I grew up a bit and became interested in botany Dr. Jelliffe's description of the flowers of Prospect Park served as a guide to me in my learning.

"I first really came under Jelliffe's influence when I entered P. & S. in the early years of this century. Jelliffe was then an instructor in Pharmacology and was in charge of the laboratory course. He taught us how to prepare drugs and made it interesting to learn. His rare knowledge of botany gave life to a course which might otherwise have been dull.

"From those days until to-day I have never been long away from Jelliffe's influence. During the college course there was little real training in learning. Most of the teaching was by lecture and as a result Quizzes were formed to supplement the college course. Those who were wealthy joined Elliot's Quiz and those of us who were less fortunate would have been badly off had not Jelliffe started his Quiz for the poor boys. How he found time to run it, is more than I shall ever know nor how he could afford it. A number of the students never paid him anything. But he did it and he and those whom he attracted to him ran a good Quiz. With his versatility he taught many subjects and taught them so that one learned. He did it simply because he was the kind of person who did things like that.

"During the interne days at City Hospital Jelliffe was one of our attending neurologists. . . . For us he made neurology a subject of vital interest and this speaker was [led] by Jelliffe's hand into the field of his life's work in those wards of the old City Hospital.

"By this time Jelliffe was more than a teacher to me. We met again at Kraepelin's *Fortbildungs Kurs* in Munich in the fall of 1909. There we sat together as students during the day and played together as friends in the evenings. Again we worked together in the old Neurological Institute on 67th Street. We worked together in the clinic and in the wards and still he taught me those things I needed to know. His thorough grounding in anatomy and clinical neurology together with his truly remarkable grasp of the literature, made him a still more inspiring teacher. His enthusiasm for neurology, his devotion to accuracy and his strict scientific honesty, at times made a young

3. Henry Alsop Riley, "Jelliffe: The Neurologist," *JNMD*, 89 (1939), 537.

man think him a harsh critic, but one learned that one made fewer mistakes if one followed Jelliffe's advice. He expected me to be as good as himself—a goal I have been striving for ever since and never reached."[4]

Eulogies

As these comments suggest, Jelliffe's personality was of more than ordinary importance in shaping the ways in which he and his work affected other people. At the time of his death, too, a number of the memorialists spoke effusively about the power of Jelliffe's presence, each one reminiscing about his own encounters and impressions. Even given the restraints imposed by the occasion, these statements help in defining such an elusive element as personal influence.

Brill, always articulate, provided one set of impressions. "I experienced a sense of relief at the thought that Jelliffe was now at rest. For Jelliffe's last years seemed extremely burdensome, the gradual dissolution of his outwardly impressive organism continued apace with his grim determination to hold onto life. He was well aware that his life was ebbing away, but with his wonted tenacity he exerted his utmost to stave it off as long as possible. . . .

"I spent a very pleasant evening with him just before he left for his beloved home at Huletts Landing, Lake George. We smoked and talked for hours as we were wont to do in times gone by, his mind was perfectly clear and there was no evidence of pain or discomfort, yet as I left him I could not stop the thought that this would be our last meeting.

"He, too, must have thought of it, for in the midst of our pleasant chat he reverted twice to thoughts of death. Once he bewailed his declining memory and reminded me that until it began to fail him, it had always been *ne plus ultra*. These were the words he used and I readily agreed with him, for Jelliffe, as all who knew him can testify, had a prodigious memory. I deliberately turned away from this sad theme but he soon came back to it and spoke freely yet not at all lugubriously of his coming death. . . .

"Jelliffe's life represents a fascinating panorama of an outstanding American scientist. He was known to the world as a prominent neuropsychiatrist but, like many pioneers in this field, Jelliffe though starting as a neurologist, gradually swung over to psychiatry and then became fully engrossed in psychoanalysis. . . . I remember well our arguments and discussions of Freud and his theories, which started when we first met in 1908 and continued until he became a firm adherent of psychoanalysis. I would, therefore, call Jelliffe a psychoanalytic psychiatrist but, speaking more broadly, I would designate Jelliffe as a versatile scientist whose interests encompassed not just neurology, psychiatry, and psychoanalysis, but the whole range of mental science."[5]

4. Louis Casamajor, "Jelliffe: The Man," *JNMD*, 89 (1939), 543–544.
5. A. A. Brill, "In Memoriam, Smith Ely Jelliffe, October 27, 1866–September 25, 1945," *JNMD*, 106 (1947), 221–222.

Another colleague—and sometime adversary in psychoanalysis—C. P. Oberndorf, recalled some of his experiences with Jelliffe. "My first contact with Dr. Jelliffe left me with a profound respect for his scientific sincerity and humility and this feeling of admiration for his intellectual integrity continued during the thirty-five years of intimate association with him. It so happened that in 1908, fresh from my hospital internship, I went abroad to prepare myself in the specialties of neurology and psychiatry— for these two subjects had at that time not been separated in clinical practice. In Berlin I became acquainted with a recent graduate of the College of Physicians and Surgeons of New York also interested in the same field. When I told him that I had been accepted to work at the clinic of Professor Theodore [sic] Ziehen at the famous Charité Hospital, he said, 'You know, Dr. Jelliffe is working there,' in a tone of great awe and respect, 'he taught me pharmacology—he has a great mind.'

"When I reported for duty a few days later a towering, vigorous looking, middle-aged man recognized in me a fellow American and introduced himself in a hearty, yet simple way, 'I am Jelliffe, I'm working here, too, as a "volunteer."' And in the humble role of a volunteer, the lowest position in the scale of the hospital staff which adhered rigidly to all the Prussian Army's formality in regard to rank, the already distinguished Jelliffe clicked his heels and saluted in approved military fashion a pedantic professor who gradually dwindled in stature during ward round discussion in the light of Jelliffe's brilliancy. But Jelliffe had decided to abandon his teaching and researches in pharmacology and devote himself to a new field in which his training had been limited. He did not consider it beneath his dignity to renew his education at the bottom."[6]

An oratorical version of impressions of Jelliffe was presented by Foster Kennedy, the neurologist.

"It is hard to think that Smith Ely Jelliffe, with his great Johnsonian figure, his twinkling, intelligent eyes, his bland, genial smile on his broad face, will not be seen again at our table. . . .

"I once called him the lineal descendant of the French encyclopedists, taking all knowledge for his province, though one wondered sometimes if he did not find books, as Stevenson put it, 'a mighty poor substitute for life.' His thought had often a mystical garment. . . .

"But his great attribute was zest. He had to drive right on, carried forward in time on the succeeding waves of every new idea, a powerful, vigorous, emotional man, with color that radiated every assembly in which he sat."[7]

This sample of formal reactions of colleagues who survived and honored Jelliffe shows that they perceived not only the versatility and broad range of

6. C. P. Oberndorf, "The Literary and Historical Contributions of Dr. Smith Ely Jelliffe," *JNMD*, 106 (1947), 228–229.
7. Foster Kennedy, "Smith Ely Jelliffe," *JNMD*, 106 (1947), 233.

interests of the man but an enthusiasm or zest that impressed virtually every-one. Moreover, the testimony was unanimous that his intellectual unpre-dictability was fascinating and at the same time reminded his associates not only of the vastness of human knowledge but of its rapidly changing and developing nature.

A Patient's Impressions

One relatively extensive document of impressions of Jelliffe exists which portrays him from a different point of view and with a little ambivalence. Yet the impressions do not vary markedly from those of Jelliffe's colleagues. The author of this set of reminiscences was Mabel Dodge Luhan, who was a patient of Jelliffe's shortly before World War I, at a time when she lived in New York and encouraged, indeed, collected, avant garde and other in-tellectuals whom she drew into her social circle—many of whom she mentions casually in the following account.

"In the morning I decided I must have help from outside and I thought of Dr. Jelliffe, whom I had been to see when Genevieve Onslow frightened us so that night we experimented with *peyote*.

"I drove into New York and called upon him, and we sat in his office. He was a tall, portly, clean-shaven man dressed in black, and his plump face was enlivened by a pair of small, intelligent green eyes.

"'Jung has taught us,' he said, 'that when one reaches an impasse, it is because he is unable to function in the way his own particular nature wishes. When we try to force ourselves to go in directions contrary to the psyche, she rebels. You do not like your present life. Why?'

"I launched into a description of my situation with Maurice. It was a great relief to talk, to tell it all. . . . to tell how I hated things about him even while I loved him and was unable to live without him.

"I enjoyed my visits three times a week to Jelliffe's office. He had a speculative mind with an amusing intuition. As he turned my attention more and more upon the inner workings of my own nature, curious spiritual events began to occur, and my starved perceptions, that had been centered for months upon Maurice, reveled in the new direction of interest. It became an absorbing game to play with oneself, reading one's motives, and trying to understand the symbols by which the soul expressed itself.

"Psychoanalysis was apparently a kind of tattletaleing. I was able to tell, not only everything about myself, but all about Maurice. I grew calm and self-sufficient, and felt superior to him in the evening when, returning from New York, I found him still in the grip of his nervous fears and worries.

"I tried to tell him about the system and how it worked, but he hated it and said it all revolted him. When I told Jelliffe this, he exclaimed:

"'Ah, naturally! He has a resistance. Whenever people particularly need psychoanalysis, they have a great resistance to it.'

"When I went to his office I always noticed a grave, sweet-looking woman sitting in an alcove at the end of the hall working upon papers, and I asked him who she was. He told me she was an old patient of his and of particular interest. 'She has cured herself of manic-depression,' he said, regarding me with an intent gaze. 'I have written up her case for the *Review*. You must read it. You know that she is my proof that by understanding and hard work these manic-depressives may free themselves.'

"One of the most interesting speculations Jelliffe went in for was apparently a new field never worked much before—the set of symbols that compose all the parts of the body. The respiratory organs, he said, stood for human aspiration, the breath was no less than the Breath of God. Failure in aspiration resulted in a breaking down of the lungs, the bronchial tubes, or the larynx. The creation, birth, and development of the soul could be reckoned in these parts, and they corresponded with the lower organs of sex where creation on another plane was effected. 'As below, so above.' The creative word issued from the throat of man when he reached the true Power of manhood, and this was the birth of the mystic Rose on the Cross of the medieval Rosicrucians.

"The appearance of a cancer in a person signified hatred. It was the parasite eating away the vitality of man. The bowels were the vehicle of the money power, excrement was gold, hoarded or distributed in circulation. . . . Ah, there were many fascinating explanations of the mystery of the body. Jelliffe had written a great volume that showed the body and its ills at three levels: the somatic, the psychic, and the symbolic. . . .

"Jelliffe had been curious about the Finney Farm constellation and I had asked him for a week-end. In the morning he had visited the Green House and talked to Bayard. He had seen the two large, green macaws that stayed out there, and had observed them with a small, knowing, psychoanalytical smile. He had studied in diplomatic silence the picture Marsden Hartley was painting on the floor of the living room while Bourgeois hammered up and down the piano. [Marsden] Hartley told Jelliffe his picture was called 'Handsome Drinks,' and the doctor made out a glass of milk, a glass of champagne, and the Communion Cup. Before dinner he had found Bobby making sketches for a play, out on the dining-room table. These drawings decided him that Bobby [Robert Edmond Jones], too, needed psychoanalysis, and before long I led him unresisting to Jelliffe's office.

"The first time I had seen Dr. Jelliffe I remember him coming towards me, then, in his office: tall, in a black suit of smooth cloth, a little paunchy, his small, green eyes set rather close together, were speculative upon one. 'A Roman Catholic priest,' I had thought at once, for there was something all over him that was like that: in his glance, in the smooth, fine texture of his pale skin, and in his bearing. He was commanding, quizzical, sure of himself, and not to be moved. His features were small and fine, and there was a kind of impudence playing over them. His face looked as though he had put on a lot of thick make-up and wiped it off so frequently that its contours were modeled by this massage. Actors' faces often have this modeled surface.

"Next, I remember him sitting beside me on the pale blue Louis Seize couch at 23 Fifth Avenue, probing me with his inquisitive eyes, asking me questions; and then it was I confided to him my curious hankering to cut off my hair. This interested him very much. No women cut off their hair in those days, and I had lovely brown coils in figure eights over my ears. Nice hair. But, oh! I longed to cut it with a physical yearning. I was dying to feel short locks against my ears—the *shorn* feeling that must follow the fatal clip-clip. I knew in advance the light and airy sensation that would come from a Dutch cut. I had seen illustrations in Howard Pyle's books, done by Maxfield Parrish that showed me how I would look! Yes, for a long time, now, I had wanted to cut my hair off, and I knew I'd be doing it one of those days, only I never arrived at the right and courageous moment of *doing* it! Jelliffe considered me gravely.

"'And who do you know that has long hair like rays? *Who* is it that you want to shear?'

"'What do you mean? *I* don't know. Who?'

"'Phoebus Apollo!' he answered me with fearful solemnity, his little jowls quivering slightly. 'The Sun!'

"These unfamiliar quirks of his mind entertained me immensely. '*What* an amusing man!' I thought. But I disbelieved him. I loved the sun, I thought. It was the moon I did not like. . . .

"It was interesting to watch my soul provide exciting subjects to discuss with Jelliffe. Whenever things got dull, something would turn up from down below to keep the ball rolling—and he and I chased it about. We talked for hours. He told me more strange and fascinating oddities and now I have forgotten them nearly all! Sometimes I argued with him by letter and he would reply.

> My Dear Mrs. Dodge:
> I am sorry you feel I dogmatize: I myself am dogmatic that I have no right to do so. As a thorough-going sophist and pragmatist my own philosophy cannot and must not be imposed on another of different experience. With Protagoras, I hold, since we do not any of us act quite alike, so therefore we cannot perceive quite alike and that the only necessity for conformity in thinking is concerned with those things which are "necessary to live" as I have quoted it so often to you! We vary concerning those things which are not needed for a bare existence and may conduce to a life that is "beautiful and good." I feel sure you cannot find therein a dogmatic philosophy.

I think my dogmatism is concerned with the evidences of your unconscious solely. If your unconscious indubitably says, "This I wish to do—but I, my conscious, knows, it will lead to death, and not to a life that is beautiful and good," then I must confess I am dogmatic. "You can't and you need not try." This is not forcing a philosophy upon you. This is only telling you you are trying to do the impossible. Perhaps I fail to get this distinction over; if so, then surely I am at fault.

I am not one whit involved in forcing people to do anything. I am only trying to be a mirror in which one may read why one cannot do certain things in certain ways. If my reading and experience and knowledge of evolution has taught it to me from another side, I should not use that overmuch, else it might seem I was putting myself in front of the mirror.

Those things which are most strongly felt as resistances are the direct results of the patient's and analyst's blind spots. One must be very careful regarding the great tendency to displace the affect, born of the resistance, to something quite foreign to the situation.

I hope I can help you to see this on Monday. I am glad you can formulate my dogmatism, as you have; it is one of my difficulties, more born of the desire to hurry people along than to make them conform. I am after all a wretched conformist myself and to be held up as a single pattern, machine maker of souls—although perhaps an hyperbolic way of taking your phrase—is a shock.

"I am afraid I did not learn much about myself with Jelliffe, but I did get a very complete line on *him*, and on Bayard, and on Leo [Stein], and I enjoyed my outings in his office. . . .

"Seeing Jelliffe welcome Bayard's appearance in my dreams, I asked him slyly:

"'Do you really think that flirtation is a form of sublimation—a suitable outlet?'

"'Surely,' he replied. 'At times it may become the necessary and constructive tool that one requires.'

"'For an amputation, you mean?' I asked him quickly. For I had never admitted to him that Maurice *was* detrimental to me. I never admitted it. I was never really disloyal to the relationship that I clung to, I only wanted it *fixed up* so that we could be happy, and anyway, these new ideas faded away at home. He smiled at me:

"'Come! Come!' he murmured, reassuringly. 'I do not want anything for you that you do not want for yourself. This is *your* affair. You yourself have that in you which will decide what is best. Your judgment, not mine, will solve your problem.'

"That was the way he threw me back upon myself."

In the end, Luhan found that Jelliffe was not providing her with what she felt she needed, and so she turned from him and "Jung's method which Dr.

Jelliffe purported to practice" and went to Brill, who seemed to suit her
better. Meantime she had introduced Jelliffe further into New York intellectual circles and through him had done a great deal to extend psychoanalytic
thinking among an important group of people in the arts.[8]

All of these memories, written for a variety of reasons by different people,
confirm a pattern in Jelliffe's life: he was a warm, effusive person, given to
enthusiasms that he would go to unusual trouble to follow. However much
he controlled his inner thoughts and feelings, other people saw him as powerful and spontaneous as well as fun loving. It was no wonder that when a
play was made up for some medical meeting high jinks, his colleagues cast
Jelliffe as The Id.[9]

A Daughter's Memories

Yet the ebullient personality and encyclopedic knowledge were largely but
public aspects of the man. Jelliffe operated on many levels. The young Jelliffe
who followed any number of interests and touched many groups at once was,
in the phases of his maturity, still possessed of many facets that showed up
in different circumstances. Jelliffe's various dimensions appear particularly
well in the warm, informal memoir that his daughter, Helena Jelliffe Goldschmidt, recorded in 1978.

"I never heard my father raise his voice. We as children were never scolded
or spanked, nor was an issue made of our impertinence. We were five children, Sylvia, Winifred, Ely, Leeming, Helena. We were all born at 271 West
71st Street, New York City. We moved to 64 West 56th Street on June 16,
1903, a large, five-storey brownstone house, and on June 18, 1904, Father
bought our summer home at Huletts Landing, New York, on Lake George.

"Mother managed all of this as well as writing all of Father's French,
translating French medical works, etc. He told me many times, 'Your mother
was a most remarkable woman.' I also remember his telling me, 'Your mother
has real wit.' Her 'at homes' on the first Wednesdays of the month were
stimulating because there one could meet many persons from the world of
the arts. Mother was a botanist and horticulturist, having a large vegetable
and flower garden at the Lake. We all worked in the garden, and she helped
Father in every possible way.

"Every room in 64 West 56th Street was lined with books, and every bit
of wall space in the Den at the Lake. One section was devoted to detective
stories, and other sections to early editions, Greek and Latin classics, French,
German, and English books. His private library in the Den, at Huletts Landing, about two thousand books, burned in a fire in 1953.

8. Mabel Dodge Luhan, *Movers and Shakers* (New York, 1936), pp. 439–457, 498. See
Acknowledgments.
9. H. A. Riley to Jelliffe, 29 May 1931.

"Dinner was the highlight of the day. Each of us had the opportunity, in turn, to tell what happened during the day. There were guessing games, and one week we spoke French and the next week German at the table. There was a little match box on the table with a slit; should we forget the proper language for the week, we forfeited one penny out of a ten-cent allowance. We learned very quickly not to forget.

"In 1909 we, the family and Grandmother (Father's mother) and cousins, spent a year in Europe: Weggis, Switzerland; Dresden, Germany; Vaumoise and Paris, France. Father was studying in Munich, attending conferences, etc. We had a lovely apartment at 13 Bismarck Platz, Dresden, that Fraulein had procured for us. (Our staff at West 56th Street consisted of Margaret, cook; Nellie, waitress and parlour maid; and Fraulein, German governess.)

"It was a very warm and happy household. Father presided at the dinner table, and every meal was a gourmet delight, always with the proper food, for Father, being a chemist, thought that the chemistry of food was important. I recall discovering that it was his voice when, at Christmas, he would climb up to the roof and speak down the chimney to us as Santa Claus. I thought what a wonderful Father to do this all these years in the cold and snow when I did not know then and thought that it was Santa Claus.

"Mother managed that we five children had our own special talents so there was no quarreling. Sylvia was a bibliophile. Winifred loved to cook and garden. Ely became an expert fisherman, supplying us with fresh perch or brook trout or black bass from the Lake for breakfast. Leeming was the athlete and did all heavy chores, helping Will Borden, our farmer, with the horses, cows, haying, etc. Helena was the dancer, giving performances in the garden to raise money for the Guild of the Mountain Grove Memorial Church at Huletts Landing, or in school plays.

"Summers at the Lake were paradise. We all had our daily privileges: gardening, picking vegetables, getting the mail by motor boat or horse and buggy (if the Lake was too rough for boating), making jams and jellies, picking apples or pears in the orchard and packing them to be sent down to 56th Street for the winter. We had honey bees (three hives) and packed 100 pounds of honey each summer. Special Christmas gifts to our uncles were a barrel of apples and honey. Everything we did was never called a chore but a privilege.

"A special treat would be to go to the Den where Father worked. Mother built a great fireplace at one end while Father was in Europe in 1908 attending medical meetings. In the Den Father had huge glass cages in which were all manner of stuffed birds and small animals which we could study and ask questions about. These were wonderful times with Father, and many times Dr. William Alanson White would be visiting and be with us. The great treat as well was when Doc White (that is what we called him) came for the Fourth of July bringing the most magnificent fireworks, fire crackers, etc.

Leeming would build the chute on the dock facing north at the Point to launch the rockets, which would burst and drop into the lake. One year we had paper balloons of various shapes and colors, one of which when inflated became a pink paper elephant. We sent it wafting north on the breeze. I have often wondered about the reactions of persons on the other side of the lake enjoying their cocktails and suddenly seeing a pink elephant floating by in the sky.

"Summers at the Lake 1911–1915 each child had a friend to visit so there were nine or ten children, Father, Mother, Fraulein, Grandmother, and two maids, a total of fourteen or fifteen people. Sylvia wrote plays, one especially I recall was called 'The Witch of Ende.' Father was the producer and stage manager, and he had to pull the curtains between acts. He was perched upon two branches of a great pine tree—the curtain was rigged on these branches—and at the performance he was laughing so hard at our antics that he almost fell out of the tree.

"We had music lessons and studied ballet, swimming, rowing, canoeing, and tennis. Father taught us to operate the Fay & Bowen motor boat. In 1929 Father bought his twenty-eight-foot Gar Wood speed boat, a special treat for everyone when he invited friends for a boat ride. Father's sister, Lulu (Louise J. Long)—we called her Tante—was an accomplished musician and gave us our music lessons. After her husband died she taught and produced many successful pupils. I remember her inviting me to meet Paderewski at his studio in New York.

"Father had a very sweet tooth. The nicest thing you could give him was a box of chocolates or a quart of ice cream. He had a two-week menu written up for Klara, the cook-housekeeper, to follow. His suppers (dinners) were superb. A special treat would be to be invited to his crêpe suzette dessert party. Klara made the crêpe and Father the special sauce, the recipe for which had been given him by the maître d' of Maxim's Restaurant in Paris. I watched Father make this sauce, which I now make with his recipe in his chafing dish which he gave me. During prohibition Father made wines, benedictine liqueur, and scotch. While I was in Europe I would send him labels from our wine bottles until he wrote to say that he could buy the labels a dime a dozen in New York. The benedictine was excellent.

"During the summer of 1916 Father took Sylvia to visit Indian reservations in the West and study Indian lore. Sylvia spoke seven languages as well as Indian. I became ill, and upon Father's return he put me to bed for forty-two days. Sylvia read to me, and Father was always there. That fall I went to Miss Shipley's Boarding School, in Bryn Mawr, Pennsylvania. Sylvia was at Bryn Mawr College at the time, and Father came often to see us.

"In 1917 Father married Belinda Dobson. After Shipley School I went to the Packer Collegiate Institute in Brooklyn, staying with Grandmother, Father's mother, and Tante, his sister, at 196 66th Avenue, Brooklyn. Leeming was there for a year until he went to Yale (class of 1923). He graduated summa cum laude and was captain of the Yale swimming team and held many other honors.

"At Packer my friend, Chici Chittenden was stage struck and had a wish to become a great dramatic actress. I said, 'That is easy; my father knows John Barrymore.' This was 1920, and Arthur Hopkins, producer, and Robert Edmond Jones, scene and costume designer, were producing Shakespeare's *Richard III* with John Barrymore at the Plymouth Theatre on Broadway. I asked Father if Chici could play in the production. He said, 'My dear, I think this can be arranged.' Then I thought, 'How foolish that I should get *her* on the stage,' and I asked Father if I could play as well, to which he said, 'I am sure this can be arranged.' Father was very interested in the theatre, in art, and in music, and he related it to his work. He gave his suggestions how Ophelia should sing her Mad Song in *Hamlet* (John Barrymore, 1922). I played in this and in *Macbeth*, with Lionel Barrymore, in 1921.

"In 1922 I went to Barnard College. When I entered college, he said, 'I know if you study very hard, you can be a cum laude. We have enough cum laude in the family,' referring to Sylvia and Leeming. 'I want you to keep your ears and eyes wide open, there are other things in life. But you MUST pass.' I followed his advice.

"I recall a number of Father's sayings.
'If you want a thing well done, do it yourself.'
'All my life I have been on the firing line.'
'I do not wish to be a big frog in a small pond but a big frog in a big pond.'
'If something is worth doing, it is worth doing well.'
'There is safety in numbers' (he approved of my having many beaux).

"To be with him a few minutes, to talk to him, he could solve all your problems with the greatest ease, giving you the utmost confidence and a feeling that you had wings and could go out and conquer the world. Father was generous with his time and his money as far as his family was concerned. He loved his children and his ten grandchildren and was interested in our welfare as we grew up and married. I remember his telling me, 'You must blow your own horn; no one will blow it for you.' And, 'Man needs only three things in life: 1. Work. 2. Two good meals a day. 3. A good bed to sleep in.'

"I heard Father lecture at Teachers College. The subject was way above my head. Then he said he would explain in layman's language, and then it was so simple and clear and easily understood. With his interest in theatre and knowing Arthur Hopkins, Jones, and Barrymore, he learned much of stage presence and elocution and became a superb speaker on and off stage.

"In October 1925, I met Carel Goldschmidt of Amsterdam, Holland. He had come to America to study the manufacture of Bayuk cigars in Philadelphia. He proposed, and I said that he would have to speak with my father, who then invited us for dinner. After dinner, Carel and Father had a pleasant interview in Father's office. After Carel left, I asked Father, 'What do you think of him?' Father said, 'I think he is the nicest young man I have ever met.' So we had a whirlwind courtship.

"In Amsterdam we met Professor Ben Brouwer, Holland's foremost neurologist and a great friend of Father's. He would always stay with him at 56th Street while visiting the States. At a dinner party given by Professor Brouwer, I met several young doctors who were very awed and impressed with Father's work. They asked if he was still alive. I said, 'Very much so. We have just returned from a visit, and one evening were dancing and drinking champagne at the Crystal Room of the Ritz Carlton Hotel until four in the morning.' Father was an excellent dancer.

"He and Belinda visited us in Amsterdam in 1928 and 1930. In 1934 Father invited us and our two sons, Dolf and Smith Ely, to visit at the Lake.

"In 1924 Father divided the Lake George property into five sections, each of us receiving twenty-five acres and shore front. I inherited the Mansion.

"We came back to Lake George in the summers of 1936, 1938, 1939, and then 1940 for good, as Holland was occupied by the Nazis and we could not go back. These were happy summers, and we saw a lot of Father as the Den is on the lake shore, and the Mansion on top of the hill. He was ill in 1944 and asked Carel to take over the running of the *Journal of Nervous and Mental Disease* and have Dr. Nolan Lewis as editor. Father and Carel enjoyed each other, having respect for each other's abilities. The doctor and the businessman got along famously.

"In the spring of 1945, Father was at Mt. Sinai Hospital, very ill. A young intern came to the room and asked, 'Well, Doctor, what seems to be the matter with you?' 'That, young man, is for YOU to find out,' replied Father. A few months later we were called, as it seemed to be the end. But it was not at all. Carel and I were greeted by Father's saying, 'How nice of you to come,' and singing Gilbert and Sullivan songs from *The Mikado*. I knew that Father would not die in the hospital but at his beloved Lake in his own bed, which he did."

These informal recollections suggest that Jelliffe's family life provided an arena that both complemented and supplemented his professional activities. They also provide insights into the inner workings of the public figure—the stage presence, the translating, the combination of work and vacation. Finally, the recollections particularly sketch some of the situation that caused Jelliffe to put such a high value on his life at Lake George—even to postponing his death until he could return there.

As the other testimony shows, Mrs. Goldschmidt's sense of her father's personal impact was not just that of a daughter. Each person whose reminiscences were recorded had a similar sense of impact, each in his own way.

The differences between them, indeed, underlined the complexity of Jelliffe. He was complex not only, as has several times been observed, in his work, but also on the personal level. The total evaluation of the man is therefore correspondingly difficult. External signs, from publicly expressed esteem to formal honors, show that he was important, but it is incumbent in summary to show as precisely as possible why and how.

Formal Evaluations of Jelliffe's Medical Contributions

Beyond memorial statements and the few short biographical articles, formal evaluations of Jelliffe's work are very few in number. In 1932, A. Chiabov, a colleague unknown to Jelliffe, reviewed his work for an Italian journal devoted to schizophrenia. Chiabov emphasized Jelliffe's sense of the complexity of the interrelationship between organic and psychological functioning. After reviewing Jelliffe's clinical contributions, Chiabov evenhandedly described Jelliffe's historical and speculative writings. At the end of his straightforward summary, Chiabov concluded,

"These are not the only publications of the author; he has an extremely large number of them. But even from these his personality seems to me to stand out and his tendency to generalize and to construct his hypotheses, some of which, when they become too precisely formulated, like those upon the various periods of the psychogenetic growth of the mind, cannot help leaving me very skeptical and very little persuaded. I shall not permit myself to discourse upon his psychoanalytic convictions, because I am too little acquainted with psychoanalysis and I do not succeed in understanding them, but it seems to me that in conclusion it can be said that, as the author [Jelliffe] himself affirms, there are still so many anatomical and physiological problems to resolve, that it is best to confine one's self to these. . . ."[10] Chiabov's reaction to Jelliffe's work was not unlike that of his American colleagues: the ideas were stimulating, especially as Jelliffe tied together widely disparate phenomena and elucidated the complicated nature of the biological and psychological workings of human beings.

At about the same time, a Brazilian, Arthur Ramos of Bahia, undertook a more systematic and comprehensive review of Jelliffe's contributions, emphasizing that Jelliffe "admits no opposition between soma and psyche, integrating them in the entirety of the personality." Ramos himself tried to integrate Jelliffe's clinical observations into his speculative schema of evolutionary psychobiology. More than any other commentator Ramos felt the unity in Jelliffe's work that provided a basis to describe him as representing a particular viewpoint. "In forming his own concepts," wrote Ramos, "Jelliffe utilizes psychoanalytic postulates with striking originality." Where Jelliffe

10. A. Chiabov, "A Group of Works of Smith Ely Jelliffe, M.D.," tr. Louis Villano, *Psychoanalytic Review*, 23 (1936), 59–67; the quote is from p. 67.

was eclectic, Ramos wrote, it was eclecticism of a far different order from most.

"Smith Ely Jelliffe is one of the chief spokesmen of the American bio-dynamic and evolutionist school. His far-reaching work reflects again the fundamental view of Stanley Hall and has in it such an element of personal value that it must be considered as a doctrinal body of legitimate originality and independence. Jelliffe grants the contributions of psychoanalysis in full measure, as subsidiary and independent factors to his own viewpoints, which comprise a dominantly tolerant and eclectic orientation. That eclecticism, however, has nothing in common with the attitude peculiar to certain *touristes* of science who live in order to use the results of this or that school without critical selection. It is governed by the demands of the monistic attitude in science, the results and philosophical orientation of which he has progressively evidenced in his work.

"Jelliffe's major aim is to discover the common base which unifies different elements in the mental sciences; to speak the universal language that would lessen separation between laborers in a common work and to which Claude Bernard has referred in a phrase that he has many times repeated: 'There will come a time when the physiologist, the philosopher and the poet will have to speak the same language and understand each other.'

"Evolution, the psychology of experience, behaviorism, psychoanalysis: each has a place in his preparation proportionate to its value as penetrating means for further understanding the main subject of his inquiries, Man."[11] Ramos, as his exposition suggests, was perhaps more sympathetic to Jelliffe's aspirations than effective in conveying exactly how the unity worked out.

What is perhaps most remarkable about Ramos's synthesis of Jelliffe's ideas is that it is almost unique. Most Americans were as uncomfortable as Chiabov with Jelliffe's speculative turn of mind. From Jelliffe's point of view, he was more modern than they, because he was working with complexity rather than very precise and tidy theory. As early as 1916 he wrote in his "Technique" articles: "There is no adequate definition of transference. In fact the whole attitude of this series of articles is one distinctly opposed to the utilization of definitions. Definitions are too apt to be sterile condensations of the meaning of words rather than dynamic principles for the understanding of things. Hence I shall not try to define transference, I shall attempt to describe it."[12] Decades later he was still struggling to capture in prose the multifarious interrelationships in each patient's malfunctioning and to relate the illness to general scientific principles.

11. Arthur Ramos, "A Bio-Dynamic and Evolutional Orientation of Psychoanalysis, Smith Ely Jelliffe: His Work," tr. E. Locke-Lewis, *JNMD*, 84 (1936), 667–675. Jelliffe was of course not a follower of G. Stanley Hall.
12. Smith Ely Jelliffe, "Technique of Psychoanalysis," *Psychoanalytic Review*, 3 (1916), 26.

Robert Powell, the leading historian of psychosomatic medicine, groups Jelliffe with Dunbar and other holistic advocates of psychosomatics. Later workers in psychosomatic medicine used the term and cited Dunbar and even Jelliffe, but their orientation was fundamentally toward disorders of single organs. "The days of Meyer, White, and Jelliffe," notes Powell, "were rapidly passing, and with the approach of World War II there occurred a marked sophistication of psychophysiologic instrumentation, as well as an influx of European analysts. Many physiologists, working at an organ level, with an occasional glance at the patients' conscious emotions, disdained . . . 'superficial' concern with the patients' movements, postures, muscle tension, and unconscious processes." The holists were interested in treating patients rather than "ultimate etiologies or mechanisms," Powell points out, but midcentury medicine left them, including Jelliffe, and went a different direction, linking specific organs with specific pathologies and psychopathologies.[13]

Evaluating Facets of Jelliffe's Work

Jelliffe's contemporaries who did not see the unity in his work tended instead to view him in two ways. The first was as a person who worked in certain nicely categorized areas—editing, teaching, clinical neurology, certain areas of psychiatry, bibliography, history of neuropsychiatry, psychoanalysis, and later psychosomatic medicine. The second way of viewing Jelliffe was as an inspirational figure. Since virtually no one, then or since, used Jelliffe's synthesis at all extensively, probably the best approach to evaluating his work is to break it up into categories, as his contemporaries—except Ramos—did and then take account of the inspiration that he provided. These categories suggest how Jelliffe's disparate contributions built up and he affected people's views in many small ways that cumulated into substantial significance.

The task of evaluating Jelliffe is complicated by the fact that the record of his work does not fit easily into the usual modes of analysis. In general, certain conventional indicators are available for measuring the impact that physicians and scientists have had. Typically, important figures had students who spread both the teacher's viewpoints and his reputation. Or the famous person originated some specific idea or ideas that are more or less easy to trace. Or, finally, the person may have left clear influences on specific institutions. In the case of Jelliffe, any of these guideposts are few and far between.

The way that Jelliffe lacked institutional demonstration and magnification of his influence is particularly striking in the instance offered by his Jungian period. When quite unwittingly he was instrumental in furnishing a platform for Jung's crucial dissent from Freud, at Fordham in 1912, Jelliffe was using

13. Robert Charles Powell, "Healing and Wholeness."

an institutional base. Yet in the years immediately succeeding, when Jelliffe's therapy and writings embodied important Jungian elements, his influence was not reinforced by hospital or teaching institutions. He influenced Louise Brink in his own office, who contributed some restrained but Jungian expositions to the technical literature, but hardly anyone else of whom there is record.

Insofar as Mabel Dodge Luhan's salon was an institution, Jelliffe may through that medium have conveyed ideas in an important way to segments of the artistic and intellectual world, so that leading thinkers not only talked about psychoanalysis but accepted imaginative and literary and a more or less Jungian version of psychoanalysis as the genuine coin. But Jelliffe was certainly not a Jungian in the way that Beatrice Hinkle and James Oppenheim were, and they were interconnected with the New York literati more than was Jelliffe.

Jelliffe did follow Jung in his use of assistants, in his ideas about a collective, Lamarckian unconscious, in his style of seeing and interpreting symbolization, and in his flights of imagination, but Jelliffe was never more than an eclectic, and his potential as an advocate of Jung diminished proportionately as he did not work through schools, professional societies, and other social institutions. It was as a Freudian in the post-1925 period that Jelliffe had direct influence for a few years within, particularly, the New York Psychoanalytic Society.

Jelliffe did teach many students—in pharmacognosy, in pharmacology, in neuropsychiatry, and in the private quiz. Letters and occasional testimony such as Casamajor's give glimpses of "Windy" Jelliffe's helpfulness and the quality of his teaching. Some idea of what and how he taught appears in his textbooks and published clinical lectures. Mostly, however, the impact of his services as teacher, however important, has to be inferred.

Jelliffe did not develop disciples or form a "school" that might have had palpable influence and perpetuate his name. Neither his son-in-law, the strongly independent Gregory Stragnell, nor his successor as editor, Nolan D. C. Lewis, represented or advocated a recognizably Jelliffean point of view. The younger man with whom he became most closely associated, Karl Menninger, used Jelliffe less as a teacher than as a father figure to help mobilize trends already present in a mature practitioner. Menninger recalled how cordial the Jelliffes were to him when he was just starting out and how "Jelliffe talked to me incessantly about Freud and Jung and psychoanalysis and complexes and libido, always as if they were the most respectable and timely topics; this was most astonishing to me." Menninger also recalled Jelliffe's role in a crucial case:

"I can remember my own conversion—that moment in which the forces of repression yielded to the mounting pressure of what we call reason. My critical-point case—my Dora—was intelligent and good-looking, but she was a persistent sleepwalker. I made a careful examination, and came to the conclusion that the diagnosis was either (1) epileptic equivalent, or (2) hysteria major.

"I told her this. But she said she didn't care what the diagnosis was; she wanted treatment. She said it was very embarrassing to wake up prowling around in her parents' bedroom, looking for something—she didn't quite know what—that her father kept hidden and which would change her completely if she could acquire it. This reminded me of some of the 'nonsense' I had read in psychoanalytic journals, so I wrote to Jelliffe about her. I told him I had no couch but I could borrow a chaise longue. He wrote back for me to use anything, just get her to talk. This wasn't at all difficult, and I listened to her once a week. But soon I had heard enough to make me go out and buy all the books on psychoanalysis that I could find."[14]

Jelliffe was important to Menninger, but Brill and others also impressed Menninger, and aside from his case—a single instance—there are no other records of analysts for whom Jelliffe was a critical figure in their decision to practice psychoanalysis. As an old friend wrote Jelliffe in 1929, "You are one of the few men who really take a comprehensive view of the whole subject of disease, so-called. I am sure you will have many followers in the future but as yet they are, unfortunately, rather few."[15]

Jelliffe did not become deeply—or more than transiently—involved with any institution after he drifted away from the Brooklyn Institute of Arts and Sciences. He was not a pillar of any hospital or medical school or professional group—although he served all of them as a responsible professional should. In 1920, just after the *Archives* incident (Chapter 2), Jelliffe served on the Organization Committee of the Association for Research in Nervous and Mental Disease and in the mid-1920's on the American Psychiatric Association Committee on the Legal Aspects of Psychiatry. But the only institution with which he could be identified was the *Journal of Nervous and Mental Disease* and the publications associated with it, the monograph series and the *Psychoanalytic Review*. In this area his influence was of a more particular kind.

Jelliffe's successors at the *Journal* did not feel constrained to follow any of his policies or even his format. He maintained a journal according to the standards of his times, and later editors did likewise for their times. In one sense, then, Jelliffe's impact as an editor is represented simply in the cold print of the volumes for which he was responsible. Beyond the book reviews, which were extremely important, Jelliffe also left his mark on the other contents of the *Journal*. On the one-hundredth anniversary of the *Journal of Nervous and Mental Disease*, one of the then chief editors, James B. Mackie,

14. Karl Menninger, *A Psychiatrist's World* (New York, 1959), pp. 846, 850.
15. E. W. Taylor to Jelliffe, 23 September 1929.

offered his impressions of the way that Jelliffe had shaped the content of the *Journal.*

"He looked for fresh material, new approaches. He found them most often with the young. An author's professional prestige bore no relationship to the acceptance of his manuscript. Jelliffe had few 'editorial policies,' nor was he given to the publication of personal editorials.

"With his encyclopedic mind, his enormous energy and his freedom from the constraints of a demanding sense of self-importance or a demanding institutional allegiance, he evaluated new work for its soundness, for its originality, and very often for its practicality. Any new idea was apt to find its way into the *Journal* and then into one of his textbooks. Although he admired deft style and clarity, he was fully aware that new ideas were often produced by the uneven processes of a groping mind in flux. He did not demand from himself or from his colleagues instantaneous clarity or beautifully paced prose. That could come later. . . .

"He was an editor's editor. Yet he never wrote a word on the fine points of the craft he mastered. His primary focus was on the work, its process, and its product."[16]

Jelliffe as editor functioned as a teacher, teaching his readers what he presented and teaching his contributors, at the very least, that they should do a thorough search of the literature before writing on any subject. For out of Jelliffe's awesome mastery of the medical literature, he could almost always find relevant items that an author had overlooked or that would at least add clinical, scientific, or historical depth to a paper. That work upgraded American and, to some extent, world medicine, especially neurology, psychiatry, and psychoanalysis. But the exact impact or influence was subtle, virtually impossible to document, and must be left as inferential as that of his role as formal teacher. Only the corpus of learning that he assembled, and which now is for the most part bound on library shelves, is palpably permanent.

Through his own writings, both in and outside of his journals, Jelliffe put a vast amount of technical and scholarly material before the public, both professional and general. The bibliography appended to this book shows a productivity that is immense. To that record should be added abstracts, book reviews, and unsigned contributions. Mackie estimates that from 1902 to 1944 alone Jelliffe published 1500 substantial contributions in addition to sixteen books as author or coauthor. But again, evidence as to what the impact of this writing was on readers is pretty well unknown. Some publications, particularly the *Text-Book,* were clearly very important in the field. Some of the rest may well have been ephemeral, although stimulating other workers at that time. Stimulation is a major function of scholarly and scientific

16. James B. Mackie, "1902–1944: The 42–Year Editorship of Smith Ely Jelliffe, A Practical Mystic," *JNMD,* 159 (1974), 305–318.

publication, an important avenue through which the intellectual stranger introduces intellectual change.

The ideas in Jelliffe's writings were never quite specific enough that they can be traced as such, distinct from the contributions of others. He devised nothing like an Oedipus complex or organ inferiority or a projective mental test that anyone could identify and know that Jelliffe had elucidated that particular series of ideas. The only exception might have been his scheme of stages of human development, and it was, as has been noted, in fact very seldom employed by other writers (perhaps because of his unusually heavy dependence on the idea of recapitulation). More typical were his ideas on psychosomatics, which were similar to Groddeck's and which, in any event, came too early for the institutionally effective founders of psychosomatic medicine, who did not draw on his work in a concrete way as they might have.[17] So with many of his efforts. The Jelliffe and White textbook probably influenced a number of writers of other textbooks in the field of nervous and mental disease to take a more dynamic approach; but many forces operating at the time could also have pushed them in that direction, and so certainty is impossible. With the exception of the textbook Jelliffe himself did not make particular claims of priority, although he sometimes felt wronged. In 1934, for example, he remarked to a correspondent, "I was in on the Clark and Atwood studies (1912), in fact first gave him the speculations as to the erotic significance of the movements [in epilepsy]. I have letters showing this."[18]

Jelliffe did work up some enthusiasm for his role in developing psychoanalytic ideas into psychosomatics. "The organic disease material is all original," he assured a popular writer in 1932, adding ironically, "Even papa Freud says so. . . ."[19]

Nevertheless, even among relatively sympathetic psychoanalysts, Jelliffe was isolated as an extremist or an eclectic—or, as in other projects, his efforts were abortive, as in the case of his work on technique: "I think my contribution, first in the *Psychoanalytic Review* and then in book form, 1920, was the first book in English devoted to the *Technique of Psychoanalysis*. While I am not very proud of it yet it went through two editions . . . and would have had more had it not been my first conflict with White. He did not think a second edition would sell. He was wrong but I knuckled under when it came to a much needed third revision and White was timid about its sales value and other resistances I do not care to go into."[20]

17. Iago Galdston, "The Roots of Psychosomatic Medicine," *Canadian Medical Association Journal*, 70 (1954), 127–134, for example, ignores Jelliffe entirely.
18. Jelliffe to C. J. C. Earl, 17 November 1934. It is not certain what letters are referred to, if indeed they have survived.
19. Jelliffe to Grace Adams, 26 March 1932. See Sigmund Freud, "A Short Account of Psycho-Analysis," *Standard Edn.*, vol. 19, p. 209.
20. Jelliffe to Ives Hendrick, 13 December 1939.

As has been suggested earlier, many of Jelliffe's medical contributions were written on the wrong level of discourse to elicit intellectual resonance from his contemporaries. In 1917 he attempted to express how he was trying to avoid being either a "fatuous enthusiast" or an "asylum routinist." Improvement was needed, he said. "Therefore if, in the present outlines, my emphasis should be laid upon certain hypothetical sides of the problem, it is with the conviction that it is with hypotheses we work; we must use them to get ahead; if they fail, reject them as fast as they show their insufficiency, and seek for more. It has always been the essential defect in the attitude of the extremists just mentioned that the enthusiast has had so many useless hypotheses intermingled with the good ones, and the so-called practical man has hung on too long to the previously useful ones after new valuable points of view have been offered."[21]

But what Jelliffe offered involved too many generalities, whatever the virtues of the specific content of what he was saying. In 1915, for example, just in surveying the routine presentations of colleagues in the New York Neurological Society, he put all of the papers into a theoretical/schematic framework that made his viewpoint seem unfamiliar rather than familiar to the audience of specialists.[22]

One standard, though not necessarily satisfactory, way of measuring impact and influence is to aggregate references to a person's work in the publications of other important figures in a field or in intellectual areas generally. Thus, for example, Alfred Korzybski, in his famous *Science and Sanity* (1933), utilized Jelliffe's stages of life and quoted him elsewhere in the volume, mentioning his name among fifty-five thinkers from Aristotle to Wittgenstein who influenced Korzybski's work. But it turns out that for two years Korzybski was working at St. Elizabeths Hospital, and of course White's influence assured that Korzybski knew Jelliffe's work.[23] Measuring such uses does indicate influence, but with such a complex burden—would Korzybski have known about Jelliffe without White? is not White's endorsement of Jelliffe "influence" anyway? etc.—that the inquiry becomes disorderly.

The fact remains that after *Citation Index* began appearing in 1967, Jelliffe's work was cited in several scientific writings almost every year. His botanical work might well be expected to appear because of the cumulative nature of systematics, but in fact papers citing his work on multiple sclerosis, Huntington's disease (possibly another cumulative subject), the sequellae of encephalitis, and sometimes psychoanalysis also continued to show up. Even the Jelliffe and White textbook after thirty or forty years was still cited

21. Smith Ely Jelliffe, "The Treatment of the Schizophrenic (Dementia Praecox) Patient," *International Clinics*, 27 (1917), 164.

22. Smith Ely Jelliffe, abstracted in *JNMD*, 42 (1915), 507–511.

23. Alfred Korzybski, *Science and Sanity: An Introduction to Non-Aristotelian Systems and General Semantics* (Lancaster, Pa., 1933).

occasionally for standard viewpoints. Although the incidence might appear light in view of the large numbers of books and papers that Jelliffe published, still the citations provide tangible evidence of enduring quality.

The foregoing brief survey of formal evidences of Jelliffe's impact suggests, again, substantial influence but a tantalizing vagueness about just what the influence was. His name continued for a long time to be remembered in connection with work on a few subjects—not only Huntington's disease and the flora of Long Island but psychosomatics and brain disease. Certainly his Lamarckianism was not remembered, nor, ultimately, his use of the death instinct. In later psychoanalysis the idea of energy, which was central to Jelliffe's viewpoint, came to be considered useless and misleading. Of course all of these superseded ideas were also held by Freud, and they did not seriously damage his reputation. Jelliffe, too, added to scientific and medical knowledge and systematized it, and the record shows enduring reputation beyond the contemporary honors bestowed by his peers.

The Puzzle of Jelliffe's Influence

Yet the testimony of Jelliffe's contemporaries was that he fulfilled an important function in his own day and age in addition to contributing directly to knowledge. His personal impact may have been even more important than the exact content of his publications. (It may be worth remarking that his contemporaries remembered him as a tall figure, but he was in fact, as noted in his passport [Chapter 1], at most just very slightly above average for his day.)

What is contradictory, then, is Jelliffe's feeling of isolation from his contemporaries and his concurrent general conformity to convention as he knew it in both behavior and attitude, whether singing hymns as a young man or making alcoholic beverages in his home during prohibition. In some ways Jelliffe was alone, truly the intellectual stranger who could lead others into new areas. He was not a part of the scientific and medical establishment. He could not influence the granting of increasingly important foundation funds. Indeed, when the Rockefeller Foundation turned to supporting the neurosciences in the 1920's and 1930's, no one could at first have provided better information on continental European laboratories and workers than Jelliffe. The Rockefeller officials never consulted him. Some social/professional groups remained relatively closed to him—he was sixty years old before he was finally elected into the exclusive Vidonian Club in which New York psychiatrists provided light entertainment for each other, an arena in which Jelliffe's colleagues knew he was outstanding.[24]

Yet Jelliffe was truly eminent, outstanding among the 150,000 physicians in the United States as well as among specialists throughout the world. When

24. Early on he was active in the more broadly cultural Charaka Club, as is reflected in part in the Bibliography.

a medical traveler sympathetic to Jelliffe's point of view, Paul Schilder, then still of Vienna, reported on his colleagues in America in 1929, he singled out Meyer as the most eminent, and he gave special attention also to White. Schilder mentioned Jelliffe and White in connection with their textbook, but Jelliffe's psychosomatics in addition got special discussion. Other American psychiatrists received even less attention. From Schilder's dynamic point of view, then, Jelliffe was a distant third on the list of important Americans— but he was, nevertheless, third.[25] And he represented a viewpoint, not leadership.

Jelliffe associated his feelings of isolation with the "extremist" label that was put on his ideas. Writing to an English friend in 1923, Jelliffe commented on what happened when he gave his paper, "Psychopathology and Organic Disease:" "I tied it on the dog at the A.N.A. and they are still wondering what kind of fool I am." Ten years later he mentioned to another correspondent his long-standing contention that electrical stimulation (a standard therapy in neurological cases) had no physiological effects, "but the noses are still in the air, as I am the proverbial bad boy in our Neurological Society and a Freudian over 65."[26]

Jelliffe's sense of isolation had an important by-product: he was quick to encourage promising work of other nonestablishment or unconventional thinkers. Trigant Burrow, for example, was grateful for Jelliffe's sympathy when the Freudian "clique" pointedly ignored Burrow's ideas at the Bad Homburg Congress in 1925. Even more important, as Casamajor, Mackie, and others pointed out, Jelliffe identified with and supported young people in the profession. He thought of himself as a fresh influence and at the age of sixty-one wanted recognition for "my jumping on the old hard shells." A few years later he concluded that he himself was not an old conservative and neither was he a young radical, which meant that he had to be an "old radical."[27]

His willingness as editor and discussant at meetings to publish and encourage the work of younger members of the profession was of great importance in shaping not only his publishing ventures but the careers of many young physicians and scientists. Lawrence Kubie, one of the young Turks of psychoanalysis in the 1930's, noted that Jelliffe "showed a rare generosity of spirit, especially perhaps toward the young." As Kubie recalled, "On one occasion I criticized a paper of his both inaccurately and with a curious kind of meanness which I regretted immediately after it appeared, and have never ceased to regret. His reply was straight from the shoulder and unsparing,

25. Paul Schilder, "Amerikanische Psychiatrie," *Der Nervenarzt*, 2 (1929), 476–481. Schilder's view was of course not typical of European psychiatry, which tended not to be dynamic.

26. Jelliffe to S. A. K. Wilson, 12 January 1923. Jelliffe to W. Burridge, 13 May 1933.

27. Jelliffe to H. S. Sullivan, 1 June 1928. Jelliffe to Elbert Lenrow, 20 October 1936, Additional Papers. Trigant Burrow to Jelliffe, 19 October 1925.

but nonetheless warm and forgiving, and even accepting wherever possible. This is what marked the man as unique, and stirred in his critics a combination of admiration and humility."[28]

Jelliffe had his opinions and occasionally made harsh evaluations, some published, for example, in book reviews, others expressed only in his correspondence. He was quite capable of writing privately and knowingly that someone "gives me a pain in the neck" (in this case Karen Horney).[29] And one can imagine authors squirming in the days when he signed his reviews and wrote such things as: "The best we can say is that the work is of grab bag construction, containing an unassorted collection of statements, many of which are of value, many are rubbish. . . . a little knowledge of psychiatry would have done him no harm."[30] Or: "This is the type of book that retards the rational development of psychiatry for its readers. It is didactic, devoid of any ray of modernity and suggests a hopeless quagmire of conservatism, and an ignorant conservatism at that."[31] Or, again: "Barbers need diplomas, but any fool is competent to treat mental disorders, and unfortunately there are thousands of them doing it."[32]

What is most significant, then, is that despite his feelings of isolation and his ability to express dislike and disapproval, Jelliffe maintained a significant standing in his profession and specialty. His colleagues did not always know exactly what his contribution was; Adolf Meyer when asked to the 1938 celebration carefully avoided mentioning anything specific but finally concluded vaguely that Jelliffe "is doing a remarkable job." In what respect, he did not say.[33]

One asset of Jelliffe's did make him formidable: his command of the literature. Thus in 1924 C. K. Mills of Philadelphia described Jelliffe as the best-equipped American in his knowledge of the neurological literature.[34] It is easy to understand Brill's remark that Jelliffe's "contemporaries did not all love him but they all esteemed and admired him" after reading the way that he treated an eminent critic, Archibald Church of Chicago, in discussion at the 1920 American Neurological Association meetings. Church no doubt understood not only the content and courtesy but the overtones of Jelliffe's reply to him. Church had commented that Jelliffe had overlooked the literature on a supposedly significant spirochete reported in cases of multiple

28. Lawrence S. Kubie, "Smith Ely Jelliffe," *JNMD*, 159 (1974), 79. C. McCord to Jelliffe, 14 May 1938, wrote a tribute to this characteristic of Jelliffe.

29. Jelliffe to Otto Fenichel, 2 March 1940.

30. Smith Ely Jelliffe, review of Hollander, *The First Signs of Insanity*, in *JNMD*, 40 (1913), 750.

31. Smith Ely Jelliffe, review of Younger, *Insanity in Every Day Practice*, in *JNMD*, 38 (1911), 381.

32. Smith Ely Jelliffe, review of Tyson, *The Practice of Medicine*, in *JNMD*, 37 (1910), 144.

33. A. A. Brill to Adolf Meyer, 10 November 1937, Adolf Meyer Papers.

34. C. K. Mills, in *Semi-Centennial Volume of the American Neurological Association, 1875–1924* (New York, 1924), p. 19.

sclerosis. In reply, according to the published report of the discussion, Jelliffe "said that after Dr. Church had given him credit for erudition, he could ill repay this compliment by confessing ignorance of the whole mass of recent literature concerning the finding of a new spirochete in some patients with multiple sclerosis. Of course, that was an old story. He thought that Dr. Church had probably seen for the last two years in the *Journal of Nervous and Mental Disease* his abstracts of this work, not only of Kuhn and Steiner's original claims but of Siemerling and others, and vigorous protests concerning the whole subject. In fact, in the May issue of the *Journal* a critical collective abstract and careful discussion of the whole of Kuhn and Steiner's theory was to be found. He thought he had made it perfectly clear that this type of case was outside of this discussion; such types, or any new ones, could be included under the specific infectious types of disseminated cerebrospinal disease. In reply to Dr. Church, he would be discourteous not to acknowledge the validity of his point, but he had already excluded from his discussion that whole group."[35]

Menninger, who obviously came to feel very close to Jelliffe, tried in an obituary notice to make some distinctions about the nature of Jelliffe's personal impact.

"My teacher, Ernest Southard, died in 1919. His brilliant and catholic mind was nonetheless capable of stubborn prejudices, and one of these prejudices was against psychoanalysis. Yet it was through him that I had met Smith Ely Jelliffe of New York, one of the most vigorous and most gifted of the protagonists of psychoanalysis at that time. Dr. Jelliffe was like Dr. Southard in his catholicity of mind and in his brilliance; he was less philosophical than Southard but more erudite and far more experienced clinically. I remember with deep gratitude how he took me under his wing after Southard died—me, a youngster fresh out of my hospital training, unknown to anyone in the field. Dr. Jelliffe introduced me to people, to experiences, and, above all, to ideas. He took me into his home, where I was impressed no less by the thousands of volumes of neurologic and psychiatric wisdom than by the infinite variety of home-made wines and liqueurs and the enormous collections of fungi, mosses, and pressed botanical specimens.

"It was Jelliffe who introduced me to clinical psychoanalysis; prior to that time I had known only the published material of Freud, Jones, Brill, Frink, and others. In those days a personal analysis was not regarded as a necessary prerequisite to the clinical practice of psychoanalysis, and it was Jelliffe who first encouraged me to try the experiment of listening for a time to free associations and judging for myself whether or not they had any clinical meaning. I recall a private meeting of a few psychoanalysts in New York to

35. *Transactions of the American Neurological Association*, 1920, pp. 251, 253. A. A. Brill, "In Memoriam," p. 226.

which Dr. Jelliffe took me, at which one of the members of the group [Horace Frink] described in considerable detail his own personal experiences in analysis with Professor Freud, subsequently discussed by all those present as if it were an ordinary clinical case."[36]

Esteem and admiration were not just formal or personal in the case of Jelliffe but entered into the very nature of his importance. Because of his eminence he was at the least able to gain serious consideration for a wide variety of ideas. In 1936, for example, Harry A. Parkind, in a formal review of the neuropsychiatric field for the year, made an almost unprecedented (in that annual series) editorial preface to his summary of a paper of Jelliffe's: "To many it will seem that he has gone too far in attributing to psychoanalytic mechanisms genetic powers in the development of physical disease." But, said Parkind, "any psychiatric concept advanced by Smith Ely Jelliffe merits widespread attention."[37]

As an extremist, then, Jelliffe's reputation and esteem made his influence potent. Like any extremist, Jelliffe played a social role in moving colleagues toward his position, for they could advance a substantial distance and still, compared to him, appear to themselves and others to be both progressive, and balanced and moderate. The more respect and visibility that he had, therefore, the more influence he exerted, even though he appeared to be isolated and without immediate adherents who would go all the way with him. Insofar, then, as Jelliffe took the unconventional stand that illness is in very substantial part an expression of the patient's life themes and the symptoms symbolizations of his/her strivings and failures, Jelliffe often moved even people who explicitly voiced their disagreements toward his position, and he therefore contributed to this type of thinking, although not usually his own formulations, in the mid-century decades. This indirect influence made Jelliffe formidable indeed, the catalyst for many small intellectual breakthroughs.

Jelliffe's contemporaries saw him as a prophet, as someone who was not exactly in tune with the times but whose time was yet to come.[38] Often this was explicit, and in 1933 Jelliffe was delighted when Freud publicly complimented his ideas as "a part of the medicine of the future."[39] That same year Roy R. Grinker, Sr., who later was a major figure in psychosomatics, wrote from Vienna where he was taking psychoanalytic training to say that he had just read through the whole file of the *Journal of Nervous and Mental*

---

36. Menninger, *A Psychiatrist's World*, pp. 826–827.

37. Harry A. Parkind, in *Yearbook of Neurology, Psychiatry and Endocrinology*, 1936, p. 308.

38. See in general John C. Burnham, "From Avant-Garde to Specialism: Psychoanalysis in America," *Journal of the History of the Behavioral Sciences*, 15 (1979), 128–134.

39. Jelliffe to Karl Menninger, 17 April 1933. Sigmund Freud, "Psychoanalysis: Exploring the Hidden Recesses of the Mind," tr. A. A. Brill, in *These Eventful Years: The Twentieth Century in the Making*, 2 vols. (New York, 1924), vol. 2, p. 523.

Disease, and he "saw how Jelliffe changed from an enumerator of visits to the out-patient dept to the most dynamic figure in American Psychiatry."[40]

The Meaning of Personal Influence

Jelliffe was therefore particularly important as an inspirational figure in medicine. Despite his occasional ability to offend, he was, as all witnesses agreed, personally charming. Lewis recalled that Jelliffe "was such a witty conversationalist that, at various medical society dinners, I often noted considerable competition among his colleagues to obtain a seat at his table."[41] This impression carried over into the realm of public speaking, an area in which personal influence showed up particularly well. Jelliffe tried to be an elocutionist, like his father, and with considerable success. In 1936 five hundred people were present to hear him after his colleagues chose him to inaugurate the prestigious "Lectures for the Laity" series of the New York Academy of Medicine.[42]

When he was seventy-six, Jelliffe looked back and reviewed the way he functioned as a public speaker. "Through imitation, conscious as well as unconscious, I became something more than a stumbling speaker either with prepared addresses and/or with discussions of medical topics (neuropsychiatric) from the floor. Having been gifted or penalized by this capacity, after an early introverted humility that kept me in my seat, I later decided to take every opportunity to have 'my say,' the which, often accompanied by an aptitude for the humorous, became well known and many opportunities for discussion were embraced to the edification and amusement of my audiences. My medical confrères were insistent upon my being put on the program and I acquiesced and flatter myself that on such occasions there was usually a large audience. Whether such sought for edification or for amusement I would not attempt to differentiate. Probably it was both and since I had allied myself early with the Freudian conceptions, I believe my discussions contained features of interest, both because of the material itself that came up for discussion and for the better oratorical as well as pedagogic methods of my delivery. I had a good voice, could be heard all over the audience chamber.

"Thus, from the ages of fifty to seventy, after which time I rarely attended medical meetings, save those of smaller local interests, psychiatry, psychoanalysis and the like."[43]

He was, then, aware of the power of impression and his ability to sway his hearers. His speculation that he might have made more progress by using demagogic techniques to further his ideas was noted above (Chapter 3). To a correspondent Jelliffe remarked that, on one occasion when he spoke on

40. Roy R. Grinker, Sr., to Jelliffe, 7 October 1933.

41. Nolan D. C. Lewis, "Smith Ely Jelliffe, 1866–1945, Psychosomatic Medicine in America," in *Psychoanalytic Pioneers*, p. 233.

42. *New York Times*, 9 October 1936.

43. Smith Ely Jelliffe, "Little Signs of Parathyroid Disturbance," *Journal of the Mount Sinai Hospital*, 9 (1942), 579.

very short notice, he was insufficiently prepared and so "carried my audience by useful elisions and . . . elocution. . . ."[44]

Jelliffe's impact therefore can be understood both in terms of the explicit content of his communications and in terms of implicit communications also. As an inspirational figure he operated in two ways. In many contexts he did not bring his readers and hearers specific ideas and information as much as he did modes and possibilities of thinking. A New England physician wrote him in 1915: "Your lectures at the Post Graduate on psycho-analysis made the greatest impression on me of anything that has occurred during my life. . . . I am indebted to you for a great awakening."[45] Jelliffe carried others where they might not otherwise have gone in their thinking. He was of course concerned with the strictly cognitive, but on several levels, including abstracting, generalizing, and making new connections between ideas. In the second place, he functioned as an ideal figure, a role model, even a conscience. He affected, therefore, the attitudes of his audiences as well as their formal knowledge and thought processes. Hence the additional importance of his personal presence, his public personality, and his elocution. It was in both his cognitive and attitudinal communications, then, that Jelliffe acted as the cultural stranger, bringing an outsider's view and with it new intellectual possibilities.

Two generations felt Jelliffe's impact in person and in print. One flourished in the early twentieth century. That generation he confronted with far-ranging scholarship, with scientific medicine, with social concerns (in medical journal editorials), and above all with psychotherapy, psychoanalysis, and psychological thinking and interpretation. The second generation constituted the intellectual and medical and especially psychiatric world of the 1920's, 1930's, and 1940's. His holistic approach and his sense of the interdependence of the complicated mental and physical functioning of each human being helped prepare the way not only for psychosomatic medicine and the neurosciences but for the burgeoning of all of the health sciences that took place after World War II and for the complicated physiological measuring upon which so much of medicine came to depend.

Jelliffe did not, it is true, directly affect the younger members of that postwar generation. But he did act as a grandfather figure for them. He had taught their teachers, for whom he was the advocate of certain standards. It was an impressive mark to leave and another impressive generation to mark.

Just what, then, was Jelliffe's image? What were the main features of the ideal figure? Of course each person viewed him idiosyncratically. But through

44. Jelliffe to Jacob Feigenbaum, 2 May 1935.
45. Owen B. Ames to Jelliffe, 9 June 1915. Lawrence S. Kubie, "Smith Ely Jelliffe, 1866–1945," in Derek Denny-Brown, ed., *Centennial Anniversary Volume of the American Neurological Association* (New York, 1975), p. 183, noted that not all of Jelliffe's contemporaries followed him or learned from him: "Some . . . felt that his hypotheses sometimes took dangerous leaps and that he did not always stop to gather sufficient evidence for his speculations."

all of the testimony and writings a certain consistent theme came through: Jelliffe stood for a familiar figure, the physician who was also learned and literate, above all a thinker and not just a technician. To this day both the thorough bibliographies and the many scholarly allusions in his papers are very imposing. When Ives Hendrick was attacking Jelliffe in 1928 (Chapter 3), he specifically focused on Jelliffe's erudition. Jelliffe's letters to Jung and Freud also illustrate his thoughtful, cultured style.

This ideal of clinician as intellectual was one of the lasting legacies not merely of Jelliffe but of Victorian science and medicine in general. Jelliffe simply embodied it for a large number of M.D.'s and other thinkers. A leading French colleague sensed Jelliffe's essence in recalling "delightful conversation on Greek drama, botanics, pharmacology, neurology, psychiatry, psychoanalysis in the truly Gallic vein which is yours."[46]

Jelliffe tried to know not just a narrow specialization, or even a field, but all knowledge—what a liberally educated person ought to know. And he tried to be cultured, to maintain the ideal of the physician as a gentleman who knew what standards were in high culture, in science, and in human decency. This was the young man who had a conventional *Wanderjahr* in Europe and sampled all of the conventional things—the best in medicine and science and also the best in music and theater. He ultimately knew Barrymore as well as Jung and Freud. This was the young professional who settled into his birthplace and enjoyed local, provincial ties, but at the same time read several languages and knew physicians and their research and other intellectuals all over the world.[47]

Jelliffe was a medical leader who would not be tied down to a particular twentieth-century social structure. In the realm of ideas, too, his speculations were in a mode more typical of the nineteenth than the twentieth century. Brill in his eulogy characterized Jelliffe as a naturalist. In his medical work Jelliffe tended to jump directly from the case history to generalization without the rigorous intermediate theorizing that marked the new generations in psychoanalysis and the neurosciences, especially after 1925 or so. His Victorian level of discourse was increasingly anachronous in his old age. But even then he stood for breadth as well as intensity, for perspective and learning as well as laboratory technique. Jelliffe, the learned physician, upheld ideals as well as standards at the same time that he advocated innovation.

46. R. Brequet to Jelliffe, 17 September 1930.
47. David A. Hollinger, "Ethnic Diversity, Cosmopolitanism and the Emergence of the American Liberal Intelligentsia," *American Quarterly*, 27 (1975), 133–151, depicts one of the major contexts in which Jelliffe operated.

(top) Susan Emma Kitchell Jelliffe, age 47, mother of Smith Ely Jelliffe.
(bottom) William Munson Jelliffe at the time of his marriage (1856).

Smith Ely Jelliffe, age 6–7 months (1867).

(*top*) *Louise Jelliffe (Mrs. Walter Pratt Long), Smith Ely Jelliffe's sister (1895).*
(*bottom*) *William Munson Jelliffe at age 60.*

Smith Ely Jelliffe, age 24 (October 1890).

Helena Dewey Leeming, wife of Smith Ely Jelliffe, probably about the time of her marriage.

Members of P & S class of 1889. Standing (left to right): John L. Andrews, Morton R. Peck, Frank L. Hupp. Sitting (left to right): Louis F. Bishop, James P. Warbasse, Smith Ely Jelliffe.

The Jelliffe Quiz (1898). Standing (left to right): William H. Alle, Frederic J. Hughes, Mr. Nesbitt, William B. Crawford, (?), Mr. Kismale, Oliver P. Hump-stone, John E. Jennings, Everett W. Gould. Sitting (left to right): Linnaeus La Fetra, Morton R. Peck, Smith Ely Jelliffe, Mr. Armstrong, Frank H. Knight.

(top) Smith Ely Jelliffe, age 33 (June 1900), before Norway trip.
(bottom) Jelliffe's Den at 231 West 71st Street, New York City (1902).

*(top) Kraepelin and students (Munich, Summer 1906). Standing (left to right):
Alzheimer, Lüttge, Kraepelin, Vostein, Jelliffe, Perusini, (?), Busch, Probst, Rehm,
(?). Sitting (left to right): Hermann, Wittenberg, Gaupp, (?), Cotton, (?), Achucarro,
Rohde, Cudden.
(bottom) White, Jelliffe, and Gregory (aboard ship, 1907).*

Jelliffe's children: Sylvia, Leeming, Winifred, Helena, and Ely (Dresden, Christmas 1908).

(top) Jelliffe's office at 64 West 56th Street, New York City.
(bottom) Putnam, Jelliffe, Timme, and (sitting) McNaughton (Plattsburg, Summer 1918).

(top) *Jelliffe, age 60–62.*
(bottom) *Jelliffe at work in the neurological library at Huletts Landing, Lake George (ca. 1936–1938).*

(top) The Den at Huletts Landing, Lake George, (mid-1930's).
(bottom) Exterior view of the Den at Lake George (mid-1930's).

(top) Jelliffe, age 70.
(bottom) Louise Jelliffe (Mrs. Walter Pratt Long).

(top) *Jelliffe's bookplate.*
(bottom) *Sample of Jelliffe's shorthand used in recording case histories.*

Smith Ely Jelliffe, M.D. Portrait by Mary Foote, undated. Photograph from the Mary Foote papers, Beinecke Library, Yale University (see comment following letter of 9 July 1923).

II

Jelliffe's Correspondence with Sigmund Freud and C. G. Jung

Edited by WILLIAM McGUIRE

Freud's German Letters
Translated by Ralph Manheim

C. G. Jung (1875–1961) and Jelliffe both attended the First International Congress for Psychiatry, Neurology, Psychology, and the Nursing of the Insane, at Amsterdam, 2–7 September 1907, and it is evident that they met during the congress. Jelliffe had sailed from New York in mid-August, with a party of doctors including William Alanson White, M. S. Gregory, and D. B. Delevan. Jelliffe and White, as official delegates of the United States to the congress, carried certificates issued by the secretary of state.[1] None of the Americans gave papers. Jung, however, presented one[2] in the section on psychiatry and neurology, which had as its topic "New Theories on the Origin of Hysteria." The principal paper on that occasion was delivered by Pierre Janet, restating his own theory of subconscious fixed ideas. Gustav Aschaffenburg, the second speaker, attacked Freud's theory of hysteria and in particular his emphasis on sexuality. Jung, third on the program, outlined the psychoanalytic technique and said that his own clinical experience confirmed all of Freud's principles. His performance was stormy—he exceeded his time limit and refused to stop speaking until he was called to order by the chairman, whereupon he strode out angrily. The fourth paper was given by a Dutch physician who was a friend of Jelliffe, Professor Gerbrandus Jelgersma, of Leiden, and the only notation that Jelliffe jotted anywhere in the printed program of the session was a reference to Jelgersma and the feeling-toned complex. He made no comment on Jung's controversial paper, though he knew Jung's work on dementia praecox, having cited it favorably

1. Jelliffe's scrapbook for 1907 (Additional Papers) contains the program of the congress, the certificate of the secretary of state appointing him a delegate, the manifest of the S. S. *Zeeland* listing him and the other three doctors as passengers, the program of a dinner aboard the S. S. *Königin Luise* on the westbound voyage in late September, and other memorabilia. Details of the congress are from Jung's letters to Freud, 4 Sept. and 11 Sept. 1907 (Jelliffe was mentioned in neither), in *The Freud/Jung Letters*, and from Ellenberger, pp. 796–798.

2. "Die Freud'sche Hysterietheorie," *Monatsschrift für Psychiatrie und Neurologie* (Berlin), 23 (1908); tr., "The Freudian Theory of Hysteria," *Coll. Works*, 4, pars. 27 ff.

in a paper he had given the previous June.[3] Further polemics against Freud
and Jung marked the next day's discussion period. Ellenberger has called
the two-day debate one of the "great discussions" in the development of
psychoanalysis, and, according to Nolan D. C. Lewis, Jelliffe listened with
interest and made Jung's acquaintance.[4] One may speculate that Jung cordially invited the Americans to pay a visit to Zurich. By that time, he had
had at least two American pupils at the Burghölzli Mental Hospital, where
he was senior staff physician: Frederick W. Peterson, of New York, and
Charles Ricksher, of the Boston area, both physicians, had spent several
months at the great hospital and had separately collaborated with Jung on
research, which subsequently was published in English.[5] A. A. Brill would
soon arrive from New York to work at the hospital.[6] Jung evidently had a
serviceable command of spoken English by then; besides his school studies,
he had spent two months in London in early 1904.[7]

After the congress ended, on 7 September, Jelliffe, White, and Gregory
set off on a half-sightseeing, half-professional excursion. They visited Liège
and Nancy (where Bernheim demonstrated hypnotism for them), then traveled south through Switzerland on their way to Italy. The party evidently
stopped in Zurich, though Jelliffe recorded the event only twenty-five years
later (and there is no record of it on Jung's part). They lunched, he said,
with Jung and his Swiss colleagues Alphonse Maeder and Franz Riklin,
presumably at the Burghölzli.[8] In Italy, the Americans paid calls on psychiatrists in several cities. They sailed home 24 September from Bremen.

When Jung and Freud made their famous trip to the United States in
September 1909, for the conference marking the twentieth anniversary of

3. Jelliffe, "Some General Reflections on the Psychology of Dementia Praecox," *Journal of
the American Medical Association*, 50 (1908), 202 ff., read at the fifty-eighth annual session of
the American Medical Association, Atlantic City, June 1907; Jung, *Über die Psychologie der
Dementia praecox: Ein Versuch* (Halle, 1907); tr., "The Psychology of Dementia Praecox," *Coll.
Works*, 3.

  4. Nolan D. C. Lewis, "Smith Ely Jelliffe: Psychosomatic Medicine in America," in *Psychoanalytic Pioneers*, p. 225. White states in *Forty Years of Psychiatry* (NMDMS 57, 1933), p.
33, that he met Jung on that occasion, and one may infer that Jelliffe likewise met Jung.

5. With Peterson, "Psycho-physical Investigations with the Galvanometer and Pneumograph
in Normal and Insane Individuals," *Brain*, 30:2 (July 1907); with Ricksher, "Further Investigations on the Galvanic Phenomenon and Respiration in Normal and Insane Individuals,"
Journal of Abnormal Psychology, 2:5 (Dec. 1907–Jan. 1908); both republished in *Coll. Works*,
2.

6. Jung to Freud, 15 Feb. 1908, n. 2, in *The Freud/Jung Letters*. While at the Burghölzli,
Brill undertook the translation of Jung's *The Psychology of Dementia Praecox*, and, after his
return to New York in 1908, F. W. Peterson collaborated with him. Their work was published
as NMDMS 3 (1909). No correspondence between Brill, Peterson, Jelliffe, White, and Jung
concerning this project has come to light. Brill retranslated the work alone for republication in
the same monograph series in 1936 and wrote a reminiscent introduction, which was reprinted
in a paperback edition of Jung's monograph (Princeton, 1974).

7. Personal communication from Franz Jung.

8. "Glimpses of a Freudian Odyssey," *Psychoanalytic Quarterly*, 2 (1933), 318–329, quoted
in Part I, ch. 2, above; and below, Jelliffe to Freud, 6 Mar. 1939. No earlier documentation of
Jelliffe's visit to Zurich has been found. Alphonse Maeder (1882–1971), Swiss psychotherapist,
and Franz Riklin, M.D. (1878–1938), psychiatrist, at the Burghölzli 1902–1904, both remained
with Jung after his dissension from Freud.

Clark University, at Worcester, Massachusetts, there was no question of again meeting Jelliffe, who was in Paris for a year of study abroad. As recounted in Part I, he had brought his family to Europe in October 1908 and had gone first to Vienna for the Third International Congress for the Relief of the Insane,[9] where he could have met the director of the Burghölzli, Eugen Bleuler.[10] He did not, in any case, meet Freud. Next, Jelliffe and his family spent six months in Berlin, where he worked with Theodor Ziehen and Hermann Oppenheim and met the psychoanalyst Karl Abraham. After a sojourn of six more months in Paris, where he studied with Janet, Joseph Babinski, and Joseph Déjérine, Jelliffe and his family sailed home to New York in early fall 1909, at about the same time that Freud and Jung were sailing back to Europe. Within a few months, Jelliffe was serving on the staff of the New York Neurological Institute. There, one of his colleagues was Brill, who, after his months at the Burghölzli and his attendance at the first psychoanalytic congress, at Salzburg in April, had already declared himself a psychoanalyst.[11]

There is no evidence that Jelliffe saw Jung again when the latter made a hurried trip to the States for a week, in March 1910, to treat a patient in Chicago.[12] Nor is there any correspondence extant between them until 1912. Though Jelliffe had been following events in the psychoanalytic world through the *Jahrbuch für psychoanalytische und psychopathologische Forschungen*, to which he subscribed, and other publications, it is not likely that in 1912 he was aware of the growing rift between Jung and Freud. He had, as recounted in Part I, joined the medical department of Fordham University, and together with William J. Maloney organized its International Extension Course in Medicine, in September,[13] to which several distinguished figures were invited: Henry Head, of London, the editor of *Brain;* Gordon Holmes, also of London, authority on the physiology of the nervous system; William Alanson White; and others, including Jung, who, it was announced, would talk on "mental mechanisms in health and disease." His subject was in fact "The Theory of Psychoanalysis"[14]—a deceptive title, for Jung's theory had by now deviated from Freud's, and his Fordham lectures actually constituted a critique of Freudian psychoanalysis. Jung's first letter to Jelliffe—or the earliest that has survived—was the following:

9. "Glimpses of a Freudian Odyssey," p. 323. Jelliffe filled a scrapbook with memorabilia from the 1908–1909 year abroad, in Additional Papers.
10. Freud to Jung, 15 Oct. 1908, in *The Freud/Jung Letters.*
11. Jung to Freud, 15 Feb. 1908, in ibid. See also Jones, 2, ch. 2, 1908. Cf. above, Part I, ch. 2.
12. Letters of March 1910 in *The Freud/Jung Letters.*
13. "Glimpses of a Freudian Odyssey," p. 325; anon., "The International Extension Course in Medicine," *Fordham Monthly,* 31:1 (Nov. 1912); H. W. Kirwin, "James J. Walsh—Medical Historian and Pathfinder," *Catholic Historical Review,* 45:4 (Jan. 1960), 428. Walsh, dean of the Fordham Medical School, organized the Extension Course. Cf. also *The Freud/Jung Letters,* p. 513, and Jung to Freud, 11 Nov. 1912.
14. First published, tr. Edith and M. D. Eder and Mary Moltzer, in the first three issues of the *Psychoanalytic Review,* 1:1 (Nov. 1913) through 2:1 (Jan. 1915); see *Coll. Works,* 4.

Jung to Jelliffe

Dr. med. C. G. Jung, LL.D.
Privatdocent der Psychiatrie
1003 Seestrasse
Küsnach-Zürich

May 13, 1912[1]

Dear Dr. Jelliffe,

I accept your kind invitation to stay in your house during the time of my lectures. I am very grateful for this arrangement, because life in hotels in New York is somewhat disagreeable.

As I already told you, I hope or expect to be in N. Y. on September 18 (*Kaiser Wilhelm II*).

Very truly yours,
Dr. Jung.

The Extension Course, attended by nearly a hundred teachers and practitioners, was evidently a success. The New York *Sun* congratulated Fordham University on the "progressive and humane spirit manifested in this novel and worthy medical enterprise." Honorary degrees were bestowed on several of the lecturers. Jung's (in absentia) was an LL.D. (his second), for "his contributions to psychoanalysis and above all his demonstrations in word associations, time reactions, and the measurement of emotional stress."[1] He was the subject of an interview on the psychology of Americans, in the *New York Times*.[2] Afterward, Jung visited White at St. Elizabeths Hospital, where he spent a week or so in analytical research on the dreams and visions of Negro patients.[3]

---

1. Handwritten letter, signed, on Jung's letterhead. All of Jung's letters to Jelliffe were written in English. The LL.D. was Jung's honorary degree at Clark University. (Letterheads will not in general be reproduced after a first instance. Unless otherwise indicated, Freud, Jung, and Jelliffe wrote from their respective homes in Vienna, Küsnacht, and New York.)

---

1. *Fordham Monthly*, 31:1 (Nov. 1912).
2. "America Facing Its Most Tragic Moment," *New York Times*, 19 Sept. 1912, magazine section, p. 1, reprinted in *C. G. Jung Speaking*, ed. William McGuire and R. F. C. Hull (Princeton, 1977), pp. 11 ff.
3. Jung to Freud, 11 Nov. 1912, and p. 513, in *The Freud/Jung Letters*.

Jung to Jelliffe

28.XI.1912[1]

My dear Dr. Jelliffe,

I must apologize that I did not write you for so long a time and that I did not yet send you the manuscript. When I came home I found work simply piled up and the ocean trip was so rough, that I couldn't work on bord. Thus it became impossible for me to revise the manuscript. I have now done half of it. A considerable part of my time also was taken by a disagreeable complication in our "Internationale Verein."[2] In Vienna namely they suddenly put out Stekel,[3] but he took the official *Zentralblatt* with him, having the publisher on his side. Thus it came out as if Freud had been put out by Stekel. We had a little private congress in Munich in order to settle all these difficulties. Now I have still to go to Wiesbaden, in order to deal with the publisher Bergmann. I hope to finish revising my manuscript within a few days.

I found a nice relief by Rossellino,[4] which I hope will please you. I also arranged the question with the custom house, so that you have to pay no duty.

Please, give my best regards to Mrs. Jelliffe and cordial greetings to your children.

Yours faithfully,
C. G. Jung.

During 1913, Jelliffe and White succeeded in establishing the *Psychoanalytic Review*, published quarterly. Jelliffe recalled twenty years later, in his "Glimpses of a Freudian Odyssey," that they invited Freud to contribute and that "Freud's reply . . . was not very cordial."[1] The aim of the editors, in any case, was to be broadly inclusive, as suggested in the description quoted in Chapter 2. The first issue contained the opening installment of

---

1. Typewritten letter, signed.

2. Jung, president of the International Psychoanalytic Association since 1910, had called a special meeting of the branch society presidents on 24 November in Munich, to discuss Stekel's dissension.

3. Wilhelm Stekel (1868–1940), one of the four original members of Freud's psychoanalytic group; editor of the *Zentralblatt für Psychoanalyse*, at first an official organ of the Association. Because of Stekel's dissenting views Freud favored his withdrawal, taking the *Zentralblatt* (published by J. F. Bergmann) with him, and so it came about.

4. Antonio Rossellino, Florentine sculptor of the 15th century. Mrs. Carel Goldschmidt (Helena Jelliffe) recalls that the relief, a Madonna and Child, in a gold frame, hung in the parlor for many years and was evidently sold by her stepmother at auction in 1954. According to John Pope-Hennessy, the authority on the sculptor, the original of the relief cannot be established, and Jung's gift must have been a copy, possibly of papier-mâché. (Personal communication.)

---

1. See below, commentary preceding Freud to White, 17 July 1914.

Jung's *The Theory of Psychoanalysis* and his congratulatory letter to the new *Review*. The original of the letter has not been discovered, nor any preliminary correspondence that may have passed between Jung and Jelliffe or White. *The Theory of Psychoanalysis* was reprinted as Nervous and Mental Disease Monograph 19, in 1915.

Letter from Doctor Jung[1]

It is most welcome news to learn of Doctors Jelliffe and White's foundation of a broadly planned journal, which aims at the compilation of general psychological literature, and which therefore may be expected to fill a gap that the existing forms of psychology have rendered painfully evident. Each of these forms deals with a special domain, such as philosophical psychology, which is largely transcendental, experimental or physiological psychology, which has been accused, not without cause, of being physiology rather than psychology, and medical psychology, which through the psychoanalytical method of Freud has now come to encroach freely upon the domain of normal psychology. The complex psychic phenomena are left practically unexplained by the first two forms of psychology, whereas the psychoanalytical method of medical psychology has started a line of inquiry which would seem to have a general range of application.

Two problems in particular are adapted to exert an activating effect upon normal psychology. One of these is the recently elaborated dynamic interpretation of the psychological experience, which endeavours to explain the psychic manifestations as equivalent energy transformations. The other problem is represented by symbolism, which comprises the structural analogy of the intellectual functions, in their onto- and phylogenetic evolution. Medical psychology naturally came closest to these problems, as being most likely to observe, examine and analyze the mode or origin of powerful affects or extraordinary psychic structures. The delusional structures of the insane, the illusions of the neurotic, and the dreams of normal as well as abnormal individuals have also afforded abundant opportunities for studying the remarkable analogies with certain ethnological structures.

In my paper on the "Changes and Symbols of the Libido,"[2] a faint attempt has been made at sketching these relations, not in order to propound a finished theory, which would be beyond me, but simply to stimulate further research

---

1. *Psychoanalytic Review*, 1:1 (fall 1913). Reprinted in *C. G. Jung: Letters*, ed. G. Adler and A. Jaffé, vol. 1 (Princeton and London, 1973), pp. 28 ff.

2. *Wandlungen und Symbole der Libido* (Leipzig and Vienna, 1912), originally published in *Jahrbuch für psychoanalytische und psychopathologische Forschungen* (Leipzig), 3:1 (1911), and 4:1 (1912); tr. Beatrice M. Hinkle as *Psychology of the Unconscious: A Study of the Transformations and Symbolisms of the Libido* (New York and London, 1916).

in a direction which appears extremely promising. It is beyond the powers of the individual, more particularly of physicians, to master the manifold domains of the mental sciences which should throw some light upon the comparative anatomy of the mind. Hence I welcome as a most opportune plan the idea of the editors to unite in their journal the contributions of competent specialists in the various fields. We need not only the work of medical psychologists, but also that of philologists, historians, archaeologists, mythologists, folklore students, ethnologists, philosophers, theologians, pedagogues and biologists.

I am free to admit that this enterprise is ambitious and highly creditable to the liberal and progressive spirit of America. The collection of comparative material, to place on a firmer footing the available results of medical psychology, is an inviting task for the near future. Especially in the realm of symbolism, a wide territory is here opened up for students of the several mythologies and religions. Another task is set in the transference of the dynamic interpretation to the problems of the history of culture. The collaboration of all these forces points towards the distant goal of a genetic psychology, which will clear our eyes for medical psychology, just as comparative anatomy has already done in regard to the structure and function of the human body.

I wish the best of success to this new venture and trust that it will not fail to arouse an active interest also on the part of the non-medical faculties.

C. G. Jung

When Jung wrote to Jelliffe again, more than a year later, he had broken definitely with Freud and was on the way to leaving the psychoanalytic movement entirely. Personal correspondence between him and Freud had ended in January 1913.[1] In March and April, Jung was again in New York lecturing, but there is no evidence that he and Jelliffe met.[2] Late in the year, after the acrimonious Fourth Psychoanalytic Congress at Munich in September, Jung resigned the editorship of the *Jahrbuch*.[3] Ernest Jones, in London, wrote Jelliffe on 24 November 1913: "It seems quite impossible for Vienna and Zurich to come to any kind of terms, so it will be better if they separate altogether, when each can develop without personal emotions on the lines that suit him best—and the best man win!"[4] Jones's uncharacteristic evenhandedness may reflect his growing belief that Jelliffe was becoming a Jungian. A year earlier Jones had taken the lead in organizing the "Committee,"

---

1. Jung to Freud, 9 Jan. 1913, in *The Freud/Jung Letters.*
2. Jung to Freud, 3 Mar. 1913, in ibid.
3. Ibid., pp. 549, 550.
4. Jelliffe papers, Library of Congress, Washington, D.C.

composed of the five psychoanalysts closest to Freud, dedicated to defending psychoanalysis against its adversaries.[5]

The temper of the time is illustrated by Jung's remarks in a postcard to White, postmarked 11 November 1913: ". . . We have a bad time over here. Freud discredited me personally in a letter to Dr. Maeder. And I had to withdraw from the *Jahrbuch* therefore. Fr. is working with nice means against all those who don't strictly believe in the dogma. We are going to found a sort of periodical for psychological researches like the *Jahrbuch* but smaller."[6]

Jung to Jelliffe

13.XII.13[1]

Dear Dr. Jelliffe,

Today I received the first copy of the *Psychoanalytic Review*.[2] I have read your article with great interest and I am generally pleased with the nice looking of the new journal. I hope it will have a large circulation. I want to subscribe for the journal. The copy I got was destined to the Editor of the *Jahrbuch*. I kept the copy assuming that you will send another copy to the new Editor Dr. Abraham,[3] Rankestrasse 24, Berlin, W. Please tell me to whom I have to send the money. The situation in Europe is rather unsettled. People don't understand my viewpoint. Well, it seems, that it has to be so. I have no intention to publish anything serious in the next future. My view seems to be too indigestible to a scientific stomac. But I am busy at work.

I hope that you and your family are all well. Please give my best regards to Mrs. Jelliffe and the children.

Yours sincerely,
Jung.

Freud had not yet met either White or Jelliffe, but evidently White had written him. The following letter—the only one that Freud wrote White, as far as we know—is apparently the "not very cordial" one that Jelliffe recalled

---

5. Jones, 2, ch. 6.
6. From the W. A. White Archives, as quoted in A. R. T. D'Amore, "William Alanson White, Pioneer Psychoanalyst," in idem, ed., *William Alanson White: The Washington Years 1904–1937* (Washington, 1976), p. 83.

---

1. Handwritten letter, signed.
2. As noted above, the first issue contained the opening section of Jelliffe's paper "The Technique of Psychoanalysis" (continued thereafter for many issues, as indicated in the Bibliography) as well as Jung's "The Theory of Psychoanalysis" and Jung's congratulatory letter.
3. Karl Abraham, M.D. (1877–1925), German psychiatrist; on the staff of the Burghölzli 1904–1907 and afterward in Berlin, where he founded the Berlin Society of the International Psychoanalytic Association. He and Eduard Hitschmann, M.D. (1871–1957), in Vienna, took over the editorship of the *Jahrbuch der Psychoanalyse* (as renamed). As noted above, Jelliffe had met Abraham while in Berlin in 1908–1909.

in his "Glimpses," though it was written many months after the appearance of the first issue of the *Psychoanalytic Review*, in the fall of 1913. It would appear that Freud was invited to contribute *after* the appearance of that issue, with Jung's contributions, which Freud had probably seen, or at least heard of. A week before this letter was written, Jung and the entire Zurich Society had voted to withdraw from the International Psycho-analytic Association.[1] Meanwhile, Freud had published his polemic directed at Jung (and Adler), "On the History of the Psychoanalytic Movement."[2] Ironically, it was this piece which, in Brill's translation, appeared in the *Psychoanalytic Review* in 1916.

Freud to White

Karlsbad 17.7.14

Villa Fasalt[1]

Dear Dr. White,

Thank you for acknowledging my communication, from which you can gain some idea of the present state of affairs in ΨA.[2]

I must own, however, that your request for a contribution to your *Review* surprises me, and I will tell you why. If I am misinformed, I shall be glad to be set right.

I am told that Dr. Jelliffe once refused to pay membership dues to the New York Society on the ground that he had no money for a foreign publisher. This, I feel, amounts to considering psychoanalysis from the standpoint of business rather than of science. Moreover, the *Review* has been founded at a time when, as you yourself stress in your letter, it is still difficult to fill it with worthwhile contributions. The way in which the *Review* makes up for this deficiency with translations may be commercially justifiable, what with the lack of copyright in America,[3] but strikes me as unseemly. I find it difficult

---

1. *The Freud/Jung Letters*, p. 552.
2. "Zur Geschichte der psychoanalytischen Bewegung," *Jahrbuch der Psychoanalyse*, 6 (1914); tr., *Standard Edn.*, 14.

---

1. Handwritten letter, signed, in the file of personal correspondence of William Alanson White, Records of Saint Elizabeths Hospital, National Archives, Washington. Freud wrote on his usual letter paper, but he was at Karlsbad, the health resort in Bohemia, where he was having treatment (Jones, 2, 193 f./172). The letter was first published by D'Amore in *White: The Washington Years*, pp. 88 f., in another translation.
2. Freud's "communication" to White has not been found, nor White's reply. The abbreviation ΨA = psychoanalysis or psychoanalytic. (Freud always used a capital alpha, Jung a lower-case alpha.)
3. This curious statement may help explain some of Freud's apparently cavalier actions in giving translation rights away, which caused Jones and others much grief. The United States had, for many years, not protected foreign authors, but after 1891 did recognize copyright of works published in foreign countries. Freud was obviously unaware of this.

to regard the *Review* as anything other than a competitor, founded exclusively for business reasons,[4] of the *Inter. Zeits. f. ärztl. Psychoanalyse*.[5] The cause would have been much better served if the psychoanalytic literature had been allowed to remain centralized for a good while yet, until experience had time to catch up with interest in America. This judgment of the *Review* is further supported by Jelliffe's intimacy with Jung, who in spite of his presidency has never lifted a finger for the International Association or its organs, but only pursued his own aggrandizement.[6]

Under these circumstances, I do not feel able to help your journal over the difficulties to which you refer. But I shall be very glad if these lines can move you to clarify and perhaps correct the information at my disposal.

Yours faithfully,
Freud

Jung to Jelliffe

5th of March 1915[1]

Dear Professor,

I was very glad to have your letter and to hear from you.

I will send you everything as soon as I get home. But since 3 months they don't let me. I am still with the army in a little town where I have plenty of practical work and horseback riding.

I was very interested to hear about the progress of your *Review* which is a very good looking thing indeed.

Dr. Long is a very distinguished woman doctor who is in a rather leading social position in London. She is collecting some of my writings in order to publish them.[2]

Until I had to join the army I lived quietly and devoted my time to my patients and to my work. I was especially working about the two types of

---

4. In view of Jelliffe's being criticized for making a profit on journalism (see Part I, ch. 2), this comment must have been particularly galling. See his comment in the letter to Freud, 6 Mar. 1939.

5. The first issue of the *Internationale Zeitschrift für ärztliche Psychoanalyse*, under Freud's editorship, had appeared in Jan. 1913.

6. Jung resigned the presidency of the International Psychoanalytic Association only on 20 Apr. 1914, in a circular letter to the presidents of the branch societies (*The Freud/Jung Letters*, p. 551).

---

1. Handwritten letter, signed. In spite of the usual letterhead, Jung was at an Army post in the Valais, southern Switzerland, having been called to active duty in the medical corps. Jelliffe's letter to Jung is lost.

2. Constance E. Long, M.D., edited *Collected Papers on Analytical Psychology* (London and New York, 1916), comprising fifteen papers by Jung.

psychology[3] and about the synthesis of unconscious tendencies. The problem is: When you analyze a patient, then you reintegrate a great amount of libido split off formerly. How can the patient apply this libido so that it doesn't more fall back into regression. Certain lines have to be constructed, so that the libido can be applied progressively—This is the great problem. I sacrificed everything else in order to devot *all my time* to the elaboration of this problem. I found many interesting things.

Actually I don't write at all, but I have the intention to write a small article about the two types after a while, when I am free again.

We have bad times in Europe. The uncertainty is great.

In these days the incurable wounded of the French and the German army pass through Switzerland. I have seen them yesterday. It is terrible.

You have no idea how mad people in Germany, France and England have become since the war. In Switzerland we are rather normal. It is a most psychological war. It will leave certain traces in the European mind, which will be of great interest.

My best regards to Mrs. Jelliffe and to your whole family and to Dr. White.

> Yours sincerely,
> *Jung.*

Jung to Jelliffe

> 228 Seestrasse
> Küsnacht-Zürich[1]
>
> [late July 1915]

Dear Dr. Jelliffe,

Your problems are very difficult and indeed they cannot be answered in a letter. The thing I always have seen to be necessary is the analysis of the analyst himself. It is astonishing, how many problems are settled, when the one point in the analyst himself is settled. I really cannot tell you much of

---

3. Jung's first work on psychological typology was his lecture to the Fourth Psychoanalytic Congress at Munich, Sept. 1913, published in French in *Archives de psychologie*, 13:52 (Dec. 1913) and in English, tr. Constance E. Long, "A Contribution to the Study of Psychological Types," in *Collected Papers* (1916). (*Coll. Works*, 6.)

---

1. Handwritten letter, signed. Jung was living at the same place in Küsnacht, but the houses had been renumbered and the spelling of the village name had been changed. The letter was undated, but Jelliffe wrote at the top "ans'd. Aug. 16, 1915." His letter to Jung has not been found.

Mrs. Evans.[2] She has spent some time with Miss Moltzer.[3] Perhaps you write once directly to her, but I am doubtfull, whether she can give you any further information on account of the indispensable analytical discretion. I only can tell you how I behaved in the case of my assistant: I trusted the cases entirely to her with the only condition, that in case of difficulties she would consult me or send the patient to me in order to be controled by myself. But this arrangement existed in the beginning only. Later on Miss M. worked quite independently and quite efficiently. Financially she is quite independent being paid directly by her patients. It is very important, of course, that you keep close analytical contact with an assistant, else you risk constant mistakes. I arranged weekly meetings with my assistant, where everything was settled carefully and on an analytical basis. It looks to me, as if Mrs. Evans were an able woman to whom private cases could be trusted under the conditions mentioned above.

The sky of Europe becomes more and more dark. We are in a pretty uncomfortable situation on our island. It is interesting to see, how difficult it is even with us, to maintain the order against the madness of the people. The general madness is most infectious—you hardly can imagine this abyss of primaeval foolishness which usurped the european mind. One sees no end. More than one million of men are either killed or uncurably wounded, and crippled.

Yours sincerely,
Dr. Jung

Jung to Jelliffe

2.I.1917[1]

Dear Dr. Jelliffe,

I thank you very much for your kind card I got from America. My time was filled with much work and military service. My publisher told me, that he is ready to issue a second edition of the *Dementia praec.* after the war. I want to tell you, that I still get the *Journal of Nervous and Mental Disease.* About one year ago I returned a copy in order to notify, that I don't want

---

2. Elida Evans, an American psychotherapist, had worked analytically in Zurich. See Part I, ch. 3.

3. Maria Moltzer (1874–1944), daughter of a Netherlands distiller, became a nurse as a protest against alcoholic abuse. From 1910 she worked as a lay analyst in Zurich under Jung's supervision, and attended the Weimar Congress in 1911. She was co-translator of Jung's "The Theory of Psychoanalysis," in the *Psychoanalytic Review.*

---

1. Typed postcard, signed. Jelliffe's card from Arizona has not been found. This was undoubtedly the trip on which he took his daughter Sylvia (Part I, ch. 4).

it. But the numbers kept on coming. I can't afford to pay so many journals.
I never subscribed for the journal.
I hope you are well. My best wishes for the new year!

Yours very truly

Jung

I got a letter from Mrs. Evans. Is she a good worker?[2]

Jung to Jelliffe

[(?) August 1917][1]

Dear Dr. Jelliffe,

I am answering your letter of June 20th on a card, because I am afraid,
that a letter would not pass through. I am actually on duty for about 4
months. I am commanding officer in charge of the British Interned in Switzerland.[2] Thus I am taken away from my work completely. As soon as I am
back again, I try to finish a rather long paper about the types. I have published
a book (Psychology of the unconscious processes).[3] It is a short presentation
of analytical conceptions and their development in the last years. It will be
published in the IId edition of my *Collect. Papers.*[4] I am happy to say, that
our development in Zurich is rich, but still internal. Nothing particular is
published yet. Times are unfavorable now. I thank you for all personal news.
With us everything is unchanged and quiet. Everything else is swallowed by
the war. The psychosis is still increasing, going on and on. Science has a
bad prognosis.

Yours cordially

Jung.

---

2. Handwritten postscript. Evans had begun working in New York as a psychotherapist under
Jelliffe's supervision. They jointly published "Psoriasis as an Hysterical Conversion Symbolization: A Preliminary Report," *New York Medical Journal,* 104 (1916); see Part I, ch. 2. Another
joint publication appeared in 1919: "Psychotherapy and Tuberculosis," *American Review of
Tuberculosis,* 3, pp. 417 ff. Evans and Jung kept in contact, and Jung wrote an introduction to
her book, *The Problem of the Nervous Child* (New York, 1920); *Coll. Works,* 18, pp. 805 f.
Agreeing with Evans in rejecting Freud's view, Jung wrote, "Infantile sexuality is the most
frequent symptom of a morbid psychological attitude."

1. Handwritten postcard, signed and undated. Jelliffe wrote the date of receipt, 17 August
1917.
2. At this time, Jung commanded an internment camp at Chateau-d'Oex (Vaud).
3. *Die Psychologie des unbewussten Prozesse* (Zurich, 1917). G. Stanley Hall wrote Jelliffe on
Nov. 20, 1917, urging its translation in the Monograph Series: "It seems to me one of the most
important things in the psychoanalytic field for years, whatever we think of it." Nothing came
of that, but cf. the next note.
4. *Collected Papers on Analytical Psychology,* ed. Constance E. Long, 2d ed. (New York and
London, 1917): "The Psychology of the Unconscious Processes," tr. Dora Hecht. In a later
revision it is in *Coll. Works,* 7.

Jung to Jelliffe

Aug. 25th 1919[1]

My dear Professor,

I was very glad indeed to have news from yourself and your family. I was interested to hear of the development of Ψα in the United States. With us the movement is spreading fast too, but has not yet reached the universities with the exception of Geneva and Oxford. Recently a book on psychotherapy has been written by a German privatdocent, Schultz,[2] wherein justice has been done to Ψα. There is a great amount of discussions going on between the different doctrines and their believers. I think you are wise to concentrate upon the essentials. This is certainly the best way to establish scientific truths. I don't participate in the disputes at all and I content myself to work out the things as I see them. Of course I have not the same eyes as Freud or Adler, but I think, it is the duty of every scientific author, to develop his views and to leave them to the public. We have all sorts of disagreements in our little country and there is a large groupe of Freudians fighting against myself as if I were the devil himself. At all events our movement lives. I always think of the word of that lawyer trusted with the code Napoléon by the emperor himself. When one year after the publication that lawyer came to Napoléon with a long list of desirable changes and improvements, the emperor said: "Mais comment? Est-ce que le code est mort?" and the lawyer answered: Non, Sire, il vit."

I only can send you a few publications of mine. Some are about to be printed. I was chiefly busy with a rather large book about the problem of attitude.[3] I am now in the last chapter.

General conditions over here are not just pleasant and the outlook is dark. In spite of the fact that travelling is very difficult still, I have been in England for two months. I was invited by the R.S. of Med., the Aristotelian Soc. and the S.P.R.[4] There is great interest in our new psychology.

Yours sincerely,

Dr. Jung.

Please give my best compliments to Dr. White.

---

1. Handwritten letter, signed; not on letterhead.

2. J. H. Schultz, *Die seelische Krankenbehandlung: Psychotherapie* (Jena, 1919).

3. *Psychologische Typen* (Zurich, 1921).

4. In London during July, Jung gave three lectures: on 4 July "The Psychological Foundations of Belief in Spirits" to the Society for Psychical Research, published in the society's *Proceedings*, 31:79 (May 1920) (*Coll. Works*, 8); 11 July "On the Problem of Psychogenesis in Mental Disease" to the Royal Society of Medicine, Section of Psychiatry, Annual Meeting, published in the society's *Proceedings*, 12:9 (Aug. 1919) (*Coll. Works*, 3); 12 July "Instinct and the Unconscious" to a symposium of the same name, at a joint meeting of the British Psychological Society, the Aristotelian Society, and the Mind Society, published in the *British Journal of Psychology*, 10:1 (Nov. 1919) (*Coll. Works*, 8).

Jung to Jelliffe

21.I.1920[1]

Dear Professor,

I thank you very much for the overwhelming amount of reprints you recently sent me. I admire your efficiency and I wonder, how you are able to be so fertile beside all your other work. During the war I published very little. Now I have finished a book about Psychological Types, which soon shall be translated into English.[2] I am now publishing my books in Switzerland, as Germany is done for a long time. I just recently heard from a Professor, that the Universities are rapidly depopulating on account of the fact that mental workers are less paid then workmen—not to speak of Austria. I am sending you a reprint of my contribution to a Symposium of the Aristotelian Society. I have not yet received your third edition.[3] I should be very glad indeed to have it. Ps.a. is rapidly spreading in England, not so in France nor in Italy. In Germany and in the countries of the centre and the east there is agony, and no Ps.a. I have not seen Rivers: *Dreams and Primitive Culture*,[4] but I thank you for the reference.

My best wishes for 1920.

Yours sincerely

Dr Jung

Jung to Jelliffe

April 2 1920[1]

Dear Professor,

Thank you very much for your reprints and particularly for your new book on the technique of $\Psi\alpha$.[2] I wondered why my modeste contributions to the science of $\Psi\alpha$ so often are quoted only indirectly. I think it is a fundamental mistake when the creative libido is called sexual, as it will be impossible to prove that f.i. all living beings are nothing but condensations along with the string of sexuality. It looks to me as if sexuality were a subdivision of the creative energy. Is the instinct of nutrition nothing but sexual? And what is

---

1. Typewritten letter, signed; the letterhead is rubber-stamped.
2. The translation, entitled *Psychological Types; or, the Psychology of Individuation* (London and New York, 1923), was the work of the British psychiatrist H. G. Baynes, M.D., a pupil of Jung's. In *Coll. Works*, 6.
3. Jelliffe and W. A. White, *Diseases of the Nervous System*, 3d ed. (Philadelphia, 1919).
4. W. H. R. Rivers, "Dreams and Primitive Culture," *John Rylands Library Bulletin* (Manchester), 4 (1917–1918).

---

1. Handwritten letter, signed.
2. *The Technique of Psychoanalysis*, 2d ed. (NMDMS 26, 1920).

the use of calling every manifestation of life sexual? What is sexuality then, when everything is sexual? Or is it permissible to make everything essentially dependent upon sexuality because of the famous "inter faeces et urinas nascimur"?[3] Or should one treat St. Peter's Cathedral in the chapter about nest-building? Through such a disproportionate use of the term "sexuality," the latter dissolves itself into a philosophic and metaphysical concept like "matter" in the famous philosophic materialism of 1870–80.[4] It is nothing but a philosophic sexualisme, but no science any more. And moreover—how can we assume any scientific opinion about the quality of the basic life energy, of which we perceive manifestations only? Even sexuality is such a manifestation. I can't help it, I am quite unable to appreciate such reductive and monotonous explanations as Freud's sexualism. It is nothing but a sort of physiology that shows the partial dependence of certain psychological processes upon sexuality. I am convinced that it is a most unscientific encroachment, when the Psyche becomes subordinate to the sexual instinct. This is a theory of a morbide character, as it shows that the psyche of its originator only can conceive of a psychology where *one* instinct prevails to such an extent that it became an obsession, an "idée obsédante," a morbid religious concept, that spreads about everything. It explains that fanatic [. . .][5] of Freud and his school. Fanatism and dogmatism are overcompensated doubt.

I hope you will not mind my opposition.

I have my summer vacations from July 15th to Aug. 31st.

Recently I published a book about the question of typical psychological attitudes.[6] It is of course only a psychological book, that contains little of pathology. It deals with normal psychology and thus it is not Freudian at all. I don't know whether you are interested in such researches or not. In the case you should like to read it, I would love to send you a copy.

Yours sincerely

C. G. Jung.

---

3. "Between feces and urine are we born." Jung attributed the saying to St. Augustine when he used it in his seminar on Dream Analysis, 1928–1930 (ed. William McGuire, in press), though it has not been possible to locate it in Augustine, Freud attributed it to "the Early Christian Father" when he quoted it in "Bruchstück einer Hysterie-Analyse," *Monatsschrift für psychiatrische Neurologie*, 18 (1905); tr., "Fragment of an Analysis of a Case of Hysteria," *Standard Edn.*, 7, p. 31, and he occasionally quoted it later.

4. Jung is probably alluding to the German biologist and philosopher Ernst Heinrich Haeckel (1834–1919), who wrote prolifically on evolutionary and other aspects of materialistic philosophy, particularly in the 1870's.

5. Illegible.

6. *Psychologische Typen*. Jelliffe's library, now at the Institute for Living, Hartford, contains the 1923 English translation, with no inscription by Jung, and the 1937 reprint of the German/Swiss edition.

Jung to Jelliffe

15.VII.1920[1]

My dear Doctor Jelliffe,

It has been a regret to me that I have had no opportunity to reply to your interesting letter of February last.

The conception of a psychological stratification[2] that you outline is attractive as a theoretical formulation but evidence I think is still wanting that such a stratification is found in practice. I should be interested to read your reports of cases whose material strongly suggests the analogy of geological formation, but it seems to me that an analogy bearing such concrete interpretations requires a very great deal of evidence to justify it as a scheme of practical utility.

I regret to say that no recollection occures to me connected with the name Stragnell[3] and I have no note of his having worked with me.

With very kind regards

Yours sincerely

Dr. Jung.

Jung to Jelliffe

Dec. 18th 1920[1]

My dear Professor!

Many thanks for your interesting letter of Nov. 6th.

I got a long report from Dr. Katz[2] about his experiences in U.S. including

---

1. Typewritten letter, signed. Jung used a sheet of his obsolete "1003 Seestrasse" letterhead and crossed out the house number.
2. Concerning "psychological stratification," cf. the next letter.
3. Gregory Stragnell, M.D. (1888–1963), neuropsychiatrist and editor, married to Jelliffe's eldest daughter Sylvia.

---

1. Handwritten letter, signed. Jelliffe's letter of 6 Nov. 1920 has not been found.
2. Johann Rudolf Katz, M.D. (1880–1938), Dutch analytical psychologist. In 1916, he had married Fanny Bowditch (1874–1967), of Boston, who in 1912 had been referred to Jung by James J. Putnam, M.D. (1846–1918), for psychoanalytic treatment. Katz, who worked with Jung and Maeder from 1915, had probably come to Zurich through Maria Moltzer, also of Amsterdam, who took over Fanny Bowditch's case under Jung's supervision. In Sept. 1920,

a fine description of the things that happened with the Freudians.[3] He also told me, that he got most stimulating impressions from your views. I await with keen interest your exposition and the material you have gathered from such organic cases.[4] This is a chapter not accessible to me, as I have no such cases among my patients.

Well I should mind the trade-unionism i.e. the dumping system of Jones and Co.[5] C'est par ordre du Moufti! The Pope in Vienna is most revengeful and tries his best to extinguish any trace of myself. Happily enough I have not set my mind upon such vain successes, else I should regret the amazing amount of misunderstanding I encounter everywhere.

With regard to the Palaeopsychological formulation[6] I think it is indisputable that a principle analogous to geological stratification exists and that f.i. dreams often give the impression of a certain integrity in the psychological stratification.

With my best wishes for a happy Xmas and New Year, I remain yours
sincerely,
C. G. Jung

In mid-July 1921, Freud went to a favorite spa, Bad Gastein, in central Austria, for the benefits to be had from its thermal springs. He and Jelliffe first met there, apparently shortly before 13 or 14 August, as Jones tells us that on the latter date Freud joined some of his family at another resort in

---

Katz and his wife were in Boston visiting her family. Jung had given him a letter of introduction to White, and after Katz had called on him in Washington, White wrote to Jelliffe (6 Nov. 1920): "I enjoyed Katz tremendously. I can imagine that the contingent you speak of may have been pretty critical of him, but it seems to me that he is worth listening to. I wish I knew more about just what his attitude and Jung's attitude is. If they have anything to say about narcissistic psychoses we certainly ought to listen to them, because Freud has closed the door so far as any help is expected from his attitude. Katz and I had a fine time together and I liked him immensely personally." (Jelliffe Papers, Library of Congress.) Jelliffe also met Katz, who while in the United States gave illustrated lectures in various cities on psychoanalysis of the Zurich school. (White Papers, National Archives.)

3. See Jelliffe's comments quoted in Part I, ch. 3.

4. I.e., cases in Jelliffe's psychosomatic practice.

5. Jung's precise allusion in this sentence is unclear. Ernest Jones had taken the lead in early 1919 to reorganize the national psychoanalytic societies, including the Swiss Society, replacing the one that Jung had headed before the war, and Jones also took over from Ferenczi the acting presidency of the International Association, because of the inaccessibility of Budapest just after the war. It seems more likely, however, that Jung is referring to some recent event, perhaps an occurrence at the Sixth International Psychoanalytic Congress at the Hague in early Sept. 1920. (See Jones, 3, ch. 1.) It is also conceivable that Jung was alluding to Jelliffe's experiences with the New York Psychoanalytic Society (Part I, ch. 3).

6. Jelliffe not long afterward published an article, "Paleopsychology: A Tentative Sketch of the Origin and Evolution of Symbolic Function," *Psychoanalytic Review*, 10 (1923), which contains some passing references to Jung's work. Also see below, his letter to Jung, 28 Aug. 1932, and Part I.

the Austrian Alps, Seefeld,[1] near Innsbruck, and Jelliffe in his "Glimpses" (Part I, ch. 2) describes how he gave Freud a box of cigars as he was about to take his train. Jelliffe wrote to White from Bad Gastein:

"[Freud] was very nice to me, and we spent the afternoon talking about everything. He was taller and larger than I had pictured him—heavier with a distinct stoop. The precise discussion of many points was not reached, but he had a fine stroke and cut into things very sharply and clearly. Bergson, he says, he does not understand. The indeterminism of pragmatism leaves him too uncertain, hence his Platonic-Kantian absolutism. As for Adler he has little use. Jung's recent material—particularly the prospective function of the dream—he called 'trash,' and he was content with the activities of his many pupils. He was very much interested in our organic work and told me of one of his pupils in Baden-Baden[2] who was carrying on quite a similar type of analyses and with the same ideas we have been working on."[3]

This, Jelliffe's first trip to Europe since the war, was very extended, from 31 May to 21 October. He and his wife spent the week of 6 July in Zurich, at the elegant Hotel Baur au Lac, and called on Jung.[4] After Bad Gastein, the Jelliffes visited Vienna, Berlin, Amsterdam, and London. Throughout their tour of Europe, Jelliffe had personal meetings with some three dozen

---

1. Jones, 3, ch. 3.

2. Georg Groddeck, M.D. (1866–1934), who like Jelliffe was sometimes called "the father of psychosomatic medicine." He is known today chiefly for his concept of "the It" (*das Es*), a term adopted by Freud in English as "the id." See *Das Buch vom Es* (Vienna, 1923), tr. (anon.) as *The Book of the Id* (NMDMS 49, 1928), often reprinted in popular editions. (Martin Grotjahn, "Georg Groddeck: The Untamed Analyst," in *Psychoanalytic Pioneers*, pp. 308 ff.)

Perhaps as a consequence of his conversation with Jelliffe, but also because of his acquaintance with Jelliffe's publications, Freud stated the following in an article on psychoanalysis that he wrote in summer 1922 for a German encyclopedia: "Some analysts (Jelliffe, Groddeck, Felix Deutsch) have reported too that the analytic treatment of gross organic diseases is not unpromising, since a mental factor not infrequently contributes to the origin and continuance of such illnesses." (*Standard Edn.*, 18, p. 250.) And again in fall 1923, for an American publication: ". . . voices have been raised among therapists (e.g. Groddeck and Jelliffe), maintaining that the psychoanalytic treatment of serious organic complaints shows promising results, since in many of these affections some part is played by a psychical factor on which it is possible to bring influence to bear." (*Standard Edn.*, 19, p. 209.) Jelliffe and Groddeck were by this time already in correspondence. See Part I, ch. 4.

3. This passage of the letter is quoted, without date, by Lewis in *Psychoanalytic Pioneers*, p. 226.

4. Jelliffe told White of his visit to Jung in a letter that has not come to hand, but White's reply is available. (28 July 1921, from Merrill, Clinton Co., New York, near the Canadian border.) Extract: "I have your two letters, of the 7th from Basle & of the 11th from Zurich. . . . I am especially interested in what you say about Jung. I am anxious to get a clear idea of what he is doing but many of the indications point to something woozy—Katz with his 'inner voice' and now you unable to understand him & his getting mad in a discussion. What's the matter? He needs some of the soothing balm that I from time to time have to [illegible] about in your footsteps & apply to those you have discoursed with on the way. . . . By the way, had Jung recd. a copy of my *Foundations*? What did he say about it? . . ." White was referring to his *Foundations of Psychiatry* (NMDMS 32; Washington, 1921), a copy of which is not now in Jung's library.

distinguished psychiatrists and neurologists.[5] He must have sent offprints of his articles to many of them, including Freud, upon returning to New York.

Freud to Jelliffe

Dec 11 1921[1]

Dear Dr. Jelliffe,

I thankfully acknowledge the receipt of your papers and promise to send you the new (fifth) volume of my Sammlung[2] as soon as it is given out.

Sincerely yours

Freud

Freud

20 Dec. 1921
Vienna IX, Berggasse 19[1]

Dear Dr. Jelliffe,

Many thanks to you (and Dr. White) for the new lot of parcels. I am eagerly looking forward to the promised textbook.[2] An active scientific exchange between America and Europe in matters of ΨA is much to be desired. Perhaps that will put an end to the talk about different schools of ΨA, and it will be generally agreed that there is only psychoanalysis.

In return for your parcels I am planning to send you my most recent publications in English translation. In the not too distant future, I hope.

You will forgive my admission that I have not been able to read anywhere near all your papers. In your chapter on ΨA literature, I was struck by one inaccuracy: you say that the *Intern. Zschr.*[3] was suspended during the war

---

5. Lewis lists twenty-eight in *Psychoanalytic Pioneers*, p. 230. The other information about the 1921 sojourn in Europe is from the scrapbook that Jelliffe devoted to it. Jelliffe gave a lengthy report of his trip to the New York Neurological Society ("A Neuropsychiatric Pilgrimage," *JNMD*, 56, 1922), in which he mentioned numerous neurologists he met (probably Lewis's source) but, perhaps out of consideration for his audience, he included neither Freud nor Jung nor any other psychoanalyst.

---

1. Handwritten postcard, signed; in English.
2. Vol. 5 of Freud's *Sammlung kleiner Schriften zur Neurosenlehre* (Collected Short Papers on the Theory of the Neuroses) appeared in 1922.

---

1. Handwritten letter, signed. The salutation is in English.
2. Jelliffe often wrote to correspondents that he was busy revising Jelliffe and White, *Diseases of the Nervous System*. The next edition appeared in 1923. See below, Jelliffe to Freud, 21 May 1923.
3. See above, Freud to White, 17 July 1914, n. 5.

and has now begun to appear again. In fact, there was no interruption during the war: it was merely thinner and appeared less frequently.

American physicians who wish to take up self-analysis with me are advised to sign up for 1 October of the coming year and to allow sufficient time, at least four to six months, for the course.

With kind regards,
Yours sincerely,
Dr. Freud

Jung to Jelliffe

Dec. 23rd 1921[1]

Dear Professor,

Thank you for your letter! I analyzed Libbin[2] personally like any other patient and only as far as it went i.e. until it became quite obvious, that he should do reasonable and honest work f.i. finishing his studies at the university. This he did not, but he wanted to draw me out, which I refused. Then Miss Potter[3] turned up in order to get analysed, but I had no time for her. Thus I only had some interviews with her in the presence of Mr. Libbin. If I would be asked, whether I should call a man like Libbin my pupil, I would say: no—He is just as much informed about analysis as any ordinary patient, who has read my books, having found his way back *to his reality* through the dissolution of his resistances.

Libbin, being a Jew, has a racial intuition and that makes him cling to my name. There his idealisme comes in. He probably would do better (f.i. financially), if he stayed with Freud's views or any other tangibilities.

Hoping you had a good return to your country I remain with my best Christmas wishes

Yours sincerely,
C. G. Jung

During the next year and a half, Jelliffe's correspondence with both Freud and Jung appears to have lapsed, though he evidently sent them his publications. Freud, on a postcard of 11 June 1922, briefly acknowledged several parcels, one of which contained *Psychoanalysis and the Drama* (Nervous and Mental Disease Monograph Series 34, 1922), which Jelliffe wrote in collaboration with Louise Brink. On 12 January 1923, Jung sent Jelliffe a postcard

---

1. Handwritten letter, signed.
2. Thomas Libbin later may have worked in association with Jelliffe as a lay analyst. See Part I, ch. 3.
3. Grace Potter, M.D. (1874–1943), psychoanalyst, studied with Freud, Rank, and Jung. In a letter of 3 Apr. 1925 to Brill, Jelliffe called her "unreliable."

thanking him for an offprint of "Psychopathology and Organic Disease," *Archives of Neurology and Psychiatry*, 8 (1922). The professional gift-giving was to some extent reciprocal, as the next letter indicates.

Jelliffe to Freud

May 21 1923.[1]

Dr. Sigmund Freud,
9 Berggasse,
Vienna 19, Austria
My dear Professor Freud:

Kindly accept my thanks for your courtesy in sending me your last study on *Das Ich und das Es*.[2] I have read it with much interest and I hope with profit.

I am still much in the dark concerning the ubw.,[3] not only as a philosophical concept, but especially in the practical everyday work in psa. Your essay is very stimulating—especially in connection with the "Jenseits."[4]

I am uncertain whether you ever received the 4th Edition of our *Diseases of the Nervous System*. I asked my publishers to forward to you a copy from me at the same time with some others. I want you to have it.[5]

With sincere regards and best wishes,

Very truly yours,
[*Smith Ely Jelliffe*]

---

1. Carbon copy of typewritten letter. This is the earliest of Jelliffe's letters to either Freud or Jung that has come to light.

2. Published in late Apr. 1923; tr. 1927, *The Ego and the Id*, under which title it is translated in *Standard Edn.*, 19. This was Freud's first use of the term *Es* (= Id), for which he makes acknowledgement to Groddeck (*Standard Edn.*, 19, p. 23).

3. *Ubw.* = *Unbewussten* = *Unconscious*, abbr. as *Ucs.* in *The Ego and the Id*, where Freud made considerable use of the term. It was largely superseded in psychoanalytic terminology by "id."

4. *Jenseits des Lustprinzips* (Vienna, etc., 1920); tr. 1922, *Beyond the Pleasure Principle*, under which title it is translated in *Standard Edn.*, 18.

5. On a postcard dated 5 June 1923, Freud informed Jelliffe that he had the third edition and "I had no opportunity to thank you for receipt of the 4th," which in the next letter Jelliffe construed as meaning Freud had not received it.

Jelliffe to Freud

July 9, 1923.[1]

My dear Professor Freud:
Many thanks for your postal card telling me you have not received a copy
of our JELLIFFE AND WHITE, 4th Edition. I am sending you one at this
time and trust you may find some interest in it.[2]
We are about to break up for the summer. I go to my country place at
Lake George as there are many family details to work out.[3]
You may know I have three girls and two boys—all now quite grown up.
My younger son has decided to study medicine. He is now 21 and has just
graduated at Yale. One daughter married a physician and another a zoologist.
The remainder are still with me and the Lake George home is a sort of
meeting ground during the summer. Else I should come to Europe. I hope
I may get to the Psychoanalytic Congress next year.

With cordial best wishes,
[*Smith Ely Jelliffe*]

Jung's *Psychological Types* was published in London and New York during
1923, and White wrote a lengthy review of it in November for the *Psychoanalytic Review*, 11 (April 1924), 184–190. He called it "one of the most important contributions to psychoanalytic literature provided psychoanalysis be
understood in its literal, etymological sense rather than in the special sense
to which it is restricted by the strictly Freudian." He made no detracting
comment, but in a letter to Jelliffe, 14 February 1924, he wrote: "If Jung
don't write his new edition [of *The Psychology of Dementia Praecox*, which
evidently Jung had under consideration at the time] any better than he did
Psychological Types you will have to give a man a pension for life to read it."
An unsigned review, sympathetic in spirit, appeared in the *Journal of Nervous
and Mental Disease*, 60:3 (September 1924), closing: "[Jung] is in line with
the furtherance of the highest aspirations of human endeavor at all times."
Jelliffe and his wife went abroad 2 July 1924 on the French Line ship
Paris. That Jelliffe subsequently was in Zurich and saw Jung is established
in his letter to Freud of 8 June 1926; no other documentation has come to

---

1. Carbon copy of typewritten letter.
2. In a postcard of 27 July 1923, from Bad Gastein, Freud acknowledged receipt of the book.
3. For particulars on Jelliffe's routine and family, see Part I, chs. 2 and 3.

light.[1] Though he visited Innsbruck for a meeting of neurologists, it does not appear that he visited Freud, who spent July and August at the Semmering, a health resort some fifty miles southwest of Vienna. The scrapbook contains a letter written to Jelliffe somewhere in Europe on 23 July from Mary Foote, at a Parisian hotel. The letter, which was devoted chiefly to listing several "cheap small hotels" in Paris, gives the impression that the writer was on familiar terms with the Jelliffes: Mrs. Jelliffe is called "Bee," and the complimentary closing is "Affec'ly."[2] Mary Foote (1887–1968), an American portrait painter formerly of New York, had met Jelliffe possibly through her close friends Robert Edmond Jones, a prominent theatrical designer, and Mabel Dodge (later Luhan), both of whom had been analysands of Jelliffe's some years earlier (see Part I, ch. 4). Foote painted a portrait of Jelliffe in the early 1920s (see page 184). In 1926, Jones was in Zurich being analyzed by Jung—who "got right down the first days farther than Jelliffe ever got," Jones wrote to Foote[3]—and he persuaded her also to come to Zurich and consult Jung. She arrived in 1927 via China and stayed for twenty-five years. Jelliffe's 1924 scrapbook fails to reveal whether he and his wife got to Paris and saw Mary Foote.

Jelliffe to Freud

December 2, 1924[1]

My dear Professor Freud:

I have received your message and have conveyed it to Miss Brink. She is very much pleased that you should find her Wagner's Women Thesis interesting.[2]

---

1. Lewis, in *Psychoanalytic Pioneers* (pp. 230–231), quotes the following passage from a letter to an unidentified recipient "in Jelliffe's 1926 European period." In the absence of evidence that Jelliffe went to Europe in that year, it appears more likely to be a description of Jelliffe's visit to Jung in 1924: "Jung is looking fine. He was very nice and cordial except when I read a part of my paper on Paleopsychology [1923]. He made quite a fuss about mixing physiology and psychology, mind and matter, body and mind, objective and subjective, and individual and environment. The things we have come to think of in terms of complements, he insists on regarding as separate—especially physiology and psychology, which he seems to think have nothing to do with each other. I really couldn't understand him on this score. The idea of the symbol as an energy container Jung accepts in principle but will not follow. As a consequence I think he is quite tired."
2. Jelliffe's secretary, Mabel Cohen, has stated that Mary Foote was a close friend of Mrs. Jelliffe.
3. Undated letter, Mary Foote papers, Beinecke Library, Yale University.

---

1. Carbon copy of typewritten letter.
2. Louise Brink (1876–19[?]), lay psychotherapist, Jelliffe's pupil and sometime collaborator. See Part I, ch. 3. The reference is to her *Women Characters in Richard Wagner: A Study in "The Ring of the Nibelung"* (NMDMS 37, 1924).

She has worked with me a great deal, first as a patient, then as an assistant, and now upon her own, as I have tried to make her independent. As she has obtained her Ph.D. degree I feel she has earned that independent status.

I was delighted to learn that all was going well with you, and trust that your discomforts have been radically removed.

I am sending you a few of my last reprints. I am not sure whether I sent you the 50 years of American Neurology.[3]

The one on Bone Pathology[4] intrigues me considerably. The later history of this case is a little unfortunate. They were persuaded to go on with another "deep penetration" treatment, from which she had a very bad burn with gangrene of the skin. This necessitated an amputation of the leg. I have a pathological report of the tumor, but this is cold comfort in view of the interesting theoretical situation.

My patient with "nephritis"—"Psychopathology and Organic Disease"[5]— died last year. She went through an interesting regression to an older object transference situation and this really killed her as the "Object" was an adventurer and involved her money matters, and there was no way out. I am certain that were I to analyze the whole situation it would be a most illuminating contribution to certain "nephritic deaths."

I have had a series of "epileptic" cases this fall, two of whom are most fascinating, also another "bony tumor" case and one malignant lymphoma case in a brilliant artistic genius approaching 40.

Your paper on the "Passing of the Oedipus Complex"[6] has intrigued me a great deal for I have often asked myself—how do so many seem to put it away so securely.

> With sincere best wishes,
> Very truly yours,
> [*Smith Ely Jelliffe*]

---

3. "Fifty Years of American Neurology: Fragments of an Historical Retrospect," in *Semi-Centennial Anniversary Volume of the American Neurological Association, 1875–1924*, ed. Jelliffe and Frederick Tilney (New York, 1924).

4. "The Neuropathology of Bone Disease: A Review of Neural Integration of Bone Structure and Function, and a Suggestion Concerning Psychogenic Factors Operative in Bone Pathology," *Transactions of the American Neurological Association, 1924*, pp. 419–435.

5. See above, p. 208, top.

6. "Der Untergang des Ödipuskomplexes," *Internationale Zeitschrift für Psychoanalyse*, 10 (1924), 245 ff.; tr. 1924, "The Passing of the Oedipus Complex"; in *Standard Edn.*, 19, "The Dissolution of the Oedipus Complex."

Freud to Jelliffe

29.XII.24.[1]

Dear Dr. Jelliffe,

Thank you for your letter, your Christmas card, and for the offprints, which arrived today and are of the greatest medical interest. I am amazed that you manage to include the whole of neuropathology in your field of interest and still find time for our psychoanalysis.

I am at present teaching Mrs. Powers,[2] whom you know and who often speaks to me of you. She is intelligent, and I dare hope that she will learn a good deal with us.

With best wishes for the year 1925.

Yours,

Freud

Just before Christmas in 1924, Jung came to the United States as the guest of wealthy American friends in Chicago.[1] The express purpose of the trip was to visit Indian communities in the Southwest and to observe Negro life in the South. The party made a rapid circuit including the Grand Canyon, Santa Fé, Taos, and New Orleans, and on 12 January 1925 Jung was in Washington, where he looked up White as well as Senator Joseph Medill McCormick, of Chicago. He sailed from New York on 14 January, not having seen Jelliffe, whom he wrote from the ship:

FRENCH LINE

Bord S.S. "France"
Le 17 janv. 1925[1]

Dear Dr. Jelliffe,

As you probably have heard from Dr. White of my flying trip through America I want to express to you my deep regrets, that I have not been able to call on you while I was in New York. I spent only two days in New York and they were simply overcrowded with unavoidable obligations. Thus I found no chance to see you. As Washington was by far less strenuous I could

---

1. Typewritten letter, signed.
2. Lillian Delger Powers, M.D. (1866–1953), originally of California, had two years of psychoanalytic training in Vienna; around 1926 she established her practice in New York, where Jelliffe referred patients to her.

---

1. For a full account of Jung's visit, see W. McGuire, "Jung in America, 1924–1925," *Spring: An Annual of Archetypal Psychology and Jungian Thought*, 1978, pp. 37 ff.

---

1. Handwritten letter, signed; on the ship's stationery.

see White at least. My time was unfortunately quite short as the trip was rather unforeseen.

Hoping this letter will find you in good health,

I remain yours sincerely,

C. G. Jung.

Jelliffe to Jung

February 20, 1925[1]

Dr. Karl Jung
Kussnach
Zurich, Switzerland
Dear Dr. Jung:

It was a great pleasure for me to receive your letter of January 17th as well as a great disappointment in not seeing you in person. But life is so full of both aspects of reality that would we have all the nice things that we want we certainly would not survive and as for the crushing things they would soon demolish us too. This latter reflection comes in my telling you of a very deep personal loss which has come to me through the death of my younger son.[2] He was 24 years old, had gone through his University with considerable distinction, not only in [the] physical field of athletics, but in his scholarship as well and was going ahead with a great deal of individual value in medicine. We are all very unhappy about it but have to face it. I was glad therefore in a double sense to get your letter as I have always appreciated your friendship and hope that I might retain it.

Otherwise the winter has been very busy and marked with a certain amount of satisfaction.[3] There has been a large amount of routine work, some revising of previous publications, the constant grind on the *Journal* and a little free time for personal expression. This latter has not been as much as one would have liked but American life is not as quiet and restful as it might be.

I am looking forward to a trip to Europe this year which, if it comes off, will certainly include seeing you.

With cordial regards, believe me,

Very truly yours,
[*Smith Ely Jelliffe*]

---

1. Carbon copy of typewritten letter.
2. William Leeming Jelliffe (b. 6 Dec. 1900), died 21 Jan. at his home in Queens. See Part I, ch. 3. Having graduated from Yale, 1923, he was a medical student at the College of Physicians and Surgeons, Columbia University.
3. Jelliffe, as noted in Part I, ch. 3, tried to hide his mourning and lose himself in routine.

Jung to Jelliffe

15.3.1925[1]

My dear Dr. Jelliffe,

Your letter with its sad news has remembered me again of the regrettable fact that I was unable to see you when I was in New York. I did not know that you experienced such a cruel loss as the death of your son in the meantime. Let me express you my deepest sympathy and condolence.

Death has been at work recently. It has been a great shock to me to learn about the sudden death of Medill McCormick.[2] I had seen him in good health on my way through Washington. But death seems to be more cruel when it takes away the young man, who is yet but a promise.

Thank you for your letter.

Yours sincerely
C. G. Jung.

Jelliffe went to Europe with his wife in mid-August 1925, primarily to attend the meeting of the German Society for Psychiatry at Kassel on 1–2 September and the International Psychoanalytic Congress at Bad Homburg, near Frankfurt, on 3–5 September. There was a rather large American delegation at the Congress. Jelliffe read a paper,[1] and it was evident that he was taking an active part in organized psychoanalysis. He had rejoined the orthodox New York Psychoanalytic Society in February (Part I, ch. 3). Freud's poor health prevented his attending the congress, and a paper he had prepared was read on his behalf by Anna Freud. Afterward the Jelliffes visited the romantic towns of Nuremberg and Rothenburg, then Vienna, Venice, the Italian lakes, Genoa, and the Riviera before sailing from Marseilles in mid-October. Freud was again taking a rest cure on the Semmering, and Jelliffe paid him a visit on the way from Vienna to Venice.[2] He did not see Jung, who during August was at the British Empire Exhibition at Wembley, near London, and then went back home to prepare for an expedition to Africa. With two companions, Jung sailed from an English port on 15 October and proceeded through the Mediterranean, stopping at various ports, including Marseilles, en route to

---

1. Typewritten letter, signed.
2. McCormick died in Washington of a heart attack on 25 Feb. 1925.

---

1. "Psycho-Analysis and Organic Disorder: Myopia as Paradigm," *International Journal of Psychoanalysis*, 7 (1925), 445 ff.; also in German: "Psychoanalyse und organische Störung: Myopie als Paradigma," *Internationale Zeitschrift für Psychoanalyse*, 12 (1926), 517 ff. Both issues constituted a *Festschrift* for Freud's seventieth birthday.
2. Information from Jelliffe's scrapbook of the trip and from Jones, *Freud: Life and Work*, 3, ch. 3.

the Suez Canal and eventually Mombasa.[3] Jelliffe and Jung must have passed at sea.

Jelliffe to Freud

December 19, 1925[1]

My dear Professor Freud:

I have just stubbed my finger with a medicine ball (caught it on the end) and said to myself, now there is another reason why I should delay writing to my friends, which have followed close on a conjunctivitis of "Marseilles-ian?"[2] origin—pneumococcus they tell me. This put cotton pads on my eyes for a couple of weeks, and then a grippe which took all the pep out of me, and so I have delayed and delayed telling you what a happy visit I had with you at the Semmering and how I shall treasure it.

I hope you are feeling better and that the old sinus is healing. A comparatively innocuous naso-pharyngitis has kept me snorting about the house for some weeks and I know how annoying such a thing can be.

I also send you some copies of my last two papers on Bone Pathology and on Encephalitis.[3] The latter is I think most important. I have worked with the patient 6 months and he is practically completely restored. He was a severe Parkinsonian with respiratory attacks and all the character changes that threatened a deteriorating psychosis, and I only analyzed his efforts to use regressive mechanisms in your sense and Hughlings Jackson's sense[4] and have had a really brilliant therapeutic result. I am further emboldened to declare these results because one of our Philadelphia confreres had him a year under observation and was about to commit him as a hopeless schizophrenic—whose "hereditary history showed he would have [been] demented even without an encephalitis." All a piece of nonsense but an indication that I was not dealing with one of "those cases which would have recovered

---

3. Jung, *Memories, Dreams, Reflections* (New York and London, 1963), ch. 9, pt. iii; *C. G. Jung: Letters*, ed. G. Adler and A. Jaffé, vol. 1 (Princeton and London, 1973), letter to Hans Kuhn, 1 Jan. 1926.

---

1. Carbon copy of typewritten letter.
2. Jelliffe contracted an infection at Marseilles or on the ship after embarking. See Part I, ch. 4.
3. "Somatic Pathology and Psychopathology at the Encephalitis Crossroad: A Fragment," *JNMD*, 61 (1925), 561 ff; the paper on bone pathology was presumably the one cited in n. 4 to the letter of 2 Dec. 1924. Apparently Jelliffe sent Freud the same offprint more than once.
4. John Hughlings Jackson (1835–1911), English neurologist, who influenced Freud's thinking, particularly in suggesting a hierarchical model of nervous system functioning (*Standard Edn.*, 14, p. 206).

anyway." Burr describes the case in *Arch. of Neurology and Psychiatry*, July 1925, Case I.[5]

As I told you, my bone case was broken into by a deep x-ray therapy and gangrene resulted and I was left stranded as to my results, but at all events I am sure of the facts, and I did get a causative mechanism out of the way.

I am still working upon my patient with the myopia which was my subject at Bad Homburg. There is in my mind little doubt but that the castration complex took hold of the peeping mechanism—sister fixation—and played a part in the myopia. One of my ophthalmological colleagues—a singularly free observer—when I said something about it remarked, "You are probably quite correct. All my mopes are abnormal mentally"—meaning something akin to narcissism. I shall hope to round the study out in better shape. The ostensible causes of his coming for analysis were an annoying blushing and procrastination in his business. He reaches the heterosexual object only when alcoholized. His sister, unmarried, has a distinct neurosis.

Another patient, who weighed 280 pounds, an unmarried woman, a doctor, is proving another exquisite problem of self-destruction by diabetes. Her mother *Einstellung*[6] is fascinating. The mother died in childbirth. Her aunt, a nun, raised her in a convent. The aunt weighed 300 pounds—interesting identifications. One to me intriguing character trait, apropos of the mother's neglect—her animosity towards the mother who never gave her any love—is of course a definite narcissistic-homosexual fixation, but she even won't use any of the money her mother left her for herself—some $3,000 in rents from property. She has always given it to some women to help them through school, college, etc., and is now paying the way of a young woman in law school. But farther—property (left by the mother) which should at current rates yield $6,000–$10,000 she won't raise the rents. Another to me interesting masochistic situation: when younger she made several suicide attempts, but of late has done good medical work, supports herself well, but is now developing (40) a diabetes.

I had yesterday a most fascinating dream analysis which indicated a marked urinary fixation (sweet urine) as a birth (death) phantasy, which I shall hope to add to some other material I have upon diabetes.

I enjoyed your little paper on Negation,[7] just to hand, and lots of confirmatory material came to mind. I recall one analysis 10 years ago now—when a patient had described in detail all of the possible attributes of a negro porter that she had seduced (in the dream) later to a rubber doll—and tore to pieces. We spent half an hour on all of the positive traits and then I suddenly asked

---

5. Charles W. Burr, "Sequelae of Epidemic Encephalitis without Any Preceding Acute Illness," *Archives of Neurology and Psychiatry*, 14 (1925).

6. *Einstellung* = attitude, fixation.

7. "Die Verneinung," *Imago*, 11 (1925), 217 ff.; tr., "Negation," *International Journal of Psycho-analysis*, 6 (1925), 367 ff. (*Standard Edn.*, 19.)

her, "Well, if the image had been exactly the opposite who would it have been?" Naturally it concealed "myself" and her desire to tear me to pieces. She was a manic-depressive, and I first obtained from her analysis—she is in one of my psychogram diagrams in my Technique—some very suggestive material about gall bladder disease and the manic-depressive psychotic reaction which is resting in the back of my head.

My illness which while not severe was very prostrating, has kept me from any of our psychoanalytical meetings, so I have not been in touch with the group. I did not see Rank[8] even, but now I am renewing my pep, getting to the gymnasium for a little exercise, holding my analyses down from 10–4 instead of 9–7 as they would be if I let them. I am recuperating.

My youngest daughter—I have 3—is being married this month.[9] She has chosen a young Hollander who travels here and there, but she will live in Amsterdam. This places all three of my girls. My oldest boy,[10] who had a severe poliomyelitis, is still with me, and my younger son[11]—the fourth in my family—as you know died in January of this year.

Had you been better I would have talked to you about him and his death as I think I need some help in my adjustment to it. He was 25 [sic], fatherhood apart, quite a remarkable boy. He always did things thoroughly from childhood—had distinct mechanical gifts. He was in his second year in medicine. Lovable, sociable, helpful, and as sound a student as he was an all-round athlete.

This thing almost finished me as apparently there was more cathexis upon him than I imagined. Life has been quite drab at times and I am sure my infection and weakened resistance is bound up in this situation. His mother died at 48 when he was 13.[12] She had a ruptured anomalous anterior communicating artery of the circle of willis and died of ventricular hemorrhage in 10 hours. Her mother had angina pectoris and died at 56.

He and I had always been very good friends. He evidently imitated me a great deal. I almost became a chemist and then took up medicine. He was tremendously intrigued with his medicine.

I tell you all this, for I wanted to when I was in the Semmering and discuss it, but it was quite too much to ask of you.

I know I am coming round—as my dreams of his being with me are becoming fewer. I feel sure you can say something that will be helpful. My

---

8. Otto Rank (1886–1939), Viennese lay analyst, who worked with Freud from 1906 and became a member of the "Committee" of six analysts closest to Freud. In 1925, he was on the way to separating from Freud, though Jelliffe probably was unaware of this. Rank had spent the first two months of 1925 in New York and returned there after the Homburg Congress, eventually spending much of his time in the United States.

9. Helena, born in 1903, who married Carel Goldschmidt on 30 Dec. 1925.

10. Smith Ely, Jr., born in 1899, had the polio attack at the age of eight.

11. See above, 20 Feb. 1925, n. 2.

12. Jelliffe's or typist's error for 15. Mrs. Jelliffe died 3 Mar. 1916.

other boy 27 really wounds my ego. He is of the more shiftless, careless type. His polio was quite severe, and although externally he is not a cripple, he has a vast number of bad muscles. His mo.-father *einstellung* is classically infantile. He is quite outspoken in thinking I do not treat him fairly. I have to harden my heart not to baby him in all ways. He is for the most part very happy and has seen Dr. Rank quite frequently. Dr. Rank can tell you more of his personality. I want to get my antipathy to him in a better state of sublimation.

This is quite an infliction—I mean the letter.

I had hoped to arrange some exchange advertising of your Collected Works and the *Journal* with Mr. Storfer[13] and it was agreed when I left Vienna. I hope nothing has interfered. I have written him but have not heard from him. He gave me two sets of the *Gesammelte Schriften* at wholesale rates and I agreed to place an advertisement with the *Journal* and *Psychoanalytic Review* free. I am waiting to hear from him re. copy. I trust he has not been ill.

With sincere regards,
[*Smith Ely Jelliffe*]

Jelliffe to Freud

February 16, 1926[1]

My dear Professor Freud:

May I at this time send you my sincerest congratulations upon your reaching the ideal age of the Scriptures,[2] as a symbol of your Super Ego sublimation capacity. The later Pauline rendering of "preaching the Gospel to the four corners of the earth"[3] you have also most successfully carried out.

I do hope you are feeling better and send you my heartiest well wishes.

May I encroach upon your time to present to you two—to me—interesting theoretical considerations which flow out of your stimulating contributions.

For some time now I have been nursing somewhere an idea about certain types of color blindness. Some years ago I was struck by F. C. S. Schiller's very fascinating reediting of some ideas of Protagoras in his *Studies in Humanism*—particularly when he made reference to Xanthias, the son of Glaucus, who "could not tell grass from blood"—which led up to the old saying of Protagoras: "From this case and others like it I learned that truth and

---

13. Adolf (later Albert) Joseph Storfer (1888–1944), director of the Internationaler Psychoanalytischer Verlag, coeditor of Freud's *Gesammelte Schriften* and of *Imago*.

---

1. Carbon copy of typewritten letter.
2. Freud's seventieth birthday was not until 6 May 1926. Subsequently, Freud sent Jelliffe a signed printed card thanking him for his "friendly expression of interest" in his seventieth birthday.
3. Not in the New Testament, though the idea is expressed in Acts 13:47, Coloss. 1:23, etc.

reality were to each (man) as he perceived them"—i.e. the aphorism "Man is the measure of all things" attributed to Protagoras.[4]

Then certain Mendelian studies on color blindness interested me, and their sex-linked characters—which as you know brought out color blindness in the male, latent in (daughter-mother) to reappear in the (son-father). Finally, when I read your Passing of the Oedipus Complex and your Anatomical Difference papers,[5] I felt that a speculative *Verkumpfung*[6] was tenable—namely, that the taboo of the Oedipus situation and its displacement to the castration threat might have some application to this so-called sex-linked fiction of the geneticist, in that the male suffered a partial castration through his color blindness (red-green especially), details to be worked out clinically, and the (daughter-mother) escape of the same since the taboo was not biologically needed. (See Lot's daughters paradigma.)[7] One of my sons-in-law[8] has this type of color blindness, and I am greatly interested in seeing how it works out with the children. His first child, a daughter, showed an interesting anal-erotic mother situation in fecal eating quite up to 4–5 months of her life. This is to me an interesting correlation. Is this too theoretical to work out?

A second even more fascinating problem has recently come up in an analysis of a father and mother (49 and 54 years old respectively) whose daughter I saw some 6 years ago and made—for them—an instant and striking diagnosis of glioma of the brain, later confirmed, although many had floundered about on other situations.[9]

In the dream material of the mother (1926) I have become very distinctly impressed with a series of *self-impregnation phantasies*. Here there are a number of previous clinical situations happening long before. The child referred to was the only partially successfully impregnated ovum.

The mother had a right- and then a left-sided dermoid cyst. (Howard Kelly,[10] one of our most reputed Johns Hopkins surgeons, removed them.)

---

4. The British philosopher F. C. S. Schiller (1864–1937) based his studies in *Humanism* (1907) on Protagoras's dictum "Man is the measure of all things" (Plato, *Theaetetus* 160 D). The works of Protagoras (5th cent. B.C.) have not survived; his views are known chiefly from Plato.

5. See above, letter of 2 Dec. 1924, n. 6; "Einige psychische Folgen des anatomischen Geschlechtsunterschieds," *Internationale Zeitschrift für Psychoanalyse*, 11 (1925), 401 ff; tr. 1927; in *Standard Edn.*, 19, as "Some Psychical Consequences of the Anatomical Distinction between the Sexes."

6. *Verkumpfung*, meaningless word, evidently a typist's error for *Verknüpfung*, connection.

7. In Genesis 19:30–38, the two daughters of Lot got him drunk in order to commit incest with him.

8. Alfred E. Emerson, a zoologist (1896–1976), married to Jelliffe's second daughter, Winifred, suffered from red-green colorblindness. The Emersons' daughter, Helena, and son, William, were not colorblind, but Helena (married to Eugene Wilkening) had two colorblind sons. (Information from Mrs. Carel Goldschmidt.)

9. This is undoubtedly the case referred to in Part I, ch. 3.

10. Howard Atwood Kelly (1858–1943).

Then she had a 20-pound pseudo-pregnancy tumor. (Cytolytic destruction of the ovum.)

After the death of this only daughter, an extremely gifted wonder child (epileptic as diagnosed by the aforesaid other specialists), the mother developed a profound asthenic invalid reaction—in bed for 3 years—for which after 5 years she has come to me on the basis of her transference when I made the right hit re. the daughter and which, the dream material shows, was a suicide compromise reaction partially glimpsed as a protection against the breaking through of the *straf*-material.[11]

Jacques Loeb's studies[12] on parthenogenetic reproduction show up to frogs (phyletically) the possibilities of incomplete male productions on ion K. Ca. Na. Mg. stimuli.

Hence my speculative correlations between the self-impregnation (complete within the self) and the dermoid cyst and tumor formation. Naturally she is one of those hyper-morality hyper-Super-Ego-formation personalities—called by us here "Nice People."

Is this crazy? It might be, if I had not partially assimilated Vaihinger's contribution[13] to the "Als Ob" problem and a recognition of the fictional nature of such speculative activities and their partial usefulness. Certainly the gynecological-pathological speculations are entirely sterile so far as I have gone over them.

At all events, from the purely psychogenic aspect I know of no one to whom I could express them whose biological-neurological-symbolic apperceptions are as fundamental as yours, and hence my temerity in outlining them to you as a Father Imago, for criticism.

Not to overwhelm you with further detail, trusting this hazy outlining may give you my ideas.

Believe me,

Very sincerely—yes affectionately,
Yours,
[*Smith Ely Jelliffe*]

---

11. *Straf* = punishment.

12. Jacques Loeb (1859–1924), American biophysiologist of German origin, at the Rockefeller Institute, New York; published the results of his parthenogenesis researches in *Artificial Parthenogenesis and Fertilization* (1913). By "artificial" Loeb meant chemically stimulated, hence Jelliffe's mention of effective chemicals (by abbreviations of potassium, calcium, sodium, and magnesium), ranging up the evolutionary scale to frogs.

13. Hans Vaihinger (1852–1933), German philosopher; he set forth his system in *Die Philosophie des Als Ob* (1911; tr. 1924 as *The Philosophy of "As If"*), arguing that, since reality cannot be known in fact, we construct systems of thought to explain reality.

Freud to Jelliffe

28.II.1926.[1]

Dear Dr. Jelliffe,

I am indebted to you in several respects for the communications I received from you in December. Especially for your letter, which contains so much of a personal nature. I was sorry to hear of the misfortunes that have befallen you. I hope you have recovered by now, that you are fully restored to your work and pursuing your multifarious interests. In part, your letter is a continuation of our conversation on the Semmering, and much of what you say makes me regret that we cannot go on conversing in the same way. In addition to your letter, I have received quite a few of your offprints and a small check, which is no doubt attributable to you.

You may have thought my reaction none too friendly. My sentiments, I assure you, are not at fault, but these last months and weeks have reminded me rather forcibly of the progress of human infirmity, and have brought me an abundance of slight and not so slight ailments, from which I have not yet wholly recovered.[2] Under these circumstances, the correctness I ordinarily try to observe suffers; I somehow meet the most necessary obligations, but fail in many respects to live up to my intentions. Do not interpret these remarks as signs of out-and-out depression; I am merely acknowledging the effects of old age, which make themselves felt in all of us sooner or later, in me at the classical time of life. All the same, I go on with my work, and believe I may say truthfully that my interest in the activities and persons I am connected with has not suffered appreciably.

This letter will have fulfilled its purpose, if you continue to give me news now and then of your health and work.

Cordially yours,
Freud

Jelliffe to Freud

March 27, 1926[1]

My dear Professor Dr. Freud:

A momentary respite affords me the pleasure to acknowledge your good favor of February 28, 1926 and to say how pleased I am to have received it.

---

1. Typewritten letter, signed.

2. At this time, Freud was beginning a rest at the Cottage Sanitarium, Vienna, to recover from a cardiac episode. See Jones, 3, 127/120; Max Schur, *Freud: Living and Dying* (New York, 1972), pp. 389–90.

---

1. Carbon copy of typewritten letter.

I know how busy you are and hope that you will not think me overgreedy in hoping to receive an answer to what I send. I am not so and hope I can write you freely and that you should not feel any obligation to answer, especially as I am all too aware of and sorry for the difficulties under which you suffer. I have little to add to this letter save its acknowledgement of your kindness.

Here as with your group we have suffered a severe loss in the death of Dr. Polon.[2] Only two weeks last Sunday I was with him in a small group which he had gathered to discuss metapsychological problems, and now we are bereft of a bright and active mind from which we had received much stimulus and hoped to gain more. Personally I feel the loss a great deal. His was a helpful, clear, and penetrating mind, by far the best in our group in this particular field. Dr. Brill undoubtedly has written you fully about him and about our work in the New York Society.

I am pleased to report that my respiratory encephalitis case continues to improve, and that I am now quite intrigued with another. Inasmuch as this one, a young woman (with a brother who also had an encephalitis 5 years ago and is in an *Irrenanstalt*[3] as a schizophrenic), has a drug habit for sleeping and at 26 still sucks her fingers (3rd and 4th of the right hand), I expect a hard tussle. I gave her some tr. belladonna and tr. hyoscyamus[4]—in very small doses: a.a cc. o.30 9.4 hrs.—and obtained a marked regression, almost complete coma for three days, which pharmacoanalytically demonstrated to her what she was after from her drugs, following which I deprived her of all drugs, and she is coming through.

In the April issue of the *Journal*, which you will soon receive, I have begun a study[5] of the respiratory encephalitis syndromy—first the historical retrospect—and hope to develop along psychoanalytic lines the psychopathology, reporting these two cases. By the time the article is completed this second case may be added to the good results—at least I have a fairly good working transference now.

Personal situations make me wish I could arrange my economic status (sell my present house, which is wanted for business purposes) and come to Europe for 1 or 2 years. If this house selling goes through I can be moderately independent and afford the time to work up an enormous amount of collected material which heretofore has had to lie fallow waiting upon some such arrangement. If this happens I hope to be able to come to you for advice.

Otherwise our life here goes on as usual. I am busy and well, interested and happy in spite of the fact that the hopes built up that my son would

---

2. Albert Polon, M.D. (1881–1926), had psychoanalytic training in Vienna.
3. *Irrenanstalt* = insane asylum.
4. Presumably hyoscyamine.
5. "Postencephalitic Respiratory Disorders," *JNMD*, 63 (1926), 357–371, continuing over eight more issues, and published in 1927 as no. 45 in the NMDMS.

carry on have had a setback. I am daily more and more certain that the foundations you have laid down are valid and full of promise for the future. For this stimulus I am grateful and glad to acknowledge my indebtedness to you. I have over and over again stated in small and in large medical gatherings that the psychoanalytic principles gave me a real interest in medicine in the large. That through your work almost all medical problems took on a new bearing of vital import and gave me the assurance that what creative talents I might possess could find some expression.

From 1907–1910, I spent 22 months in European clinics at much economic stress because I became dissatisfied with the reigning dogmas in medicine, and finally came through to a larger philosophical conception of my task. If the more immediate stimulus came through Jung, at this time called by Maloney and myself to Fordham, where I was professor of psychiatry, still it was your influence, via Jung's activities, to which I am most vitally under obligation.

I am saying this for, as you may recall, you asked me when I first met you in 1921 at Bad Gastein what were my resistances, and I told you I felt you had misjudged Dr. White and myself, and possibly mal-advised by Jones (?) had written in a letter in response to Dr. White's request for a paper for the *Psychoanalytic Review* that we had founded the *Psychoanalytic Review* as a competitor to your interests.[6]

I do not pretend to question your reactions at the time, but do hope that your larger vision may hold us faultless even if immature, in the sincerity of our efforts towards the main issues of the situation.

Thus I do still look forward to the time when you will feel that the *Psychoanalytic Review* may have the honor of a communication from you.

I think that I have encroached upon your time enough although there are many thoughts that crowd into my mind, and close by sending you my sincerest well wishes.

I am personally not in full sympathy with Stekel's final chapter in Volume II of the *Fortschritte*,[7] even though it seems to me he longs for a reconciliation with the Father and yet cannot acknowledge his infidelity. Perhaps this is the conflict between art and science, between intuition and reality *Prüfung*.[8] How are they to be resolved in a higher unity?

Very sincerely,
[Smith Ely Jelliffe]

---

6. See above, Freud to White, 17 July 1914.
7. Wilhelm Stekel, *Fortschritte und Technik der Traumdeutung* (Vienna, 1935).
8. *Prüfung* = testing.

Freud to Jelliffe

11.IV.26.[1]

Dear Dr. Jelliffe,

I acknowledge your many personal letters with thanks. Let me take this opportunity to explain something that happened a long time ago.

It is true that I was at first very suspicious of you and of Dr. White, and that my distrust carried over to the *Psychoanalytic Review* you founded. The reason was that I first heard your name from Jung, who spoke of you emphatically as his friend at a time[2] when I was already convinced of his hostile attitude toward me. Later I met you in the company of Dr. Stekel (in 1921 in Gastein), and that again was no recommendation in my eyes. Of course you, as an outsider, could have had no exact knowledge of these personal relations. It has given me great pleasure to learn of your true opinions and intentions from our correspondence over the years, and I have been glad to correct my initial misapprehension with regard to you and Dr. White. In principle I should not be disinclined to contribute to your *Review*, but my production at the moment is very meager and may soon dry up altogether.

Do not fail to go on writing to me; the news of Dr. Polon's death came as a shock. I already thought him very capable when he was here with me, and I am told that he made considerable progress since then.

With kind regards,
Cordially yours,
Freud

Jelliffe to Freud

June 8, 1926.[1]

Dear Professor Freud:

It was a great pleasure to get your letter of April 11th and it would have been answered sooner but I have been misbehaving and trying some masochistic experiments. First I fell and dislocated my acromic-clavicular joint, left side. I learned a lot about my sleep ritual from it, as it certainly disturbed it and was very annoying. The sleep disturbance was much worse than the joint disturbance. Then I had a sharp otitis attack which fortunately subsided without any membrane puncture. So I have slowed up in my own work a bit and now am feeling quite fit again.

---

1. Typewritten letter, signed.
2. Probably after Jung's return from his visit to the United States, when he gave the Fordham Lectures, in 1912.

---

1. Carbon copy of typewritten letter.

The two volumes of the *Festschrift* have been received and I am delighted with them. I am specially pleased that my small contribution should have been included.[2]

I cannot tell you how much your letter has meant to me, and I feel you rightly understand our position. Living so far away from the focus of intense activities it is but natural that our perspectives here do not have the sharp definition as do those at the center of things. My Bad Homburg[3] visit has clarified many issues greatly.

Visiting Jung in 1924 I was amazed to learn how narrow his vision was for the general situation and how one-sided he had developed in his interests. I felt he had really ceased to be a physician, a profession which I have come to feel more and more is of great importance to be allied with. As for Stekel's last contribution in his Vol. II, it is "stupid."

I am looking forward to going to Lake George in July for a three months holiday, to revise our Text Book, and I hope to get some psa. material in more complete form for presentation.

Thanking you again for your kindness in giving me of your time,

Very sincerely,

[*Smith Ely Jelliffe*]

Jung to Jelliffe

July 21st 1927[1]

My dear Professor,

I am sorry, I cannot recall Miss Severn[2] etc.—But, as I am away from home until the beginning of Aug. I am unable to look up my books. I will do it as soon as I am home again and I will write to you once more.

Yes, Jones[3] was all right—a pleasure to work with such a fellow!

I hope you are in good health.

My best regards to yourself and to Dr. White.

Yours sincerely

C. G. Jung

---

2. See above, commentary (before 19 Dec. 1925).
3. Ibid.

1. Handwritten letter, signed. Though on Jung's home letterhead, it evidently was written elsewhere, probably at an army reserve camp, where Jung performed duty every summer, an obligation for all Swiss men. Jelliffe's letter has not been found.
2. See below, Emma Jung's letter of 16 Jan. 1928.
3. Robert Edmond Jones. See above, commentary (before 2 Dec. 1924).

Jelliffe attended the International Psychoanalytic Congress at Innsbruck, 1–3 September 1927, and his scrapbook for that year shows that he subsequently was in Austria, the Italian Alps, Amsterdam, and London. His visit to Freud is attested by a handwritten card addressed to Jelliffe at the Hotel Panhans (on the Semmering, where Freud was again on holiday): "I am free from 3.30 p.m. till 4.30 and expect to see you in this time."[1] Jelliffe did not visit Jung in Zurich during the 1927 trip.

Emma Jung to Jelliffe

16 I 1928[1]

Dear Sir,

I am finding among Dr. Jung's letters one of yours, still unanswered, where you ask about a Mrs. Elizabeth Severn.[2] Now, Dr. Jung cannot re-

---

1. Jelliffe described the visit in a letter to Ernest Jones, 24 Oct. 1927 (carbon copy in Jelliffe Papers):

"I had two very good hours with Freud. He was certainly anti-American, partly conditioned I think from Ferenczi's plaints that the Amerikanische Gruppe had not received him well. In fact, someone had suggested that he was behaving exactly as Rank had behaved, save in the fact he had his wife rather than his secretary with him, and this apparently lay behind some of the vituperation against Rank and transferred it to the Amerikanische Gruppe. The lay-analysis situation seemed to me to be the chief cause for dissent.

"He [Freud] discussed—'very frankly' as he asked if he might—the whole problem and I agreed with him in the main. I myself think the American type of scholarship is decidedly lacking in background and early training. We are a helter-skelter frontier type as yet, and the practical difficulties and exigencies threaten to prevent earnest quiet deep thinking. All this which lay in his mind, I agree with. I deplore the patchwork of my earlier training myself and struggle almost Laocoon-wise with the environment which constantly interrupts and prevents working through.

"He deplored the lack of 'leadership' in the group. This I also agree with. Where can we get it without cheap, political, democratic notions? Where genius and mountebank are indistinguishable by the mass, save for brief illumined moments, and so we went on. This led to his 'disappointment,' as he called it, with Brill and the loss of rapport there over a matter which I think I should not put on paper, but which finally dumped the applecart and left Freud quite unhappy about it. Especially as a group of the New York group stood with Brill aloof from Ferenczi—even though Brill dined him and introduced him at various meetings.

"Still, his (Brill's) opinion and mine coincide that Ferenczi was very ill advised to let himself be sponsored by a lay group, some of the chief activators of which have come from our Bolshevik Free love Feminists—and who have more brass and intrigue than anything else. This Greenwich Village bunch enveloped Ferenczi as a cloud and so the so-called more reputable people would have none of him. [. . .]"

---

1. Handwritten letter, signed.

2. American psychotherapist, author of *Psychotherapy, Its Doctrine and Practice* (Philadelphia and London, 1913); *The Psychology of Behaviour* (New York, 1917); and *The Discovery of the Self* (London and Philadelphia, 1933). The next sentence of Emma Jung's letter, referring to "Brown" and "Haywood," suggests a connection to the American writer Heywood Broun, who may have consulted Jelliffe, according to Edward L. Bernays' memoir, *Biography of an Idea* (New York, 1965), p. 631, where Bernays, as noted in Part I, says that Freud, his uncle, had

member her at all, neither under the name of Brown or Haywood. Excuse that this comes so late, maybe it's of no use to you anymore. Dr. Jung is sending you his greetings and best wishes for the New Year.

Yours truly

Emma Jung

Jelliffe to Freud

September 23, 1929[1]

My dear Professor Freud:

For some time I have been having in mind the purpose of writing you, first to offer you my best wishes, secondly to send you a copy of my *Technique of Psychoanalysis* translated into Spanish,[2] and then to confer about a young physician who came to me last winter for some advice, and finally to make a request.

It was a great pleasure to meet again your daughter at Oxford[3] and to learn that you were enjoying your work. I trust your well being continues. The meeting seemed to me to be a quite harmonious one. My own trip was very hurried. Only at the last moment could I get away to return directly to New York and to Lake George where family matters required my attention.

The translation speaks for itself. Wilson did it chiefly. Delgado went over it carefully.

Dr. John Murray[4] of Concord, N. H., 32, married, 2 children, came in to see me about his desire to specialize in neuropsychiatry. He was very anxious to do some psychoanalytic work as he had come to feel that without it there was little understanding of human activities. He has been doing general medicine and has been moderately successful. I have talked with him now several times and he is preparing himself to spend 2 years in Europe. He speaks college German only but has an alert interesting mind and it seems to me would make good material. In discussing the possibilities I went over the entire European field, with which I feel I am fairly conversant, and it finally reduced itself to this, that I advised him to go to Vienna, and I would write this part of my letter to learn if you would be interested in working with him. If you would that would definitely decide his plans. He would come over in January 1930 in time to get in the Post Graduate course in

---

recommended Jelliffe as an analyst, and Bernays relayed the advice to Broun. According to Broun's son, Heywood Hale Broun, his father had analytical interviews with a man in Boston (personal communication).

1. Carbon copy of typewritten letter.
2. *Técnica del Psicoanálisis*, tr. Honorio F. Delgado and Paul Wilson (Segovia, 1929).
3. The Twelfth International Psychoanalytic Congress was held at Oxford, 27–31 July 1929.
4. John M. Murray, M.D. (1896–).

neuropsychiatry. This, I told him, was a good general orientation, and then he would work intensively at his analysis and his neuropsychiatry with Marburg and Pötzl,[5] and do some internal medicine, in which he is quite proficient.

He has interested me as a very likely young man, hence this rather long letter.

With one final matter would I detain you a moment. Dr. White and I have our differences as to some of the material he publishes in the *Psychoanalytic Review*. I make no apology for it; I simply state it. He assumes the chief editorial activity. We would both welcome, however, something from you. Here we certainly would be united in our desires. We have not asked you since the beginning. I believe it would be difficult to formulate any adequate explanation why we have not done so in this long interval. Others perhaps may know better than we. At all events the *Review* is forging slowly ahead, pays for itself and, I trust, is representing "psychoanalysis" better and better. There is still much room for improvement.

With sincere best wishes,

[*Smith Ely Jelliffe*]

Freud to Jelliffe

Oct. 12th 1929
temporarily Berlin-Tegel[1]

Dear Dr. Jelliffe,

Your letter takes me back into a time of unlimited capacity of work, when it meant nothing to me to accept a new patient or write a new paper when asked for it. This time has passed away and it is not reasonable to expect it coming back. Now I feel it is enough for me to have five patients, I will find six of them for a time when I return to Vienna. So I see I cannot take Dr. Murray. I am sorry for it, I should liked to have him work with me, as you recommend him. I have no doubt you will give him good advice as to whom he should go. Alexander[2] as you know is most popular with American Doctors, he is excellent no doubt, but I cannot see why he should have the privilege of instructing Americans and why accomplished analysts like Ei-

---

5. Otto Marburg, M.D. (1874–1948), then director of the Neurological Institute, University of Vienna; from 1938 in the United States. Otto Pötzl, M.D. (1877–1962), psychiatrist and professor at the University of Vienna.

---

1. Handwritten letter in English, on Freud's Vienna letterhead. Freud was at the Tegel Sanatorium (in a suburb north of Berlin) undergoing treatment by the oral surgeon Schroeder (Jones, 3, 155/146).

2. Franz Alexander, M.D. (1891–1964), psychoanalyst, originally of Budapest, in Berlin 1920–1930, thereafter in Chicago.

tingon, Sachs, Rado at Berlin or Nunberg and Federn at Vienna should be left aside.[3] But you will find it out for yourself.

The same cause accounts for my answer to your request. I am again sorry I cannot comply with it. It is too hard for me to write. I have published practically nothing in the last year and a half and if I am working now on a new pamphlet[4]—the continuation of *Future of an Illusion*[5] in a way—my excuse is I intend it to be the last thing I will ever publish.

As regards the ΨA *Review* I think Dr. White behaved towards me in a rather queer way. My explanation was he feels a good deal of resistance against Analysis and I had to be glad that he dislocated it from Analysis and turned it over to me personally. I cannot remember I ever got a single copy of the *Review*. I understood, the *Review* was rather his work than yours.

I look forward to the arrival of the Spanish[6] translation of your Technique and congratulate you on the occasion.

I may return to Vienna in two weeks.

Yours with kind greetings,

Freud

Jelliffe to Freud

November 26, 1929[1]

Dear Professor Freud:

It was very kind of you to write me so full and explicit a letter and I appreciate it very much. I had delayed answering it until I had had the opportunity of going over it with those parts of interest to Dr. Murray.

He came in to see me yesterday and I showed him the letter and he has decided to go first to Vienna and then let the matter of his analysis shape

---

3. Max Eitingon, M.D. (1881–1943), of Russian origin, reared in Leipzig, in Berlin 1909–1934 (where he founded the Psychoanalytic Policlinic), later in Palestine. While a voluntary assistant at the Burghölzli, Zurich, he was Freud's first follower to visit him from abroad, and later was a member of the "Committee." Hanns Sachs (1881–1947), lay psychoanalyst, originally from Vienna; trained in Berlin; after 1932 in Boston. Sandor Rado, M.D. (1890–1972), originally Hungarian, trained in Berlin; after 1931 in New York. Hermann Nunberg, M.D. (1884–1970), originally Polish; worked at the Burghölzli, Zurich, and, after 1914, Vienna; in the United States from 1931. Paul Federn, M.D. (1871–1950), Viennese, adherent of psychoanalysis from 1904; after 1924, "all who called upon Freud were automatically referred to Federn, who presented to Freud only those cases of particular clinical interest" (Edoardo Weiss, article on Federn in *Psychoanalytic Pioneers*, p. 149); in New York from 1938.

4. *Das Unbehagen in der Kultur* (1930), tr. Joan Riviere as *Civilization and Its Discontents* (London and New York, 1930), under which title it is in the *Standard Edn.*, 21.

5. *Die Zukunft einer Illusion* (1927; finished in September, published in November), tr. W. D. Robson-Scott as *The Future of an Illusion* (London, 1928), under which title it is in the *Standard Edn.*, 21.

6. Freud learned Spanish as a hobby in his teens.

---

1. Carbon copy of typewritten letter.

itself without any suggestions on my part and after meeting the different analytical workers. I am going to give him a letter of introduction to you and I know you will discuss with him the various opportunities better after first meeting him.

He has a very excellent mind and a very free, frank and open personality and will make, I think, an excellent worker in the field. He has an excellent opening on his return at one of our men's colleges along lines with are developing in Yale, Princeton and other colleges where they are deeply interested in the use of psychoanalysis to aid the students in their problems. This movement has taken on very wide proportions here chiefly through the "Mental Hygiene" Societies,[2] all of whom are becoming more and more oriented to psychoanalysis and more and more favorably. There are deep resistances it is true but the superficial stupidities are becoming fewer and fewer.

I have read with much interest Thos. Mann's essay[3] and have suggested to Dr. White that it be translated and that he should publish it in the *Review*. It would be quite apropos at this time in view of Mann's recent honors.[4] Should he wish to do this I trust we may have the sanction of the Verlag.

I am quite sure that Dr. White is quite free from either personal resistances or resistances to psychoanalysis. I can say this since I know him so well and what analysis I have had has been from him chiefly. His position in Washington, as a part of the Government, gives him a definite insight into practical measures of propaganda. He knows the political methods by which large extensions of ideas are made possible, and since his time is so occupied with his official position as Superintendent of the leading psychiatric hospital in this country he cannot do individual analytic research. His whole hospital from the nurses up is all analytic however. He chiefly is of service as he travels a great deal, addresses many Societies all over the States, and is greatly in demand. He outlines the principles of psychoanalysis everywhere and has done more for its extension over the U. S. A. than any one other individual. I think you should know this.

As for the *Review*, the clerical side of it is attended to by one of his secretaries in his off time. I wish I had known you had not received copies. It is an inadvertance which is inexcusable, and I take upon myself much of the blame since I could have consulted our mailing list and seen if your name

---

2. Mental hygiene literature for these years contained a large number of accounts of attempts to improve the mental health of college students. See, e.g., Austen Fox Riggs and William B. Terhune, "The Mental Health of College Women," *Mental Hygiene*, 12 (1928), 559–568.

3. "Die Stellung Freuds in der modernen Geistesgeschichte," *Psychoanalytische Bewegung* (Vienna), 1:3 (1929); tr. H. T. Lowe-Porter, "Freud's Position in the History of Modern Culture," *Criterion*, 12 (1933), 549–570; *Psychoanalytic Review*, 28 (1941), 92–116.

4. Mann was awarded the Nobel Prize in Literature for 1929, which had been announced shortly before.

was on it or not. I am sending you copies of this year's numbers thus far issued and will see that you receive further issues.[5]

At our last meeting of the New York Psychoanalytic Society we passed the resolution to admit properly trained lay analysts to the Society.

I am still busy on my studies on oculogyric crises in post-encephalitis cases and also some post-encephalitic tics. They are enormously interesting. I trust I shall be able to publish a small monograph on the situation.[6]

It may interest you to hear that Dr. Powers[7] has been doing some most excellent work.

With sincere regards and best wishes for your continuance in health. Believe me,

> Very sincerely yours,
> [*Smith Ely Jelliffe*]

Jelliffe to Freud

January 18, 1930[1]

My dear Professor Freud:

It was a great pleasure to receive from you a copy of your *Das Unbehagen in der Kultur*.[2] A very excellent despatch about the book had appeared in the *New York Times* only this very week,[3] and so I was prepared for it. You had also written me about it.

So kindly accept my sincere thanks. Here all are well and busy. The Society is well attended and the members are working earnestly.

For myself, I have been well and also occupied. I was made the President of the American Neurological Association this year and am anxious to present an address which shall deal with psychoanalytic principles.[4] The matter is still very nebulous in my mind. We have had some antagonistic expressions from former presidents, but I think I shall avoid polemics. I have thought for some time that what you have discussed as "condensation"[5] says all that

---

5. Freud sent Jelliffe a postcard on 10 December gratefully acknowledging receipt of the *Psychoanalytic Review*, vol. 16.

6. Jelliffe published several papers on this subject in 1929 and subsequently (see Bibliography). For the eventual monograph, see below, Jelliffe to Jung, 16 May 1932, n. 2.

7. See above, 29 Dec. 1924, n. 2.

---

1. Carbon copy of typewritten letter.

2. See above, Freud to Jelliffe, 12 Oct. 1929, n. 4. Though dated 1930, the book was printed and available during December 1929 (Jones, 3, 158/148).

3. *New York Times*, 13 Jan. 1930, p. 3: "Freud Sees Aims of Man as Futile," unsigned dispatch from Vienna, of column length.

4. "Psychiatry of Our Colonial Forefathers," *Archives of Neurology and Psychiatry*, 24 (1930); also in *Transactions of the American Neurological Association*, 56 (1930).

5. Freud first dealt with the principle of condensation in dreams in *The Interpretation of Dreams* (1900), ch. 6, sec. (A): *Standard Edn.*, 4, pp. 279 ff.

the "Gestalt theory"[6] has to offer, and even more since the concept affords a method of dismembering the "Gestalt" or "engram," and hence is a better mode of approach. This I hope I can make as a part of my study, in which I wish to go still deeper into structural foundations and thus combine or rather get under the more neurological concepts, which are those of the major portion of the Association.

I am still trying to go on with my oculogyric crises in encephalitis and their relation to the anxiety, guilt situation—and also some leads as to the catatonic *Haltung*[7] in its hostility reaction component as picked out in Parkinsonism.

With cordial regards and best wishes,

Sincerely,

[*Smith Ely Jelliffe*]

Jung to Jelliffe

Küsnacht, Oct. 13th [1931][1]

My dear Jelliffe,

It is nice to hear of you again after many years.

I just want to tell you that I see no point in sending my papers to your journal. You surely know that I am a mystic according to American standards.[2] So I think that it will be theological journals that might refer to my papers. I have noticed that my medical colleagues find it particularly hard to understand my ideas. I therefore should prefer not to disturb the peace of their mind. The things that I have written in the last years are only psychological stuff, which I suppose is Chinese to the readers of your journal. You will excuse therefore if I prefer not to enter upon your proposition.

Sincerely yours

C. G. Jung

---

6. The school of Gestalt psychology, emphasizing the whole rather than distinct parts, dates from just after the turn of the century in Germany. Adherents brought Gestalt theory to the United States in the 1920's and after.

7. *Haltung* = bearing, posture. Cf. Jelliffe, "Vigilance: The Motor Pattern and Inner Meaning in Some Schizophrenics' Behavior," *Proceedings of the Association for Research in Nervous and Mental Disease*, 75 (1930); also *Psychoanalytic Review*, 17 (1930).

---

1. Typewritten postcard, signed; postmarked 14 Oct. 1931. Jelliffe's letter which it answers is missing.

2. Characteristically, W. A. White, reviewing Jung's *Two Essays on Analytical Psychology* (tr. H. G. and C. F. Baynes; New York and London, 1928) in the *New York Herald Tribune*, 30 Dec. 1928, stated that "these essays will be welcomed by Jung's admirers and followers in this country, but will serve only to confirm the suspicions of the more orthodox Freudians of his nonscientific and mystical tendencies." In 1931, a book of a still more definitely mystical inclination appeared: with Richard Wilhelm, *The Secret of the Golden Flower* (tr. C. F. Baynes; New York and London), an ancient Chinese Taoist text with Jung's psychological commentary.

SMITH ELY JELLIFFE, M.D.
64 WEST 56TH STREET
NEW YORK
October 23, 1931[1]

Dr. Carl Jung
Kussnach
Zurich, Suisse
Dear Dr. Jung:

I have your note and was disappointed to get it. First as to your feeling about the criticism which you locate here as to "mysticism." I have never heard it here. I have read of it in certain European medical literature but was unaware that in America they even had any ideas of what mysticism really was. With our abundant supply of hemi-semi-demi-morons it strikes me, personally, as strange that anyone, and least of all you, would have any feelings to waste about such matters.

Then again I was disappointed as I have always enjoyed reading your works and would naturally be glad to have them in reprint form available for reference and be saved the burden of going to the library to consult them. I had specially wanted your address at Berne (*Schw. m. Woch.*)[2] and your papers before the Psychotherapeutic Congresses.[3]

As to the reviewing of them in the *Journal of Nervous and Mental Disease,* this is of secondary consideration as all such reviewing and abstracting which I do is usually done in the form of collected abstracts, in which I try to show the development of various views concerning questions of neurology and psychiatry—a bit formal perhaps, but one has to consider the audience. I was not writing as from the *Psychoanalytic Review,* as Dr. White does all of this kind of work on that.

I write you this more or less fully as you were kind enough to follow up my postal request.

I am sending you a couple of recent things of mine which may interest you.

---

1. Typewritten letter, signed; from the C. G. Jung Archives, courtesy of Franz Jung.
2. *The General Bibliography of Jung's Writings (Coll. Works,* 19) lists no address at Berne published in the *Schweizerisches medizinisches Wochenschrift.* However, the 29 Aug. 1929 issue of that journal contained an English translation, by Cary F. Baynes, of "Problems of Modern Psychotherapy," which Jung had given as a lecture to the Psychotherapeutische Gesellschaft, Munich, on 21 Mar. 1929. The Baynes translation later appeared in *Modern Man in Search of a Soul* (1933).
3. Besides the foregoing, these included "The Aims of Psychotherapy" (*Coll. Works,* 16), address to the Fourth General Medical Congress for Psychotherapy, Bad Nauheim, Apr. 1929, and "The Practical Use of Dream-Analysis" (ibid.), to the Sixth General Medical Congress for Psychotherapy, Dresden, Apr. 1931.

With sincere regards,
Smith Ely Jelliffe

Jelliffe wrote on 16 February 1932, to Gardner Murphy, professor of psychology at Columbia University: "The more of Jung I read the less I can comprehend him. I make serious efforts, but he reads more and more like Husserl and similar philosophers[1] and I have a hard time fitting it into the actual concrete processes. I know from many years of patient waiting how stupid (repressed) one can be about looking at things in different ways but I can't see Jung very clearly."

Freud to Jelliffe

15.5.1932
Vienna IX, Berggasse 19[1]

Dear Dr. Jelliffe,
    I never found out whether or not the twins I spoke of in the passage[2] you cite were monozygotic, and it is certain that I cannot find out now. I do know for sure, however, that they always lived together and were inseparable up to the time of their final secondary school examinations.
    Your remarks about Dupuytren's contracture[3] would certainly be of interest to me, but I am too far from the subject to venture an opinion.
                                        Yours sincerely,
                                        Freud

---

1. See below, Jelliffe to Jung, 5 July 32, n. 5.

---

1. Handwritten letter, signed. Jelliffe's letter which it answers is missing.
2. Presumably in "The Psychogenesis of a Case of Homosexuality in a Woman" (1920), *Standard Edn.*, 18, p. 159, n. 1.
3. Cf. Jelliffe, "Dupuytren's Contracture and the Unconscious," *International Clinics*, 41 (1931). The French surgeon and anatomist Guillaume Dupuytren (1777–1834) first described this psychogenic deformity of the hand in 1831.

Jelliffe to Jung

May 16, 1932[1]

My dear Dr. Jung:

As I have just published a small study on Compulsions in the Oculogyric Crises of Encephalitis,[2] I take occasion to send you a copy with my compliments and expression of regards.

I have just started reading Wilhelm's *Secret of the Golden Flower*[3] and it promises to be most fascinating. I feel illy prepared and although I went through an uncle's collection of Max Müller's "Sacred Books of the East"[4] in my twenties, little of it stuck for lack of a proper training. I am looking forward to a pleasurable enterprise.

May I also ask about something that interests me in a recent autobiographical sketch in Murchison's recent *History of Psychology in Autobiography*, Vol. 1,[5] where McDougall, p. 211, writes as follows: "I, therefore, found opportunities to visit C. G. Jung at Zurich and to be analyzed, so far as that process is possible for so hopelessly normal a personality as mine. I made an effort to be as openminded as possible; and came away enlightened but not convinced."[6] This, I take it from the context, was in 1920.

Apart from the inherent evidence of nonsense in the statement itself as to his "hopelessly normal personality," I am intrigued to know what process did he actually go through, how long and what did it all amount to?

If I am indiscreet in asking such a question pay no attention to it. In another place he has stated "he took some dreams to Jung to be analyzed" which seems to bear out the notion that he thought an analysis consists of a dozen or more "conversations."

Here life flows on as usual. I have been much occupied all winter and hope to present further material of my "Dupuytren's Contracture Case" of which I think I sent you a reprint. If I did not I would like to send you one, and if you feel it worth while, get your comment upon it.

When I read a part of my "Oculogyric Crises" paper before our Neurological Association, especially that phase when I quoted "Lift up thine eyes to the hills whence cometh thy help,"[7] I had the joy of being called a "mystic."

---

1. Typewritten letter, signed; from the C. G. Jung Archives, courtesy of Franz Jung.
2. *Psychopathology of Forced Movements and the Oculogyric Crises of Lethargic Encephalitis* (NMDMS 95; New York, 1952).
3. See above, Jung to Jelliffe 13 Oct. 31, n. 2.
4. Translations of the chief Oriental religious writings, in fifty-one volumes, ed. Friedrich Max Müller (1823–1900), originally German; from 1846 he was at Oxford University.
5. Carl Murchison, *History of Psychology in Autobiography*, vol. 1 (Worcester, Mass., 1930).
6. William McDougall (1871–1938), English psychologist, after 1920 in the United States; at Harvard until 1927; thereafter at Duke University. Jung discussed McDougall's views in "The Therapeutic Value of Abreaction" (1921), *Coll. Works*, 16, pars. 255 ff.
7. Psalm 121:1: "I will lift up mine eyes unto the hills, from whence cometh my help" (A.V.).

So you see why I wrote about your "feeling." To me it was comic, for as yet I fail to know what these people here think is "mystic." Levy-Bruhl's last work on the "Surnaturel"[8] has interested me greatly even though he adds little to what he has already written.

With sincere best wishes,
Smith Ely Jelliffe

Jung to Jelliffe

June 7th 1932[1]

My dear Dr. Jelliffe,

Thank you for sending me your interesting study on "Compulsion" etc. I don't know whether I am bound to medical discretion in McDougall's case, as he designates himself as a hopelessly normal personality. I probably had no right to consider his case as one that would fall under the conception of medical discretion. There isn't much to be indiscreet about anyhow. It was really as he states it: a very few dreams taken to Dr. Jung in order to have an argument about it, and withholding if possible all reactions which could be disagreeable. It was, as you suspect, a very modest number of conversations and anything else but a submission to the actual procedure of analysis of which, I'm afraid, Prof. McDougall has not the faintest idea. I like however his experiments with rats[2] and wouldn't argue that point with him, but people who are absolutely innocent of psychology, I find, are usually profoundly convinced of their psychological competence.

Well, I'm thoroughly glad that they spotted your mysticism. Now you know how damn easy it is to get a nice name.

I wish you every good luck for the study of the *Golden Flower*.

You have sent me "Dupuytren's Contracture and the Unconscious." I don't feel competent to judge the neurological aspect of the case. Concerning the few hints you give to the psychological material hardly enable me to say something of the psychological aspect. Thus far it seems it is the material you would get practically anywhere in organic as well as in functional diseases.

Sincerely yours,
C. G. Jung.

---

8. Lucien Lévy-Bruhl, *Le Surnaturel et la nature dans la mentalité primitive* (Paris, 1921). Jung drew heavily on the theories of primitive psychology adduced by Lévy-Bruhl (1857–1939).

---

1. Typewritten letter, signed.
2. McDougall, "An Experiment for the Testing of the Hypothesis of Lamarck," *British Journal of Psychology*, 17 (1927), 269–304. McDougall worked with laboratory rats to collect evidence in support of Lamarckianism, i.e., the inheritance of acquired characteristics. As noted in Part I and elsewhere, Jelliffe persisted in Lamarckian beliefs long after they became untenable in Anglo-American science; some of Jung's ideas also reflected Lamarckian assumptions.

Jelliffe to Jung

July 5, 1932[1]

My dear Dr. Jung:

It was a great pleasure to get your letter and to receive confirmation of what I had felt to be true from McDougall's own statements—in his written articles—that he had seen you but a few times—had his dreams analyzed, etc. His autobiographical sketch in "Murchison's" series, Clark University Biographies, is "charmingly naive." I make free to send you my "review"[2] on the volume. It contains a short note on what I wrote re McDougall.

I was particularly intrigued by what you said of the "Dupuytren" and would like to ask you more about this situation. If it encroaches on your time forget it. It is only a beginning but I can get no help from anyone here, for in spite of much "holistic" talking everyone seems to be a parallelist, and the body and mind are not one but separated as Plato originally disembodied the psyche.

It is true that this kind of material is familiar in the organic disturbances. My deep interest in them—psychologically—if I may say so, came more from your talks at my home[3] than from any other source. Since then I have been at the organic and am perfectly certain there is much to be accomplished.

The few hints I obtained from you about the variation in quantitative dynamics in dream symbols I have tried to work out more and more. I can get no help from any of the orthodox fellows here—they simply do not get what one is after and the very meager hints from Freud's works hardly go beyond the organ identifications: even though these are important. Prison = skin: for instance at times—hence generalized psoriasis in some unconscious criminals—and even "arthritic bondage" with some. One I talked about with you very briefly one evening—not over five minutes—I have followed from afar. This year he finally—after 20 years—did get indicted and may finally get in jail.

This is but one of a host of side problems in the organic sphere which I have been mulling over.

My chief difficulty is with the "*quantitative*" situations and their recognition. The therapeutic situation is of importance, but I count that secondary just now—since I have never taken on a distinctly organic case for analysis per se. All of the "organic material" has come up as a part of an accompanying and probably related "neurosis."

Your hint as to "archaic" symbolizations has been very fruitful, but how to measure the "*amounts*" of regressive or fixated libido keeps me thinking.

---

1. Carbon copy of typewritten letter.
2. *JNMD*, 76 (1932), 418–419.
3. In Sept. 1912. See above, Jung to Jelliffe, 13 May 1912.

Thus my very poorly expressed thought about the "Centaur" dream of my Dupuytren's Contracture case and the multiple sclerosis material. The McCormick[4] with multiple sclerosis—whom you know—had such dreams and I have others, and incidentally some Boston neurologists last week would diagnose the Dupuytren chap as a "multiple sclerosis."

Hence this long letter to you, even though I am half persuaded you count me "not so hot"—as an Americanism would put it. I presume I ought to comprehend Husserl, and Klages and Prinzhorn and Kronfeld and even Jaspers,[5] but frankly I find them hard sledding. Have you a pill or a powder—that might, as with the case of "Thomas," help my unbelief?

With sincere regards,
[*Smith Ely Jelliffe*]

Jung to Jelliffe

July 18th, 1932[1]

My dear Dr. Jelliffe,

The trouble with you is that your interest is concentrated upon the darkest spot natural science has ever hit upon, namely the place where, metaphorically speaking, the soul joins the body. Personally I don't believe in such a place existing, because I believe in an incomprehensible living thing that to our mind has two aspects, a physical and a psychical one. I firmly believe that any disturbance on any side produces a parallel disturbance in the other side. I hold, for instance, that a man with a chronic skin disease has a peculiar psychology, and a man with a peculiar psychology will have a peculiar physical ailment. Intuitive types, for instance, seem to be suffering often from ulcer of the stomach or other intestinal trouble. But the trouble with all these observations is that they suffer from a great deal of uncertainty, chiefly on account of a most insufficient psychological understanding. The absence of exact methods and measurements is indeed most deplorable. Yet there are certain possibilities of measuring intensities. Take for instance the method

---

4. Unidentified. But cf. Jung to Jelliffe, 28 Aug. 1932, n. 6.

5. German philosophers: Edmund Husserl (1859–1938), founder of phenomenology; Ludwig Klages (1872–1956), psychologist and graphologist; Hans Prinzhorn (1886–1933), psychiatrist, pupil of Klages; Arthur Kronfeld (1886–19[?]), psychiatrist, critic of psychoanalysis; Karl Jaspers, M.D. (1883–1969), influenced the existential school. Of the five, only Klages is mentioned in Jung's writings, and in a critical way, for his "gradual rejection of reality and negation of life as it is" ("Wotan," 1936, *Coll. Works*, 10, par. 575 and n. 3.).

---

1. Typewritten letter, signed.

of the accumulation of complex indicators in the association experiment.[2] If you simply count the frequency of complex indicators, you get a sort of measurement of the at least actual importance of a certain complex. You also can measure emotional intensities by the usual psychophysiological methods. Yet when it comes to an analytical case, i.e. a human individual, then things get so atrociously complicated that you simply can't keep up with exact demonstrable methods. Then truth becomes a mere probability or statistical average, a state of uncertainty which is very like the state of things in the interior of an atom.

The psychophysiological connexus is an impenetrable mystery, which, as I said above, represents two sides, the physical end, which is fairly obvious, and the psychical end, which is far from being obvious yet. Despite of the fact that the psychophysiological connexus is of the most fascinating interest, I gave up every direct attempt to understand it, because I felt that our psychological knowledge is much too insufficient to allow a clear understanding of its cooperation with the physis. Therefore I have pushed on my psychological investigations as far as possible in order to clear up the psychological end of the business.

In comparison with the fatness of the organic side of your "Dupuytren" case, the psychological side is of appalling thinness. Much more ought to be known there, in order to justify the smallest attempt to elucidate the psychophysiological nature of the case. In your whole work, as far as I'm aware of it, your psychological conceptions are overshadowed by the organic. It looks almost as if your psychological process were a mere appendix and epiphenomenon of the physical substratum. I handle the soul as a factor sui generis, a dignity which we quite naturally attribute to the physiological process. As long as we deny the psyche the character of an autonomous factor we are always tempted not to take it seriously. But if we accredit the psyche with autonomy, then you begin to handle it with the same seriousness which you bestow upon the physiological process. The psychological analogy to the physiological process is *phantasy*.

Now this statement is, I admit, most awkward, but the autonomy of the psychological factor shows the most in phantasy. As the physiological process is the expression of organic life, so the phantastical process is the expression

---

2. Jung developed and applied the word-association tests while on the staff of the Burghölzli Hospital, and he published the first report "Experimentelle Untersuchungen über Assoziationen Gesunder" ("The Associations of Normal Subjects"), jointly with Franz Riklin, in the *Journal für Psychologie und Neurologie*, 3–4 (1904); a dozen more papers followed, through 1909. (It was Jung's act of sending Freud the first collected volume of his *Diagnostische Assoziationsstudien* in Apr. 1906 that set in motion their correspondence.) The test consisted of a list of expressly chosen words which were read to the subject in a timed sequence; the subject was to react with an associated word, and the presence of affective factors, or of "complexes," could be indicated by the reaction word given, a delayed reaction time, and psychophysical symptoms gauged by the galvanometer and pneumograph.

of the inorganic, psychological life. As soon as you admit this idea, you have to seek for the underlying phantasy process. It is an unfortunate fate that Freud's point of view has done everything to obliterate the reality of the phantasy process. Freud's theory is like the theory of Christian Science referring to the unreality of the physical illness, it denies psychical reality. I tried therefore to establish the true and unadulterated nature of the phantasy process, and it is really astonishing to see what extraordinary material you discover then. It is the material that wells forth for instance in a psychosis, the stuff you find there in a distorted form is present everywhere and it functions all the time. But our consciousness has an almost insane resistance against acknowledging its reality. I must say, I wouldn't dare to tackle the psychology of any organic case without getting the patient first into that frame of mind that allows him to produce the underlying phantasy process.

If ever we are to discover the nature of the psychophysiological connexus, it will be by the knowledge of the phantasy process—I am planning to write about this process soon.[3]

With sincere wishes,

Yours cordially,
C. G. Jung.

Freud to Jelliffe

10.8.1932[1]

Dear Dr. Jelliffe,

I cannot tell you anything about Jastrow's book.[2] He wrote to say it had been sent and that he hoped I would not take his criticism amiss. In my reply, I assured him that I would not, which sounds polite but is actually an insult, since it amounts to saying: I don't care in the least what you may write about me.

But the book has not come. After many weeks I informed him of the fact and he promised to send me another copy immediately. This one has not arrived either.

---

3. Jung subsequently published no work expressly on the fantasy process, though in "Zur Empirie des Individuationsprozessess," his lecture at the first Eranos conference, Ascona, Switzerland, August 1933 (*Eranos Jahrbuch 1933*, Zurich, 1934), he analyzed a series of fantasy-images painted by an analysand. See the revised version, "A Study in the Process of Individuation," *Coll. Works*, 9, pt. i.

---

1. Handwritten letter, signed. Jelliffe's letter it answered is missing.
2. Joseph Jastrow (1863–1944), professor of psychology at the University of Wisconsin, popularizer of psychology. The book in question was *The House That Freud Built* (New York, 1932).

With kind regards,
Yours truly,[3]
Freud

Freud to Jelliffe

17.8.1932[1]

Dear Dr. Jelliffe,
I received Jastrow's book today and have looked through it. Now I understand your hesitation about how to deal with it. It is really one of the stupidest and most arrogant pieces of criticism that our Analysis has ever suffered.

Cordially yours,
Freud

Jelliffe to Freud

August 22, 1932[1]

My dear Professor Freud:
Kindly accept my thanks for your favor of the 10th instant. I wrote my review[2] and sent it to Drs. White and Brill and they were of different opinions as to the desirability of publishing it. White and also Feigenbaum[3] thought it better to ignore the book entirely. Brill would be more aggressive and believed I should publish my rather pungent criticism. I am still undecided.

Inasmuch as in preparation for the hoped-for possibility of getting to Wiesbaden[4] I have been forehanded and prepared in advance my August, September, and October issues of the *Journal of Nervous and Mental Disease*, it could not appear before November. The book is so insidiously malicious and so uninformed yet with the glitter of apparent complete understanding that it becomes especially difficult to know just how to deal with it. Hence my appeal to you and the others.

---

3. English in original.

---

1. Handwritten letter, signed.

---

1. Carbon copy of typewritten letter.
2. A review of the aforementioned book by Jastrow, unsigned but certainly by Jelliffe, appeared in *JNMD*, 79 (1934), calling the book "unimportant" and "approaching the mendacious." It included a statement from Brill, also strongly critical.
3. Dorian Feigenbaum, M.D. (1887–1937), co-founder of the *Psychoanalytic Quarterly*.
4. International Psychoanalytical Congress, in late Aug. 1932.

There has been for some time a matter which I have been thinking about and looking for help. When Ferenczi[5] was here I tried to get some suggestions but was not quite free enough and our contacts were not sustained. It was probably mostly my own inhibitions and resistances.

As you know, the problem of irreversible conversion processes has interested me a great deal. These as factors in a direct or indirect causative role of organic disease have for years intrigued my curiosity. A number of my papers have dealt with it, but all too fragmentarily. My myopia as castration[6] and my Dupuytren paper are the most explicit statements of the situation. I am even more deeply convinced than these papers indicate of the validity of the whole conception. These are results of displaced cathectic processes. In the myopia patient the punishment for "peeping" and the "greediness for ocular grasping" are extraordinarily clear.

This patient, in my opinion, would have been a schizophrenic if he had not displaced the whole conflict to the myopia-producing process. As it is he remained with a part of the unresolved conflict as a "pathological blusher." It all came on when he renounced masturbation.

The problem revolves about the possible "measurement of affect" as made evident or indicated in the symbolization process. You may recall I first approached this in a generalization as to "paleopsychological levels" using the term I believe Jung first used, "thought fossils."[7] Can one draw valid ideas concerning quantitative factors from the paleopsychological age of the symbolizations employed in the dream process?

I touch upon this in my Dupuytren paper—apropos of the "Centaur" figure in the dream.

I think there is no need of elaborating the idea to you. The *continuance* of conversion is readily understood as repetition, with longer or shorter intervals of compulsion discharge. This chronic factor is fairly evident in its results, if not in the repetition of wish, but *how much* affect is trying to get through the organ, and *how registerable*, this is my problem. The term "archaic" symbolization is helpful, but what nuances indicate "archaic" features in somewhat the same sense that we know that certain "Equisetums" of the

---

5. Sandor Ferenczi was in the United States from late Sept. 1926 until 2 June 1927, having been invited originally to lecture at the New School for Social Research, New York. He continued his stay for further lecturing and analyzing, and "engaged in training analytically eight or nine people, mostly lay. . . . These and other activities brought him into conflict with the New York analysts, who had on January 25, 1927, passed strong resolutions condemning all therapeutic practice by non-medical people. Relations became more and more strained as the months went on until he was almost completely ostracized by his colleagues" (Jones, 3, pp. 134, 142/127, 134).

6. See above, commentary before 19 Dec. 1925, n. 1.

7. The term "thought fossils" is not found in Jung's published writings, though it is an apt figure for the archetypes.

Carboniferous were mighty giants when compared with the Equisetums[8] that still love to cluster along the cinder paths of our railroads? Certainly a Centaur copulative wish in the dream is dynamically more loaded then usual. How use the idea when it is displaced to sadistic grasping of the hands (and feet) that gets into a "phyletic" musculature which at the present stage is no longer voluntary muscle, but the left-over connectus tissue remnants of what once functioned as muscle—in an analogy, as the dwarf Equisetums of today compare with those giants that laid down our coal beds.

Is the whole idea fantastic? I don't think so—I believe a lot of "organic" chronic diseases follow this general idea, but how get it into some demonstrable form? All of Groddeck is suggestive but it does not get down to the minute steps of the processes.

With best regards and good wishes and regrets that I shall not be able to get to Europe this year and present my respects in person,

Very sincerely,

[*Smith Ely Jelliffe*]

Jelliffe to Jung

August 28, 1932[1]

My dear Dr. Jung:

Thank you for your very stimulating letter. I am certainly in trouble in more senses than one in trying to get at certain problems of disorder through the psychological portals.

I am at one with you as to the "doubt" that there is a "place" where the soul joins the body. In fact I cannot reconcile myself to any psychophysical parallelism or even interactionism. Whether I start with body or with the hormé,[2] I am driven first to the recognition there is *matter* (define it as one will, i.e. organs) and then there is *something* both mechanistic and vitalistic— which we call *life*—and finally something which we call *mind*. The "holistic" or emergent evolution aspect appeals to me, that matter, life, and mind represent a *condensation synthesis* of certain aspects of energy transformations.

---

8. The equisetums, or horsetails, are primitive plants surviving from the paleozoic Carboniferous period when, growing to the size of trees, they contributed to coal deposits.

1. Carbon copy of typewritten letter.
2. In "On Psychological Understanding," which Jung read in English before the Psycho-Medical Society, London, 24 July 1914, he used this term and stated: "In my German publications I have used the word *libido*, which seems to be too easily misunderstood in English. *Horme* is the Greek word for 'force, attack, press, impetuosity, violence, urgency, zeal.' "— *Journal of Abnormal Psychology* (Boston), 9:6 (Feb.-Mar. 1915), 385 ff.; cf. *Coll. Works*, 3, par. 418, n. 16. The paper was reprinted as an untitled supplement to "The Content of the Psychoses" in *Collected Papers on Analytical Psychology*, ed. Constance E. Long (London and New York, 1916; 2d ed., 1917); see pp. 347–348, n. 2.

In all of this I feel I am not far from your thought. The problem of specific quantitative variations registerable in the psychological field intrigues me greatly and hence my appeal to you and my thanks that you should try to aid me.

If one rests upon a variable qualitative constitutional background as present *au fond*, it appears one is blocked. If the idea be accepted that heredity is but transmitted acquired experience, it would appear to me that environment had been uniform over so long a time that so far as human beings are concerned they are fundamentally alike. If so, then how get at the dynamics of repression, which ontologically operates with the variations we find and which can be "typed"? Types then have "als ob"[3] values in spite of their complexities.

I am glad to get your suggestions re. the association method as throwing light on the intensity of complex investiture. I had neglected this clear aid and had been grasping in the blue for some help from symbolic distortion and/or archaic symbolizations.

You are quite just in your comparison between the fatness and leanness of my "Dupuytren case." Faute de mieux I had to get it out and was not ready to bring forward the enormous amount of psychological material that would give it any semblance of justification from the "wish psychology" or phantasy aspect. I have reams and reams of phantasy material.

I think that I really envisage the "soul" as preponderant and not an appendage to the structure. There is no dynamics in structure per se. Structure only guides and tends to compel "patterns" of performance. So in that I feel I can be entirely with you and quite follow you in the "phantasy" analogy of psychological to physiological. The latter to me, as yet, is purely "descriptive." In a previous paper (Vigilance)[4] when I say that without the psychic factor even a spinal-cord reflex is not explained—so my allegiance to the organic, save as the material necessary to act, is not so profound as it would appear.

The appearance in the dream life of the "collective unconscious" symbolizations (paleopsychological thought fossils I have designated them mindful of your phrase "thought fossils") always awakens my interest, for I am fairly certain here is where quantitative affective factors may be registerable. At the same time I would like help to clarify in my mind those aspects of such symbolizations which may be but the expression of temporary regression adaptations (the theriomorphic symbols in alcoholism, for instance) or those which may be permanently operating fixation factors at such old levels. I

---

3. *Als ob* = "as if," a term from Vaihinger; see above, Jelliffe to Freud, 16 Feb. 1926, n. 13.
4. See above, Jelliffe to Freud, 18 Jan. 1930, n. 7.

once hazarded an "Ovidian"[5] theriomorphic level along geological analogy lines. It is all very crude I know, still highly speculative, but the host of issues intrigue me.

If it does not bore you any thoughts you care to express would be appreciated. I tried to get from Ferenczi some ideas as to the methods of measuring *malignant conversions* but he evaded the whole thing.

You probably have followed the McC. situation closely.[6] "Cancer of the Liver." Here is certainly speculative material as to correlation of power through "possession." As you once expressed it, "she thought she could buy everything."

With sincere best wishes,
[Smith Ely Jelliffe]

Freud to Jelliffe

25 Sept. 1932[1]

Dear Dr. Jelliffe,

Thanks for your letter. I still think you should chastise this man Jastrow, your criticism is so sound and powerful and your voice is listened to in your country.

As for the other, more interesting problem, I am sure you too have found that when you are pursued by a problem no one can help you. One must always work these things out for oneself. I can only give you my opinion, which is that your ideas are far from fantastic, and that you are on the right track. Perhaps all we can do for the present is to collect observations of cases in which an organic disorder has clearly been substituted for a psychic one. I, too, have made such observations. Let us leave the archaic and quantitative aspects to speculation.

With deep regret that I shall not see you in Europe this year—you know how uncertain the future is for me—.

Cordially yours,
Freud

---

5. The allusion is to the Latin poet Ovid's *Metamorphoses,* in which transformations to animal forms (theriomorphism) are recounted as features of classical myths.

6. The allusion is to Edith Rockefeller McCormick (b. 1871, d. 25 Aug. 1932), of Chicago, who with her former husband, Harold F. McCormick, had first consulted Jung in Zurich in 1909; see *The Freud/Jung Letters,* 150 F, 151 J. Edith McCormick subsequently lived in Zurich, underwent analysis with Jung, and was a patron of analytical psychology as well as of musicians and writers. Later she returned to Chicago, where she died. The American press sedulously covered her private life, last illness, and death.

1. Handwritten letter, signed. The first paragraph is in English in the original.

Jung to Jelliffe

Oct. 16th 1932[1]

My dear Professor,

I must apologize for my long silence. Unfortunately I was quite unable to look after my correspondence these last months on account of too many obligations. We just had an Indological "Seminar" here by Prof. Hauer and Zimmer from Tübingen and Heidelberg about the philosophy of the Tantra Yoga,[2] a thing, you might say, miles apart from psychology. Yet, when you get into the depths of what I call the collective unconscious you encounter problems that have been tackled in certain ways by other times and civilisations. This is of course an entirely different aspect from your psychological point of view, which is the standpoint of natural science. You know that this was my way of approach too, but I had to recognize the fact that there are other aspects, since the human mind is not only the mother of Natural Science but of many other things just as well. And surely these other aspects are very helpful to the understanding of what "Psyche" means. Even from the standpoint of the Scientist it is indispensable to know the matter which one is dealing with and thus to know the reasons why one gets stuck with the usual experimental methods, by which we thought we could tackle the psychological problem. The latter is a great deal more intricate than one expected. Of course this is no reason why one should not try to invent new and better methods with the hope to subject at least a part of the psychical process to accurate investigation and quantitative definition.

Within the strictly psychical realm, where exact measuring is not possible, we surely ought to get at least to a qualitative equivalent of measurement, namely to diagnostic qualities. I think I see what you mean when you speak of the animal visions of alcoholics (you could add narcosis dreams, hashish, mescalin and other visions) or the specifically distorted symbols in schizophrenic processes. In order to investigate such problems it is indispensable that we know first how normal phantasy—i.e. the normal unhampered psyche—works. We ought to know the normal average symbols produced by the Unconscious first, because, only on the basis of such knowledge we would be able to recognize and to define accurately the pathological variations. Since many years I am concerned with this task, which is—by Jove—no mean

---

1. Handwritten letter, signed.
2. J. Wilhelm Hauer (1881–1962), Indologist and theologian, University of Tübingen, gave six lectures in English on Tantra or Kundalini Yoga at the Psychologischer Club, Zurich, 3–8 October 1932. Heinrich Zimmer (1890–1943), also an Indologist, University of Heidelberg, contributed explanatory remarks. Jung gave a "psychological commentary" in four lectures on 12–26 October and 2 November. The entire seminar was issued privately, in multigraphed form, in both English and German versions, as *The Kundalini Yoga*. This form of yoga is a Hindu discipline based on the symbolism of a serpent, "kundalini," coiled at the base of the spine and ascending through five centers, "chakras," to the brain.

enterprise. I have come across some peculiar variations, which seem to be reliable. F.i. when you compare normal phantasy with pathological material you are always struck by the fact that normal symbols always point to a particular significance which they "try" to elucidate. This tendency is increasingly absent in patholog. material. There is a peculiar lack of cohesion and synthesis. The same in phantasy pictures, f.i. in schizophrenia: there you often find lines, so-called "Bruchlinien,"[3] that split the picture. In toxic cases the tendency to meaningful synthesis is substituted through a tendency to repetition of the same motive. (Many mice, c——,[4] flies, beetles or variations of size (mescalin).) For toxic symbols (in visions) endless variation without improvement in significance is characteristic, the same with fever visions. Another important pathological symptom is the admixture of elements which destroy or upset the intended significance, particularly so in schizophrenia. You mention Mrs. McCormick in your letter. She was such a case of latent sch[izophrenia] and was very much on the edge when I treated her. She dreamt right in the beginning of her analysis of a tree struck by lightning and split in half. ("Bruchlinie"!) This is, what one calls a "bad" symbol. Another case, that suffers now from hallucinations and ideas of perseveration, formerly produced pictures with "Bruchlinien," breaking lines, thus f.i.[5]

A great and puzzling problem is the "intended meaning" of "significance" of a symbol. It hangs together with the much bigger problem, whether the unconscious symbolization has a meaning or aim at all or whether it is merely reactivated stuff, i.e. relics of the past. I must say, I am inclined to assume that the archaic material is merely a means to an end. It is, as far as I can see, used for the purpose of synthesizing a meaning which the conscious mind has not attained to yet. This is, I know, a pretty bold hypothesis, which has to be proven yet, but it would be a logical result of the assumption that the psyche is a purposive system of functions. Long and careful researches have shown me that my hypothesis is not far from the truth. I am actually busy with a book about this matter.[6] When we once know the average normal

---

3. "Fracture lines." Jung's earliest work on schizophrenia was *Über die Psychologie der Dementia praecox: Ein Versuch* (Halle, 1907) = *The Psychology of Dementia Praecox*, tr. A. A. Brill and Frederick W. Peterson (NMDMS 3, 1909): retr., *Coll. Works*, 3. He published occasionally on the subject throughout his career. No explanation of the "Bruchlinien" occurs in his publications.

4. Illegible word. The allusion in this sentence is to hallucinations induced by the alkaloid drug mescaline. In a paper he wrote late in life, Jung stated that "experiences with mescalin[e] and related drugs encourage the hypothesis of a toxic origin" of schizophrenia ("Recent Thoughts on Schizophrenia," 1956, *Coll. Works*, 3, par. 548), and he recalled his speculation about that hypothesis in *The Psychology of Dementia Praecox*, par. 195.

5. For Jung's drawings inserted at this point, see the facsimile (p. 248).

6. See above, Jung to Jelliffe, 18 July 1932, n. 3. Jung did not actually publish a new *book* (other than a collection of essays, *Wirklichkeit der Seele*, 1934) until *Psychology and Religion* (1938; in *Coll. Works*, 11).

Toxic symbols (in visions) endless variation without improvement in significance is characteristic, the same with fever visions. Another important pathological symptom is the admixture of elements, which destroy or upset the intended significance, particularly so in schizophrenia. You mention Mrs McCormick in your letter. She was such a case of latent Sch. and was very much on the edge, when I treated her. She dreamt right in the beginning of her analysis of a tree struck by lightning and split in half. ("Bruchlinie"!) This is, what one calls, a "bad" symbol. Another case, that suffers now from hallucinations and ideas of persecution, formerly produced pictures with Bruchlinien, breaking lines, thus f.i.

A great and puzzling problem is the "intended" meaning or significance of a symbol. It hangs together with the much bigger problem, whether the unconscious symbolization has a meaning or aim at all or whether it is merely reactivated stuff i.e. relics of the past. I must say, I am inclined to assume, that the archaic material is merely a means to an end. It is, as far, I

Page from Jung's letter to Jelliffe, 16 October 1932. Photograph from the Library of Congress.

line of the unhampered creative process of the unconscious, then we possess the diagnostic criterion for an accurate definition of pathological products. But as yet we do not possess a normal phenomenology of the creative process. It needs just masses of careful observations, carried out by different observers, also a lot of comparative material.

My work is unfortunately frequently interrupted by public lectures, particularly in Germany where I seem to be subject to a most inopportune popularity.[7]

Hoping you are in good health,
I remain, my dear Professor,

> Yours
> Sincerely
> C. G. Jung.

Jelliffe to Freud

January 9, 1933[1]

My dear Professor Freud:

The copy of your new *Einführung*[2] has reached me with your compliments and I thank you very sincerely for it. Thus far I have only glanced through it hoping soon to settle down and enjoy it. Dr. Brill has told me he was reading it and I have asked him to review it for the *Journal*.

We had a very pleasant dinner last Tuesday as you may already have heard.[3] The dining room was filled with an extremely attractive group of well wishers. They were all friends of the movement and there were none of the Jastrow or other ambivalent types. It was a great pleasure for me as I have watched the Society's growth since the beginning although not as a charter member, which was largely accidental.

My own small contribution was an after-dinner outline of my "Freudian Odyssey"[4] [which] I hope to finish in literary form and will send it to you— D. V.

---

7. The bibliography of Jung's writings (*Coll. Works*, 19) lists no published lectures in Germany during 1932. His involvement with the International General Medical Society for Psychotherapy did not begin until June 1933.

---

1. Carbon copy of typewritten letter.
2. *Neue Folge der Vorlesungen zur Einführung in die Psychoanalyse* (Vienna, 1933). The book actually appeared on 6 Dec. 1932 (Jones, 3, pp. 186/174 f.), and Freud evidently dispatched Jelliffe's copy immediately. As *New Introductory Lectures on Psycho-Analysis* (London), an English tr. by W. J. H. Sprott appeared later in 1933; James Strachey's tr. is in *Standard Edn.*, 22.
3. Meeting of the New York Psychoanalytic Society, 3 Jan. 1933.
4. "Glimpses of a Freudian Odyssey" appeared subsequently in the *Psychoanalytic Quarterly*, 2 (1933), 318–329. Jelliffe stated (318n) that he had presented an earlier version to the society on 27 Dec. 1932, to celebrate the twenty-first anniversary of its founding by Brill.

Wishing you the best of the season and with expressions of personal affection,

Believe me,
Very truly yours,
[*Smith Ely Jelliffe*]

Jelliffe to Freud

January 28, 1933[1]

My dear Professor Freud:

I wish to thank you for your courtesy in sending me a personal copy of your New Lectures. I appreciate it very highly.

I have thus far read only the two opening chapters but I feel the same stimulation that I have always enjoyed in reading your works. I still prefer to read them in German as they convey a more profound significance than when Englished, save occasionally when the translator has a deep and thorough feeling of the English language. Joan Riviere's translation of your *Ego and the Id*,[2] for instance, delights me in this regard.

Dr. Brill has promised me a review for the *Journal*, and as he is to make it a part of a program of our Neurological Society meeting next week it will probably be written shortly.

We had our annual meeting of the New York Psychoanalytic Society last night and Dr. Brill was re-elected as President. I declined as Vice-President because I have been getting hard of hearing and it makes it specially difficult to preside at meetings and carry on business when one does not hear everything. Dr. Lewin was elected Vice-President. Dr. Zilboorg was made Secretary and Dr. Meyer remains Treasurer.[3]

The affairs of the Institute are prospering mildly in spite of real difficulties.

I hear from time to time that you are working and I hope that you will be able to give us many more stimulating studies.

As for myself I am fairly busy with a number of interesting patients. I am working further on the "Myopia" patient that I reported on some time ago.[4] Also the "Dupuytren's Contracture"[5] one. Here the "sadistic" material is absolutely "incroyable." These and other matters connected with the *Journal* keep me out of mischief.

---

1. Carbon copy of typewritten letter.
2. *Das Ich und das Es* (Vienna, 1923), tr. Joan Riviere, London, 1927; rev. tr. by Strachey, *Standard Edn.*, 19.
3. Bertram D. Lewin, M.D. (1896–1971); Gregory Zilboorg, M.D. (1890–1959); Monroe Meyer, M.D.
4. See above, Jelliffe to Freud, 22 Aug. 1932, at n. 6.
5. See above, Freud to Jelliffe, 15 May 1932, n. 3.

With sincere best wishes,
[*Smith Ely Jelliffe*]

Jelliffe to Freud

February 7, 1933[1]

My dear Professor Freud:

I have been reading lately a review of the psychoanalytic conceptions by J. de la Vaissière, a Jesuit, *Archives de philosophie*, Vol. 8, 1932.[2] On page 16 he quotes from the French edition of your "Ma Vie": "Je veux mentionner expressément que le nom de Janet pendant mon séjour à la Salpêtrière ne fut même pas prononcé"—d'autre part Janet a fait à la Société française de psychiâtrie la déclaraction suivant—"Le point de départ du freudisme, c'est le séjour de Freud à la Salpêtrière et la reproduction de nos conversations à cette époque."[3]

He then wonders why such a contradiction can come to be.

I have for some time been aware of these two statements and have looked up Janet's life and work and have some letters from him.[4] He graduated in 1881 at the age of 22 from l'ecole supérieure of Paris. He then went to a lycée at Châteauroux near Orleans as a teacher in philosophy 1881–1883.[5] He then obtained a similar place at the Lycée in Havre 1883–1889. The first psychological work he ever published was on Mme. B. (Léonie), whom he observed in Havre with Dr. Gibert for 10 days in Sept.–Oct. 1885. These observations on somnambulism he presented before the newly founded so-

---

1. Carbon copy of typewritten letter.

2. Jules de la Vaissière, "La Théorie psychanalytique de Freud: Etude de psychologie positive," *Archives de philosophie*, 8 (1932). La Vaissière (1863–1941) was a pioneer of Catholic pedagogy based on the data of modern psychology.

3. Jelliffe's punctuation and accents have been corrected in this passage. The first sentence is quoted from Freud, *Ma Vie et la psychanalyse* (Paris, 1928), tr. Marie Bonaparte from "Selbstdarstellung," in Grote's *Die Medizin der Gegenwart in Selbstdarstellungen* (Leipzig, 1925), 4, pp. 1–52. As tr. J. Strachey, "An Autobiographical Study," *Standard Edn.*, 20, p. 13, it reads: "I should therefore like to say explicitly that during the whole of my visit to the Salpêtrière Janet's name was never so much as mentioned." The last sentence, which La Vaissière quoted from Janet, could not be documented. Ellenberger, p. 485, states: "In July 1889 Freud. . . . went to the International Congress of Psychology in Paris. It is likely that he saw Janet there, although there is no record of their meeting." Pierre Janet (1859–1947) made significant contributions to the development of dynamic psychology and psychopathology.

4. These letters cannot be located.

5. According to Ellenberger, pp. 335 f., who consulted other primary sources, Janet taught at Châteauroux for four months in 1882–1883.

ciety of "physiological Psychology" on Nov. 30, 1885.[6] Charcot[7] was president of the society. You were in Paris in the fall of 1885. (Just when did you go to Paris and how long did you stay?) Have you any recollection of attending this meeting and hearing this paper, as this would have been a time when you might have met Janet?

Certainly neither of you then could have talked about the ideas which later were developed, as Janet seems to infer. At all events Janet came to Paris to study medicine in 1889 and took his degree in 1893 with his thesis on "Hysteria," "Les Accidents" et "Les Stigmates."

I believe Janet is incorrect, and in my review[8] of this Vaissière study I may present this whole matter. I am not certain whether it is worth while. But I would like to hear from you on the points raised in this letter if you feel disposed to discuss them.

> With sincere best wishes,
> [*Smith Ely Jelliffe*]

Freud to Jelliffe

10.2.1933[1]

Dear Dr. Jelliffe,

Your communication has of course been of the utmost interest to me. It is one more fragment of the future medicine for which you are preparing the way. The next number of the *Internationale Zeitschrift* will carry a study by Weizsäcker, the German internist, which is another contribution to what you, I believe, call holism.[2]

I remember—and would like once again to apologize for—my unfriendliness at our first meeting (in Gastein?).[3] I was suspicious, because I had seen

---

6. "Note sur quelques phénomènes de somnambulisme," *Bulletins de la Société de psychologie physiologique*, 1 (1885), 24–32, as cited by Ellenberger, who states (p. 338) that the paper was read to the society in Paris by a relative of Janet's, and "it is not known whether Janet was present."

7. Jean-Martin Charcot, M.D. (1825–1893), director of the Salpêtrière, which he developed into the greatest neurological clinic of its time. Freud studied at the clinic from October 1885 until February 1886, and during this period his interest in psychopathology was awakened. Freud translated two of Charcot's books into German, with Charcot's authorization.

8. No review by Jelliffe has been traced.

---

1. Handwritten letter, signed. Published (in tr.) in *Psychoanalytic Pioneers*, p. 266, where it is misdated 2 October 1933. It is a reply to Jelliffe's letter of 9 Jan. 1933. In a letter of 21 Feb. 1933 to Dr. Lillian Powers, Jelliffe asked her to transcribe and translate this letter for him, as his "mastery of the script is very insecure."

2. Viktor von Weizsäcker (1886–1957), "Körpergeschehen und Neurose: Analytische Studie über somatische Symptombildung," *Internationale Zeitschrift für ärztliche Psychoanalyse*, 29 (1933), 16–116. Freud wrote "holism" in English.

3. See above, commentary preceding Freud to Jelliffe, 11 Dec. 1921, and Freud to Jelliffe, 11 Apr. 1926.

you in the company of Stekel. Since then I have learned to esteem you for the breadth of your interests and knowledge, the freedom of your thinking, and your worth as one of the strongest pillars of Analysis in America. I am sorry to hear that you are being inconvenienced by the impairment of your hearing. Since my operation in 1923 only one of my ears has been functioning. The other is still holding out, but when a man is as old as I have become the death instinct[4] has an easy time of it.

Even if I should go on living for a while, you must not expect me to contribute much of any significance to science. (My father and eldest brother died between the ages of 81 and 82.)[5] But I shall always be glad to see others develop any suggestions I have been able to give them.

With kind regards,
Cordially yours,
Freud

Freud to Jelliffe

18.2.1933[1]

Dear Dr. Jelliffe,

Let the following observations be my last word concerning my relations with Janet:

1) I went to Paris in October 1885, and stayed until a month before Easter 1886.

2) I have never seen Janet and never exchanged a word with him.

3) If he delivered a lecture in November 1885 in Paris under the chairmanship of Charcot, I knew nothing of it and was not present.

4) During my stay at the Salpêtrière, I never heard the name of Janet mentioned. The first to mention this name in my presence was Dr. J. Breuer in Vienna, some time after 1893.[2]

Please dispose of this information as you see fit.

Yours sincerely,
Freud

---

4. "Death instinct" in English.

5. Jakob Freud (1815–1896); Emanuel Freud (1832–1914), a half-brother. Max Schur, *Freud: Living and Dying* (New York, 1972), comments extensively on Freud's attitude toward death.

1. Handwritten letter, signed.

2. Josef Breuer, M.D. (1842–1925), Viennese physician, first to use the cathartic method to treat hysteria; collaborated with Freud in writing *Stüdien über Hysterie* (Leipzig and Vienna, 1895), tr. J. and A. Strachey, "Studies in Hysteria," *Standard Edn.*, 2.

Freud to Jelliffe

18.2.1933[1]

Dear Dr. Jelliffe,

Permit me the following slight correction to yesterday's communication about Janet.

I said the first person to mention the name of Janet in my presence was Dr. J. Breuer *after* 1893. But our "Preliminary Communication,"[2] in which Janet is cited, already appeared in that year. Therefore, it would be correct to say: shortly *before* the year 1893.

Yours sincerely,
Freud

Jelliffe to Freud

April 17, 1933[1]

My dear Dr. Freud:

Your highly esteemed letter of February 10th has been on my desk as well as on my conscience, for it was very pleasant to get it and not very courteous of me not to have written you before this.

I was much pleased that you have deemed some of my efforts as worthy of commendation. It heartens me to go on. I know there is a rich field for fruitful study here, and although it is difficult to pin it down in symbols that are in line with mechanistic science and hence verifiable and usable, I have constantly before me the stimulus of your conceptions and example.

I have long since felt that I was perhaps more to blame in re. our first meeting than you. In true American simplicity—perhaps stupidity—I was not alert to the contrary winds of doctrine that were blowing in the psychoanalytic movement, and it has only been after my contacts with X that[2] I realized and have increasingly come to feel he was not very trustworthy as a scientist. A clever, inspirational, intuitive personality maybe, but hardly the one who had much to offer save a bright gathering of material made possible by another's ideas.

---

1. Handwritten letter, signed. Both letters carry the date indicated.
2. Breuer and Freud, "Über den psychischen Mechanismus hysterischer Phänomene (Vorläufige Mitteilung)," sec. 3–5, *Neurologisches Centralblatt*, 12:2 (15 Jan. 1893), 43–47; tr., "On the Psychical Mechanism of Hysterical Phenomena: Preliminary Communication," *Standard Edn.*, 2. The reference (p. 12 of the latter) is to "the two Janets," Pierre and his uncle Jules, a physician.

---

1. Carbon copy of typewritten letter.
2. The carbon copy is blurred because of an erasure, but this is almost surely the reading. "X" must stand for Stekel.

Even today at Doctor Feigenbaum's it was a pleasure to learn from Dr. Deutsch[3] that you were still busy, and only the other day I was glad to get "Warum Krieg"[4] and Dr. Brill who was in consultation with me today has promised to review it.

The new English edition of *The Interpretation of Dreams*[5] has also arrived and I am delighted to see it. It still has much that I am striving to master.

My winter's work has been very attractive. I have been kept busy but as you know, as with the other physicians, we have had to reduce our fees considerably and what with increased taxes, were not the cost of living appreciably diminished, we would all only just about come out even; especially as most of our invested savings are unproductive. On the whole perhaps it is childish to be talking of this in view of the real hardships through which Austria has been going.

It has given me great sorrow to see the wave of anti-semitism sweep over Germany[6] and we are here, in the main, all enraged at it. There must be something essentially superior in a race that can stimulate so much envy and persecution and as I reflect on our psychiatric and neurological sciences we would indeed be poor without that which has come from this racial source.[7]

With sincere appreciations for your kind letter,

> Believe me with best greetings,
> Very truly yours,
> [*Smith Ely Jelliffe*]

---

3. Felix Deutsch, M.D. (1884–1964), analyst and specialist in psychosomatic medicine, had recently come to the United States from Vienna with his wife, the analyst Helene Deutsch (1884–1982).

4. *Warum Krieg?* (Paris, 1933) was an extended letter by Freud in reply to one from Albert Einstein, both written in response to a request from the International Institute of Intellectual Co-operation of the League of Nations; tr. J. Strachey, "Why War?" *Standard Edn.*, 22.

5. This was the 3d ed. (London and New York, 1932) of the Brill tr. (1913), "completely revised and largely rewritten by various unspecified hands" (ed. note by Strachey, *Standard Edn.*, 4).

6. Hitler had been appointed chancellor of Germany by President Paul von Hindenburg on 30 Jan. 1933, and his National Socialist government was voted dictatorial powers on 23 Mar. Anti-Jewish policies were put into effect in early April.

7. A source of information about events in Germany was Ernest Jones, who wrote to Jelliffe on 25 Apr. 1933: "We are having a hectic time over here with political refugees. Some seventy thousand Jews got away from Germany as the blow was falling. Among them are most of the German Psycho-Analytical Society; I only know of four or five members still left in Berlin. The persecution has been much worse than you seem to think and has really quite lived up to the Middle Ages in reputation. It is a very Hunnish affair." Jelliffe replied, on 19 May 1933: "We have been getting letters from the German Jew difficulty. It is tough as I see it more clearly and the whole mess is incomprehensible to me. Of course the schieber [grafters] did buy up much of the real estate—at least this seems a real grudge—but it is all too pitiful." (Jelliffe Papers, Library of Congress.)

Freud to Jelliffe

Vienna XIX, Strassergasse 47[1]
2.8.1934

Dear Dr. Jelliffe,

I value your letter as a mark of your friendly feelings toward me. I was especially interested in your paper on quinidine[2] since I myself have been using it in the treatment of my bothersome extrasystoles, without side effects incidentally.

My hearing is not what it used to be either, but I manage, and at the age of 78 I have a certain right to deafness, a right which I contest in a man your age. I am very sorry to hear that this infirmity inconveniences you in your work and social life. Be that as it may, we are all in the same boat. As for me, this last segment of my life is not being made easy for me.

So much in this world escapes the rule of justice, and so it is with the honors accorded me on the occasion of the fiftieth anniversary of the introduction of cocaine. I should not really have been named along with Koller. It is true that I published a study on coca and foresaw its use as an anaesthetic, but I turned over the idea of experimenting with it to a friend, who botched it. I did not directly influence Koller.[3]

We would be enjoying a lovely summer holiday in a charming suburb of Vienna if political conditions permitted. News of the death of German president Hindenburg[4] has just reached us. No one can say what consequences the German development may have for our poor Austria.

---

1. Handwritten letter, signed. Freud was spending the summer in a house in Grinzing, a rural suburb. Jelliffe's letter to which this one replies has not survived.

2. "Acroparesthesia and Quinidine: A Query and a Quest," *JNMD*, 79 (1934), 631–651.

3. Freud's experiments with cocaine, in summer 1884, led to his article "Über Coca," *Zentralblatt für die gesamte Therapie*, 2 (July, 1884); tr. in *Cocaine Papers*, ed. Robert Byck (New York, 1974). The friend who "botched" (*verdarb*) the idea was the ophthalmologist Leopold Königstein (1850–1924), to whom Freud, upon leaving for a visit to his fiancée, had suggested that "he should investigate the question of how far the anaesthetizing properties of cocaine were applicable in diseases of the eye. When I returned from my holiday I found that not he, but another of my friends, Carl Koller . . . , whom I had also spoken to about cocaine, had made the decisive experiments. . . ." ("An Autobiographical Study," orig. 1925, in *Standard Edn.*, 20, pp. 14–15). The ophthalmologist Koller (1857–1944), later in New York, had indeed been influenced by Freud, in that the latter had informed him of his work on cocaine. It was Koller who pursued the significant research, and he, as Freud wrote (ibid.), "is therefore rightly regarded as the discoverer of local anaesthesia by cocaine." See Jones, 1, ch. 6, "The Cocaine Episode." For the observance of the fiftieth anniversary of the introduction of cocaine, see Hortense Koller Becker, "Carl Koller and Cocaine," *Psychoanalytic Quarterly*, 32 (1963), reprinted in Byck, ed., *Cocaine Papers*, pp. 293, 316.

4. President Hindenburg died on 2 Aug. 1934. Subsequently Hitler assumed the presidency through plebiscite.

Wishing you the best of health,
Cordially yours,
Freud

Jelliffe to Jung

January 30, 1936[1]

My dear Dr. Jung:

In the recent very interesting and informing work of Olga v. Koenig-Fachsenfeld,[2] I find some references to your Seminar protocols and am minded to ask you if by any chance these are available. Maybe those of Mary Foote's are?[3]

I also note the citation of a work on "Die praktische Verwendbarkeit der Traumanalyse,"[4] the publisher is not noted, and also your newest work on *Wirklichkeit der Seele.*[5] I am hopeful that my request to get such for review in the *Journal of Nervous and Mental Disease* may be granted.[6]

I know that you may have taken umbrage at some of my comments from time to time but I wish you to know how highly I esteem you and your work, even if at times I cannot see eye to eye about certain situations.

For instance, I am quite at variance on the "normal" problem. That there may be established structural so-called "norms" for the microscopical appearances and even the functional product variations for a kidney cell I grant. From kidney experience laid down in structuralized form—i.e. kidney cell

---

1. Typewritten letter, signed; from the C. G. Jung Archives, courtesy of Franz Jung.

2. Olga von Koenig-Fachsenfeld, German analytical psychologist. The book was *Wandlungen des Traumproblems von der Romantik bis zur Gegenwart* (Stuttgart, 1935), for which Jung wrote a foreword (tr. in *Coll. Works*, 18, pars. 1737–1741).

3. For Mary Foote, see commentary following Jelliffe to Freud, 9 July 1923. Since 1929, besides being in analysis with Jung, Mary Foote had been attending his weekly English seminars, editing the transcripts ("Notes" or "protocols") of them, and supervising their private publication, partly at her own expense. Jung had begun to conduct such seminars for his analysands and pupils as early as 1920, but only in 1925 was a seminar systematically transcribed. The principal seminars, all edited by Mary Foote, were "Dream Analysis," 1928–1930; "Interpretation of Visions," 1930–1934; and "Psychological Analysis of Nietzsche's Zarathustra," 1934–1939. Their publication (by Princeton University Press) is in progress.

4. Jung delivered this lecture to the Sixth Congress of the Allgemeine ärztliche Gesellschaft für Psychotherapie, Dresden, 31 Apr. 1931, and it was published in the *Bericht* of the Congress; tr. Cary F. Baynes and W. S. Dell as "Dream Analysis in Its Practical Application," *Modern Man in Search of a Soul* (New York and London, 1933), pp. 1–31. Jelliffe's library (now at the Institute for Living, Hartford) contains a copy of *Modern Man* (1934 printing), but no indication of when he acquired it.

5. *Wirklichkeit der Seele; Anwendungen und Fortschritte der neueren Psychologie*, with contributions by Hugo Rosenthal, Emma Jung, and W. M. Kranefeldt (Zurich, 1934). The work cited in n. 4 was republished in *Wirklichkeit*; tr., "The Practical Use of Dream-Analysis," *Coll. Works*, 16.

6. No review of this work of Jung's was published in *JNMD*.

form may show phasic modifications from a more centralized type.[7] I think it methodologically wrong to assume intent, or predicate a "centralized type" by which the movement in the phase is to be judged pathological. The "normal" in my way of seeing must from lack of universal statistical verification be built up the other way, i.e. by the plotting of the curve of the phasic movements. Just for a moment consider how the "normals" of yesterday no longer exist, in any of the biological sciences—much less those of the day before yesterday.

When the survey would include the highly complex "Seele" phases—just see what the "normal" phenomenology was when Catholicism was the regnant social sanction—or any other credo within the limited boundaries of its own votaries.

How could the less evident "projection" mechanisms ever have been partly revealed without "paranoid" projection phenomena—and how "normal" or "pathological" are certain of such "projections"—or will they be in a hundred or two hundred years. I think I object to a deductive, a prioristic attitude towards the "normality" abstraction. I have no objection to its functioning as a purely "als ob"[8] fiction, but as a fixed postulate I am still from Missouri. Hence my lifted eyebrow as I read in the Introduction to the Koenig-Fachsenfeld book, "top of p. IV," your statement as to variation from Freud and your judgment as to his position in which I cannot concur.

I also am desirous of knowing just how you come to the conclusion that your psychiatry stems from Paris.[9] While it is true that Janet's Ph.D. thesis, *L'Automatisme psychologique,* appeared in 1889, he had not yet begun to do any work in Paris. He was in a Lycée at Havre from 1883–1889 and his material came from physicians in Havre—"Dr. Gibert and Léonie—Mme. B." He did not join the Salpêtrière group until about the time of Charcot's illness, 1890–1891 maybe.[10]

When Freud was with Charcot in 1885, Janet was in Havre. His "Hysteria" book 1893 was his M.D. thesis. His "Léonie"—*spoken* of in Paris in 1885—never was *shown* there.

---

7. The seemingly incomplete sentences here and in the paragraph that follows are as written.

8. "As if"; see above, Jelliffe to Freud, 16 Feb. 1926, n. 13.

9. Jung wrote, in his foreword to the Koenig-Fachsenfeld book: ". . . the psychology of the neuroses . . . had been developed almost simultaneously by Freud in Vienna and by Pierre Janet in Paris. My own course of development was influenced primarily by the French school and later by Wundt's psychology. Later in 1906, I made contact with Freud, only to part company with him. . . . It was chiefly considerations of principle that brought about the separation, above all the recognition that psychopathology can never be based exclusively on the psychology of psychic disease, which would restrict it to the pathological, but must include normal psychology and the full range of the psyche" (*Coll. Works,* 18, par. 1737).

10. Janet began his medical studies in November 1889 and, from 1890, worked under Charcot at the Salpêtrière (Ellenberger, p. 340).

As for French psychiatry at this time, it was nil. So I wonder just why you omitted Bleuler's name as you went to Burghölzli some time about 1905 I believe[11]—and as I understand it from reading the "Diagnostic Word Associations" study[12]—the term "complex" was a joint creation of yours and of Bleuler's. Correct me if I am wrong on this point.

I have wearied you by this long letter but I have been meaning to write you for some time and further wondering if an exchange might be arranged between your *Centralblatt für Psychotherapie*[13] and the *Journal of Nervous and Mental Disease*.

With best wishes and my belated congratulations on your 60th birthday,[14]

Very sincerely,
Smith Ely Jelliffe

Jung to Jelliffe

February 24th 1936.[1]

Dear Dr. Jelliffe,

The reports of my seminar are mere protocols which are exclusively destined to members of the said seminars. They wouldn't be fit for scientific use. I don't think that my volume *Wirklichkeit der Seele* has any interest for you because it is merely psychological and has nothing to do with your medical point of view.

I'm quite willing to answer your questions. I owe a great deal of mental stimulation and of knowledge to Janet, whose lectures I followed in 1902 in Paris. I also got a great deal from his books. I certainly owe a very important psychological point of view to his psychology. I never denied the fact that my psychiatry comes from Bleuler's clinic. I was there already in 1900.

---

11. "On December 10, 1900, I took up my post as assistant at the Burghölzli Mental Hospital"—Jung, *Memories, Dreams, Reflections* (New York, 1963), p. 111. Eugen Bleuler, M.D. (1857–1939) was then director.

12. See next letter, n. 2.

13. Jung had become editor of the *Zentralblatt für Psychotherapie und ihre Grenzgebiete* (Leipzig) in late 1933.

14. Jung's sixtieth birthday had been 26 July 1935.

---

1. Typewritten letter, signed. Published in *C. G. Jung: Letters*, ed. Gerhard Adler and Aniela Jaffé, vol. 1 (Princeton and London, 1973), pp. 210–211.

The concept of "gefühlsbetonter Komplex" as it is used in the association-test is really my own invention,[2] if one doesn't insist that the word "complex" has been used in many other ways before my time. But I'm not aware of the fact that it has been used in the particular way I have been using it. When you study Kraepelin's experimental work about associations (Aschaffenburg etc.) you don't find any systematic consideration of this fact, nor in the experiments of Wundt's school.[3]

I quite agree with you that normality is a most relative conception. Yet it is an idea without which you can't do in practical life. It is quite certain that from century to century or even from month to month our point of view changes, yet there is always a stock of human beings or of facts which represents the average functioning, and which is called "normal." If this conception wouldn't exist, we also couldn't speak of something abnormal, by which term we express the fact that certain functions or events are not conforming to the average course of events.

It is quite true that the reason why I couldn't continue to collaborate with Freud was the fact that everything in his psychology was reductive, personal and envisaged from the angle of repression. A thing which seemed to me particularly impossible was Freud's handling of dreams, which looks to me like a distortion of facts. The immediate reason for my dissension was the fact that Freud in a publication[4] identified the method with his theory, a fact that seemed inadmissible to me, because I am convinced that one can apply a scientific method without believing in a certain theory. The results obtained by this method can be interpreted in several ways. Adler[5] for instance interprets neurosis in a very different way, [and] the same Freud's pupil Silberer[6] has quite clearly shown, independently of myself, that one can interpret in what he called an anagogic way. I think a psychologist has to consider these

---

2. Jung first used this term ("feeling-toned complex") in the earliest of his Studies in Word Association, written with Franz Riklin, "Experimentelle Untersuchungen über Assoziationen Gesunder," *Journal für Psychologie und Neurologie*, 3–4 (1904); tr., "The Associations of Normal Subjects," *Coll. Works*, 2, par. 314; cf. par. 167, n. 18. In a paper published the next year, "Die psychologische Diagnose des Tatbestandes," *Schweizerische Zeitschrift für Strafrecht*, 18 (1905), 369 ff., Jung stated that the concept originated with the psychiatrist Theodor Ziehen (1862–1950), in an 1891 work, and he cited the contributions of the psychiatrists Emil Kraepelin (see below, Jelliffe to Freud, 6 Mar. 1939, n. 8) and Gustav Aschaffenburg, M.D. (1866–1944), and the psychologist Wilhelm Wundt (1832–1920). Tr., "The Psychological Diagnosis of Evidence," *Coll. Works*, 2, pars. 728–733.

3. Jung further elaborated the contributions of Kraepelin, Aschaffenburg, and Wundt in "Die psychopathologische Bedeutung des Assoziationsexperimentes," *Archiv für Kriminalanthropologie und Kriminalistik*, 23 (1906), 1145–62, orig. a lecture, 1905. Tr., "The Psychopathological Significance of the Association Experiment," *Coll. Works*, 2, pars. 863 ff.

4. Probably *Totem and Taboo* (1913), the first part of which appeared in 1912: "Die Inzestscheu," *Imago*, 1:1 (March).

5. Alfred Adler, M.D. (1870–1937) adhered to psychoanalysis until 1911 and then founded the system he called Individual Psychology.

6. Herbert Silberer (1882–1922), Viennese psychoanalyst and writer on alchemical symbolism.

different possibilities and it is my sincerest conviction that it is much too early for psychology to restrict itself to a one-sided reductive point of view. If you carefully study Freud's paper "Die Zukunft einer Illusion"[7] then you see which the results are. Freudian psychology reaches [*sic*] in a field that simply cannot be reduced to Freudian premises, if one studies actual facts without bias.

Concerning the exchange of the *Zentralblatt für Psychotherapie* and *Journal of Nervous and Mental Disease*, I have handed on your request to the "Redaktion."[8]

Yours truly

C. G. Jung.

I am sending you a German reprint[9] from which you can see something of my point of view. No need of quarrelling about detail!

Jelliffe to Jung

April 15, 1936[1]

My dear Professor Jung:

Your good letter of February 24th has lain in my portfolio for some time. I have picked it up and reread it, but more particularly I have been struggling with the collected papers of your 60th birthday collection[2] and your Individuation's Problems of the Dream.[3] I have read it twice and am still not clear about the way by which the symbolic interpretations are arrived at.

I went over the Vogt Journal[4] and reread your Association Studies and thus oriented myself re. the origin of the term "Complex." I have for a long time realized the advance step over the Aschaffenburg, Wundt, Kraepelin studies. I used to play the game myself following Münsterberg[5] and when

---

7. *The Future of an Illusion* (orig. 1927; tr. 1928).

8. *Redaktion* = editorial office.

9. "Traumsymbole des Individuationsprozesses," *Eranos-Jahrbuch 1935* (Zurich, 1936), an offprint of which, signed by the author, is in the Jelliffe Collection, Institute of Living. Tr. W. Stanley Dell, "Dream Symbols of the Process of Individuation," in *The Integration of the Personality* (New York, 1939; London, 1940); later revised as Part II of *Psychology and Alchemy* (orig. 1944), *Coll. Works*, 12.

---

1. Typewritten letter, signed; from the C. G. Jung Archives, courtesy of Franz Jung.

2. *Die kulturelle Bedeutung der komplexen Psychologie* [The cultural significance of complex psychology], ed. Psychological Club, Zurich (Berlin, 1935), a 625-page *Festschrift* for Jung.

3. See previous letter, n. 9.

4. *Journal für Psychologie und Neurologie* (Leipzig), ed. Oskar Vogt, M.D. (1870–1959). Jung's *Diagnostische Assoziationsstudien* were published in the *Journal*, 3–9 (1904–1907).

5. Hugo Münsterberg (1863–1916), psychologist, originally German, at Harvard after 1892, who popularized the use of the association test and its physiological analogues.

your Association Study was translated[6] I was aware of the definite forward step.

I think I was a bit perplexed about your apparent antithesis between normal and pathological—the former as applied to a class, in the Aristotelian sense, as differing in fundamentals from the pathological. I think your statement has been that Freud dealt with the "pathological" and hence the differences. A falling tower of Pisa and a leaning one are obeying identical gravitational laws. The analogy may be a non-sequitur but pathological phenomena have quantitative more than qualitative variations I am certain.

I am much disturbed myself at my own stupidity in understanding the processes behind dream formation. I know Silberer's work. You may recall I translated his "Mysticism" book[7] and I do hold in mind many of the hints and suggestions you gave me back in 1912 and later and have found them very helpful, but I still labor and am much in the dark.

I am thinking just now of a dream of an involution depression patient in which what apparently was the opposite of a "reduction in symbolic statement." It stepped up the scale instead of the one I once related to you as "going from the Ocean Liner, to the inside of the liner and then to a row boat and then to a raft and then to a desert Island" and to which you said *suicide!*—which some time later when he was under J. J. Putnam's[8] care he did. And this other patient who stepped up the quantities did the same. When I heard of the dream I thought to myself I wonder if this "opposite" has relevancy to the suicide wish and later I learned it must have.

I shall get the dream series[9] and see if I can learn something from them and rereading your recent work. I try to get something from Dr. Hinkle[10] but to me she is so naive that I am helpless with the Persona and Anima.[11] It is too simple.

As for Adler his rejection of the significance of the reproduction instinct in human affairs by a wave of the hand and the statement "he does not have to marry" as settling all that too has its asinine aspect that puts me entirely

---

6. *Studies in Word-Association . . . under the direction of C. G. Jung*, tr. M. D. Eder (New York, 1918; London, 1919); Jung's contributions retr. in *Coll. Works*, 2.

7. *Probleme der Mystik und ihrer Symbolik* (Leipzig, 1914), tr. S. E. Jelliffe, *Problems of Mysticism and Its Symbolism* (New York, 1917).

8. James Jackson Putnam, M.D. (1846–1918), professor of neurology at Harvard, founder and first president of the American Psychoanalytic Association (1911).

9. Jelliffe may be referring to Jung's seminar on "Dream Analysis," 1928–1930.

10. Beatrice M. Hinkle, M.D. (1872–1953), American adherent of Jung from as early as the Third Psychoanalytic Congress, Weimar, September 1911; translator of his *Symbole und Wandlung der Libido = Psychology of the Unconscious* (1916); later, director of a private sanitarium at Washington, Connecticut. Hinkle and Jelliffe had been colleagues at the Post-Graduate Medical School and Hospital around 1912.

11. Technical terms in analytical psychology: *persona*, the aspect of personality that an individual shows to the world; *anima*, personification of the feminine nature of the man's unconscious.

out of sympathy with the I. P.[12] save as to its opportunistic demagogue value for the American "mob."[13]

Do you know anything of Lungwitz's *Lehrbuch der Psychobiologie?*[14] This has been my latest thorn in the flesh. Is it worth while putting on the whole crown? I am still struggling with "Numbers."[15]

With best wishes and renewed appreciation for your courtesy,

Very sincerely,

Smith Ely Jelliffe

A week earlier, Jelliffe had received from the poet and psychiatrist Merrill Moore, M.D. (1903–1957), of Harvard, a letter (8 April 1936) criticizing an editorial Jung had published in the *Zentralblatt für Psychotherapie*, 6:3 (Dec. 1933), his first statement as editor. It includes the controversial statement: "The differences which actually do exist between Germanic and Jewish psychology and which have long been known to every intelligent person are no longer to be glossed over, and this can only be beneficial to science. [. . .] At the same time, I should like to state expressly that this implies no depreciation of Semitic psychology, any more than it is a depreciation of the Chinese to speak of the peculiar psychology of the Oriental" (*Collected Works*, 10, pars. 1014–15). Moore wrote: "I think that is a most amazing utterance for the leader of a school of modern psychotherapy to make. I would be very much interested in knowing what your personal reaction to it is." Jelliffe replied (18 April 1936): "Yes, I have read the Jung editorial [. . .] and have written him about it and had a couple of letters—but he side steps as usual." No correspondence between Jelliffe and Jung on that subject has come to light.

Jung to Jelliffe

April 30th, 1936[1]

Dear Professor Jelliffe,

Thank you for kindly sending me the interesting "Consideration of Julian Green."[2] I have seen Lungwitz' book. It didn't appeal to me. There are too

---

12. = Individual Psychology.

13. As Jelliffe's correspondence shows, he had had experiences with Adler that made a most unfavorable impression.

14. Hans Lungwitz, *Lehrbuch der Psychobiologie*, vol. 1 (Kirchhain, Niederlausitz, Germany, 1933).

15. The reference to "Numbers" is obscure. It might refer to a discussion of number symbolism in Jelliffe's article on Julien Green, which he had sent to Jung. See the next letter, n. 2.

---

1. Typewritten letter, signed.

2. *University of Virginia Magazine*, 94 (March 1936), 171–178. The French novelist Julien Green (1900–) was born of American parents who had settled in France.

many people busy in science that learn words which they use to complicate things. I'm sure if I had a chance to have a personal talk with you, I could show you all the necessary points, but the written word is a damnably tricky thing because one never knows exactly how to read it. Primitive language needs as you know a lot of gesticulation. People therefore can't talk to each other in the night, so they light a fire, because mere sound won't do. So when you want to understand one of my papers you better light a fire first so that you can see where I am serious and where I smile.

Sincerely yours,

C. G. Jung.

Jelliffe to Freud

May 20, 1936[1]

My dear Professor Freud:

May I at this time send an additional word of congratulations to that already tendered you from the banquet table of some days past.[2] As I read from almost innumerable sources in our medical and daily press the expressions of homage and praise my narcissism is the more thrilled that it has been my privilege to have known you and more especially to have found through the stimulus of your thought a world of enjoyment about me. As in my first enthusiasms as a youth Spencer, Huxley, Lewes and Darwin[3] offered something about the world that was satisfying so I first felt and have continued to feel that your conceptions gave me a binding grasp of life's processes which still thrills me in my daily life and work. For this I am most truly thankful and grateful.

I need not relate how since 1910 my early discussions with Brill and White gave more precise direction to my thought which first in 1907 began to be really acquainted with your activities. Nor is it incumbent to tell you how ever since then the feeling of satisfaction and security has steadily augmented as I try to understand human behavior in its various manifestations. For all this I feel indebted to you and thrust these words upon you.

And now to another small question. In Rickman's list of your works[4] there are two mentioned: one on the Flusskrebs (1882) and one on a new method

---

1. Carbon copy of typewritten letter.

2. 6 May 1936 was Freud's eightieth birthday, and during that same month the American Neurological Association held a dinner in Freud's honor, at which Jelliffe read a paper, "Sigmund Freud as a Neurologist," which, expanded, was presented to the Section on Neurology and Psychiatry of the N.Y. Academy of Medicine on 9 Feb. 1937 (*JNMD*, 85, 1937). Freud, in May 1936, was made an honorary member of the association.

3. The evolutionary thinkers Herbert Spencer (1820–1903), T. H. Huxley (1825–1895), George Henry Lewes (1817–1878), and Charles R. Darwin (1809–1882). See Part I, ch. 1.

4. John Rickman, M.D. (1891–1951), *Index Psychoanalyticus 1893–1926* (London, 1928).

of studying Faserverlauf (1884),[5] but the sources are not given. Could you supply these? Also was the "Multiple Neuritis" paper published in complete form in any regular publication or was it a "Sep. Abd." as cited in *Neur. Ztbl.*, 5, 251, 1886.[6] Where could it be found complete? I have found all of the others and have them in photostat or printed form. I am desirous of completing the collection.

As you probably know, Dr. Brill has finally completed an English translation of your *Studies in Hysteria*[7] and this important missing number in the series of your works is made available—all too late.

I have been rereading Dr. M. Dorer's *Historisch Grundlagen* and more particularly her chapter "Zur Persönlichkeit und Lehre und Freunde," p. 118.[8] On p. 63 I find a reference to the "neue Method." I assume this is one of the missing citations, but have not checked up in our Academy Library.

Here I find much about the Vienna school of your student days that interests me. I have been reading some of this now for years. It was on a wintry day in 1890 that I first stuck my nose in the Obersteiner-Meynert laboratory[9] and had it [so] gruffly bitten off that I beat a hasty retreat. My German consisted of a trip on the Rhine steamer, a day in Zurich and a hasty flight to Vienna where I had been told they gave courses in English. I took none, may it be remarked, but plugged away at the language (and without any help of a "Schatz").[10] I am still romantic about Vienna at 70. Hence my desire to get some reflection of your judgment on the Dorer book—if you feel free to express it.

I also would revert to an old question re. the Janet history. As you know I have persistently tried to correct the oft repeated error of so many who place Janet among the early Charcot students. I have letters from Janet himself about this. But I am interested to know if you recall when you first became acquainted with his 1889 doctorate thesis (Ph.D.) *Les Automatismes psychologique*—or whether you ever read an earlier study of his in the *Revue philosophique* of 1886?[11] or when in Paris in 1885–1886 ever attended the newly founded society of "psychologie physiologique"—Nov. 30, 1885, of which Charcot was first President and Paul Janet, Pierre Janet's uncle, vice-presi-

---

5. See the next letter, n. 2 and 3.

6. Ibid., n. 4.

7. NMDMS 61 (1936). The Brill tr. was replaced by that of James and Alix Strachey, *Standard Edn.*, 2 (1955).

8. Maria Dorer, *Historische Grundlagen der Psychoanalyse* (Leipzig, 1932). (The chapter Jelliffe mentions: "Concerning Personality, Studies, and Friends.") For the "neue Method," see the next letter, n. 3.

9. Theodor Meynert, M.D. (1833–1892), director of the Psychiatric Clinic, in whose laboratory for cerebral anatomy Freud worked, 1882–1886. Heinrich Obersteiner, M.D. (1847–1922), German neuroanatomist.

10. Lit., treasure; a girl friend. See Part I, ch. 1.

11. "Les Actes inconscients et le dédoublement de la personnalité pendant le sonambulisme provoqué," *Revue philosophique*, 22 (1886), cited by Ellenberger, p. 413, n. 78.

dent. I think I have written you about this before but I do not find it among my letters.

Tonight I am feeling quite "deprimé."[12] I have a severe auricular fibrillation and could not get to the New York Psychoanalytic Society which is to discuss the rules and regulations for the Institute—a preliminary copy of which I enclose herewith. I am writing this while the cardiac machine is flopping all over the lot. I write everything in long hand and my secretary deciphers it as best she can.

My apologies for this long letter.

> With sincere well wishes,
> [*Smith Ely Jelliffe*]

Freud to Jelliffe

> 7 June 1936
> Vienna XIX, Strassergasse 47[1]

Dear Dr. Jelliffe,

Thank you kindly for your letter and your congratulations. I hasten to answer your questions.

I have no recollection of reading Dorer's *Historische Grundlagen*. The name sounds familiar, but I cannot find the book here in my summer home.

The paper on the Flusskrebs appeared in 1882 in the *Sitzungsber. der K. Akad. d. Wissensch.*, III Abtheilung, January issue.[2]

A new method for the study of the "Faserverlauf" appeared in the *Centralblatt für d. med. Wissensch.* 1884, No. 16.[3]

Acute multiple neuritis in *Wiener Med. Wochenschrift*, No. 6, 1886.[4]

I first came across Janet's "Automatisme" between 1891 and 1892. In Paris in 1885/6 I had never heard his name. Janet could have put an end to all the slanders connected with our relations by making a statement. He never did.

I hope the illness of which you write has passed.

> Cordially yours,
> *Freud*

---

12. *deprimé* = depressed.

---

1. Handwritten letter, signed.

2. "Über den Bau der Nervenfasern und Nervenzellen beim Flusskrebs," *Sitzungsberichten der Königlichen Akademie der Wissenschaft*, 3 Abt., 85 (1882). ("On the Structure of the Nerve Fibers and Nerve Cells of the Crayfish.")

3. "Eine neue Methode zum Studium des Faserverlaufes im Centralnervensystem," *Zentralblatt für den medische Wissenschaft*, 22:11 (1884). ("A New Method for the Study of Nerve Tracts in the Central Nervous System.")

4. "Akute multiple Neuritis der spinalen und Hirnnerven," *Wiener medische Wochenschrift*, 36 (1886) ("Acute Multiple Neuritis of the Spinal and Cranial Nerves.") For Freud's abstracts of the papers cited in nn. 2–4, see *Standard Edn.*, 3, pp. 230, 231, 236.

Jelliffe to Jung

July 9, 1936[1]

My dear Dr. Jung:

Your good letter of April 30th I brought with me to my summer camp, also your 60th birthday volume and the Individuation paper.[2] I had read your 1934 Eranos paper on the Collective Unconscious[3] and enjoyed it greatly and am now for the second time going through the Individuation brochure. Could you send me the Eranos, 1934 paper, if you have a reprint.

It has been of much interest to "light a fire" as you suggest, and to follow your sign language as closely as I could. In fact since I have been getting a bit deaf of late I have been paying a little more attention to sign talking; lip reading is a bit beyond me but I find it helps and so I shall watch more for your smile.

Your comment on Lungwitz was appreciated. He is terribly verbose but that seems a generalized notion many of us have re. the other fellow.

Another matter has just come up. Dr. Strong[4] has written me about your writing to him re. the Dementia Praecox monograph.[5] You may recall, or I seem to, that at one time you thought you might revise and elaborate it. This anticipation was one of the factors that determined our letting it lapse in our series, although there was a steady though small call for it.

Inasmuch as American Psychiatry has become very analytically minded and for other reasons Brill has wanted us to reprint, now for two years, and we finally decided to do so. As he, Brill, wished also to have us do the original *Studien über Hysterie* which has never been Englished, we finally made an arrangement with him to do both books and they are now in galley proof at

---

1. Typewritten letter, signed; from the C. G. Jung Archives, courtesy of Franz Jung.

2. See Jung to Jelliffe, 24 Feb. 36, n. 9.

3. "Über die Archetypen des kollektiven Unbewussten," *Eranos Jahrbuch 1934*. Tr. W. Stanley Dell, "Archetypes of the Collective Unconscious," in *The Integration of the Personality;* later, revised, in *Coll. Works*, 9, i.

4. Archibald McIntyre Strong, M.D. (1881–1941), psychiatrist at Presbyterian Hospital, New York, and analytical psychologist.

5. *The Psychology of Dementia Praecox*, tr. Frederick W. Peterson and A. A. Brill (NMDMS 4, 1909). It had gone out of print and the NMD Publishing Co. had sold the rights to Kegan Paul, Trench, Trubner & Co., London. Brill wanted to reprint, and Kegan Paul offered to

the present writing. Brill revised and corrected his old translation and Peterson[6] wrote he would rather retire so it will appear as it really is, Brill's own work.

Now as to the Bailliére, Tindall matter, Brill and White and I have no objections to its inclusion in your collected work.[7] We do feel however in view of Brill's putting up the money for this revised copy, that if Bailliére, Tindall and Co. are very anxious to include it they might be willing to offer some cash inducement. This will go to Brill. Dr. Brill was also interested to know what translation was to be used. Your reaction to this suggestion would be appreciated.

When I have gone over the Individuation brochure again I hope to write to you about it.

I presume you know Meinertz's contributions. I am struggling with one of his recent ones in the *Zeitschrift für Neurologie*[8]—also with Bachofen[9] and Bernoulli, which latter author I note you refer to in your Eranos lecture.

With sincere regards and best wishes,

Smith Ely Jelliffe

Freud to Jelliffe

12 July 1936[1]

Dear Dr. Jelliffe,

I am surprised to find that I still have something to say about my stay in Paris and my relations with Janet, and must correct your views in the matter. I arrived in Paris in October, 1885, and stayed until Easter 1886. If a new psychological society was founded there in 1885, I heard nothing of it. My statement that while in Paris I never heard the name of Janet stands fast.

---

return the rights for five pounds. W. A. White, who handled business matters for the firm, approved the transaction and wrote a check for the amount required, sending it (6 Mar. 1936) with the comment, "What is the mystery back of Brill's urgent desire to reprint this monograph? It reminds me of a squabble over the exhumation of a more or less worthless skeleton that has been buried for centuries." Subsequently, Strong wrote Jelliffe (18 June 1936) at Jung's request, saying that another London house, Bailliére, Tindall & Cox, wanted to republish Jung's *Collected Papers on Analytical Psychology* (1916; 2d ed., 1917) with the *Dementia Praecox* monograph added, and requested permission.

6. In an introduction to his new translation, Brill wrote, "Dr. Peterson, whose ideas about psychoanalysis have changed materially, was not inclined to collaborate with me this time. *Tempora mutantur*. . . ."

7. By "collected work" Jelliffe means *Collected Papers on Analytical Psychology*.

8. S. Meinertz, "Zur Wissenschaftsstruktur der seelischen Krankenbehandlung," *Zeitschrift der gesammte Neurologie und Psychiatrie*, 156 (1936).

9. Johann Jakob Bachofen (1815–1887), Swiss jurist, historian, and social philosopher.

---

1. Handwritten letter, signed.

I cannot regret Schilder's[2] resignation from the Psa. Association as much as you do. His opposition to self-analysis and his restriction of the analysis of students and patients to a few months are deviations of such fundamental importance that I must declare him unsuited to teaching psychoanalysis, quite regardless of whether others are more or less suited than he. Moreover, he left of his own free will. As you know, the Psa. Association first refused him permission to teach and then, quite inconsistently, granted it.

Wishing you the best of health and a fine holiday,

Yours,

Freud

Jung to Jelliffe

August 1st, 1936[1]

Dear Dr. Jelliffe,

Thank you for your kind letter. I will see what Bailliére & Tindall & Co. are intending to do in the matter of the Dementia Praecox book. If Dr. Brill doesn't object we might use his translation. But I must speak first to Dr. Cary Baynes[2] who is doing translation work for me and see what she thinks about this matter. You will hear either from me or from her about the decision we have come to.

I'm sorry I have no reprints of my 1934 Eranos paper. There never have been any reprints unfortunately.

About the Bernoulli you mention, there are two of them. The one I mentioned in my paper is Professor of history of arts at the Federal Technical University of Zürich.[3] The other is Carl Albrecht Bernoulli,[4] a philosophical writer who is chiefly famous for editing Nietzsche's letters. I know Meinertz personally. I don't think that you should wrestle too much with his publications. He is involved even for German-speaking people. As you know there

---

2. Paul Ferdinand Schilder, M.D. (1886–1940), Viennese psychiatrist, a psychoanalyst from 1920; from 1930, in New York. Jelliffe was a sponsor of Schilder when he entered the United States: see Part I. It appears that a letter to Freud from Jelliffe mentioning Schilder is missing.

1. Typewritten letter, signed.
2. Cary Fink Baynes, M.D. (1883–1977), American nonpracticing physician, in Zurich during most of 1921–1936 as a pupil of Jung. She edited his 1925 seminar and translated several of his works, in addition to *The Secret of the Golden Flower* (1931) and the *I Ching, or Book of Changes* (1950). At this time, Jung considered her his official translator.
3. Rudolf Bernoulli (1880–1948) lectured at the 1935 Eranos Conference on "Spiritual Development as Reflected in Alchemy and Related Disciplines," the paper Jung cited (cf. *Psychology and Alchemy, Coll. Works*, 12, par. 332); tr. Ralph Manheim in *Spiritual Disciplines*, ed. Joseph Campbell (New York, 1960).
4. Karl Albrecht Bernoulli (1868–1937), whose literary work included writings on Bachofen.

are scientists who make complicated things simple and others who make simple things complicated.

Sincerely yours,

C. G. Jung.

Jung to Jelliffe

August 4th, 1936[1]

Dear Dr. Jelliffe,

It appears that Bailliére & Tindall are rather anxious to have if possible some article of mine which has not yet appeared in English. The idea of getting them to take the Dementia Praecox paper grew out of the wish to have that reappear in English. Since you are now taking care of that in a very satisfactory way, we have decided not to pursue the matter with Bailliére & Tindall.[2]

Thanking you very much for your friendly cooperation.

Sincerely yours,

C. G. Jung.

No further letters between Jelliffe and Jung have survived, and it appears that their friendship, tenuous as it was by this time, soon dwindled to nothing. There is no evidence that the two men met when Jung attended the Harvard Tercentenary Conference of Arts and Sciences in September 1936 and subsequently lectured to the Analytical Psychology Club of New York. In September 1937, Jung delivered the Terry Lectures at Yale University (they were published as *Psychology and Religion*, New Haven, 1938; *Collected Works*, 11) and gave a seminar in New York during late October, again sponsored by the Analytical Psychology Club. Jelliffe attended at least one of the sessions. The documentation: Ernest Jones to Jelliffe, 1 December 1937: "I hope you Americans are not being drawn into the ramp of Jung's Gesellschaft für Psychotherapie which is labelling itself international, aims at including 'all forms' of Psychotherapy and intends to hold a Congress in England next July." Jelliffe to Jones, 15 December 1937: "As to the Jung ramp I have not heard of it here. They keep their movements very dark and in the Goering-Jung *Zentralblatt* is about all we hear of it. [. . .] I saw Jung this fall. He was distinctly his age and gave a very religious preachment to a lot of female admirers. I was not much impressed, quite the reverse. He seems to have reverted to his pastoral ancestor." The seminar in New York was actually based on Jung's Eranos lecture of 1935, "Traumsymbole des Individuations-

---

1. Typewritten letter, signed.
2. Writing Jelliffe on 29 June 1936, Strong indicated that he favored the publication of Brill's new edition of *Dementia Praecox* and would make an appropriate suggestion to Jung. Bailliére, Tindall & Cox did not, in any case, reissue *Collected Papers*.

prozesses," which he had sent to Jelliffe in early 1936 (see Jung to Jelliffe, 24 February 1936, n. 9).

A little more than a year later, Jelliffe made the following estimate of Jung, in a letter to A. A. Roback, M.D. (17 January 1939): "Years ago I came to a general conviction that Jung was quite a Janus-faced person. He was not a scientist, but more of an opportunist in doctrine and in methods. I have seen little to change this general idea hoping to modify a definite admiration for his undoubted ability."

Freud to Jelliffe

Vienna, 23 September 1936[1]

Gratefully acknowledging receipt of your wife's book *For Dear Life*.[2] With kind regards,

Freud

Jelliffe to Freud

February 8, 1937[1]

My dear Professor Freud:

I am sending you at this time a rough copy of a paper[2] I shall read—with some omissions—tomorrow night at our Academy of Medicine—Dr. Brill presiding before the Section on Neurology and Psychiatry. Later I hope to publish it either in the *Journal of Nervous and Mental Disease* or the *Archives of Neurology and Psychiatry*.

I send it chiefly to learn if there are any gross errors or misconstructions. Such I would not like to have appear in print. Dr. Sachs[3] was to have discussed it but will be away. He has made some slight corrections which are not included in this copy.

I would have sent it along before but for pressure of many things.

If you have the time and inclination to read it and visé it, I would much appreciate it.

With sincere best wishes,

[*Smith Ely Jelliffe*]

---

1. Handwritten postcard, signed.
2. Belinda Jelliffe's autobiographical novel (New York, 1936). Freud's courtesy in acknowledging such a gift at this trying time of his life is the justification for preserving this trivial message.

---

1. Carbon copy of typewritten letter.
2. See below, Jelliffe to Freud, 17 June 1937, n. 2.
3. Bernard Sachs, M.D. (1858–1944), neurologist, professor at Columbia. See below, Jelliffe to Freud, 17 June 1937, n. 3.

Freud to Jelliffe

23 February 1937[1]

Dear Dr. Jelliffe,

You have undertaken a thankless task, that of calling attention to my pre-analytic papers, which are today so far from me. Your account is accurate except for a few details, which I am rectifying out of sheer pedantry:

p 3   It is not true that I was refused the position of assistant at the Physiological Institute. I failed to obtain it because no such position was available. Places had not yet been found for Exner and Fleischl. I often heard that I would have been next. Brücke was well disposed to me; in the end, when he learned of my material situation, he only said that he would not have wished to take responsibility for guiding me into a research career.[2]

p 5   Stricker, Schenk and A. had worked in the Physiological Laboratory in earlier years. They were never to be found there in my time.[3]

p 13   Note: I translated the last volume of J. St. Mill's Works, edited by Theodor Gomperz.[4]

p 15   Primarius Dr. Scholz,[5] not Professor. (An old fool!)

p 17   Meynert was very open-minded in his dealings with me in those years. He had no influence on my work.

p 26   0.5 cocaine! You mean 0.05, I should think.[6]

That's all. Perhaps your article will have some influence on those who still like to believe that I pulled psychoanalysis out of my hat.

Cordially yours,
Freud

---

1. Handwritten letter, signed.

2. Freud spent 1876–1882 in the Physiological Laboratory, or Institute, at the University of Vienna under the great physiologist Ernst Wilhelm von Brücke (1819–1892), whose assistants were Ernst Fleischl von Marxow (1840–1891) and Sigmund Exner (1846–1926). See Freud, "An Autobiographical Study" (1925), *Standard Edn.*, 20, pp. 9–10.

3. Salomon Stricker, M.D. (1834–1898), professor of pathology; Samuel Leopold Schenk, M.D., professor of embryology; the name abbreviated by "A." could not be identified; no name fitting the case was mentioned in Jelliffe's published article.

4. In 1880, Freud translated vol. 12 of John Stuart Mill's *Gesammelte Werke* (containing essays on social problems and on Plato) at the request of the editor, Theodor Gomperz (1832–1912), famous professor of classical philology.

5. Franz Scholz, M.D., superintendent of the neurological section of the General Hospital of Vienna, where Freud was physician 1884–1885. Freud on another occasion referred to him as "a fossil and feeble-minded" (Jones, 1, 218/199).

6. In Freud's experiments with cocaine he took 0.05 gram of cocainum muriaticum in a 1 percent water solution. See above, Freud to Jelliffe, 2 Aug. 1934, n. 3.

Jelliffe to Freud

April 13, 1937[1]

My dear Dr. Freud:

It was a great pleasure to get your letter and to make the corrections you suggested. Instead of the paper's having been an "undankbare Arbeit," I found it full of interest and well worth while. I think I obtained a better vision of what was going on in the natural sciences in Vienna during the years I was just starting grammar school and was first wearing long pants.

As I went through the "Sitzungsberichte"—the Academy has not the volume of your "Lappenorgan" study[2]—I could see you then about 20–21 as I saw myself studying medicine and in the botanical laboratory at Columbia working up some plants from the "Solenhofen State" areas and making microscopical studies on the conducting vessels in various woods to further experiments on chemical fireproofing.[3]

It was most gratifying to read the papers of Exner, of Claus[4] and of the others in 1876, 1877, 1878 and on through half a dozen years.

Our own N. Y. Academy of Science, some 10 years later, interested me greatly and the new Museum of Natural History was a constant refuge.[5]

It was with added pleasure that I read the Bruns paper[6] after I had mine finished. It enabled me to turn back and help my own.

Dr. White's death[7] has been a very unhappy one for me. We had worked together now for 40 years and I shall miss his good counsel and friendship. The editing of the *Psychoanalytic Review* will fall upon my shoulders, for a time at least, until the business of the partnership agreement shall be straightened out. If it continues under my editorship, for I had little to do with the

---

1. Carbon copy of typewritten letter.

2. "Beobachtungen über Gestaltung und feineren Bau der als Hoden beschriebenen Lappenorgane des Aalls," *Sitzungsberichte der kaiserlichen Akademie der Wissenschaften* (Vienna), Math.-naturwiss. Kl., 1 Abt., 75 (1877), the first paper that Freud wrote for publication, reporting his observations on the configuration and finer structure of the lobed organs in eels described as testes, for which he dissected 400 eels at the Zoological Experimental Station at Trieste. See Jones, 1, 41/37 f. Jelliffe was evidently reading at the library of the New York Academy of Medicine.

3. For Jelliffe's work in botany, see Part I, ch. 1. No publication is recorded on the experiments here mentioned. "Solenhofen state" alludes to a type of limestone.

4. Carl Claus (1835–1899), professor of zoology at Vienna, who had appointed Freud to his fellowship at Trieste.

5. The American Museum of Natural History, on Central Park West, was founded in 1869 and its construction was begun in 1877. It formerly contained the premises of the New York Academy of Sciences, which later removed to its own building on East 63rd St.

6. Presumably Rudolf Bruns, "Sigmund Freuds Leistungen auf dem Gebiete der organischen Neurologie," *Schweizer Archiv für Neurologie und Psychiatrie*, 37 (1936), a study of Freud's achievements in the area of organic neurology.

7. White died at St. Elizabeths Hospital on 7 March 1937, aged sixty-seven.

choice of papers published, certain changes will be instituted. It has been rather stationary for the past four or five years.

With cordial best wishes,
Very sincerely,
[*Smith Ely Jelliffe*]

Jelliffe to Freud

June 17, 1937[1]

My dear Professor Freud:

At this time I send you the reprint of the paper you so kindly viséd.[2] I trust I have left no "boners" in it.

I gave a short abstract viva voce at the meeting of the American Neurological Association about two weeks ago and had both a large and encouraging audience. You will be a bit amused at the parapraxis of Dr. Sachs who discussed my presentation. He said a number of very pleasant things quoting your own statement as once made that he was a "braver Mann." Then in recounting how Anton, Starr, he, and "who was the fourth" at the same laboratory table in Meynert's laboratory, he brought down the house.[3] Everybody recognized the lapsus and it all went off very merrily.

Dr. Adolf Meyer[4] discussed very well the general biological foundations and significance of your work. All in all it was a very satisfactory period in the day's deliberations. I have thought you might be interested.

Owing to Dr. White's death I shall take over the entire management of the *Psychoanalytic Review* and the Monograph Series. I am a bit old to pile on this extra burden but I wished to keep the thing intact until I could pass it on to reliable hands.

Dr. Brill has consented to join in on the *Psychoanalytic Review* and I think we can aid the general situation materially if nothing seriously interferes with my present state of well being.

My country home in the Adirondacks waits for me and in two weeks I shall be gone from the city for a few months.

---

1. Carbon copy of typewritten letter.

2. "Sigmund Freud as a Neurologist: Some Notes on His Earlier Neurobiological and Clinical Neurological Studies," *JNMD*, 85 (1937).

3. With Sachs at Meynert's laboratory in 1882 were Gabriel Anton, M.D. (1858–1933), Austrian neurologist; Moses Allen Starr, M.D. (1854–1932), professor of neurology at Columbia, Jelliffe's teacher and sponsor, an outspoken adversary of psychoanalysis; and "the fourth," Freud, whose name Sachs forgot, or pretended to forget, at the meeting in 1937. The occasion is described by C. P. Oberndorf, "Forty Years of Psycho-Analytic Psychiatry," *International Journal of Psycho-Analysis*, 30 (1949), 158.

4. Adolf Meyer, M.D. (1866–1950), originally of Zurich, in the U.S. after 1892, and in 1937 professor of psychiatry at Johns Hopkins University. This address is not in his *Collected Papers* (Baltimore, 1950–1952).

With cordial regards and best wishes,

Very sincerely,

[*Smith Ely Jelliffe*]

Jelliffe to Freud

August 16, 1938[1]

Professor Sigmund Freud
39 Ellsworthy Road
London, N.W. 3, England[2]
My dear Professor Freud:

Having just obtained your London address I have no further excuse to delay my word of sympathy for the "slings and arrows of outrageous fortune" that have compassed you about. Also to express to you the hope that you will find some peace and comfort in your new home, a country I have always found a joy and a comfort, as well as a stimulus.

It has been my good fortune to have been asked by the editor of the *American Journal of Sociology*, Dr. Burgess,[3] to say something about your work and its place in psychiatry. I sent it off to them this morning but am not very proud of it. It was not as simple as my small paper on your work as a neurologist, a reprint of which I think I sent you. If there be time, when the galley proofs come, I shall send one to you and request your visé. I wish it might meet with your approval. I have no one to talk such matters over with intimately since Dr. White died and I needs must let it go forward without his kindly critique.

If some time you feel you have a word for or about the *Psychoanalytic Review* I trust you will favor me with it. During Dr. White's illness, for he had been sick a year or more, the *Review* suffered from lack of attention. I hope I shall be able to bring it into a more representative position. But I too am not as young as I would like to be and find it increasingly difficult to edit and finance all by myself. Fortunately I have had much encouragement from the new arrangements which have begun.

With sincerest well wishes,

Smith Ely Jelliffe

---

1. Typewritten letter, signed; from the Sigmund Freud Collection, Library of Congress.

2. Freud, with his wife and daughter Anna, left Vienna on 4 June 1938 and arrived two days later in London, where they took up residence in a rented house.

3. Ernest S. Burgess (1886–1966), professor of sociology at the University of Chicago. Jelliffe's paper was "Sigmund Freud and Psychiatry: A Partial Appraisal," *American Journal of Sociology*, 45 (1939).

Freud to Jelliffe

August 23, 1938

39 Elsworthy Road

London, N.W. 3[1]

Dear Dr. Jelliffe,

Thank you so much for your kind word of sympathy. I am happy to be here after my experience in what is now Germany.

Looking forward to the proofs you announce. I hope you are sure of all the assistance I can give you without influencing your judgement. I feel hurt by the behaviour of American analysts in the matter of Lay-Analysis and in their relation to the I.P.V.[2] Nor are they, it seems, very fond of me. But this does not affect my relation to you which is to remain undamaged.

Hoping you will be all right for a long time to come

Yours sincerely
Freud

Freud to Jelliffe

Oct. 18, 1938

20 Maresfield Gardens
London N.W. 3[1]

Dear Dr. Jelliffe,

Here I am at last settled in relative security, glad to have escaped the furor teutonicus, waiting for patients who so far have not yet arrived. I have overcome another of my "habitual" operations and am still fit to work.[2]

Among the immigrants in New York, there is one man, Dr. Jekels,[3] not only a distinguished analyst, but also a very good friend of mine. I would like to hear that you can do something to ease his situation by sending him patients etc.

---

1. Handwritten letter, signed, in English. Published in *Psychoanalytic Pioneers*, p. 227.
2. = Internationale Psychoanalytische Verein (International Psycho-Analytical Association). At the International Psycho-Analytical Congress in Paris at the beginning of August, a sharp difference of opinion had arisen, essentially over the question of lay analysis, between the Americans (anti) and the Europeans (pro). Jelliffe's relationship to the lay analysis controversy is described in Part I, ch. 3.

---

1. Handwritten letter, signed, in English. Published in *Psychoanalytic Pioneers*, p. 228. Freud struck out the previous street address and wrote in the new one, which is also in N.W. 3 (Hampstead), where the Freud family had moved on 16 September 1938.
2. On 8 September, Freud had undergone a severe operation for his chronic oral condition.
3. Ludwig Jekels, M.D. (1867–1954), Viennese-educated Polish psychiatrist, a psychoanalyst since 1908.

You promised to send me some proofs of an essay of yours in which I should be personally interested.

Yours with kind regards

Sigm. Freud

Jelliffe to Freud

November 4, 1938[1]

Prof. Sigmund Freud
20 Mansfield Gardens [*sic*]
London, England
My dear Professor Freud:

I had been hoping ere this not only to answer your cordial letter of August 23rd but also to send you the galley proof of the article I sent to the *American Journal of Sociology* on August 15th. Only last week I asked for information as to its progress. As it was to be part of a symposium its delay may have been due to derelict contributors. At all events I hope to hear from Prof. Burgess, the editor, shortly.

A few days after getting yours of August 23rd word also came from Dr. Jones that you had made a successful journey through the surgical country and yours of October 18th confirming this good news gives me happiness for your sake and rejoicing with all your well wishers.

In your first note you comment on the lay analyst situation. In principle I am in definite agreement with you. In practice there are, as you no doubt know, difficulties of more than one kind. I hardly need emphasize what a long and arduous fight it has been to even regulate the practice of medicine, and keep it from a horde of parasites, of which the Christian Scientists are not the worst variety. Chiropractors, osteopaths, mental healers, soothsayers, etc., etc., and others have been brought to boot, in some states, and medical practice acts have been sharpened and codified. It may be, in the long run that "error will writhe in pain and die among her worshippers"[2] but "Oh Lord how long, how long" one might cry with Job[3] in mind. In New York State the medical practice act has nearly arrived at a point when any effort to "diagnose, prescribe or offer counsel or advice for disease" shall be called practising medicine restricted to duly qualified physicians. This is one of the legal hedges.

Another specific situation has grown up here in many states. This has been the entrance into mental medicine of an army of academic psychologists.

---

1. Typewritten letter, signed, from the Freud Collection, Library of Congress.
2. From William Cullen Bryant, "The Battle-Field" (1837): "But Error, wounded, writhes in pain, / And dies among his [*sic*] worshippers."
3. Actually, Isaiah 6:11.

Originally starting as intelligence testers, with their Binet-Simon-Terman scales,[4] etc., they have rushed the psychotherapy camps, and I need not dilate on this aspect of a serious and amusing situation. Especially as so many prattle about introvert and extravert, with repression and regression, with libido and the Id and other phrases, making a veritable jargon, much worse than Jastrow's caricature of *The House that Freud Built*.

You know all this but it comes to mind and I pen it. To find a well qualified, ethical and sincere lay analyst of the type of Joan Riviere, Princess Bonaparte, or your own Anna[5]—we simply do not raise them here in this generation.

As you know I had two under my wing. One gave it up as a too rigorous Super Ego made her feel uncomfortable being only an A.B., A.M., Ph.D. and a trained nurse as well. You know her as Zenia X[6] and as competent as many I know in England, but they are few and far between and are on the qui vive to be "raided" as practising medicine without a physician's license. Many of the Jung disciples are doing this and getting away with it in a fashion.[7]

The politics of a certain wing in the American Psychoanalytic I cannot stand as I never was a good politician and hate to see these efforts at preferential preeminence, to say nothing of the push for what we call "cushy jobs" as directors or this or that and which some day will animate an anti-semitic wave here as elsewhere.

I do sincerely wish we might do something better in the lay analysis situation as I am convinced we need for the good of the whole movement the support and sympathy that a wider cultural group of supporters, of the Thomas Mann type, can afford. Some are coming along, like Prof. Dollard at Yale[8] and I might mention others.

Already Dr. Jekels has written me and I shall do what I can to be of aid to him. I have taken a much longer vacation than usual this year, especially as I had to do some experimental therapeutic work on my own periodic auricular fibrillation. This has become permanent now and so I am spared the annoyance of anxiety relative to "will it or won't it" if I do this, or that.

---

4. Intelligence test devised 1905–1911 by the French psychologists Alfred Binet and Theodore Simon, revised by the American psychologist L. M. Terman, 1916; usually called the Stanford Revision of the Binet-Simon Test.

5. Joan Riviere (1883–1962), British lay analyst and translator of many works of Freud's; Marie Bonaparte (1882–1962), married to Prince George of Greece (she was the great-grand-daughter of Lucién Bonaparte, brother of Napoleon I); Anna Freud (1895–1982), in London since 1938.

6. Louise Brink; see Jelliffe to Freud, 2 Dec. 1924, n. 2, and Freud to Jelliffe, 23 Aug. 1938, n. 2.

7. It has not been possible to document this statement beyond observing that Jungian analysts then practicing in New York included lay persons.

8. John Dollard (1900–1980), well-known psychologist, then on the staff of the Yale Institute of Human Relations.

I know better what my heart can stand and what to do about it now that quinidine is no longer a hope or a prop.

There are other troubles but of these I shall say nothing save that I must take care of myself and the deafness is most aggravating. Here also experiments with hearing aids have been partly successful.

The added work after Dr. White's death on the *Review* and Monographs also had to be put into some organized form. This has been a part of my summer's work, if the organization was to be maintained. I must now edit, manage and finance the whole show. It is of interest but time consuming, and divertability must be kept in check if I hope to do any more actual observing, recording and publishing in the only sphere which seems to me to be all embracing and definitely worth while. Today I am 72 and apart from the things mentioned hardly know it. I echo your generous hope that I may be able to continue for some time.

With sincere best wishes and many thanks for your letters,

Very truly yours,
Smith Ely Jelliffe

Freud to Jelliffe

Febr. 9, 1939[1]

Dear Dr. Jelliffe,

Thanks for your highly interesting paper. No comments on my side forthcoming. I know you have been one of my sincerest and staunchest adherers through all these years. I now often laugh in remembrance of the bad reception I gave you at Gastein because I had first seen you in company of Stekel.

A remark of yours saying that Psychoanalysis has spread in U. S. more widely than deeply, struck me as particularly true. I am by no means happy to see that Analysis has become the handmaid of Psychiatry in America and nothing else. I am reminded of the parallelism in the fate of our Vienna Ladies, who by exile have been turned into housemaids serving in English households.

Yours with kindest regards
Sigm. Freud

---

1. Handwritten letter, signed, in English; published in *Psychoanalytic Pioneers*, p. 228.

Jelliffe to Freud

March 6, 1939[1]

My dear Professor Freud:

It was a pleasure to get your letter of February 9, 1939 and I appreciate very highly the generous statement of your feeling towards my interest in and advocacy of your conceptions.

I do not now recall all of the steps that led up to my interest and definite attitude, and in my little after-dinner talk at our 25th New York Psychoanalytic Anniversary[2] I skipped over many of the preliminaries. Some day I may autobiograph my impressions as I recall them.

Although my early training in college was mathematical and engineering, it was not my forte and I early turned to medicine chiefly because of my natural history interests. These were greatest in botany but also included some geologizing and beetle, bird and mollusca collecting, classifying, etc. None of these things save some superficial geology were in my engineering courses but it opened up the time-bound possibilities of evolution, and reading in Darwin, Spencer, Lyell,[3] Goethe, Pope, and Lucretius deepened and fortified this general viewpoint. Embryology in medicine naturally fell in line and I did a lot of histology with the organs of lower animals. All of this was on my own as was the botany. Then Schwendener and Kerner von Marilaun[4] swung the phyletic viewpoint in plant anatomy into the pot and naturally Haeckel's elaboration of v. Baer's[5] generalization I revelled in. The phylogeny of plants was specially entrancing as I had done a really good lot of collecting and studying since I was 16 or 17 in this branch. This also on my own. Hence the slowness in coming to the already known principles.

We had here in Cope, Leidy, Ward[6] and others active announcers of the principle in the thought realm and hence a readiness to a more monistic conception of the whole living processes. I was a rank amateur however and a voracious reader. My Wanderjahr[7] gave me German, consolidated my college French and took the mystery out of several languages.

Dr. White and I had been friends ever since 1896 when I spent a summer vacation in Binghamton, and from 1903 on he visited me in my summer

---

1. Typewritten letter, signed; from the Freud Collection, Library of Congress.
2. See above, Jelliffe to Freud, 9 Jan. 1933, n. 4.
3. Charles Lyell (1797–1875), British geologist, is best known for advocating uniformitarianism, which was a necessary antecedent to Darwin's work.
4. The botanists Simon Schwendener (1829–1919), German, and Anton Kerner, Ritter von Marilaun (1831–1898), Austrian.
5. Karl Ernst von Baer (1792–1876), Estonian-German naturalist and embryologist. Jelliffe is alluding to the idea that ontogeny recapitulates phylogeny.
6. Edward Drinker Cope (1840–1897), Joseph Leidy (1823–1891), and Lester Frank Ward (1841–1913), American evolutionists and neo-Lamarckians.
7. See Part I, ch. 1.

camp which we purchased that year. Thus began a free interchange of ideas through letters and verbal discussions. In 1906 I was fed up with the orthodox medical situation and blindly went to Kraepelin.[8] I have never regretted it, from the clinical psychiatric viewpoint. Dr. White had become enamored of Sidis and Prince[9] but I was not satisfied. Sidis I distrusted as a person and when I realized he was revamping Russian work and putting it out as his own I further repudiated him. The details of this are of interest but unimportant now. Our battles, White's and mine, over hypnoidal phenomena were royal and when I read some of your studies for the first time I had a feeling of greater security. I can remember firing some of your work at him as a final rejoinder to a hypnosis argument as he was once leaving my house and on his way to Washington.

In 1907 we met Jung, Maeder and Riklin[10] at a luncheon in Zurich and I owe much to Jung's enthusiasm at that time. Only later did I come to any real perception of the inner tensions in your original group.

Then Brill became my assistant at the Neurological Institute in 1910. We walked home through the park many an afternoon and he clarified a lot of my ideas. All this I have stated in my "Odyssey" note.[11]

I was hurt mostly by your letter to White in response to his request that you give us something for the *Review*. Neither of us were near enough to the Vienna group to know of the 1908–1909 difficulties in the parent society.[12]

But as both of us were definitely not commercially minded, as you charged, the rebuff was taken without too much protest, but with much of the spirit of the wrongly accused little boy—"We'll show papa we were not as bad as he thought."

White was much more lenient than I to methodological variants. He did not read German although his librarian[13] was an excellent German scholar and fed him all that he required. Also he had little time for individual analytic work and thus much entered the *Review* that I did not like. Sometimes I was dogmatic about it and kept some matters out.

Then I met Stekel and soon "got his number," as we say it. I lost my respect for his integrity while intrigued by his ingenuity and then became

---

8. Emil Kraepelin, M.D. (1856–1926), German clinical psychiatrist, professor at Munich, who evolved the standard system of psychiatric classification and differentiated dementia praecox (his term) from manic-depressive psychosis. For Jelliffe's work with him, see Part I, ch. 2.

9. Boris Sidis (1876–1923), emigrated from Russia, studied with William James at Harvard, and later directed a sanatorium at Portsmouth, New Hampshire; Morton Prince, M.D. (1854–1929), psychiatrist in Boston, founder and editor of the *Journal of Abnormal Psychology*. Both were pioneers in dynamic psychopathology.

10. See above, introductory remarks to these letters, n. 8. Jelliffe does not mention here meeting Jung at the Amsterdam Congress in September 1907.

11. "Glimpses of a Freudian Odyssey"; see Jelliffe to Freud, 9 Jan. 1933, n. 4.

12. The reference is presumably to the dissidence of Alfred Adler, Jung, and Stekel during 1911–1912.

13. White's librarian could not be identified.

wearied by his repetitive prolixity. Rank[14] in the meantime had become debauched by an unpleasant debacle.

All this I am recording anent the general charge of the superficiality of American thought. This I am led to reflect is often confused with catholicity and tolerance. I never have been sympathetic to a very widespread accusation of your intolerance. "Methodologies" have to be rigid in order to be proven or disproven. It is banal to state it—but so it seemed and has seemed to me that you were struggling to keep "proof" always in the foreground.

Hence my advocacy throughout the years. Even now in the dissensions in the New York Society on the death instinct I hear all around me contradictory voices but am trying to understand.

I have made this letter much too long but felt the impulse to write more than a conventional word of thanks for your last note.

With sincere regards,
Smith Ely Jelliffe

Anna Freud to Jelliffe

20 Maresfield Gardens,
London, N.W. 3.
28.9.39[1]

Dear Dr. Jelliffe,

I am sure you will not mind if I ask you for a favour at this moment.

Now, after my father's death,[2] his doctor, Dr. Max Schur,[3] is leaving for America. He has looked after him for 14 years up to the very end and I am immensely grateful to him. He is an excellent man and I am sure he will make his way somehow. But if there is anything you could do to help him along, would you do it? I should be very thankful.

This has been a difficult year for all of us.

Very sincerely yours
Anna Freud.

---

14. See above, Jelliffe to Freud, 19 Dec. 1925, n. 8.

---

1. Handwritten letter, signed, in English.
2. Freud died at home on 23 Sept. 1939.
3. Max Schur, M.D. (1867–1969), Vienna internist, became Freud's physician in Mar. 1929, and attended him to the end of Freud's life. Schur became a psychoanalyst in 1932 and carried on his career in New York from 1939 on. He wrote *Freud: Living and Dying* (1972).

Anna Freud to Jelliffe

16.10.39.[1]

Dear Dr. Jelliffe,

I have been very touched by your letter[2] to me about my father. You knew him both personally and scientifically and, I think, much better than all those who only met him in these last years. I am always sorry that I was not with him in the earlier days of his work and his difficult times with the world around. I should have liked to help him then. I really only came in when most of his battles were fought and won already.

This last year of his life was not made easy for him. He enjoyed life in England and we made his new home here very pleasant and the way he liked it. Only the malignancy of his cancer grew worse and worse. He underwent a most painful X-ray and Radium treatment with the greatest courage. But it was all no good.

Thank you once more for what you said in your letter.

Sincerely yours
Anna Freud.

---

1. Handwritten letter, signed, in English.
2. Missing.

Chronology of Events in the Life of Smith Ely Jelliffe

1866
October 27, born in New York City
1882
Graduates from Brooklyn public schools
Enters Brooklyn Polytechnic Institute
1886
Completes "scientific course" at Brooklyn Polytechnic
Enters College of Physicians and Surgeons, Columbia University
1889
M.D., College of Physicians and Surgeons
1889–1890
Internship, St. Mary's General Hospital, Brooklyn
1890–1891
Wanderjahr in Europe
1891
Opens practice in Brooklyn
1894
Joins faculty of New York College of Pharmacy to teach pharmacognosy
Marriage to Helena Dewey Leeming
Moves home and office to 231 West 71st Street, New York City
1896
Summer appointment at Binghamton State Hospital and meets William
    Alanson White
1897
Appointed assistant in neurology, Vanderbilt Clinic, Columbia University,
    and Presbyterian Hospital
Begins work with *Journal of Nervous and Mental Disease*
1899
Appointed associate editor, *Journal of Nervous and Mental Disease*
1900
Appointed editor, *Medical News*

1901
December, purchases *Journal of Nervous and Mental Disease*
1903
Appointed instructor in materia medica and therapeutics, College of Physicians and Surgeons
Moves home and office to 64 West 56th Street
1904
Last botanical publication
Purchase of property at Huletts Landing on Lake George, New York
1905
Medical News merged into *New York Medical Journal*, with Jelliffe as coeditor
Publication of Jelliffe's translation of Dubois's classic on psychotherapy
1906
Study in Munich
1907
Termination of all Columbia appointments
Further study in Munich
Attends Amsterdam Congress and meets Jung there and in Zurich
Finally commits himself to the specialty of nervous and mental diseases
Founds, with White, *Nervous and Mental Disease Monograph Series*
1908
Resigns from *New York Medical Journal*
1908–1909
Study in Berlin and Paris
1909–1910
Visiting physician, Hospital for Nervous Diseases
Adherence to psychoanalysis
1911
Begins teaching in Post-Graduate Medical School
1912
Instrumental in bringing Jung to lecture at Fordham
1913
First psychoanalytic publication
Founds, with White, the *Psychoanalytic Review*
1915
Publishes major nervous and mental disease textbook in collaboration with White
1916
Death of Helena Leeming Jelliffe
1917
Appointed coeditor, *New York Medical Journal*
Marriage to Bee Dobson
Termination of medical school teaching and hospital appointments
1918
Assumes full editorial responsibility for the *Journal of Nervous and Mental Disease*
President, American Psychopathological Association

1919
Business office of monograph series moves to Washington
Resignation as coeditor of *New York Medical Journal*
Rival journal, *Archives of Neurology and Psychiatry*, founded
1921
First meeting with Freud
1925
Readmitted to orthodox New York Psychoanalytic Society
1929
Last trip abroad
1929–1930
President, American Neurological Association
1937
Death of White
Assumes editorship of *Psychoanalytic Review* and monograph series
1938
Testimonial dinner
1941
Sells personal library to Institute of Living
1944
Gives up editing
1945
September 25, dies at Huletts Landing, New York

Generations
Summary of Jelliffe's Genealogical Researches

I   THOMAS JELLIFF
- B: Norwalk, Conn., possibly by 1703; bought land, Poplar Plains 1741–1743
- M: Catherine Fillow prior to 1749
  3 sons: Thomas, WILLIAM, Richard
- D: Date unknown; but later than 1754

II   WILLIAM JELLIFF
- B: 1752 (2d son)
- M: Huldah Sturgis on Dec. 7, 1771
  10 children (8 sons, 2 daughters): (CAPT) WILLIAM, Sturgis, Aaron, Hezikiah, Zalmon, David, Gould, Hiram, Polly, Rachel
- D: 1823

III
- (CAPT) WILLIAM
- B: Oct. 29, 1772
- M: Polly Taylor
  5 children (2 sons, 3 daughters): Maltby, WILLIAM BURR, Polly, Almira, Julia (or Julaura)
- D: 1814

IV
- WILLIAM BURR
- B: March 20, 1806
- M: Ann Eliza Raymond
  2 sons 1 daughter grew up: Angelina Elisabeth, WILLIAM MUNSON, Samuel Gould
- D: Feb. 26, 1886

V

WILLIAM MUNSON
B: April 8, 1835
M: Susan Emma Kitchell
1 daughter 2 sons grew up: Annie Louise,
SMITH ELY
D: Nov. 30, 1898

VI

SMITH ELY
B: Oct. 17, 1866
M: Helena Dewey Leeming
5 children (2 sons, 3 daughters): Sylvia,
Winifred, Ely, Leeming, Helena
D: Sept. 25, 1945

Smith Ely Jelliffe, M.D.

| B Oct. 27, 1866. N.Y.C. |
| M Dec. 20, 1894. Brkln, N.Y. |
| D Sept. 25, 1945 Hulett's Ldg. N.Y. |
| R 64 W. 56th St. NYC & Hulett's Ldg. |

Ambrose Kitchell

| B Dec. 31, 1774 M |
| D Mar. 12, 1854 R |

Ambrose Ward Kitchell

| B Mar. 13, 1808 |
| M Nov. 11, 1833 |
| D Nov. 21, 1884 |
| R |

Bettsy Mulford

| B   D |

Susan Emma Kitchell

B Sept. 15, 1836
D Nov. 2, 1921

William Mulford

| B Oct. 1, 1781 M Jan. 30, 1806 |
| D June 15, 1869 R Hanover Neck, N.Y. |

Ann Eliza Mulford

B Mar. 13, 1811
D Mar.   1906 ?

Catherine Campfield

| B Jan. 30, 1786 D Mar. 13, 1833 |

Bibliography of Smith Ely Jelliffe

Prepared by JOHN E. SAUER

Because of numerous errors and occasional omissions in the published and unpublished bibliographies of Smith Ely Jelliffe's works, an attempt was made to compare each entry listed below with the original. An asterisk following an entry indicates that, although Jelliffe at some point listed the item, a copy of the original was not obtained, and, therefore, the citation may not be completely accurate. Entries are listed according to the year of publication. Where an article appeared in more than one journal in the same year, it is listed as an entry with both references. Where an article appeared in more than one journal in different years, an entry is listed for each year and each is cross-referenced.

This Bibliography is not exhaustive. While it does include all books, monographs, and journal articles signed by Jelliffe, the Bibliography does not include all of his published works. Only substantial obituaries are included in this list, not the brief notices of death which Jelliffe frequently contributed. Also omitted are unsigned editorials. Two other important types of writing not included in this Bibliography are abstracts and book reviews. Alexander Grinstein, in *The Index of Psychoanalytic Writings* (New York, 1956), lists 422 abstracts written by Jelliffe between 1915 and 1940 and twenty-nine book reviews written between 1914 and 1942. Representative of the volume of his work in this area of abstracting and reviewing in the period before 1914 are the figures for 1903. Jelliffe abstracted thirty-five articles and reviewed twelve books for the *Journal of Nervous and Mental Disease* alone in that year. Even as late as 1923, during the period when Jelliffe was most active in writing, revising, and editing, he contributed nine reviews and twelve abstracts to that same journal. After 1919, book reviews there generally were unsigned, and Jelliffe contributed many of them.

All journal titles are listed as they were at the time of publication of the cited article. Because of the many citations in the *Journal of Nervous and Mental Disease*, the title is given as *JNMD* throughout the Bibliography, as in the footnotes.

1890
List of Plants of Prospect Park. *Brooklyn Daily Eagle Almanac*, 5:75–76.

1891

Addition to List of Plants of Prospect Park. *Brooklyn Daily Eagle Almanac*, 6:94.

1893

The Chicago Water in the World's Fair Grounds. *American Monthly Microscopical Journal*, 14:310–311.

Notes on the Flora of Long Island. *Science*, 22:6.

A Preliminary List of the Microscopical Animals Found in the Brooklyn Water Supply. *American Monthly Microscopical Journal*, 14:289–290.

A Preliminary Report on the Vegetable Organisms Found in Ridgewood Water Supply. *Bulletin of the Torrey Botanical Club*, 20:243.

A Preliminary Report Upon the Microscopical Organisms Found in the Brooklyn Water Supply. *Brooklyn Medical Journal*, 7:593–617.

1894

The Aniline Stains. *American Monthly Microscopical Journal*, 15:152–155.

Cryptogamic Notes from Long Island-I. *Bulletin of the Torrey Botanical Club*, 21:266–268.

Cryptogamic Notes from Long Island-II. *Bulletin of the Torrey Botanical Club*, 21:489.

A Further Contribution to the Microscopical Examination of the Brooklyn Water Supply. *The Brooklyn Medical Journal*, 8:588–604.

The Microscope in Pharmacy. In *Coblenz Handbook of Pharmacy*. Philadelphia: Blakiston.★

A Report of Two Cases of Perforating Ulcer of the Foot, with Notes and Bibliography. *New York Medical Journal*, 60:458–464.

Some Dangers Resulting from the Use of Cows' Milk. *Babyhood*, 10:293–297.

1895

The Adulteration of Insect Powders by the Addition of Powdered Stems. *Druggists Circular*, 39:4–5.

Cryptogamic Notes from Long Island-III. *Bulletin of the Torrey Botanical Club*, 22:274–275.

Essentials of Vegetable Pharmacognosy. New York: D. O. Haynes and Co. With Henry H. Rusby.★

Outlines of Plant Histology: Pharmaceutical Era. New York: D. O. Haynes and Co.★

1896

Some Observations on the Strophanthus Seeds of the American Market. *Druggists Circular*, 40:101–102.

Strophanthus Hispidus and Strophanthus Kombé. *Druggists Circular*, 40:284.

1897

Contribution to the Study of the Blood in General Paresis. *State Hospital Bulletin*, 2:397–420.

Further Notes on Some Moulds Found in Medicinal Solutions. *Druggists Circular and Chemical Gazette*, 41:246–247.

Local Cryptogamic Notes. *Bulletin of the Torrey Botanical Club*, 24:412. With Henry C. Bennett.

Microscopical Characteristics of Powdered Colchicum, Aconite, Squill and Jalap. *Druggists Circular and Chemical Gazette*, 41:350–351.

Preliminary Notice Upon the Cytology of the Brains of Some Amphibians: I. Necturus. *Journal of Comparative Neurology*, 7:146–154.

A Report Upon Some Microscopical Organisms Found in the New York City Water Supply. *New York Medical Journal*, 65:722–727. With Karl M. Vogel. Also in *Journal of Pharmacology*, vol. 5.*

Some Cryptogams Found in the Air. *Bulletin of the Torrey Botanical Club*, 24:480–481. Also in *Studies, Department of Pathology, College of Physicians and Surgeons*, vol. 5.

On Some Laboratory Moulds. *Journal of Pharmacology*, 4:279–294. Also in *Studies, Department of Pathology, College of Physicians and Surgeons*, vol. 5.

Some Moulds and Bacteria Found in Medicinal Solutions. *Druggists Circular and Chemical Gazette*, 41:94–95. Also in *Journal of Pharmacology*, 4:255–263.

A Study of Some of the Nutlets of the Official Labiates. *Druggists Circular and Chemical Gazette*, 41:34–35.

1898

Bibliographical Contribution to the Cytology of the Nerve Cell. *Archives of Neurology and Psychopathology*, 1:441–463.

Microscopical Characteristics of Powdered Ipecacuanha and Belladonna. *Druggists Circular and Chemical Gazette*, 42:286. Also in *Journal of Pharmacology*, 5:257–260.

Microscopical Characteristics of Powdered Rhubarb and Senna. *Druggists Circular and Chemical Gazette*, 42:7.

Microscopical Characteristics of Vanilla. *Journal of Pharmacology*, 5:35–36.

Microscopy. *Journal of Pharmacology*, vol. 6.*

Pharmacognosy Reprint. *Journal of Pharmacology*, vol. 6.*

Some Notes on the Pharmacognosy of Ergot. *Merck's Report*, 7:163–164. Also in *Journal of Pharmacology*, 5:73–78.

1899

Revision of Charles H. May, *Anatomy, Physiology, and Hygiene; For Use in Primary and Intermediate Schools*. 4th Edition. New York: Wm. Wood and Company.

Clinical Notes on a Case of Syringomyelia. *JNMD*, 26:227–230.

Revision of Lawrence Wolff. *Essentials of Medical Chemistry, Organic and Inorganic*. 5th Edition. Philadelphia: W. B. Saunders.

The Flora of Long Island. Lancaster, Pa.: New Era Printing Company.

Microscopical Characteristics of Cassia Cinnamon. *Druggists Circular and Chemical Gazette*, 43:98–99.

Microscopical Characteristics of Powdered Cascara. *Druggists Circular and Chemical Gazette*, 43:50.

Microscopical Characteristics of Powdered Hyoscyamus and Belladonna Leaf. *Druggists Circular and Chemical Gazette*, 43:74–75. Also in *Journal of Pharmacology*, 7:8–10.

Microscopical Characteristics of Powdered Male Fern. *Druggists Circular and Chemical Gazette*, 43:27.

Morphology and Histology of Plants. Lancaster, Pa.: Science Press. With H. H. Rusby.

Notes on the Histology of Podophyllum. *Druggists Circular and Chemical Gazette*, 43:196.

Notes on Powdered Drugs: Coca and Cannabis Indica. *Merck's Report*, 8:202–203.
Notes on Sarsaparilla. *Merck's Report*, 8:52–53.
The Pharmacognosy of Mentha Piperita. *Druggists Circular and Chemical Gazette*, 43:252.
Report of a Case of Alcoholic Multiple Neuritis, with Autopsy. *Medical Record*, 56:37–46. With J. H. Larkin. Also in *Studies, Department of Pathology, College of Physicians and Surgeons*, vol. 7.
Translation (with H. L. Jelliffe) of G. Levi, Research on Comparative Cytology of the Nervous System of the Vertebrates. *Alienist and Neurologist*, 20:439–463.
Some Notes on the Pharmacognosy of Cubebs. *Druggists Circular and Chemical Gazette*, 43:172.

1900

Translation and arrangement of F. R. von Höhnel, Animal Wools and Hairs. *Journal of Pharmacology*, 7:189–194, 206–216, 223–237. Final installment with Ernestine Wolwitz.
Liquorice Root. *Druggists Circular and Chemical Gazette*, 44:112.
Abstract and translation of F. R. von Höhnel, The Microscopical Examination of Paper. *Journal of Pharmacology*, 7:28–34, 45–51.
Notes on the Pharmacognosy of Digitalis. *Druggists Circular and Chemical Gazette*, 44:176.
The Pharmacography of Cloves. *Druggists Circular and Chemical Gazette*, 44:4.
Translation (with H. L. Jelliffe) of G. Levi, Research on Comparative Cytology of the Nervous System of the Vertebrates. *Alienist and Neurologist*, 21:337–360.
Sickness in the House. *Puritan*, pp. 576–582.*
Synopsis of Lectures on Materia Medica and Therapeutics of F. W. Peabody, M.D. New York: Dougherty.*

1901

Cocaine Analgesia of the Spinal Cord. *Popular Science Monthly*, 59:280–283.
Diseases of the Nervous System. In Glentworth R. Butler, *The Diagnostics of Internal Medicine*, pp. 942–1005. New York: D. Appleton and Co. With A. B. Bonar.
Insects as Carriers of Disease. *Munsey's*, 25:707–713.
Some Observations, General and Technical, Made at the Craig Colony. *Medical News*, 79:846–848.

1902

Influenza and the Nervous System. *Philadelphia Medical Journal*, 10:1041–1044.
Revision of George Butler, *Materia Medica*. 4th Edition. Philadelphia: W. B. Saunders.
Pharmacognosy. *Journal of Pharmacology*, vol. 9.*

1903

Consciousness. Pain. Other articles. In Albert H. Buck (ed.), *A Reference Handbook of the Medical Sciences*. New York: Wm. Wood and Co.*
Death by Electricity and Lightning. In vol. 1, *Peterson and Haynes Textbook of Legal Medicine*, pp. 245–263. 2 vols. Philadelphia: W. B. Saunders.
Hypnotics, Analgesics and Resultant Drug Addictions. *Journal of the American Medical Association*, 40:571–573.

Idiocy, Imbecility and Feeblemindedness. In vol. 1, *Peterson and Haynes Textbook of Legal Medicine*, pp. 663–682. 2 vols. Philadelphia: W. B. Saunders.

Pharmacognosy. New York: Alliance Press.*

Some Notes on the Opium Habit and Its Treatment. *American Journal of the Medical Sciences*, 125:786–799.

The Work of a Neurological Dispensary Clinic. *JNMD*, 30:482–488. With L. Pierce Clark.

1904

Additions to "The Flora of Long Island." *Torreya*, 4:97–100.

Revision of John C. Shaw, *Essentials of Nervous Diseases and Insanity, Their Symptoms and Treatment.* 4th Edition. Philadelphia: W. B. Saunders and Co.

An Introduction to Pharmacognosy. Philadelphia: W. B. Saunders and Co.

Laboratory Exercises in Materia Medica. New York: Dougherty. With N. A. Bastedo.*

Multiple Sclerosis, Its Occurrence and Etiology. *JNMD*, 31:446–455.

Notes on Principles of Materia Medica. New York: Alliance Press.*

Some Notes on Dispensary Work in Nervous and Mental Diseases. *JNMD*, 31:309–317.

A Visit to Gheel. *Medical News*, 85:151–154.

1905

Revision of Charles H. May, *Anatomy, Physiology, and Hygiene; For Use in Primary and Intermediate Schools.* 5th Edition. New York: Wm. Wood and Company.

Dispensary Work in Nervous Diseases. *JNMD*, 32:449–453.

Examination of the Nervous System. In Glentworth Butler, *The Diagnostics of Internal Medicine*, pp. 513, 591, 1011–1079. 2d Edition. New York: D. Appleton and Company.

Multiple Neuritis in Wood Alcohol Poisoning. *Medical News,* 86:387–390.

Translation and editing of Paul Dubois, *The Psychic Treatment of Nervous Disorders.* New York: Funk & Wagnalls. With William A. White.

Some Notes on Neuritis and Its Treatment. *Merck's Archives*, 7:375–379.

The Urine and Feces in Diagnosis. Philadelphia: Lea Brothers and Co. With Otto Hensel and Richard Weil.

1906

Aphasia, Hemiparesis, and Hemianaesthesia in Migraine. *New York Medical Journal*, 83:33–36.

Charaka and His Times. *Proceedings of the Charaka Club*, 2:21–29.

Dispensary Work in Nervous and Mental Diseases. *JNMD*, 33:234–241.

Drug Addictions. Preliminary Report of the Committee in Section on Nervous and Mental Diseases. *Journal of the American Medical Association*, 46:643–644.

The Dutch Physician in New Amsterdam and His Colleagues at Home. *Medical Library and Historical Journal*, 4:145–161.

Two Unusual Epileptic Histories. *Medical Record*, 69:500–502.

1907

Dispensary Work in Nervous and Mental Diseases. *JNMD*, 34:691–698.

Hemilingual Atrophy of Traumatic Origin. *JNMD*, 34:194–197.

Translation of Nikolaus Gierlich, Periodical Paranoia and the Origin of Paranoiac Delusions. *Alienist and Neurologist*, 28:303–329.

Translation of Joseph Grasset, *The Semi-Insane and the Semi-Responsible*. New York: Funk & Wagnalls.

The Signs of Pre-Dementia Praecox: Their Significance and Pedagogic Prophylaxis. *American Journal of the Medical Sciences*, 134:157–182.

On Some of the More Recent Literature of Tabes Dorsalis: Pathology and Etiology. *International Clinics*, 17:257–268.

The Standard Family Physician. New York: Funk & Wagnalls. With Carl Reissig.*

1908

The Alcoholic Psychoses. Chronic Alcoholic Delirium (Korsakoff's Psychosis). *New York Medical Journal*, 88:769–777.

A Contribution to the History of Huntington's Chorea—a Preliminary Report. *Neurographs*, 1:116–124.

A Contribution to the Pathogenesis of Some Epilepsies. A Preliminary Contribution. *JNMD*, 35:243–255.

General Paresis: A Clinical Lecture. *International Clinics*, 18:219–238.

Hysteria and the Reeducation Method of Dubois. *New York Medical Journal*, 87:926–930.

Manic Depressive Insanity. A Clinical Lecture. *Kansas City Medical Index-Lancet*, 31:111–119.

The Psychiaters and Psychiatry of the Augustan Era. *Johns Hopkins Hospital Bulletin*, 19:308–312.

The Reeducation Method of Dubois. *JNMD*, 35:389–391.

Some General Reflections on the Psychology of Dementia Praecox. *Journal of the American Medical Association*, 50:202–205.

Translation and editing of *Studies in Paranoia*. *(1) Periodical Paranoia and the Origin of Paranoiac Delusions* by Nikolaus Gierlich; *(2) Contributions to the Study of Paranoia* by M. Friedmann. Nervous and Mental Disease Monograph, No. 2. New York: Journal of Nervous and Mental Disease Publishing Co.

Superior Alternate Hemiplegia—Gubler-Weber Type. *Interstate Medical Journal*, 15:715–722. Also in *City Hospital Medical and Surgical Reports*, 1:115–123.

1909

Diseases of the Nervous System. In Glentworth R. Butler, *The Diagnostics of Internal Medicine*, pp. 1029–1097. 3d Edition. New York: D. Appleton and Company. With A. B. Bonar.

Translation of Jules Payot, *Education of the Will, the Theory and Practise of Self-Culture*. New York: Funk & Wagnalls.

Superior Alternate Hemiplegia—Gubler-Weber Type. *City Hospital Medical and Surgical Reports*, 1:115–123. Also in *Interstate Medical Journal*, 15:715–722.

1910

Dementia Praecox. An Historical Summary. *New York Medical Journal*, 91:521–530.

Franciscus Sylvius. *Proceedings of the Charaka Club*, 3:14–28.*

Migraine. Neuralgia. Professional Spasms. Occupational Neuroses. Tetany. Hysteria. In vol. 7, William Osler, *Modern Medicine*, pp. 750–867. 7 vols. Philadelphia: Lea and Febiger.

Notes on the History of Psychiatry. I. *Alienist and Neurologist*, 31:80–89.

The Thalamic Syndrome. *Medical Record*, 77:305–310.

1911

Cerebellar Syndromes. *New York State Journal of Medicine*, 11:507–513.

Cyclothemia—the Mild Forms of Manic-Depressive Psychoses and the Manic-Depressive Constitution. *American Journal of Insanity*, 67:661–676.

Dementia Praecox. Boston: R. G. Badger. With Adolf Meyer and August Hoch.

Hughlings Jackson and Neurology. *Journal of the American Medical Association*, 67:1460–1461.

On Lesions of the Mid-Brain, with Special Reference to the Benedict Syndrome. *Interstate Medical Journal*, 18:817–827.

The Meningeal Forms of Epidemic Polio-Encephalomyelitis. *Journal of the American Medical Association*, 56:1867–1870.

Notes on the History of Psychiatry. II, III, IV, V. *Alienist and Neurologist*, 32:141–155, 297–314, 478–490, 649–668.

Predementia Praecox: The Hereditary and Constitutional Features of the Dementia Praecox Make Up. *JNMD*, 38:1–26.

Statistical Summary of Cases in Department of Neurology, Vanderbilt Clinic for Ten Years—1900 to 1909. *JNMD*, 38:391–412. With A. A. Brill.

Tumors of the Pineal Body. With an Account of the Pineal Syndrome, the Report of a Case of Teratoma of the Pineal and Abstracts of All Previously Recorded Cases of Pineal Tumors. *Archives of Internal Medicine*, 8:851–880. With Pearce Bailey.

Über ein malignes Chordom mit Symptomen von Seiten des Gehirns und Rückenmarks. *Zeitschrift für des Geschichte Neurologie und Psychiatrie*, 5:590–604. With John H. Larkin.

Translation of Felix Plaut, *The Wassermann Sero-Diagnosis of Syphilis in Its Application to Psychiatry*. Nervous and Mental Disease Monograph, No. 5. New York: Journal of Nervous and Mental Disease Publishing Co. With Louis Casamajor.

1912

Emergency Care of the Mentally Disordered. *American Journal of Nursing*, 12:395–401, 479–484.

The Little Signs of Differentiation of Hemiplegia, Organic and Hysterical. *Post-Graduate*, 27:876–892.

Malignant Chordoma, Involving Brain and Spinal Cord. *JNMD*, 39:1–16. With John H. Larkin.

Nervous and Mental Disease Dispensary Work. *Post-Graduate*, 27:467–482, 593–607.

Notes on the History of Psychiatry. VI, VII. *Alienist and Neurologist*, 33:69–90, 307–322.

1913

Brain of Patient with Cortical Astereognosis. *JNMD*, 40:593–594. With Louis Casamajor.

Various articles in Albert H. Buck (ed.), *A Reference Handbook of the Medical Sciences*. New York: Wm. Wood and Co.*

A Case of Acute Infective Encephalitis, Possibly of Gonococcic Origin. *JNMD*, 40:388–389. With John H. Larkin.

Day Dreams and Thinking. *Proceedings of the Mental Hygiene Congress at the College of the City of New York*, pp. 156–170, November 1912.
The Modern Treatment of Nervous and Mental Diseases. 2 vols. Philadelphia: Lea and Febiger. Edited with William A. White.
The Nervous System. *Post-Graduate*, 28:723–726.
The New York State Bar Association Questionnaire—Some Comments. *Journal of the American Institute of Criminal Law and Criminology*, 4:368–377.
Notes on the History of Psychiatry. VIII, IX. *Alienist and Neurologist*, 34:26–38, 235–248.
Translation of Joseph J. Déjérine and E. Gauckler, *The Psychoneuroses and Their Treatment by Psychotherapy*. Philadelphia: J. B. Lippincott Co.
Various articles in Thomas L. Stedman (ed.), *A Reference Handbook of the Medical Sciences*. 3d Edition. New York: Wm. Wood and Co.
Some Anomalous Tremors. *JNMD*, 40:328–330. Also in *New York Medical Journal*, 97:953–954.
Some Notes on "Transference." *Journal of Abnormal Psychology*, 8:302–309.
Some Notes on "Transference" in Psychoanalysis. *JNMD*, 40:603–604.
A Summary of the Origins, Transformations, and Present-Day Trends of the Paranoia Concept. *Medical Record*, 83:599–605.
The Technique of Psychoanalysis. *Psychoanalytic Review*, 1:63–75, 178–186, 301–307, 439–444.
1914
Compulsion Neurosis and Primitive Culture. An Analysis, a Book Review and an Autobiography. *Psychoanalytic Review*, 1:361–387. With Zenia X——.
Epilepsies and Psychoanalysis: A Query. *Medical Record*, 85:822–823. Also in *JNMD*, 41:293–296. With Frank M. Hallock.
Translation of Hans Eppinger and Leo Hess, *Vagotonia*. *JNMD*, 41:166–173, 256–260, 319–327, 468–472, 532–537, 600–603, 662–665, 730–737, 791–798; and 42:47–50, 112–119, 172–176, 247–250, 304–307, 515–518. With Walter M. Kraus. Also in Nervous and Mental Disease Monograph, No. 20. New York: Nervous and Mental Disease Publishing Co.
Intraspinous Treatment (Swift-Ellis) for General Paresis. *JNMD*, 41:44–50. Also in *Medical Record*, 85:178–180.
Translation of Otto Rank, *The Myth of the Birth of the Hero*. Nervous and Mental Disease Monograph, No. 18. New York: Journal of Nervous and Mental Disease Publishing Co. With F. Robbins.
Nervous and Mental Disease Dispensary Work. II. *Post-Graduate*, 29:576–597.
On Some Obscure Tremors, Due to Mid-Brain Lesions. *Post-Graduate*, 29:756–769.
Wilson's Disease, Paralysis Agitans or Multiple Sclerosis: A Case for Diagnosis. *JNMD*, 41:238–241. With William C. Herring.
1915
Address of Retiring President. *JNMD*, 42:507–511.
Appleton's Medical Dictionary. New York: D. Appleton and Company. Edited with Caroline W. Latimer.
A Case for Diagnosis (Specific Lesion Involving the Thalamus?). *JNMD*, 42:102–104.

Diseases of the Nervous System. New York: Lea and Febiger. With William A. White.

Hysteria. Migraines. Neuralgia. Professional Spasms. Occupational Neuroses. Tetany. In vol. 5, William Osler, pp. 654–708. *Modern Medicine.* 2d Edition. Philadelphia: Lea and Febiger.

Notes on the History of Psychiatry. X. *Alienist and Neurologist,* 36:365–371.

Specific Lesion Involving the Thalamus. *Medical Record,* 87:83.

The Technique of Psychoanalysis. *Psychoanalytic Review,* 2:73–80, 191–199, 286–296, 409–421.

Translation of Hans Eppinger and Leo Hess, *Vagotonia.* Nervous and Mental Disease Monograph, No. 20. New York: The Journal of Nervous and Mental Disease Publishing Co. With Walter M. Kraus. Also in *JNMD,* 41:166–173, 256–260, 319–327, 468–472, 532–537, 600–603, 662–665, 730–737, 791–798, and 42:47–50, 112–119, 172–176, 247–250, 304–307, 515–518.

1916

Translation of A. E. Maeder, *The Dream Problem.* Nervous and Mental Disease Monograph, No. 22. New York: Journal of Nervous and Mental Disease Publishing Co. With Frank M. Hallock.

Heine-Medin's Disease—with Medin's Original Descriptions. I, II. *Alienist and Neurologist,* 37:15–34, 271–286. With E. A. Dederer.

Notes on the History of Psychiatry. XI, XII, XIII, XIV. *Alienist and Neurologist,* 37:35–51, 158–183, 287–312, 331–346.

The Physician and Psychotherapy. *Medical Record,* 90:362–363.

Principles Underlying the Classification of Diseases of the Nervous System. *Journal of the American Medical Association,* 66:781–783. With William A. White.

Psoriasis as an Hysterical Conversion Symbolization. A Preliminary Report. *New York Medical Journal,* 104:1077–1084. With Elida Evans.

A Rejoinder: Maeder's Dream Problem and Its Critic, L. H. *Journal of Abnormal Psychology,* 11:335–344.

The Technique of Psychoanalysis. *Psychoanalytic Review,* 3:26–42, 161–175, 254–271, 394–405.

1917

Alopecia and Tetany. *Medical Record,* 91:691.

Cerebellum Disorders. Other articles. In Thomas L. Stedman (ed.), *A Reference Handbook of the Medical Sciences.* 3d Edition. New York: Wm. Wood and Co.★

Diseases of the Nervous System. 2d Edition. Philadelphia: Lea and Febiger. With William A. White.

Dispensary Work in Diseases of the Nervous System. III. *JNMD,* 45:46–56.

Dispensary Work in Diseases of the Nervous System. IV. *JNMD,* 46:333–346.

Dr. Watson and the Concept of Mental Disease. *Journal of Philosophy, Psychology and Scientific Methods,* 14:267–275.

Heine-Medin's Disease—with Medin's Original Descriptions from the Swedish. III. *Alienist and Neurologist,* 38:1–20.

The Mentality of the Alcoholic. *New York Medical Journal,* 105:629–635.

Notes on the History of Psychiatry. XV. *Alienist and Neurologist,* 38:147–159.

Priority and Progress. *Journal of Philosophy, Psychology and Scientific Methods,* 14:393–400.

Translation of Herbert Silberer, *Problems of Mysticism and Its Symbolism*. New York: Moffat, Yard and Company.

Psychotherapy and the Drama. The Therapeutic Message of Peter Ibbetson. *New York Medical Journal*, 106:442–447.

The Role of Animals in the Unconscious, with Some Remarks on Theriomorphic Symbolism as Seen in Ovid. *Psychoanalytic Review*, 4:253–271. With Louise Brink.

Translation of Alfred Adler, *Study of Organ Inferiority and Its Psychical Compensation*. Nervous and Mental Disease Monograph, No. 24. New York: Journal of Nervous and Mental Disease Publishing Company.

The Technique of Psychoanalysis. Nervous and Mental Disease Monograph, No. 26. New York: Journal of Nervous and Mental Disease Publishing Company.

The Technique of Psychoanalysis. *Psychoanalytic Review*, 4:70–83; 180–197.

The Treatment of the Schizophrenic (Dementia Praecox) Patient: A Clinical Lecture. *International Clinics*, 27:163–174.

The Vegetative Nervous System and Dementia Praecox. A Critical Résumé and Discussion. *New York Medical Journal*, 105:968–971.

The War and the Nervous System. I. Peripheral Nerve Injuries. *New York Medical Journal*, 106:17–21.

The Yellow Jacket and the Flowerly Kingdom. A Recent Dramatic Conception of the "Oedipus Complex." *Medical Record*, 91:663–666.

1918

Compulsion and Freedom: The Fantasy of the Willow Tree. *Psychoanalytic Review*, 5:255–268. With Louise Brink.

The Epileptic Attack in Dynamic Pathology. *New York Medical Journal*, 108:139–143.

Eyes of Youth: A Drama of Past Influences and Future Possibilities. *Medical Record*, 93:356–362. With Louise Brink.

I Mary MacLane—a Psychoanalytic Review and Appreciation. *Interstate Medical Journal*, 25:199–209. With Louise Brink.

Modern Art and Mass Psychotherapy. *Boston Medical and Surgical Journal*, 179:609–613.

Nervous and Mental Disturbances of Influenza. *New York Medical Journal*, 108:725–728, 755–757, 807–811.

War Neuroses and Psychoneuroses. *JNMD*, 48:246–253, 325–332, 385–394; 49:50–57, 142–148, 234–238; 50:359–368, 464–467. With Charles R. Payne.

1919

Alcohol in Some of Its Social Compensatory Aspects. *New York Medical Journal*, 109:934–936. Also in *Medical Record*, 96:821–822.

Alcoholism and the Phantasy Life in Tolstoi's Drama "Redemption." *New York Medical Journal*, 109:92–97. With Louise Brink.

Charles Hamilton Hughes. *JNMD*, 50:309–312.

Contributions to Psychotherapeutic Technic through Psychoanalysis. *JNMD*, 49:318–322. Also in *Psychoanalytic Review*, 6:1–14.

"Dear Brutus": The Dramatist's Use of the Dream. *New York Medical Journal*, 109:577–583. With Louise Brink. Also in *Woman's Medical Journal*, 27:195–204.

Diseases of the Nervous System. 3d Edition. Philadelphia: Lea and Febiger. With William A. White.

"The Jest": The Destruction Wrought by Hate. *New York Medical Journal,* 110:573–577. With Louise Brink.

Joseph Grasset. *JNMD,* 49:94–96.

Magic Above and Magic Below. *Transactions of the Charaka Club,* 5:75–82.

Paul DuBois. *JNMD,* 50:305–307.

Psychotherapy and Tuberculosis. *American Review of Tuberculosis,* 3:417–432. With Elida Evans.

Some Recent Studies on Beri-Beri and Related Types of Polyneuritis. With Preliminary Remarks on Phosphorus Function in the Dynamics of Biochemical Mechanisms. A Collected Abstract. *JNMD,* 49:522–537.

The Symbol as an Energy Container: A Preliminary Statement. *JNMD,* 50:540–550.

The Wild Duck. Psychoanalytic Review, 6:357–378. With Louise Brink.

1920

Augusto Tamburini. *JNMD,* 51:205–207.

"Dear Brutus": The Dramatist's Use of the Dream. *Woman's Medical Journal,* 27:195–204. With Louise Brink. Also in *New York Medical Journal,* 109:577–583.

Elmer Ernest Southard. *JNMD,* 51:405–408.

Encephalitis Lethargica. *New York Medical Journal,* 111:412–415.

Encephalitis Lethargica. Collected Abstract. *International Review of Medicine and Surgery,* 1:1.*

Translation of Max Schlesinger, *The History of the Symbol. JNMD,* 51:153–160, 261–268, 359–366, 438–450. With Louise Brink.

The Hysteria Group. In Tice, vol. 10, *Practice of Medicine,* pp. 329–359. New York: [publisher unknown].*

Multiple Sclerosis, the Vegetative Nervous System and Psychoanalytic Research. *Archives of Neurology and Psychiatry,* 4:593–596.

Neurology. Foreword. *International Digest of Medicine,* 1:1.*

The Parathyroid and Convulsive States. General Considerations. *New York Medical Journal,* 112:877–879.

The Pineal Body: Its Structure, Function and Diseases. *New York Medical Journal,* 111:235–240, 269–275.

Pineal Gland. In vol. 3, *Nelson's Loose Leaf System of Medicine,* p. 257. New York: T. Nelson and Sons.*

Psychoanalysis and Compulsion Neurosis. The Therapeutic Possibilities. *Psychoanalytic Review,* 7:134–147. With Zenia X——.

Psychoanalysis in the Light of Evolution. *Globe and Commercial Advertiser,* 2 November.

Psychoanalysis in the Treatment of Nervous Disease. New York: Literary Digest for the Society of Applied Psychology.*

The Symbol as an Energy Container. *Archives of Neurology and Psychiatry,* 3:206–207.

The Technique of Psychoanalysis. 2d Edition. Nervous and Mental Disease Monograph, No. 26. New York: Journal of Nervous and Mental Disease Publishing Company.

A Wizard of Dreams Outlines His New Science. *New York Times,* 8 August.

1921

Hypothyroidism and Tabes Dorsalis. A Preliminary Statement. *New York Medical Journal,* 113:383–386.

Multiple Sclerosis and Psychoanalysis. A Preliminary Statement of a Tentative Research. *American Journal of the Medical Sciences,* 161:666–675.

Psychoanalysis Winning Favor of American Physicians. *New York Herald,* 23 January.

1922

Emotional and Psychological Factors in Multiple Sclerosis. *JNMD,* 55:399–404.

Nervous System Syndromes in Influenza. In Francis Crookshank, *Influenza,* pp. 351–377. London: Heinemann and Company.

A Neuropsychiatric Pilgrimage. *JNMD,* 56:239–248.

The Pineal: Some Pathological Considerations. In vol. 2, Lewellys Barker and R. G. Hoskins (eds.), *Endocrinology and Metabolism,* pp. 35–46. 2 vols. New York: D. Appleton and Company.

The Psyche and the Vegetative Nervous System with Special Reference to Some Endocrinopathies. *New York Medical Journal,* 115:382–387.

Psychoanalysis and the Drama. Nervous and Mental Disease Monograph, No. 34. New York: Nervous and Mental Disease Publishing Company. With Louise Brink.

Psychopathology and Organic Disease. *Archives of Neurology and Psychiatry,* 8:639–651.

1923

Aesculapius and Izaak Walton. *New York Medical Journal and Medical Record,* 117:222–224.

Death by Electricity and Lightning. Mental Defect States. In Peterson, Haynes, and Webster, *Textbook of Legal Medicine.* 2d Edition. Philadelphia: W. B. Saunders Company.*

Diseases of the Nervous System. 4th Edition. Philadelphia: Lea and Febiger. With William A. White.

Launzi: Molnar's Play. *New York Herald,* 21 October.

The Mneme, the Engram and the Unconscious. Richard Semon: His Life and Work. *JNMD,* 57:329–341.

The Neuropathology of Bone Disease. A Review of Neural Integration of Bone Structure and Function, and a Suggestion Concerning Psychogenic Factors Operative in Bone Pathology. *Transactions of the American Neurological Association, 49th Annual Meeting,* pp. 419–435.

Paleopsychology. A Tentative Sketch of the Origin and Evolution of Symbolic Function. *Psychoanalytic Review,* 10:121–139.

The Pineal Body. In vol. 3, *Nelson New Loose-Leaf Medicine,* pp. 257–261. New York: T. Nelson and Sons.

Various articles in Thomas L. Stedman (ed.), *A Reference Handbook of the Medical Sciences.* 4th Edition. 8 vols. New York: Wm. Wood and Co.*

Some Reflections on the Modern School of Dutch Neuropsychiatry. *JNMD*, 57:564–568. Also in *Archives of Neurology and Psychiatry*, 9:658–661.

1924

Dutch Neuropsychiatry and Its Representatives. *Medical Journal and Record*, 120:260–266, 324–326.

Fifty Years of American Neurology: Fragments of an Historical Retrospect. In *Semi-Centennial Anniversary Volume of the American Neurological Association, 1875–1924*, pp. 386–438. New York: American Neurological Association.

Parts of Central Nervous System Which Tend to Exhibit Morbid Recessive or Dominant Characters. *Archives of Neurology and Psychiatry*, 12:380–410.

Semi-Centennial Anniversary Volume of the American Neurological Association, 1875–1924. New York: American Neurological Association. Edited with Frederick Tilney.

The Work of the New York Psychiatric Society. *Medical Journal and Record*, 119:xcii–xciii.

1925

Translation of Constantine von Monakow, *The Emotions, Morality and the Brain*. Nervous and Mental Disease Monograph, No. 39. New York: Nervous and Mental Disease Publishing Company. With Gertrude Barnes.

The Old Age Factor in Psychoanalytical Therapy. *Medical Journal and Record*, 121:7–12. Also in *JNMD*, 61:274–279.

The Sexual Life of the Child. In vol. 7, Isaac A. Abt (ed.), *Pediatrics*, pp. 796–854. 7 vols. Philadelphia: W. B. Saunders.

Somatic Pathology and Psychopathology at the Encephalitis Crossroad: A Fragment. *JNMD*, 61:561–586.

Editing of *Studies in Psychiatry, Vol. II*. Nervous and Mental Disease Monograph, No. 41. New York: Nervous and Mental Disease Publishing Company.

Chapters on Treatment of Hysteria, Headaches, Migraine, Vertigo, Epilepsy. In Forscheimer, *Treatment of Internal Diseases*. New York: D. Appleton and Company.*

Unconscious Dynamics and Human Behavior. In *Problems of Personality. Studies Presented to Morton Prince*, pp. 331–350. New York: Harcourt, Brace and Company.

1926

Postencephalitic Respiratory Disorders. Review of the Syndromy, Case Reports and Discussion. *JNMD*, 63:357–371, 467–477, 592–611; 64:29–44, 157–166, 241–260, 362–370, 503–527, 629–636.

Psychoanalyse und Organische Störung: Myopie als Paradigma. *Internationale Zeitschrift für Psychoanalyse*, 12:517–527. Also translated in *International Journal of Psycho-Analysis*, 7:445–456.

1927

The Mental Pictures in Schizophrenia and in Epidemic Encephalitis. Their Alliances, Differences and a Point of View. *American Journal of Psychiatry*, 6:413–465.

Postencephalitic Respiratory Disorders. Nervous and Mental Disease Monograph, No. 45. New York: Nervous and Mental Disease Publishing Company.

Postencephalitic Respiratory Syndromes: Phenomenology and Pathologic Considerations. *Archives of Neurology and Psychiatry*, 17:627–661.
Sex Has Thrown a Bomb into Business. *New York Herald-Tribune*, 25 September, Magazine Section. Also in Morris Fishbein and William A. White (eds.), *Why Men Fail*, pp. 69–92. New York: Century Company.

1928
On Eidetic Psychology and Psychiatric Problems. *Medical Journal and Record*, 128:80–83.
Hysteria, Migraines, Neuralgia, Professional Spasms, Occupational Neuroses, Tetany. In vol. 6, Osler-MacRae, *Modern Medicine*, pp. 654–766. 3d Edition. 7 vols. Philadelphia: Lea and Febiger.
The Hysteria Group. Revised in vol. 10, Tice, *Practice of Medicine*, pp.329–360. Hagerstown, Md.: W. F. Prior Co.*
Mme. Déjérine-Klumpke, 1859–1927. *Bulletin of the New York Academy of Medicine*, 4:655–659.
The Pineal Body. Review of Literature, 1921–1927. In *Nelson's Loose Leaf System of Medicine*, pp. 1052–1067. New York: T. Nelson and Sons.
Sex Has Thrown a Bomb into Business. In Morris Fishbein and William A. White (eds.), *Why Men Fail*, pp. 69–92. New York: Century Company. Reprinted from *New York Herald-Tribune*, 25 September, Magazine Section.
Women and the Old Immorality. *Forum*, 77:189–199.

1929
The Diencephalic Vegetative Mechanisms: The Anatomy and Physiology. *Archives of Neurology and Psychiatry*, 21:838–862.
Diseases of the Nervous System. 5th Edition. Philadelphia: Lea and Febiger. With William A. White.
Ibsen. In *The Apostle of the Psychopath; Mott Memorial Volume*, pp. 239–251. London: H. K. Lewis.
Manic-Depressive Psychosis Group. *JNMD*, 70:410–419.
Multiple Sclerosis Syndromes. *JNMD*, 70:310–320.
Narcolepsy—Hypnolepsy—Pyknolepsy. *Medical Journal and Record*, 129:269–273, 313–315.
Oculogyric Crises as Compulsion Phenomena in Postencephalitis: Their Occurrence, Phenomenology and Meaning. *JNMD*, 69:59–68, 165–184, 278–297, 415–426, 531–551, 666–679.
Oculogyric Crises: Psychopathologic Considerations of the Affective States. *Transactions of the American Neurological Association, 55th Annual Meeting*, pp. 498–523.
Poliomyelitis Group. *JNMD*, 70:535–547.
Psychological Components in Postencephalitic Oculogyric Crises: Contribution to a Genetic Interpretation of Compulsion Phenomena. *Archives of Neurology and Psychiatry*, 21:491–532.
Técnica del Psicoanálisis. Translated by Honorio F. Delgado and Paul Wilson. Segovia: El Adelantado de Segovia.*
The Theory of the Libido. In Victor F. Calverton and Samuel D. Schmalhausen (eds.), *Sex in Civilization*, pp. 456–471. New York: Macauley Company.
Unkinking the Mind: A Discussion of Psychoanalysis. *Hygeia*, 7:33–35.

The Vegetative Nervous System and the Ionic Milieu. *JNMD*, 70:206–209.
1930
Head Injuries—Delayed Hemorrhage—Concussion. *JNMD*, 72:422–426.
Meningitis Group. *JNMD*, 71:57–64, 201–208.
Neurosyphilis—Older and Newer Contributions. *JNMD*, 72:171–181, 300–308, 426–436, 572–590, 670–687.
Oculogyric Crises: Psychopathologic Considerations of the Affective States. *Archives of Neurology and Psychiatry*, 23:1227–1247.
Ophthalmic Migraine. *JNMD*, 72:291–300.
The Parathyroid; Calcium Metabolism, and Tetany Reactions. *JNMD*, 71:303–311, 450–459.
Psychiatry of Our Colonial Forefathers. *Archives of Neurology and Psychiatry*, 24:667–681. Also in *Transactions of the American Neurological Association*, 56:1–18.
Psychotherapy in Modern Medicine. *Long Island Medical Journal*, 24:152–161.
Some Random Notes on the History of Psychiatry of the Middle Ages. *American Journal of Psychiatry*, 10:275–286.
Vigilance, the Motor Pattern and Inner Meaning in Some Schizophrenics' Behavior. *Psychoanalytic Review*, 17:305–330. Also in *Proceedings of the Association for Research in Nervous and Mental Disease*, 1931, p. 75.*
What Price Healing? A Fragmentary Inquiry. *Journal of the American Medical Association*, 94:1393–1395.
1931
Cerebral Hemorrhage and the Apoplexies in General. *JNMD*, 74:217–231.
Comments on Brain Tumors. *JNMD*, 73:420–427, 542–549.
Dupuytren's Contracture and the Unconscious: A Preliminary Statement of a Problem. *International Clinics*, 41, Series 3:184–199.
Translation of Max Neuburger, The Historic Past of German Neuropathology. In *Essays in the History of Medicine*, pp. 69–87. New York: Medical Life Press.
The Immediate and Remote Effects of the World War on the Nervous System. Psychopathology and War Residuals. *Proceedings of the International Congress of Military Surgeons*, pp. 273–289.
Translation of W. R. Hess, *On the Interrelationships between Psychic and Vegetative Functions*. *JNMD*, 74:301–320, 511–528, 645–653, 726–735. With Louise Brink.
Poliomyelitis. *JNMD*, 74:761–768, 75:70–79.
The Schizophrenic Group. *JNMD*, 74:347–360, 543–557, 664–669, 751–761.
Some Historical Phases of the Manic-Depressive Synthesis. *JNMD*, 73:353–374, 499–521.
Vegetative Nervous System and Blood Vessels. *JNMD*, 73:652–656.
Vegetative Neurology: Gastrointestinal and Skin and General. *JNMD*, 73:78–88, 223–232.
Vigilance, the Motor Pattern and Inner Meaning in Some Schizophrenics' Behavior. *Proceedings of the Association for Research in Nervous and Mental Disease*, p. 75.* Also in *Psychoanalytic Review*, 17:305–330.
1932
Emil Kraepelin, The Man and His Work. *Archives of Neurology and Psychiatry*, 27:761–775.

Psychoanalysis. In *Collier's Encyclopedia.*
Psychopathology of Forced Movements and the Oculogyric Crises of Lethargic Encephalitis. Nervous and Mental Disease Monograph, No. 55. New York: Nervous and Mental Disease Publishing Company.
Psychopathology and Organic Disease. *New York State Journal of Medicine,* 32:581–588.
Some Brief Notes, Old and New, on Brain Tumor. *JNMD,* 76:65–70, 184–187, 268–280.
Some Fragmentary Reflections on Masculine Superiority. *Medical Journal and Record,* 135:337–340.
Some Present and Past Observations on the Optic Nerve and Its Disorders. *JNMD,* 76:385–396, 483–494, 608–622.
1933
Amyotonia Congenita, Thomsen's Disease; Myotonia Congenita, Oppenheim's Disease. In *Cyclopedia of Medicine.* Philadelphia: F. A. Davis and Company.*
The Death Instinct in Somatic and Psychopathology. *Psychoanalytic Review,* 20:121–132.
Dr. Bancroft and Psychiatry. *JNMD,* 77:385–401.
Emil Kraepelin, Psychiatrist and Poet. With Reproduction of Schwalbe's Discussion. *JNMD,* 77:134–152, 274–282. With Louise Brink.
Glimpses of a Freudian Odyssey. *Psychoanalytic Quarterly,* 2:318–329.
The Heart: Muscle and Nervous System. *JNMD,* 78:64–77.
The Myotonic Pupil: A Contribution and a Critical Review. *Journal of Neurology and Psychopathology,* 13:349–358.
Nervous Diseases Following Accidents. In Sydney C. Schweitzer, *Trial Manual for Negligence Actions,* pp. 710–731. New York: Baker, Voorhis and Company.
Die Parkinsonsche Körperhaltung: Einige Betrachtungen über Unbewusste Feindseligkeit. *Internationale Zeitschrift für Psychoanalyse,* 19:485–498.
Psychoanalysis and Internal Medicine. In Sandor Lorand, *Psychoanalysis Today: Its Scope and Function,* pp. 293–306. New York: Covici-Friede.
Thomsen's Disease (Myotonia Congenita). Report of Case and Review of American Literature. *Journal of the American Medical Association,* 100:555–560. With Lloyd Ziegler.
What! No Pictures? *Journal of Criminal Law and Criminology,* 24:1019–1024.
1934
Acroparesthesia and Quinidine: A Query and a Quest. With Report on American Literature on Acroparesthesia. *JNMD,* 79:631–651.
Historical Notes on Constitution and Individuality. *Archives of Neurology and Psychiatry,* 32:359–376.
L. Pierce Clark. *American Journal of Psychiatry,* 13:1153–1155.
The Narcolepsies. Cryptogenic and Symptomatic Types. *Archives of Neurology and Psychiatry,* 31:615–634. With J. Notkin.
The Narcolepsies. *American Journal of Psychiatry,* 13:733–737. With J. Notkin.
The Pyknolepsies. *American Journal of Psychiatry,* 14:679–692. With J. Notkin. Also in *Archives of Neurology and Psychiatry,* 33:752–763.

1935

Affective or Emotional Participation in Disease Processes. *Health Examiner*, 5:12–14.

The Amyotrophic Lateral Sclerosis Syndrome and Trauma. *JNMD*, 82:415–435, 532–550.

Diseases of the Nervous System. 6th Edition. Philadelphia: Lea and Febiger. With William A. White.

Dynamic Concepts and the Epileptic Attack. *American Journal of Psychiatry*, 92:565–574.

The Meaning of Sex to the Psychoanalyst. *Urologic and Cutaneous Review*, 39:797–802.

Ophthalmic Migraines. In *Cyclopedia of Medicine*, p. 943. Philadelphia: F. A. Davis Company.*

The Psychopathology of the Oculogyric Crises and Its Funeral [Oration] by Dr. Lawrence S. Kubie. *Psychoanalytic Quarterly*, 4:360–366.

The Pyknolepsies. *Archives of Neurology and Psychiatry*, 33:752–763. With J. Notkin. Also in *American Journal of Psychiatry*, 14:679–692.

Santiago Ramón y Cajal, M.D. *Transactions of the American Neurological Association*, 60:234–236.

1936

The Bodily Organs and Psychopathology. *American Journal of Psychiatry*, 92:1051–1076.

Charles Loomis Dana, M.D. *JNMD*, 83:622–637.

Children's Problems: A Generalized Approach. *American Journal of Orthopsychiatry*, 6:406–411.

A Consideration of Julian Green. *University of Virginia Magazine*, 94:171–178.

The Ecological Principle in Medicine. *Bulletin of the Neurological Institute of New York*, 5:199–201.

Infantile Sexuality. In Victor Robinson (ed.), *Encyclopedia Sexualis*, pp. 407–415. New York: Dingwall-Rock Ltd.

Medicine, the Law, and Juvenile Delinquency. *Journal of Criminal Law and Criminology*, 27:503–514.

Mental Attitudes vs. Health. *Hygeia*, 14:710–712.

Editing and Revision of John F. Meagher, *A Study of Masturbation and the Psychosexual Life*. 3d Edition. Baltimore: Wm. Wood and Company.

1937

Charles Loomis Dana, 1852–1935. *Transactions of the American Neurological Association*, 62:187–193.

Les Concepts Dynamiques et la Crise Épileptique. *L'Encéphale*, 32:15–25.

Dr. Roback's "Fifty Years of the Dissociation School." *JNMD*, 86:369–372.

The Ecological Principle in Medicine. *Journal of Abnormal and Social Psychology*, 32:100–121.

The Origin and Nature of the Hypoglycemic Therapy of the Psychoses. *JNMD*, 85:575–578.

S. A. Kinnier Wilson, M.D., *JNMD*, 86:743–748.

Sigmund Freud as a Neurologist. Some Notes on His Earlier Neurobiological and Clinical Neurological Studies. *JNMD*, 85:696–711.

The Skin: Nervous System and the Bath. *Medical Record*, 145:93–98.

Some Notes on Poisoning by *Clitocybe Dealbata* (sow.) *Var. Sudorifica* (Peck). *New York State Journal of Medicine*, 37:1357–1361.

Why Do Such Things Happen? *Cosmopolitan*, July, p. 56.*

William A. White. *JNMD*, 85:626–634.

William A. White. *Medical Record*, 145:309.

William A. White, M.D. *Psychoanalytic Review*, 24:210–230.

William Alanson White. *Mental Hygiene*, 21:291–293.

1938

The Ecological Principle in Medicine. *Confina Neurologica*, 1:134–136.

The Historical Background of Psychiatry. In New York Academy of Medicine, *Milestones in Medicine*, pp. 1–36. New York: D. Appleton-Century.

James Ramsay Hunt, M.D. *JNMD*, 87:394–402.

1939

The Christian Formulation and Medicine. *Psychiatric Quarterly*, 13:705–710.

The Editor Himself and His Adopted Child. *JNMD*, 89:545–589.

General Reflections on Psychosomatic Monism. *New York State Journal of Medicine*, 39:1017–1021.

I. Seth Hirsch, M.D.: An Appreciation. *Radiology*, 33:111–114.

James Ramsay Hunt, 1874–1937. *Transactions of the American Neurological Association*, 64:219–222.

Julian Green: Le Visionnaire. *University of Virginia Magazine*, 100:2–4, 23–25.

Open Letter to Dr. Ernest Jones. *International Journal of Psycho-Analysis*, 20:349–352.

Sigmund Freud and Psychiatry: A Partial Appraisal. *American Journal of Sociology*, 45:326–340.

Sketches in Psychosomatic Medicine. Nervous and Mental Disease Monograph, No. 65. New York: Nervous and Mental Disease Publishing Company.

1940

Hysteria. *Cyclopedia of Medicine, Surgery and Specialties*, pp. 397–418. Philadelphia: F. A. Davis Company.

The Influence of Psychoanalysis on Neurology. *Psychoanalytic Quarterly*, 9:214–215.

My Arthritis and Me. *Medical Record*, 152:85–87.

Nervous System. Nervousness. Organotherapy, or Opotherapy. Other articles in *Encyclopedia Americana*.

The Parkinsonian Body Posture: Some Considerations on Unconscious Hostility. *Psychoanalytic Review*, 27:467–479.

Sigmund Freud. *Psychoanalytic Review*, 27:129–131.

Vigilance and the Vitalistic Hypothesis. *JNMD*, 92:471–488.

1941

George W. Jacoby, 1857–1940. *Transactions of the American Neurological Association*, 67:247.

1942

Dr. Menas S. Gregory. *JNMD*, 95:257–258.

Little Signs of Parathyroid Disturbance. *Journal of the Mount Sinai Hospital, New York*, 9:578–581.

A Popular Essay on Air. *Medical Record*, 155:261–265, 415–419, 449–450.
Some Notes on Parathyroid Dysfunction. *Medical Record*, 155:523–525.
Stewart Paton, 1865–1942. *American Journal of Psychiatry*, 99:156–157.
1944
Two Morphine Color Dreams, with a Note on the Etiology of the Opium Habit.
  Psychoanalytic Review, 31:128–132.

Index